Postcolonial Cinema Studies

"*Postcolonial Cinema Studies* is an essential book that orchestrates an enriching dialogue between postcolonial studies and cinema studies, in ways that mutually illuminate both fields. Interdisciplinary and transnational, the volume goes beyond the usual Anglophone boundaries. Not only does it stretch the corpus of films to be studied, it also productively counterpoints theories, methodologies, and regions."

Ella Shohat, *New York University, USA* and
Robert Stam, *Tisch School of the Arts, USA*

"This book is a significant contribution to the study of postcolonial cinema and beyond. Global in scope yet thorough in its rigorous investigation of specific case studies of national, transnational and global cinemas, this book will probably be considered one of the definitive texts on postcolonial cinema for many years to come."

Yosefa Loshitzky, *University of East London*, UK

"*Postcolonial Cinema Studies* will be a major contribution to postcolonial research and cinematic scholarship and is on the 'leading edge' of its field."

Dr Imogen Tyler, *Lancaster University, UK*

"*Postcolonial Cinema Studies* argues that current experiences of migration, economic exploitation, militarization, racial and religious conflicts, and tensions between citizens and non-citizens are haunted by colonial and neocolonial histories globally. Impressive in its scope and its attention to diverse cinematic dimensions, the book is an important intervention in cinema and postcolonial studies."

Katarzyna Marciniak, *Ohio University, USA*

This collection of essays foregrounds the work of filmmakers in theorizing and comparing postcolonial conditions, recasting debates in both cinema and postcolonial studies. Postcolonial cinema is presented, not as a rigid category, but as an optic through which to address questions of postcolonial historiography, geography, subjectivity, and epistemology.

Current circumstances of migration and imm... militarization, economic exploitation, racial and ... citizenship and cultural

self-representation have deep roots in colonial/postcolonial/neocolonial histories. Contributors engage the tense asymmetries bequeathed to the contemporary world by the multiple, diverse, and overlapping histories of European, Soviet, US, and multi-national imperial ventures. With interdisciplinary expertise, they discover and explore the conceptual temporalities and spatialities of postcoloniality, with an emphasis on the politics of form, the 'postcolonial aesthetics' through which filmmakers challenge themselves and their viewers to move beyond national and imperial imaginaries.

Sandra Ponzanesi is Associate Professor of Gender and Postcolonial Critique, Department of Media and Culture Studies/Gender Programme at Utrecht University, the Netherlands. Among her publications are *Paradoxes of Postcolonial Culture* (2004), *Migrant Cartographies* (2005) and *Deconstructing Europe: Postcolonial Perspectives* (Routledge, 2011).

Marguerite Waller is Professor of Women's Studies and Comparative Literature at the University of California, Riverside, USA. Among her publications are *Frontline Feminisms: Women, War, and Resistance* (Routledge, 2001), *Federico Fellini: Contemporary Perspectives* (2002), *Dialogue and Difference: Feminisms Challenge Globalization* (2005), and *The Wages of Empire* (2007).

Postcolonial Cinema Studies

Edited by
Sandra Ponzanesi and
Marguerite Waller

Routledge
Taylor & Francis Group

LONDON AND NEW YORK

First published 2012
by Routledge
2 Park Square, Milton Park, Abingdon, Oxon OX14 4RN

Simultaneously published in the USA and Canada
by Routledge
711 Third Avenue, New York, NY 10017

Routledge is an imprint of the Taylor & Francis Group, an informa business

British Library Cataloguing in Publication Data
A catalogue record for this book is available from the British Library

Library of Congress Cataloging in Publication Data
Postcolonial cinema studies / edited by Sandra Ponzanesi and
Marguerite Waller.
  p. cm.
  Includes bibliographical references and index.
  1. Motion pictures—Political aspects. 2. Imperialism
in motion pictures. 3. Nationalism in motion pictures.
4. Intercultural communication in motion pictures.
5. Culture in motion pictures. 6. Multiculturalism in
motion pictures. 7. Motion pictures and globalization.
I. Ponzanesi, Sandra, 1967- II. Waller, Marguerite R., 1948-
PN1995.9.P6P68 2011
791.43′6581—dc23   2011019514

ISBN: 978-0-415-78228-9 (hbk)
ISBN: 978-0-415-78229-6 (pbk)
ISBN: 978-0-203-18147-8 (ebk)

Typeset in Garamond and Gill Sans
by HWA Text and Data Management, London

In memoriam
Emory Elliott

Contents

Figures

Contributors

Jude G. Akudinobi earned his PhD in Cinema-Television from the University of Southern California and teaches in the Department of Black Studies, at the University of California, Santa Barbara. His works on African cinema have appeared in *Iris*, *The Black Scholar*, *Nka: Journal of Contemporary African Art*, *Social Identities*, *Third Text*, *Research in African Literatures*, *Meridians*, amongst other publications and anthologies. Dr Akudinobi's research interests span the complexities of cultural politics, postcolonial literatures, media, and cinemas. His current projects include a book on the creative and discursive configurations of Nigeria's effervescent film culture, Nollywood.

Kanika Batra is Assistant Professor at Texas Tech University, in the department of English. She specializes in postcolonial literatures and has special interests in postcolonial feminism and postcolonial queer Studies. Her articles have appeared in *The Journal of Commonwealth and Postcolonial Studies* and *Interventions: International Journal of Postcolonial Studies*. In 2001 she published a monograph on *Caribbean poetry: Derek Walcott and Edward Brathwaite* for the Indira Gandhi National Open University, India. Her new book entitled *Feminist Visions and Queer Futures in Postcolonial Drama: Community, Kinship, and Citizenship* was published with Routledge in 2010.

Ruth Ben-Ghiat is Chair of the Department of Italian Studies and Professor of Italian Studies and History at New York University. She is the author of *Fascist Modernities: Italy 1922–45* (2001, 2004), and the editor of *Gli imperi: dall'antichità all'età contemporanea* (2009), and (with Mia Fuller) of *Italian Colonialism* (2005, 2008). Her essay for this volume is taken from her new book, entitled *Fascism's Empire Cinema: Histories and Journeys of Italian Conquest and Defeat*. She has also completed research for *Italian Prisoners of War and the Transition from Dictatorship*.

Shohini Chaudhuri is Senior Lecturer in the Department of Literature, Film, and Theatre Studies at the University of Essex. She is author of *Contemporary World Cinema: Europe, the Middle East, East Asia and South Asia* (2005) and *Feminist Film Theorists* (Routledge, 2006). Her research interests include feminist and postcolonial studies, world cinema, cultural theory, and psychoanalysis. She has published on these topics in the journals *Camera Obscura*, *Screen*, *Strategies: Journal of Theory, Culture and Politics*, and *South Asian Popular Culture*, and in the edited collections *New Punk Cinema* (2005), *Film Analysis: A Norton Reader* (2005), and *Storytelling in World Cinemas* (forthcoming).

Julie Codell is Professor of Art History at Arizona State University, and affiliate in Film and Media Studies, English, Gender and Women's Studies, and the Center for Asian Research. She has published 140 books, book chapters, articles, reviews and encyclopedia entries on film, Victorian culture (art, literature and the press) and India under the Raj (art and Indian modernism, craft production, travel narratives, and the Indian press). She wrote *The Victorian Artist* (2003) and *Images of an Idyllic Past: Edward Curtis's Photographs* (1988); edited *Transculturation in British Art* (2012), *Photography and the Imperial Durbars of British India* (2011), *The Political Economy of Art* (2008), *Genre, Gender, Race, World Cinema* (2007) and *Imperial Co-Histories* (2003) and co-edited *Encounters in the Victorian Press* (with L. Brake, 2004) and *Orientalism Transposed* (with D. S. Macleod, 1998), currently being translated into Japanese (2013). Her writings on film include her Blackwell's reader and essays and book chapters on the 1930s empire film *Rhodes of Africa*, John Huston's *The Man Who Would Be King* and imperial ideology, François Truffaut's *L'Enfant sauvage* and autobiography in film, Robert Bresson's *Lancelot du Lac* and deconstruction, and *Robocop* and the techno-body.

Sabine Doran is Assistant Professor of Comparative Literature and German at the University of California, Riverside, where she was also Director of the German Program from 2005 to 2008. She received her PhD (2004) in Comparative Literature from the Free University of Berlin, and was a DAAD scholar and Visiting Researcher at Stanford University from 1996 to 1999. She has also held appointments at Oberlin College (2004–2005) and the Free University of Berlin Summer University (2002–2005). At UC Riverside, she has organized many colloquia and seminars, including a Mellon Workshop on "Affect, Technicity, Ethics" (2006–2007). Professor Doran's research concerns the intersection between visual art and literature, particularly color theory and synaesthesia. Her most recent article, "Synaesthesia in European Film Theory," was published in the collection *European Film Theory* (Routledge, 2009). Her current book project is *Portrait of a Modern Color: Figuring Yellow in Art, Literature, and Film*.

Hamish Ford is a lecturer in Film, Media and Cultural Studies at the University of Newcastle, Australia. His teaching and research interests include: contemporary world cinema and postcolonialism; cinematic time and negativity; post-war European modernist film; cinematic affect; film and authorship; and the relationship between European philosophy and film studies (especially Frankfurt School, phenomenology, and Deleuze). His latest publication is "Broken Glass by the Road: Adorno and a Cinema of Negativity", in *New Takes in Film and Philosophy* (Havi Carel & Greg Tuck, eds., Palgrave Macmillan 2011), and he has just completed work on a monograph taking in the areas of cinema, philosophy and modernist studies entitled *Challenging Negativity and Time: Post-War Modernist Cinema Up Close.*

Claudia Hoffmann is an Andrew W. Mellon Postdoctoral Fellow in the Humanities and a visiting assistant professor in the Department of Film, Television and Digital Media and the African Studies Center at the University of California, Los Angeles. Her publications engage with diasporic Nollywood filmmaking in the United States and questions of identity, transnational discourse, and the significance of the cinematic city. She is currently working on a book-length study on the cinematic representation of a clandestine African diaspora in the works of African, North American, and European filmmakers. Her research emphasizes how different cinematic aesthetics and filmmaking traditions recreate the global spaces that undocumented African migrants occupy in Europe and the United States.

Anikó Imre is Associate Professor of Critical Studies in the University of Southern California's School of Cinematic Arts. Her work revolves around film and new media theory, global television, national and transnational media, postcoloniality, global consumption and mobility, studies of identity and play, media education, and European media. She is the author of *Identity Games: Globalization and the Transformation of Media Cultures in the New Europe* (MIT Press, 2009), editor of *East European Cinemas* (Routledge, 2005) and *The Blackwell Companion to East European Cinema*, and co-editor of *Transnational Feminism in Film and Media*, (Palgrave, 2007) and *Popular Television in Eastern and Southern Europe* (Routledge, 2011).

Priya Jaikumar is Associate Professor at the University of Southern California, in the School of Cinematic Arts. Jaikumar's research has focused on the problem of interpreting historical change in cultural industries and aesthetic forms, in particular the break from colonial relations dominating the nexus of Britain, India and the dominions. Her book *Cinema at the End of Empire: A Politics of Transition in Britain and India* challenges the rubric of national cinema dominant in film studies to detail the intertwined film histories of a declining empire and a nascent nation. Her scholarly work on questions of state power, cultural regulation, film form and feminism has also appeared in *Cinema Journal*, *The Moving Image*, *Post Script*, *Screen*, *World Literature Today*, and in recent anthologies such as *Hollywood Abroad* and *Transnational Feminism in Film and Media*. Currently, she is working on architecture, photography and cinema in the colonial context.

Mariam B. Lam is Associate Professor of Comparative Literature and Southeast Asian Studies at the University of California, Riverside, with affiliations in Media and Cultural Studies, Women's Studies and Labor Studies. She specializes in Vietnamese, Southeast Asian and Asian American literature, film, popular culture, gender and sexuality, translation, tourism and diasporic community politics. She is founding co-editor of the *Journal of Vietnamese Studies* and Director of the UCR Southeast Asian Studies Research Program, SEATRiP (Southeast Asia: Texts, Rituals, Performance), with its particular focus on the humanities, arts and social sciences. She is currently completing two monograph projects, *Not Coming to Terms: Viet Nam, Post-Trauma* *and Cultural Politics*, which analyzes literary and filmic production and community politics within and across Vietnam, France, and the United States, and *Surfin' the Cold Wave: New Circulations of Cold War Culture and Global Capital*, which examines the neoliberal post-socialist development of film and broadcast television, ethnic media mobility and cultural educational curriculum.

Paulo de Medeiros received a PhD in Comparative Literature from the University of Massachusetts, Amherst and holds the Chair of Portuguese Studies at Utrecht University. He has published variously on issues of literary theory and contemporary Portuguese authors. Some of his articles relating to Postcolonial Studies include "Postcolonial Memories and Lusophone Literatures" in *European Review* 13.1 (2005) and "(Re-)Constructing, (Re-)Membering Postcolonial Selves" in *Stories and Portraits of the Self. Internationale Forschungen zur Allgemeinen und Vergleichenden Literaturwissenschaft*, vol. 115 (2007). He also edited a volume of essays on Postcolonial Theory and Lusophone Literatures (2007). Currently, he is writing on cruelty and inheritance in relation to a Postcolonial Europe.

Sandra Ponzanesi is Associate Professor in Gender and Postcolonial Critique at Utrecht University (NL), department of Media and Culture Studies, Graduate Gender Programme. She has been Visiting Professor at the University of California, Los Angeles and visiting scholar at the University of California, Riverside. Among her interests are the reception of postcolonial literature in relation to the literary award industry and the exploration of digital literacies of migrant youth in transnational contexts. She has published on postcolonial critique, transnational feminist theories, Italian colonial history, visual culture and postcolonial cinema. Among her publications are *Paradoxes of Post-colonial Culture: Contemporary Women Writing of the Indian and Afro-Italian Diaspora* (2004), *Migrant Cartographies. New Cultural and Literary Spaces in Post-colonial Europe* (2005) with Daniela Merolla and *Deconstructing Europe: Postcolonial Perspectives* (2011) with Bolette B. Blaagaard.

Rich Rice is Associate Professor of English at Texas Tech University in the Technical Communication and Rhetoric program. His research interests include contemporary composition and rhetoric, new media and digital rhetoric, TA training, ePortfolios, distance education, and service learning. Recent publications include *Portfolio Teaching: A Guide For Students* (2006) and *Portfolio Teaching: A Guide For Teachers of College* (2006), both co-authored with Nedra Reynolds. Forthcoming articles include "Teaching Style in Basic Writing through Remediating Photo Essays" with Ben Lauren in Basic Writing Online, "ePortfolios and the Communicative Intellect in Online Education" in an edited collection with IGI Global, and "New Media Labs as Key Technical Communication Instructional Support Spaces" in *Intercom*. His forthcoming edited collection, *ePortfolio Performance Support Systems: Constructing, Presenting, and Assessing Portfolios in Public Workplaces*, co-edited with Katherine Wills, is with Parlor Press. And he is working on a first-year composition reader with Marc Wilson and Kanika Batra called *Writing For Life: Making Sense of Communication in a Global World*.

Mireille Rosello is Professor of Literary Studies at the University of Amsterdam, the Netherlands. Her research focuses on comparative and interdisciplinary cultural studies of contemporary objects and visual or textual narratives (twentieth and twenty-first-century literatures, popular culture, cinema, television and new media), and more specifically on two areas of inquiry: Diasporic Studies (especially European, North African and Caribbean voices) and Gender Constructions (queer theories and performativity). Her most recent publications are *The Reparative in Memorial Narratives: Works of Mourning in Progress* (2009), *France and the Maghreb: Performative Encounters* (2005), and its French version *Encontres Méditerranéennes: Littératures et cultures France-Maghreb* (2006). She is working on two collections of articles on "What's Queer about Europe" and "European multilingualism."

Marguerite Waller is Professor of Women's Studies and Comparative Literature at the University of California, Riverside. She has also taught as a Fulbright Lecturer at the Université de Haute Normandie in France and at the Eötvös Loránd University in Hungary. Her teaching and research interests include medieval and Renaissance European literature, transnational feminist dialogue, national, transnational, and postcolonial cinema and media, border art and theory, immigrant protest, and neoliberal subjectivity. Her essays in these areas have appeared in many volumes and journals. She is the author of *Petrarch's Poetics and Literary History* (1980), and she has co-edited four anthologies: *Frontline Feminisms: Women, War, and Resistance*, with Jennifer Rycenga (Routledge, 2001), *Federico Fellini: Contemporary Perspectives*, with Frank Burke (2002), *Dialogue and Difference: Feminisms Challenge Globalization*, with Sylvia Marcos (2005), and *The Wages of Empire: Neoliberal Politics, Repressions, and Women's Poverty*, with Amalia Cabezas and Ellen Reese (2007).

Acknowledgments

First and foremost the editors thank all of those who have contributed essays to this volume. It has been a pleasure and a privilege working with them and benefiting from their insights, knowledge, and expertise in various fields. They have made this project rewarding and a unique experience.

Shaping this volume over the last years has involved the collaboration, participation, and support of many different people, colleagues, and friends. We are very grateful for our academic environments, Utrecht University in the Netherlands and the University of California at Riverside, which have provided several opportunities for exchanges, dialogues, and visits for both Sandra and Marguerite. Sandra is very thankful for the University of California system exchange with Utrecht University, which allowed her to spend a visiting fellowship at the Center for Ideas and Society at UCR in 2005, directed by the wonderful Professor Emory Elliott, who so unfortunately passed away recently. We are also grateful for the University of California-Utrecht University Collaborative Grant Program which allowed Marguerite to come to Utrecht in 2007 to teach a master class in the Graduate Gender Program, where she returned in 2009 to teach at the NOI♀SE Summer School.

We especially thank our particular departments and institutes, which have created conducive and stimulating scholarly environments. At Utrecht University we would like to thank the Research Institute for History and Culture, the Focus group Cultures and Identities, the Department of Media and Culture Studies and foremost the Gender Programme and all Sandra's colleagues (Rosemarie Buikema, Gloria Wekker, Berteke Waaldijk, Iris van der Tuin, Marta Zarzycka, Eva Midden, Babs Boter, Kathrin Thiele, Bettina Papenburg), all students and international visitors. Also many thanks to the Centre for the Humanities and in particular to Rosi Braidotti for hosting the Postcolonial Studies Initiative (PCI), directed by Paulo de Medeiros and Sandra Ponzanesi, which has launched a postcolonial film series and allowed to put into practice some of the work in this volume. Marguerite would like to acknowledge the support of several travel and research grants from the University of California Riverside Academic Senate and the invigorating collaboration of colleagues in both her departments: Comparative Literature and Foreign Languages and Women's Studies.

We are also very thankful for the acute, elaborate, and very useful suggestions provided by our anonymous external readers. We have followed most of their leads, as they were spot on. Also we would like to thank our editor at Routledge Natalie Foster and editorial assistant Ruth Moody for their support and assistance throughout the process, always responding to our many queries and ideas with timely solutions and advice.

Our enormous gratitude goes to Koen Leurs, who has worked tirelessly on this project, assisting us with a numbing array of details and handling with great expertise the increasingly technical side of preparing a book manuscript. His absolute reliability, competence, skills, and quickness have been crucial to keeping us on track and helping us maintain our bearings among the different drafts, images, and captions floating around in cyberspace. Koen went beyond the call of duty and accomplished these feats in the face of very difficult personal circumstances. Thank you, Koen.

Sandra would also like to thank Graham Huggan at the University of Leeds, for having shared with her the passion for interdisciplinarity and for pushing the boundaries of postcolonial theory into new realms. She is grateful for his collegiality, friendship, and collaboration over many years. Also Sandra thanks warmly all the "poco" friends and colleagues at Utrecht and beyond: Bolette Blaagaard, Rosemarie Buikema, Iain Chambers, Lidia Curti, Paulo de Medeiros, Paul Gilroy, Frances Gouda, Marsha Henry, Monica Jansen, Birgit Kaiser, Sabrina Marchetti, John Mcleod, Daniela Merolla, Susheila Nasta, Luisa Passerini, Pamela Pattynama, Ato Quayson, Emmanuelle Radar, Mireille Rosello, Rajeswari Sunder Rajan, Vron Ware, and many others to whom this list does not do justice.

Marguerite is deeply grateful for the ongoing friendship and support of a widening circle of "trannies" (transnational thinkers), which includes Alicia Arrizón, Alica Bardan, Michelle Bloom, Amalia Cabezas, Piya Chatterjee, Sabine Doran, April Durham, Joy Ngozi Ezeilo, Christine Gailey, Sandra Harding, Judit Hersko, D. Emily Hicks, Aniko Imre, Stephanie Jed, John Kim, Corinne Kumar, Mariam Lam, Françoise Lionnet, Cristina Lombardi-Diop, Margherita Long, Katarzyna Marciniak, Sylvia Marcos, Sante Matteo, Vartan Messier, Obioma Nnaemeka, Áine O'Healy, Tanya Rawal, Shu-mei Shih, Jeff Sacks, Jacqueline Siapno, Pasquale Verdicchio, and Ruth Wallen and many more whom our word limit does not allow her to name.

Transnational dialogues, which have sometimes involved confrontations between US and European-based theories and positionings, have in our case resulted in a long and fruitful collaboration that could not have been possible without the support of our immediate families. Our thanks go to Joost Raessens for having endured our long working hours and many Skype sessions and to our children, Lea Waller, and Oliver and Nicholas Ponzanesi, who inspire us to believe that a better postcolonial future is possible.

Introduction

Sandra Ponzanesi and Marguerite Waller

There is always a tendency to identify historical breaks and to say "this begins there," "This ends here," while the scene keeps on recurring as unchangeable as change itself.
(Trinh T. Minh-ha, *Surname Viet Given Name Nam*, 1989)

The repercussions of cultures, whether in symbiosis or in conflict – in a polka, we might say, or in a *laghia* – in domination or liberation, opening before us an unknown forever both near and deferred, their lines of force occasionally divined, only to vanish instantly. Leaving us to imagine their interaction and shape it at the same time: to dream or to act.
(Édouard Glissant, "Relation", 1997, p. 131)

What is, or what might constitute, "postcolonial cinema studies"? We do not propose "postcolonial cinema," as a genre or wish to essentialize it by fitting it into a taxonomy. The chapters and the interview we bring together in this volume envision postcolonial cinema in relation to dynamic departures from colonial paradigms of knowledge and power. It matters less what a film is thematically about and more about how it engages with history, subjectivity, epistemology, and the political ramifications of all of these. The authors in this volume focus on the elaboration and deployment of a "postcolonial lens" and on the nature of cinematic engagement with audiences through that lens. Films created and received through other optics – Third Cinema, the cinemas of exile, migration, or diaspora, feminist cinema, accented cinema, transnational cinema, world cinema – may also be engaged through a postcolonial lens. The empire films of Hollywood, Great Britain, France, fascist Italy, and other sites, reconsidered in light of postcolonial studies, become especially illuminating demonstrations of the extent to which instances of colonialism and postcolonialism are interconnected, often overlapping, and continuously interacting.

This is not to imply that postcolonial cinema is everywhere. It is constituted by and within a *conceptual* space in which making connections and drawing inferences, specifically those that are occluded by national and colonial frames, is encouraged. We discover and explore this conceptual space by breaking with universalisms and learning to navigate a fluid, situational, relational mode of knowledge production, one that requires mutual recognition and engagement as well as new methodological and aesthetic strategies.

Bringing cinema studies and postcolonial studies into a more intimate and complex relationship with each other, therefore, presented itself to the editors as, among other things, a project that was itself an instance of "postcolonial" cultural production. Both fields are deeply involved with questions of representation, and they have much to offer each other concerning the forms and legacies of epistemological violence and the role of aesthetics in reshaping the human *sensoriam* (Benjamin, 1968; Said, 1978; Trinh, 1992; Spivak, 1993; Marks, 2000). Through careful and creative orchestrations of postcolonial theoretical debates and close analyses of films, the authors in this volume have used each mode of analysis to extend the other. Several chapters also map features of postcolonial cinema in relation to the conditions of its production, distribution, and reception, which are particularly complex given their dependence upon transnational collaborations, alternative circuits of distribution, and heterogeneous exhibition venues (Batra and Rice, Hoffman, Ponzanesi in this volume).

Reviewing the entwined political, epistemological, and cinematic projects that intersect in the films under consideration here, we have found ourselves reflecting on why, in the academy, postcolonial studies and cinema studies have not engaged each other more fully before. What has stood in the way of this rather obvious intersection, and how is this resistance perhaps relevant to the goals of this volume? This missed opportunity is even more remarkable if we take into account the enormous impact that Edward Said's thinking has had on discussions of how representation, including visual representation, is implicated in the creation and policing of boundaries between West and East, between Europe and the rest, between self and other. Frantz Fanon, Ngugi wa Thiong'o, Gayatri Spivak, and Homi Bhabha, among others, have also analyzed the colonization of the imagination. All have called attention to the enduring ideological legacies of colonialism as they exceed the territory and chronology of empires, coming to permeate the values and regimes of cultures long after official "decolonization."

Legacies, disciplines, practices

In his seminal book *Orientalism*, which appeared in 1978 and has been widely translated, Said argues that Western scholarship has constructed the Orient (vaguely referring to North Africa, the Middle East, and Asia) as a means of "dominating, restructuring, and having authority over the Other" (1978, p. 3). Within the binary logic of empire, the West defined itself as superior to an exoticized, inferiorized Orient, which became the screen upon which Europe could project its own disallowed fears and desires. The representation of the Arab or Asian as mysterious, exotic, and seductive was coupled with the idea that they were inherently barbaric, criminal, and dangerous, set outside the time frame of modernity, poised in a timeless space. It has not escaped feminist theorists that Orientalism is imbricated in the construction of gender, an insight which Said himself has accepted:

We can now see that Orientalism is a praxis of the same sort, albeit in different territories, as male gender dominance, or patriarchy, in metropolitan society: the Orient was routinely described as feminine, its riches as fertile, its main symbols the sensual woman, the harem and the despotic – but curiously attractive – ruler.

(Said, 1985, p. 103)

This gendered sense of Orientalism is developed by postcolonial filmmaker Shirin Neshat, who in *Women Without Men* makes intertextual reference to Said's critique of Orientalism through the figure of Zarin by staging an interruption of the voyeuristic pleasure associated with the so called "harem" and "hammam," using stereotypically exotic compositions of figures in baths and seraglios to display suffering and anorexic bodies (Ponzanesi, this volume). It is notable that Said's thinking about stereotypes and cultural othering is still valid today, as the West's political, legal, and discursive responses to the destruction of New York's World Trade Center on September 11, 2001 further elaborate the image of the Arab and/or Muslim male as potential terrorist and contribute to a rising Islamophobia in Europe and the U.S. In her chapter, Shohini Chaudhuri explores how the techniques of Orientalist representation are applied in twenty-first-century discourses on terror, marking "others" as "unpeople," outside systems of justice and beyond the pale of human rights.

The discipline of cinema studies, however, as it was taking shape in the U.S. and northern Europe at about the same time that Edward Said's and Gayatri Spivak's projects (about which we will have more to say below) began to overlap, found its bearings in a different discursive universe. Evolving rapidly, particularly as a critique of the corporate-controlled mass media and culture of Hollywood, Anglo-American and French film studies adopted primarily semiotics, psychoanalysis, and feminist/queer theory as their theoretical reference points. Despite its critique of the capitalist visual imaginary, however, film studies tended to overlook the role of monopolistic distribution practices in the global reach of Hollywood and to attribute to its productions a universal psychic appeal. Recapitulating the colonial binary of "the West and the rest," U.S. film theory (though not film history) in particular tended to Orientalize as "art house cinema" almost all "foreign" productions, including those of Western Europe, Africa, and South America, while Asian, Indian, and East European cinemas were hardly mentioned at all. Ironically, then, the development of cinematic languages and aesthetics in Marxist-inspired film movements from early Soviet cinema to Italian neorealism, South American Third Cinema and Cinema Novo, Cuban revolutionary film, some African cinemas, and even pre-McCarthy era Hollywood *film noir*, barely figured in theoretical discussions of ideology, gender, space, time, and the political imaginary. A community of African/Third Cinema students, scholars, and filmmakers (including Haile Gerima, Julie Dash, and Charles Burnett) at UCLA, for example, mentored by Third Cinema theorist Teshome Gabriel, was so thoroughly marginalized within the university that not until 2009 was any attempt made by their home institution to recognize and collect the work of this group, known in filmmaking circles as the L.A. Rebellion (Horak, 2010).

How the center/periphery logic of colonialism operates in the constitution of academic disciplines is a question well worth pursuing, but here we simply call attention to the way in which the marginalization of film cultures other than that of "global Hollywood" has contributed to the privileging of Hollywood aesthetics, interpretive strategies, and criteria of evaluation (even when they are the object of critique) (Miller *et al.*, 2005; Shohat and Stam, 1994). Further, as feminist visual theorist Ella Shohat has pointed out, the Orientalist fantasies that Said analyzed so persuasively are consistently reproduced in stereotypical representations by Western film directors of gender, race, and ethnicity in the cultures of North Africa and Asia. *The Sheik* (1921), *Pépé le Moko* (1937), *Morocco* (1930), *Indochine* (1990), *Lawrence of Arabia* (1962), *The Sheltering Sky* (1990) and *Aladdin* (1992) are just few of the titles that confirm that films with "Orientalist traits" have existed within and without, and also before and after, colonization or imperial conquest as such (Shohat, 1998). Indeed, as Said predicted, we discover the persistence of this Orientalist paradigm in many recent films as well, ranging from *The English Patient* (1996) to *Black Hawk Down* (2001) and *Cast Away* (2000), to mention but a few.

The transformation of this landscape of academic cinema studies owes much to the work of French philosopher, Gilles Deleuze, visual culture historians and theorists Ella Shohat and Robert Stam, filmmaker and theorist Trinh Minh-ha, black cultural studies theorist Manthia Diawara, and feminist, deconstructionist, postcolonial theorist Gayatri Spivak. Deleuze's two-part study of cinematic epistemology, *Cinema 1: The Movement-Image* (published in French in 1983 and in English in l986), and *Cinema 2: The Time-Image* (published in French in l985 and in English in l989), became influential on Anglo-American film theory in the l990s once film scholars began to absorb its "anti-Oedipal" interdisciplinarity and proto-postcolonial reconceptualization of national cinemas. Several of our authors draw upon these volumes and on the discussions of noncentered, contingent, and relational, "rhizomatic" thought elaborated by Deleuze and his co-author, psychoanalyst Félix Guattari, in their *Capitalism and Schizophrenia* volumes, *Anti-OEdipus* (1972; English translation, 1984) and *A Thousand Plateaus*. (1980, English translation, 1987) Shohat's and Stam's *Unthinking Eurocentrism* (1994) and the more recent *Multiculturalism, Postcoloniality and Transnational Media* (2003), Shohat's anthology *Talking Visions* (1998), bell hooks's *Black Looks* (1992) and *Reel to Real* (1996), Lola Young's *Fear of the Dark* (1995), and Lisa Bloom's *With Other Eyes* (1999) though framed in terms of multiculturalism and race, helped open up the then largely unexplored issues of historiographical, aesthetic, and epistemological difference in both cinema studies and visual culture more generally. Gayatri Spivak was, at about the same time, forcefully demonstrating in many landmark essays – on subalternity and historiography, on the politics of translation, on developing transnational literacy, on the need to internationalize feminisms – how deeply conditioned readers and viewers are by the epistemological violence of colonialism and its legacies (Spivak, 1987, 1993, 1999).

Third Cinema and beyond

The authors and editors of this volume are indebted to all of these thinkers and many others. The editors though, would like to call attention to filmmaking projects that engaged these issues before either film studies or postcolonial studies began to emerge in the U.S./West European academy in the 1980s and 1990s. Beginning in the 1960s, a transnational "Third Cinema" announced itself as both challenging the ideological, aesthetic, and economic dominance of "First Cinema" (rooted in corporate Hollywood) and differentiating itself from the counter-hegemonic but still European, nation-state based "Second Cinema." Third Cinema was conceived as a revolutionary cinema that would focus on the masses and express their political goals through innovative cinematic forms. Referring to the poverty of its financial and technical means, but also to its embattled and subversive goals, Brazilian director Glauber Rocha espoused an "aesthetics of hunger" (1965). For Cuban Julio Garcia Espinosa it was an "imperfect cinema" whose message was more important than the technical quality of the product (1966). In their manifesto, "Toward a Third Cinema" (1969), which began with a quotation from anti-colonial writer Frantz Fanon, Ottavio Getino and Fernando Solanas positioned it as a "guerilla cinema," explicitly urging that it *not* be collapsed into "Third World," thereby challenging the persistent dichotomy between the West and the Rest. Third Cinema could be made anywhere, not just in Latin America or Africa, but even in Europe – for example, Solanas's *Tangos: el exilio de Gardel* (1985) – or North America, as was Haile Gerima's *Bush Mama* (1979), set in South Central Los Angeles. It was not politically homogeneous either. Ella Shohat, and Ranjana Khanna have called attention to the ways in which gender politics and Third Cinema sometimes missed each other, Shohat calling for a "post-thirdist" critical culture and Khanna for a "Fourth Cinema," in which women's gazes and voices would not be assimilated to the political programs of their male protagonists (Khanna, 1998; Shohat, 2003). A number of filmmakers identified with Third Cinema, though, including Gerima, were manifestly aware that gender was ideologically and socially pivotal to their projects.

Many films and manifestos of the 1960s paid homage to Fanon, including Gillo Pontecorvo's *The Battle of Algiers* (1966) and Solanas's and Getino's *La hora de los hornos/The Hour of the Furnaces* (1968). Among Fanon's arguments about the urgent necessity of a new culture and a new human being, which grew out of his work on the convergence of anti-imperial politics and psychoanalytic theory, it is his thinking about identification and the gaze that is perhaps most pertinent to colonial/postcolonial cinema studies. Long before 1970s film theory took up these issues, Fanon deployed Lacan's notion of the "*stade du miroir*" or mirror stage to explore identity and identification in their multiple psychological, cultural, historical, and political dimensions (Lacan, 2007). One of the symptoms of colonial neurosis, he observed, was the incapacity of the colonizer to identify with the colonized. The imperial gaze saw only "torpid creatures, wasted with fevers, obsessed by ancestral customs" forming "an almost inorganic background for the innovating dynamism of colonial mercantilism" (Fanon, 1963, p. 210). Applying this analysis of the imperial gaze to cinematic spectatorship, he explained how these mass media mechanisms of identification and nonidentification worked for colonized subjects, shifting with the context (an issue developed by Julie Codell in this volume), but nevertheless hegemonizing the imperial subject.

> In the Antilles, the young Negro identifies himself *de facto* with Tarzan against the Negroes. This is much more difficult for him in a European theater, for the rest of the audience, which is white, automatically identifies him with the savages on the screen.
>
> (Fanon, 1967, p. 191)

Either way, identification with an ego ideal is a zero sum game. As more recent academic work on film spectatorship has argued, it naturalizes the intersecting racial, class, and gender orders of colonial domination (Friedberg, 1990; Ravetto, 2001). The ideology of sovereign individualism, through film and other cultural productions, infiltrates the psychological and political life of those colonized, producing a society of self-alienated subjects. The manifestos of the 1960s and 1970s valorized an anti-imperialist cinema, not focused on the individual, whether as self-expressive auteur, idealized protagonist, or consumer-spectator. Third Cinema practitioners created a vision at odds with that reproduced in and through the type of dominant cinema that Fanon invoked, allowing for the emergence of what Stam and Shohat call "polycentric multiculturalism," wherein "no single community or part of the world, whatever its economic or political power, should be epistemologically privileged" (1994, p. 48).

Creating and reading postcolonial cinema(s)

If Third Cinema generally advocates class struggle and armed resistance, the postcolonial cinematic imaginary is highly sensitive to the tendency of opposition to succumb to binarism, "out of which ghouls of totalitarian thinking might suddenly emerge" as Glissant writes in his poem *Relation* (1997, p. 131). In the late 1970s and early 1980s two young filmmakers released paradigm-shifting films that departed from both nation and genre as strategies of location and identification. Not only did they not privilege a particular community or part of the world, their films were about interacting across spaces, times, histories, and languages, coming to terms with, but also departing from, the differentiations and hierarchizations created through colonial histories. Their distinctive aesthetic strategies were linked both within the films and in commentaries on them with discovering alternatives to colonialist-inflected forms of representation and knowledge production. "I am Kidlat Tahimik," the narrator says near the beginning of *Mababangong bangungot/The Perfumed Nightmare* (1977), "I choose my vehicle, and I can cross any bridge." In *Reassemblage* (1982) filmmaker and theorist Trinh T. Minh-ha says in answer to her friends' questions about what her film is about, "Not about, just nearby." Both Tahimik (a pseudonym for Philippines-based Eric de Guia) and Trinh draw connections between cinema as a medium and a postcolonial epistemology in which difference becomes originary rather than secondary, and porousness not threatening but empowering. Kidlat's "vehicle," diegetically a discarded World War II U.S. military jeep that has been elongated, gorgeously decorated, and repurposed as a "jeepney" for transporting ordinary people from place to place, also references cinema, which Tahimik as filmmaker is using to transport audiences to a "space" not governed by monopoly capitalism. (The film plays with the term "space," in part through the motif of a "Werner von Braun Fan Club" from which Kidlat eventually resigns.) Trinh's films and the essays and interviews in which she talks about her work in the contexts of both "high" theory and cinema history shuttle the "differences," "othernesses," and "hybridities" generated by totalizing ideological frames and political systems across each other in the creation of dense webs of relational meaning. As we watch the outdoor wedding ceremony of a Vietnamese American woman and a Caucasian American man in *Surname Viet Given Name Nam* (1989), it is undecideable whether we are watching a scene from "Vietnamese" history or "American" history. Indeed, without anything being said, the framing of histories, especially the recent histories of the U.S. and Vietnam, as separable seems suddenly nonsensical. The women's voices on the soundtrack, mixing Vietnamese and English, poetry and informal conversation, meanwhile, further complicate our reading of this event with their evocations of female desire. Precluding the possibility of reading the wedding as a utopian image of biculturalism, the difficulty of representing even, or especially, oneself as a postcolonial female subject emerges as Trinh's voice-over reads (in English translation) a letter (in French) from a friend who has published a book in France about Vietnamese women:

> Since the publication of the book, I felt like having lost a part of myself. It is very difficult for a Vietnamese woman to write about Vietnamese women. At least in France, where, in spite of the Mouvement de Libération de la Femme [Women's Liberation Movement], maternalism remains the cornerstone of the dominant ideology. To have everything as it should be, I should have accepted a preface by Simone de Beauvoir.

Filmmaking is translation, Trinh concludes in an interview about her own practice, and translation is an ongoing struggle, involving questions not only of language but also of power, meaning, and resistance to meaning, "a process through which the self loses its fixed boundaries – a disturbing yet potentially empowering practice of difference" ("Film as Translation", 1992, p. 133).

If the postcolonial optic is less explicitly polemical than that of Third Cinema, it is nevertheless strongly political and still concerned with authoritarian oppression. Priya Jaikumar explains in her interview at the conclusion of this volume why the postcolonial political imaginary displaces state institutions and corporate capital as privileged loci. "There are other kinds of power in the world. It is not just about capitalism" (p. 236). Accentuating semiotic and discursive interactions which may involve elderly women, janitors, or children, rather than iconic figures of freedom fighters, the filmmakers featured here as postcolonial engage with society and the "real" more obliquely, often problematizing the cinematic tools, media technologies, and distribution networks through which we receive images and information. They show these mediating structures playing a large role in how we process and respond to what we receive. Postcolonial cinema, while maintaining engagement with collectives, refocuses on the specificity of individuals. Protagonists are not presented as ego ideals or everypersons, though, but as multi-dimensional figures – often marginalized, subordinated, displaced, or deterritorialized – whose subjectivities as well as subject positions are open to the unexpected, the unpredictable, which may enter from somewhere beyond our particular epistemological ken. Hamid Naficy (2003) suggests that with these films spectators participate in a more phenomenologically complex circuit of perception than that envisaged by the ideals of Third Cinema, though we would like to keep these categories and spectatorial positions nonoppositional and mutually porous.

Further contexts and relations

Hamid Naficy (2000), Laura U. Marks (2000), the collaborative group Katarzyna Marciniak, Anikó Imre, and Aine O'Healy (2007), and other cinema studies scholars have, over the past decade, conceptualized a range of new, inter-related developments in filmmaking that intersect with our conceptualization of postcolonial cinema. Responding to rapidly shifting economic, demographic, and geopolitical circumstances around the world, cinemas of exile and diaspora, haptic cinema, transnational feminist cinema, migrant, intercultural, and hybridized national cinemas (in Europe: British-Asian, Black-British, French-Beur, African-Italian, Turkish-German, etc.) are challenging and vastly expanding visual imaginaries. Naficy has explored in great detail, not only thematically but also stylistically, the characteristics of a cinema of exile and diaspora that he has termed "accented." Accented cinema questions notions of belonging and identity, confinement within alien borders and nostalgia for "home," while exploring language use (multilingualism, orality, acousticity, accents, and inflection), modes of narration (autobiographical, epistolary, telephonic, texting [SMS], and e-mail), and the addition of haptic elements (appealing to the senses of touch and smell).

The phenomenological experience of homelessness and the politics of displacement, exile, and diaspora are also elaborated by Marks in *The Skin of the Film: Intercultural Cinema, Embodiment, and the Senses*. In her analysis of relationships between audiovisual media and cultural memory, she foregrounds what she calls "haptic visuality" (the sense of touch evoked visually – at the limits of vision) in her discussion of how memory is embedded in and embodied by the senses and therefore mediated by the very fabric and feel of film. (Sabine Doran uses both the metaphor of weaving and Marks's discussion of haptic cinema in her analysis of Raul Ruiz's *Les Trois Couronnes du Matelot/Three Crowns of the Sailor* in this volume.) "For intercultural artists it is most valuable to think of the skin of the film not as a screen, but as a membrane that brings its audience into contact with the material forms of memory," Marks writes (p. 243). By the "skin of the film" she means both the fragile financial and technical means of interstitial film production and the intercultural skin of its reception, the traces it leaves as it circulates among various audiences as an artifact that conveys the disjunctures and intervals of experience and memory in a rapidly globalizing world.

Transnational cinema and media as described by Marciniak, Imre and O'Healy in their volume *Transnational Feminisms in Film and Media* foreground the imbrication of the foreign within the domestic, demystifying the rhetoric of global progress while also questioning the legitimacy of national borders (2007, p. 3). They are sites consisting of multiple layers and connotations, which feature subjectivities emerging between national identities and the economic and political circumstances of neocolonial globalization underwriting these shifting subjectivites.

Postcolonial cinema has much in common with all of these. And, like these porous categories, the "postcolonial" rubric is intended to counteract the ghettoization of films (as "ethnic," "minority," "immigrant," "hyphenated," or even "art-house") that depart from commercial and ideological hegemonies. Yet postcolonial cinema remains a strange false friend of these categories as it connects with, but also departs from, the projects they name to pursue questions of the tense power asymmetries bequeathed to the contemporary world by the multiple, diverse, and overlapping histories of conquest and colonialism. Characters, images, and narratives move across and between contingent histories and geographies, which the temporal and spatial malleability of cinema actualizes in powerfully affective ways. Édouard Glissant likened this recursive, self-reflexive historiography to baroque art. "Baroque art mustered bypasses, proliferation, spatial redundancy, anything that flouted the alleged unicity of the thing known and the knowing of it" (1997, p. 78). In a similar spirit, Sabine Doran and Priya Jaikumar liken the diverse, nonmimetic aesthetics of postcolonial cinema to surrealism "making a dark commentary on what appears to be normal," (Jaikumar, p. 241). As the gaze is turned back upon imperial ways of knowing, feeling, and seeing, the present becomes permeable to the experiences subjugated by political domination. Recursiveness, porosity, intrusion, and haunting are some of the terms used by our contributors to talk about the ways in which these films, and/or reading them through a postcolonial lens, disable imperial paradigms of central conflict, isomorphic identity, and linear history, offering instead shifting perspectives and changing subjectivities. Diaries, wills, ruins, shipwrecks, and shadows take on agency as rationalism and mastery lose their persuasiveness.

We can make no claim to comprehensiveness. This collection of essays, grouped and sequenced to invite recursive and relational readings, does not frame postcolonial cinema as a genre or as characteristic of a particular period or place. Instead it charts possible routes to take in thinking about cinema studies and postcolonial studies together. Different perspectives and approaches are offered with the goal of sparking further postcolonial readings of cinema while using cinema to expand and deepen postcolonial critique. Such a practice is open to many trajectories and applications, which enact the overlapping of histories and temporalities, the merging of perspectives and aesthetics, and the enhancing of subaltern subjectivities and marginalized identities. In cinema, postcolonial theory's focus on colonial/postcolonial relations becomes actualized in new realms of sensory and political experience, where power relationships are relocated, shifted, and renegotiated. As neo-colonial configurations of power emerge in the contemporary world, we are reminded that the colonial hangover is far from over. Film (and media generally), because they can deal in fantasy and the imaginary, project new possibilities of resistance and subversion, particularly through the prisms of micropolitics and aesthetics. The *grand récits* break down opening space for the infinite specificities that refract larger, often repressed, miswritten, and unofficial histories of the nation, communities, classes, genders, and subaltern groups.

A recent film by Michel Haneke, *Caché/Hidden* (2004), and the heated debates and divergent readings it has unleashed in Europe, suggest the complexity of these cinematic projects. As Gayatri Spivak writes of an earlier film, *Sammy and Rosie Get Laid* (directed by Stephen Frears and written by Hanif Kureishi, 1987), which she sees as a mix of "migrant diasporic" and "diasporic postcolonial," characters and frameworks, "there is a lot to read there" (1993, p. 244), requiring nothing short of a new "politics of reading" (1993, p 251). Haneke, a filmmaker of Austrian origin but resident in France, depicts in his film how the French national identity is haunted by its repressed colonial past in Algeria. This haunting is not just an idea "out there," but takes place literally in the form of flashbacks, nightmares, and paranoia. Through an intriguing visual technique that positions anonymous digital videos as the frame within the frame, the film both visually and conceptually makes as real as quotidian "reality," the "colonial unconscious" that comes to haunt the "imaginary" of the present.

Haneke, who specializes in unraveling European bourgeois subjectivity and family life, which he depicts as often alienated and complacent, makes a postcolonial intervention in this film by showing how the comfortable world of Georges, a sophisticated French TV talkshow host, becomes disturbed by the recollection of the past, specifically his aggressiveness as a six-year old child toward an Algerian boy, Majid.

The film slowly and very indirectly unfolds the story of Majid, who lost his parents in the notorious Paris massacre of 1961, a peaceful demonstration in support of the Algerian cause that turned into a bloodbath, subsequently silenced within the police archives and the national memory. When Georges's parents wanted to adopt the orphaned Majid, violent jealousy and his desire not to share his privileges drives the young Georges to create an incident that relegates Majid to an orphanage and a life of marginality.

As an adult, the Algerian Majid lives in the outskirts of Paris in stark contrast to the affluent Georges, who lives in a chic neighborhood in the city center. After several confrontations with Georges about the authorship of the mysterious videotapes that bring the past into the present, Majid commits a gruesome and violent suicide that Georges is forced to witness. Through this action the film hints at the responsibility, personal and by extrapolation national, that Georges has to take, which until then he has repressed in order to safeguard his comfortable present.

What characterizes *Caché* as a postcolonial film (analyzed by Hamish Ford in this volume) is not only its subject matter, but also its visual style. As James Penney writes "Haneke's ingenious device [of the anonymous video tapes] presents a felicitous occasion to revisit the conceptualization of the apparatus in cinema theory" (2011). In addition to exploring the visual dynamics of France's lingering colonial guilt, the film engages with Lacan's concept of the gaze, combining, as Fanon did, the psychodynamics of postcolonial guilt with a critique of the colonial field of vision. The colonial real comes back in the form of a gaze, a gaze indexed by the videotapes left anonymously on Georges's doorstep. These tapes are shot by a camera whose status is paradoxical. "Both included and banished from the film's diegesis, this camera torments Georges with memories of his childhood, memories that we see in the form of harrowing flashbacks ... The video footage is also the film's principal means of creating suspense; it incites our desire as viewers to solve the perplexing enigma of its impossible hidden camera" (ibid.).

In *Caché* the colonial/postcolonial impasse is not resolved, however, but left open. The final shot shows the children of the two main characters having a conversation, which is inaudible to viewers, outside a French school while the end credits roll. Haneke does not offer any closure or easy solutions, either about the author of the videotapes or about the function of this final shot, which has generated wildly diverging interpretations. Haneke's film instead offers one example of how postcolonial cinema initiates ongoing interrogations, ways of questioning reality, history, memory, and identity, reformulating the conventions of cinema for the purposes of narrating, visualizing, and rendering the effects of subjugated histories and emergent subjectivities. Not all such films are as harsh as Haneke's. Comedy, fantasy, or some version of magical realism may also become vehicles of this postcolonial turn of the cinematic gaze.

Rationale of the volume

We have organized the chapters in this book into four sections: Cinemas of Empire; Postcolonial Cinemas: Unframing Histories; Postcolonial Cinemas: Aesthetics; and Postcolonial Cinemas and Globalization. Introductions to individual chapters can be found at the beginning of each of these four sections; here we offer the rationale for organizing them this way. The sections are not mutually exclusive but heuristic – proposing emphases rather than categories. Historiography and aesthetics, as our authors demonstrate, are inextricably linked, as are the projects of empire and globalization.

The first section introduces different versions of "empire film," both those popular in the years before World War II when, ironically, European empires were losing their moral, if not yet their political, legitimacy and a cluster of historical epics produced between the 1960s and 1980s in Eastern Europe. The chapters in the next section focus on the myriad ways that the films under discussion undo historiographical stability. The third section investigates the aesthetic frameworks and rhetorical strategies that the postcolonial cinematic optic has had to create and through which it becomes accessible. The last section explores the intersection of postcoloniality with globalization, emphasizing the porosity of the rubric "postcolonial cinema studies" to other frameworks and its enduring relevance to the seismic shifts of post-Cold War restructuring.

Though there are no beginnings or endings to the application of the postcolonial paradigm, to bring into focus the practices of postcolonial cinema it is important to revisit "empire cinema." As a mass media tool of European imperial projects, such productions helped shape, enforce, and naturalize the relationships between hegemonizing groups and their "dominated" others. These films magnify the role of foreign conquest in nation-building and were often intended to enhance international prestige. Cinema brought the spectacle of distant territories close to home, and helped to forge political consensus, not least by offering domestic audiences the pleasure of colonization through visual renditions of imperial mastery. Postcolonial cinema historiography offers a different lens through which to read these films, allowing us to unpack their visual codes and narrative discourses of supremacy and to discover their tensions and aporias. For author Anikó Imre, the postcolonial lens begins to make sense of the pleasures of the seemingly paradoxical "socialist national historical epic."

Our authors further emphasize that the production and reception of empire films had different fortunes in different parts of Europe, North America, and diverse colonial settings. The new technology of cinema evolved into a powerful mass medium at the height of European imperial rule, and was quickly transported to the colonies where it was influential on subsequent developments of film as an instrument of resistance and on the emergence of new national, regional, and political cinemas.

The second section of the book focuses on the reconceptualization of imperial/colonial histories and geographies. Nostalgia, memory, amnesia, trauma, denial, repression, guilt – and, not least, humor – are some of the recurrent traits of postcolonial films where identities have become unstable, and the past comes to haunt the present in the forms of ghosts, shadows, written documents, and phantasmatic spaces. These are films that do not privilege a single history or central narrative. They move toward margins and spaces between, proliferating stories and identities, which become nomadic rather than teleological. What remains vital in this unframing of histories is a political commitment to visualizing what has been invisible, untold, or discarded, opening the frame or creating frames that are not finite or conclusive. To unframe histories is to undo official and dominant accounts that exclude or marginalize subjects, creating gender, racial, ethnic, and linguistic alterities.

Postcolonial imaginaries create and depend upon postcolonial aesthetics. The authors in the third section discuss the highly original formal and rhetorical strategies that filmmakers have deployed in their projections of postcolonial historiographies, geographies, and subjectivities. Playing with margins and marginality, framing, camera angles, editing, color, texture, the relations between word and image, constitute a resistance that is at once aesthetic and political. Postcolonial cinema can be conceptualized as a "dangerous supplement" (Derrida, 1974) to national and genre cinemas; it exposes relationalities, contaminations, and zones of contact. It encourages complex reading processes (Spivak, 1993) that help us unthink ossified categories and representations (Shohat and Stam, 1994), unsettling traditional frameworks of interpretation and including perspectives, even highly elaborated epistemologies, that appear irrelevant, threatening, or absurd from within the hegemon.

The chapters in the final section address the relationship between thinking the postcolonial through cinema and postcolonial cinema's entanglements with other dynamics that exceed the postcolonial optic.

Science-fiction films, for example, often take a certain decolonization of the imagination as one of their aims, projecting futures that magnify the dark areas of the present and past. Michael Winterbottom's *Code 46* (2003) for instance, is set in a nonspecified Brave New World where cities are heavily controlled and accessible only through check points. Outside these cities, the desert has taken over and shanty towns are jammed with non-citizens – people without "papelles" (special travel permits issued by the totalitarian regime) who are forced to live primitive lives. Through the dystopian world of *Code 46*, we are summoned to reflect upon the implementation of human rights and access to citizenship in relation to the proliferation of new economic borders, securitized frontiers, and invisible technological thresholds, which currently rearticulate neocolonial relations through the exclusion of bodies, races, and minority groups marked as deviant (Stacey, 2010). In her discussion of *Children of Men* (2010), set in the not too distant 2027, Shohini Chaudhuri explores that film's engagement with the contemporary nation-state's treatment of asylum seekers and refugees as "un-people," whose vulnerable, disposable, often racialized bodies fall outside systems of justice and citizenship – a position controversially termed "bare life" by Italian philosopher Giorgio Agamben (1998).

The relationships between postcolonial cinemas and globalization also include global film industries such as Bollywood and Nollywood. Until recently, the category of Bollywood cinema (Indian film production based in Mumbai) was excluded from Western critical and theoretical appraisal both because most film scholars in the West were unacquainted with it and because it did not cohere with the aesthetic categories, particularly the privileging of realism, by which Western and world cinemas were being evaluated. However, distribution of Bollywood films to diasporic Indian communities and various transnational audiences has allowed a shift in Western assumptions about films and their quality. Bollywood is seen less as mass escapism and more as a cinema capable of renegotiating national values for domestic, diasporic, and cosmopolitanism communities.

The booming of the Nigerian video industry, often referred to as Nollywood, has emerged through an interesting intersection between the spread of digital technology, the street violence in cities like Lagos that made going to the cinema less attractive, and desire to counteract Hollywood domination through local productions focused on national and regional issues, traditions, themes, and forms of entertainment. Nollywood's digital video films enter the market through alternative distribution channels such as supermarkets, petrol stations, hair salons, and airports, and are also the object of fierce pirating. They cater to the Nigerian community both at home and in the diaspora, creating an alternative circuit of media representation and distribution.

Global exhibition through corporate marketing, a proliferation of international festivals, and low-cost video and digital channels, along with increasing co-production and the weakening of the nation-state, are all factors further problematizing the traditional categories of cinema studies. On the other hand, reproduction on DVDs and computer downloading have exponentially facilitated the distribution, reproduction, and storage of both widely and less well distributed films. These technologies hold great promise for scholars and students, making the archiving of films and access to them in the classroom far more feasible than they were two decades ago. Some of the films discussed in this book have become much more available even as our work has progressed. Postcolonial cinema is also about rematerializing and re-embodying these global flows and about the multiplication and diversification of audiences.

We thought it would be fitting to close, not by concluding, but by further expanding the discussions in this volume with Priya Jaikumar's thoughts about teaching cinema and postcolonialism in the classroom. Jaikumar shares several years' worth of experience giving students the interdisciplinary materials and tools with which to develop their own postcolonial optics. Several of her students, who are now scholars themselves, are currently investigating the Japanese empire and its aftermath in East Asian cinemas. Like Jaikumar, we are well aware that there are many more films and film cultures that need to be engaged in postcolonial film studies. We encourage our readers to carry on this project.

Bibliography

Agamben, G., 1998. *Homo Sacer: Sovereign Power and Bare Life.* Trans. D. Heller-Roazen. Stanford, CA: Stanford University Press.

Benjamin, W., 1968. The Work of Art in an Age of Mechanical Reproduction. (published in German in 1936.) *Illuminations.* Trans. Harry Zohn. Edited and with introduction by H. Arendt. New York: Schocken Books, pp. 217–51.

Bhabha, H., 1994. *The Location of Culture.* London: Routledge.

Bloom, L., 1999. *With Other Eyes.* Minneapolis: University of Minneapolis Press.

Deleuze, G., 1986. *Cinema 1: The Movement-Image* (published in French in 1983). Translated from French by H. Tomlinson and B. Hobberjam. London: The Athlone Press.

Deleuze, G., 1989. *Cinema 2: The Time-Image* (published in French in 1985). Translated from French by H. Tomlinson and R. Galeta. Minneapolis: University of Minnesota Press.

Deleuze, G. and Guattari, F., 1984. *Anti-Œdipus. Vol. I Capitalism and Schizophrenia* (published in French in 1972). Translated from French by R. Hurley, M. Seem, and H. R. Lane. London: The Athlone Press.

Deleuze, G. and Guattari, F., 1987. *A Thousand Plateaus: Capitalism and Schizophrenia II* (published in French in 1980) Translated from French by B. Massumi. London: The Athlone Press.

Derrida, J., 1974. *...That Dangerous Supplement...* (published in French in 1967). *Of Grammatology.* Translated from French by G. C. Spivak. Baltimore, MD: The Johns Hopkins University Press, pp. 144–64.

Diawara, M., 1992. *African Cinema: Politics and Culture.* Bloomington: Indiana University Press.

Espinosa, J.G., 1979. For an imperfect cinema. Translated from Spanish by Julianne Burton. *Jump Cut: A Review of Contemporary Media*, 20 (1979,) pp. 24–6. (First published in Spanish as Por un Cine imperfecto, *Cine Cubano*, 14, 1966).

Fanon, F., 1963. *The Wretched of the Earth* (published in French in 1961). Preface by J.-P. Sartre. Translated from French by C. Farrington. New York: Grove Weidenfeld.

Fanon, F., 1967. The Negro and Psychopathology. *Black Skin, White Masks* (published in French in 1952). Translated from French by C. L. Markmann, New York: Grove Press, pp. 141–209.

Friedberg, A., 1990. Theories of Cinematic Identification. In: E. A. Kaplan, ed., 1990. *Psychoanalysis and Cinema.* London and New York: Routledge, pp. 36–45.

Getino, O. and Solanas, F., 1971. Toward a Third Cinema (published in Spanish in 1969). *Cineaste*, 4(3), pp. 1–10.

Glissant, E., 1997. *Poetics of Relation.* (Originally published in French in 1990). Translated from French by B. Wing. Ann Arbor: The University of Michigan Press.

hooks, b., 1992. *Black Looks: Race and Representation.* Boston, MA: South End Press.

hooks, b., 1996. *Reel to Real: Race, Sex, and Class at the Movies.* New York, NY: Routledge.

Horak, J.-C., 2010. Forming history through the archive. Available at http://www.ithaca.edu/fleff10/blogs/archival_spaces/forming_history_through_the_archive. (Accessed March 2, 2011)

Khanna, R., 1998. The Battle of Algiers and the Nouba of the women of Mont Chenoua: From Third to Fourth Cinema. *Third Text*, 12(43), pp. 13–21.

Lacan, J., 2007. The Mirror Stage as Formative of the I Function as Revealed in Psyhoanalytic Experience. *Écrits: The First Complete Edition in English.* Translated from French by B. Fink, H. Fink, and R. Grigg. New York: W.W. Norton and Co., pp. 75–81.

Marciniak, K., A. Imre, A. O'Healy., eds., 2007. *Transnational Feminism in Film and Media.* New York: Palgrave Macmillan.

Marks, L., 2000. *The Skin of the Film: Intercultural Cinema, Embodiment and the Senses.* Durham, NC: Duke University Press.

Miller, T., Govil, N., McMurria, J., Maxwell R., and Wang, T., 2005. *Global Hollywood 2.* London: bfi Publishing.

Naficy, H., 2000. *An Accented Cinema. Exilic and Diasporic Filmmaking.* Princeton, NJ: Princeton University Press.

Naficy, H., 2003. Theorizing "Third World" Film Spectatorship: the Case of Iran and Iranian Cinema. In: A.R. Guneratne and W. Dissanayake, eds., 2003. *Rethinking Third Cinema.* New York, Routledge, pp. 183–201.

Ngugi wa Thiong'o, 1986. *Decolonising the Mind: The Politics of Language in African Literature.* Portsmouth, NH: Heinemann Books Inc. in association with Nairobi: East African Publishers K.L. Ltd.

Penney, J., 2011. "You Never Look at Me From Where I See You": Postcolonial Guilt in Caché. *New Formations: A Journal of Culture/Theory/Politics*, 70, pp. 77–93.

Ravetto, K. 2001. *The Unmaking of Fascist Aesthetics.* Minneapolis: The University of Minnesota Press.

Rocha, G., 1995. An Aesthetic of Hunger (published in Portuguese in 1965). Translated from Portuguese by R. Johnson and B. Hollyman. In: R. Johnson and R. Stam, eds., 1995. *Brazilian Cinema.* New York: Columbia University Press, pp. 68–71.

Said, E., 1978. *Orientalism.* London: Pantheon Books.

Said, E., 1985. Orientalism Reconsidered. *Cultural Critique*, 1, pp. 89–107.

Shohat, E., 2003. Post-Third-Worldist Culture: Gender, Nation, and the Cinema. In: A. R. Guneratne and W. Dissanayake, eds., 2003. *Rethinking Third Cinema.* New York: Routledge, pp. 49–50.

Shohat, E., 1998. *Talking Visions.* Multicultural Feminism in a Transnational Age. Cambridge, MA: MIT Press.

Shohat, E. and Stam, R., 1994. *Unthinking Eurocentrism: Multiculturalism and the Media.* London: Routledge, 1994.

Shohat, E. and Stam, R. eds., 2003. *Multiculturalism, Postcoloniality and Transnational Media.* New Brunswick, NJ, Rutgers.

Spivak, G. C., 1987. *In Other Worlds: Essays in Cultural Politics.* New York: Methuen.

Spivak, G. C., 1993. *Outside in The Teaching Machine.* New York and London: Routledge.

Spivak, G. C., 1999. *A critique of Postcolonial Reason: Toward a History of the Vanishing Present.* Cambridge, MA and London: Harvard University Press.

Stacey, J., 2010. *The Cinematic Life of the Gene.* Durham, NC: Duke University Press.

Trinh, M. T., 1992. *Framer Framed.* New York: Routledge.

Young, L., 1995. *Fear of the Dark. "Race," Gender and Sexuality in the Cinema.* London: Routledge.

Filmography

Aladdin, 1992, [film] Directed by R. Clements and J. Musker. USA: Walt Disney Pictures.

The Battle of Algiers, 1966. [film] Directed by G. Pontecorvo. Italy/Algeria: Igor Film.

Black Hawk Down, 2001. [film] Directed by R. Scott. USA: Philadelphia Newspaper Inc./ Sony.

Bush Mama, 1979. [film] Directed by H. Gerima. USA: Mypheduh Films.

Caché (Hidden), 2005. [film] Directed by M. Haneke. France/Austria/Germany/Italy/USA: Sony Pictures Classics.

Cast Away, 2000. [film] Directed by R. Zemeckis. USA: DreamWorks SKG.

Children of Men, 2006. [film] Directed by A. Cuaron. USA: Universal Pictures.

Code 46, 2003. [film] Directed by M. Winterbottom. UK: British Broadcasting Corporation (BBC).

The English Patient, 1996. [film] Directed by A. Minghella. USA: Miramax.

La hora de los hornos, 1968. [film] Directed by and F. E. Solanas and O. Getino. Argentina: Grupo Cine Liberacion/Solanas Production.

Indochine, 1990. [film] Directed by R. Wargnier. France: Paradis Films.

Lawrence of Arabia, 1962. [film] Directed by D. Lean. UK: Columbia Pictures.

Mababangong bangungot, 1977. [film] Directed by Kidlat Tahimik. Philippines.

Morocco, 1930 [film] Directed by J. von Sternberg. USA: Paramount Pictures.

Pépé le Moko, 1937. [film] Directed by J. Duvivier. France: Paris Film.

Reassemblage, 1982. [film] Directed by Trinh T. Minh-ha. USA: Women Make Movies.

The Sheik, 1921. [film] Directed by G. Melford. USA: Paramount Pictures.

The Sheltering Sky, 1990. [film] Directed by B. Bertolucci. UK/Italy: Recorded Picture Company (RPC)/Warner Bros, Pictures.

Sammy and Rosie Get Laid, 1987. [film] Directed by S. Frears. UK: Channel Four Films.

Surname Viet Given Name Nam, 1989. [film] Directed by Trinh T. Minh-ha. USA: Women Make Movies.

Tangos: el exilio de Gardel, 1985. [film] Directed by F. Solanas. Argentina/France:

Les Trois Couronnes du Matelot, 1983. [film] Directed by R. Ruiz. France: Film A2, Centre National de la Cinématographie (CNC).

Women Without Men, 2009. [film] Directed by S. Neshat. Germany: Essential Filmproduktion.

Part I

Cinemas of empire

Cinema's late colonial period embodied the ambiguities, possibility and fears generated by two historical paradoxes: that of colonialism's moral delegitimization before its political demise and that of its persistence in shaping modern postcolonial societies well after the end of a formal empire.

(Priya Jaikumar, 2006, p. 2)

The chapters in this section explore the complex inter-implications of colonialism and postcolonialism. They focus on cinemas of empire that orchestrated sensations of visual mastery and also offered occasions for its undermining. Film as a medium is endowed with particular formal and aesthetic properties, which can be used to promote a variety of ways of seeing. Empire films tended to legitimate the domination by metropolitan centers over colonial peripheries. Colonial images of gender, race, and class carried ideological connotations that confirmed imperial epistemologies and taxonomies, depicting natives as primitives and savages, subjects outside modernity. However, the chapters in this section analyze not only the production and naturalization of colonial epistemes, but also occasions when these epistemes are undermined by departures from dominant representational practices and the perhaps inadvertent intrusion of alternative visual codes.

Ruth Ben-Ghiat points out that the term empire cinema is not found in Italian film scholarship. Specialists of early French and Italian cinema prefer to speak of "colonial cinema." Though the two terms tend to be used interchangeably, many scholars feel that it is important to differentiate between colonialism and imperialism. Colonialism refers to the practice (conquering of the land and exploiting its resources) and imperialism to the idea driving the practice (political and economic control, but also an ideological investment). Cinema was a perfect medium with which to convey these ideological discourses, whose legacies continue to shape political and cultural landscapes long after the official end of colonization.

For Mussolini, cinema was the strongest weapon (Reich and Garofalo, 2002; Ben-Ghiat, 2001), and it was strategically used as part of an orchestrated political propaganda campaign that was meant to manufacture consent. Colonial films imaged Roman grandeur and supported Italy's model of racial superiority and virility, especially during the conquest of Ethiopia (called Abyssinia before 1935). They put the new technology at the service of imperial policies, which were glamorized by the spectacles offered to Italian audiences at home.

Empire films, which focused on glorifying the British Empire were, as Julie Codell writes, popular on both sides of the Atlantic. British actors played older British officers and American actors played younger officers, metaphorically figuring the passing of the "white man's burden" from Britain to America. Codell explores such paradoxes as the British film industry's casting of Paul Robeson, a major figure of the Harlem Renaissance and a prominent advocate of African American civil rights, as the savage "other," thereby using the same body to project both Western moral rectitude and the African "savagery" that legitimated Western domination. Similarly, the use of blackface in some empire films both signified and yet curiously de-essentialized racial difference.

Cinema served both to consolidate empires and to dismantle them. As Priya Jaikumar writes in her book *Cinema at the end of Empire*, quoted in our epigraph, cinema played a very paradoxical and ambivalent role on both sides of the imperial divide. The beginnings of cinema corresponded with the apogee of colonialism, but also to the proliferation of anti-colonial independence movements. Jaikumar, in her Postface to this volume, explores the intersection between a dying ideology, that of imperialism, and the rise of a new medium whose transportation to the colonies as an innovative technological tool resulted not only in the assimilation of its language and codes, but also the possibility of its appropriation, offering new nations a powerful tool for self-representation and decolonization.

This section concludes with an empire of a different kind, not linked to Western European dominance, but to what Bakic-Hayden (1995) calls the "nesting orientalisms" involved in the political imaginary of Eastern Europe. The Soviet Empire is just the latest phase in a history of imperial struggles over a terrain that has been multiply conquered, and where rulers and subjects often shifted roles. Anikó Imre's chapter reflects on a series of historical epics produced between the 1960s and the 1980s in the Eastern bloc, perceiving a postcolonial pattern in the thematic and ideological overlaps among them. Following a remarkably similar formula, these films consolidate "East" European nationhood vis-à-vis the Ottoman Empire, each nation portraying itself as a defender of Europe against the "Eastern" infidels. For many viewers, the Ottoman Empire was envisioned as a precursor to the Soviet Empire. Thus, these films, while intended to bolster loyalty to national communist regimes, implicitly challenge Soviet domination, ironically through a self-colonizing identification with the West. East and West, Europe and nonEurope, emerge as highly charged, but always relative terms whose use in these films uncannily prefigures economic and cultural developments in the region since the dissolution of the Soviet Union. Imre's skillful integration of post-Soviet and postcolonial perspectives unveils the workings of Cold War and post-Cold War orientalisms, and critically expands the postcolonial notion of "empire film."

Bibliography

Bakic-Hayden, M., 1995. Nesting Orientalisms: The Case of Former Yugoslavia. *Slavic Review*, 54(4), pp. 917–31.

Ben-Ghiat, R., 2001. *Fascist Modernities*. Berkeley: University of California Press.

Ben-Ghiat, R. and Fuller, M. eds., 2005. *Italian Colonialism*. New York: Palgrave.

Jaikumar, P., 2006. *Cinema at the End of Empire: A Politics of Transition in Britain and India*. Durham, NC: Duke University Press.

Reich, J. and Garofalo, P. eds., 2002. *Re-Viewing Fascism. Italian Cinema, 1922–1943*. Bloomington, IN: Indiana University Press.

Chapter 1

Italian Fascism's empire cinema

Kif Tebbi, the conquest of Libya, and the assault on the nomadic

Ruth Ben-Ghiat

The history and consequences of Italian colonialism were until quite recently little known in Italy and abroad. Italian expansionism is usually linked to the aggressions in Ethiopia (1935–1936), which was called Abyssinia before 1935, of the Fascist regime led by Benito Mussolini (1922–1945) but the foundations of this empire were laid in the liberal period, with the occupations of the East African countries of Eritrea (1890) and Somalia (1908) and the seizure of Ottoman-held Libya in 1912 (Labanca, 2002; Ben-Ghiat and Fuller, 2005; Palumbo, 2003; Andall and Duncan, 2005). This neglected history has translated into an obscured film history: the dozens of documentary and feature films made on imperial themes are little studied, apart from historical colossals such as *Cabiria* (Pastrone, 1914) and *Scipione l'Africano/Scipio the African* (Gallone, 1936) (Gili and Brunetta, 1990; Elena, 1999; Hay, 1987; Coletti, 2006). The present essay discusses the 1920s, when the Fascists laid the groundwork for the acquisition of territories that would transform the Mediterranean from Italy's "prison" into the hinge of an empire that stretched from the Levant to Africa and the Red Sea (Fuller, 2007). In the realm of cinema, the 1920s is normally considered a period of crisis; World War One decimated Italy's previously profitable and prolific national industry, dispersing underemployed Italian film professionals to the film capitals of Europe. Yet research over the last decades has revealed a more robust filmic landscape than previously imagined, as well as the influences of Italians' years abroad on their future film aesthetics, production methods, and directing styles (Ricci, 2008; Martinelli, 1978; Farassino, 2000, pp. 83–106).

I bring these filmic and imperial histories together in my discussion of the silent movie *Kif Tebbi* (Camerini, 1928), which is set and partly shot in the Tripolitanian region of Libya. It forms part of the international Orientalist trend in filmmaking, but also testifies to Mussolini's impact on Italian male stardom and the need to justify a next wave of Italian occupation that would inaugurate new levels of European colonial violence. While *Kif Tebbi* is also of interest as an antecedent for empire films of the sound era, Italians are entirely absent from its narrative; the point of view narrated is that of a Tripolitanian notable (played by the Italian actor Marcello Spada) in love with a young nomad. Such a film could not have been made a decade later, when heightened racial and pedagogical demands mandated narratives that revolved around the Italian male who resists local temptation. As such, *Kif Tebbi* offers a window into the continuities and ruptures of Italian imperial ideologies and iconographies from early to late Fascism and from silent to sound cinema. As for other European colonizers, empire served the Italians as an agent of nation-building and international prestige. Yet in both the liberal and Fascist periods, imperial ideologies were fueled by a particular Italian discourse of *ressentiment:* empire would correct a history of marginalization by the "Great Powers," giving Italy the power to refute perceptions of Italian "backwardness" (Bosworth, 1996; Fuller, 2007). The obsessive display of communications, military, agricultural, and medical technology in empire films has its origins here, and also explains why Italian colonialists demonstrated little of the "melancholy discourse of nostalgia" for the disappearing "exotic Other" that Ali Behdad has found in the French case. Any "belatedness" that haunted Italians was largely about their late start at colonization with respect to other Europeans (Behdad, 1994, p. 92).

The Mediterranean was the field of action upon which these imperial agendas depended. As Mia Fuller observes, the Mediterranean was a means of achieving Italian autonomy from Europe, as well as being central to the revival of Rome as a model of imperial power (Fuller, 2007, pp. 39–62). The Fascist construction of the Mediterranean as *mare nostrum*, a space "saturated with a timeless Roman and Italian essence," required its elision as a site of "cultural crossovers, contaminations, creolizations, and uneven historical memories" (Fuller, 2007, p. 40; Chambers, 2008, p. 28). The splitting off of the "Roman" Mediterranean from the "Oriental" Levant was one strategy to this end. In the case of Libya and Italy's Dodecanese Island possessions, this translated into a desire to "reclaim" Rhodes and other territories from Turkish influences, the Turk standing in for an unacceptable history of Oriental backwardness and lassitude. Yet this "other" Mediterranean surfaces in Fascism's empire cinema, which is haunted by the basin as a "fluid and unstable archive" of the kinds of wanderings and intercultural fusions the Fascists feared. The Mediterranean crossings that figure in almost every Italian empire film initiate travelers into unstable realms of cultural translation and personal transformation. The personages of these films about settlement never really settle, and for male protagonists the narrative lies in their confrontations with their new surroundings and in the struggle to render the body free of temptation and serviceable for Fascist goals. In these films, the frontier is thus not only a space "of interactions and interviews," as Michel De Certeau describes it, but also a space of interdictions (Chambers, 2008, p. 39; De Certeau, 1984, p. 127).

These prohibitions come to the fore in Fascist empire films when the male protagonist encounters nomadic figures. The nomad was not only a metaphor for mobility, but stood for all that the colonial occupier hated about the "messiness" and unpredictability of the colonial encounter (Atkinson, 2007, 1999; Gabriel, 1988). In empire films, this figure and its values are referenced obliquely but consistently, through a series of personages who represent transience and restlessness, and are located outside Fascist schemes of hierarchy and allegiance. European colonial discourses often romanticized the nomad as a function of a parallel mythologizing of the desert as a zone outside Western spatio-temporality, and in the postcolonial age the nomad and the nomadic have continued to serve as foils for contemporary theorizations of identity and the power of perpetual displacement (Marks, 2006; Kaplan, 1996; Deleuze and Guattari, 1986; Miller, 1998, pp. 171–208). Although similar Orientalist visions of the desert run through Italian imperial texts, including *Kif Tebbi,* empire films also assert a reterritorialization of the desert as a space for the staging of Fascist modernity and as a place where men can recover from "nomadic" influences. The colonies thus become ideal "homelands," as described by James Clifford: safe spaces where mobility can be controlled, within and across borders, and where the values of stasis and purity are asserted against the historical forces of movement and contamination (Clifford, 1997, p. 7).

The conquest of Libya and the negation of the nomadic

Libya was not Italy's longest-held colony, but it was the one the Fascists had the highest ambitions for in terms of tourism and mass resettlement, as well as the one that posed the greatest resistance to Italian rule. The brutal General Rodolfo Graziani was given the mandate of extirpating a resistance that had prevented the Italians from expanding beyond the coastal regions. The 1923 novel (with the same title) from which *Kif Tebbi* is adapted is a product of this moment. Its author, Luciano Zùccoli, traveled with Graziani's troops in Tripolitania as he did his research, reaching the conclusion that the Arab soul was "always desirous of domination and a master." This fantasy of colonial obedience informs the book's title, which translates to "as you wish" (Zùccoli, 1923, pp. ix and xi; Tamis, 2008). In 1927, the year *Kif Tebbi* was made, Mussolini approved the biggest Italian military operation since the Italo-Turkish War to rout this sustained opposition. He focused on the Cyrenaica region, where the Sanusi leadership had organized a highly effective resistance based on the use of nomadic and semi-nomadic Bedouin troops. Yet the Fascists' weapons of industrial warfare (bomber planes, poison gas) proved ill suited to fighting the Bedouin, who operated in small bands, and the regime decided to adopt a totalitarian solution. Over the next years, over 100,000 nomads and their 500,000 animals were deported by boat and on foot to newly constructed concentration camps, where they endured disease, hunger, and forced labor which caused between 40,000 and 60,000 deaths.

While these mass crimes occurred in 1930–1932, after *Kif Tebbi* was released, two points are relevant here for the larger arguments of this essay. First, Fascist persecution of the nomad was motivated by more than military strategy. As a metaphor of mobility, the nomad conjured all that Fascism feared: uncontrolled movement, ephemerality, errancy, and absence of national or territorial loyalties. For Graziani, for example, Cyrenaica was "an infected organism," and the nomad the antithesis of the dictatorship and its cult of discipline, hygiene, and hierarchy. The nomad was

> anarchic, a lover of the most absolute liberty and independence ... who uses his mobility and ease of displacement to roam immense desert territories ... nomadism must be considered an imminent danger, one that must be rigorously and definitively stopped and controlled.
>
> (Graziani, 1932, pp. 64; 119–22; Atkinson, 1999, 2007)

Second, the mass crimes in the desert perpetrated by the Fascists had grave postcolonial consequences, from the environmental tragedy of the destruction of livestock, to the disruption of an age-old nomadic way of life in the region, to the collective exile of an entire generation of Libyan notables who fled to nearby Maghreb lands, becoming nomads of a sort themselves. All were victims of a Fascist colonial policy that made of their cultures "a space of traces" born of "the dispersal of tribes and the provoked disintegration of collective memories ..." (Raybaud and Scharfman, 1993, p. 150; Ahmida, 2005; Baldinetti, 2010; Jerary, 2005).

The Fascist conquest of Libya provides the historical referent for *Kif Tebbi*, but the movie's filmic intertexts have broader horizons. The film can be located within the Orientalist trend of filmmaking launched by the wildly popular Rodolfo Valentino vehicle *The Sheik* (Melford, 1921). Orientalist films of the silent era revolve around fantasies of rescue and domination. Set in or on the way to North African deserts and other exotic locales, they follow the male protagonist as he saves the European or non-European female lead from the lascivious or brutal Arab or African (Shohat, 1997; Studlar, 1997). The male hero may be a European (*Maciste contro lo sciecco/Maciste Against the Sheik,* Camerini, 1926*)*, a Europeanized native (*Kif Tebbi*) a native who turns out to be European *(The Sheik)*, or not a hero at all, but simply a European male presence whose mentality and counsel are a foil for the barbaric native men, customs, and laws that oppress or threaten the female protagonist (*La sperduta di Allah/Allah's Lost Soul,* Guazzoni, 1929; *L'esclave blanche/The White Slave,* Genina, 1927). In their *mise-en-scène* and costume design, these movies draw on an older history of Orientalist representation as enshrined in paintings, photographs, and literature (Nochlin, 1989). The staging of the negation of female autonomy, through kidnappings and bondage, and the subsequent rescue of the woman was part of the viewing pleasure: both were salves to a Western masculinity threatened by female emancipation *and* the virile Other. Yet the aesthetic of excess that surrounded Valentino, and the liminal personal identities and gender-bending costumes that characterized protagonists of both sexes in Orientalist films, made them popular with female as well as male viewers (Studlar, 1997; Shohat, 1997).

Since so many of the Orientalist pictures were male star vehicles, it is useful to touch upon their male characterizations and their treatments of the relationship between gender and mobility to better understand the connections and differences between these works and Fascist empire films such as *Kif Tebbi*. To do this one must depart from Valentino's *The Sheik*, which has an intertextual relation with Camerini's *Maciste contro lo sciecco* as well as *Kif Tebbi*. Valentino was a racially and sexually ambiguous figure in the context of silent American cinema: he was the Latin lover and rescuer of aristocratic white women, but also an erotic object himself, whose feminization and otherness were brought forth particularly in his Oriental pictures (Hansen, 1986; Studlar, 1989; Bertellini, 2010). In *The Sheik,* Valentino plays Ahmed, a Sahara desert chieftain who rescues the intrepid British explorer Lady Diana after she is kidnapped by a rival Sheik. Ahmed is both titillated and irritated by Lady Diana's boldness, and he soon makes Lady Diana into "a helpless captive in the desert wastes," forcing her to dress *à l'Arabe.* Theatricality and performance are key to the film's spectatorial appeal, and Lady Diana's

Figure 1.1 The Sheik eyes his prisoner (Source: still *The Sheik*, 1921)

mandatory masquerade associates her with exotic dancers and an ocular regime that equates control of the gaze with male authority. Valentino looks at his prisoner with gleaming, lascivious eyes, but the arrival of a French friend calls him to his conscience. He cannot act "like a savage" – like the other Sheik who arrives who reclaim his prize, with no such scruples – because, as we find out at the close of the film, he is actually European, even sharing an English genetic patrimony with Lady Diana through his father. We have here a double set of triangulations: between good and bad Arab over the woman, and among the three men, who represent stable/unstable models of civilized Western masculinity (Raoul and Ahmed-Valentino) and Arab barbarity. Raoul is an unassuming male physical presence, the better to offset the robed splendor and dramatics of the figure of Valentino, but the movements of both men claim the desert and wanderings through it as a male space and a male prerogative (intertitles *The Sheik*; Hansen, 1986).

The Italian iterations of this genre inherited the dilemma of dealing with the overwhelming screen presence of Valentino. Released in Italy in 1924 as *Lo sciecco*, *The Sheik* was the film most responsible for Valentino's popularity there. One solution was the path of imitation, incarnated by Spada's star turn in *Kif Tebbi;* the other was rejection, as embodied by Pagano in the tellingly titled *Maciste Against the Sheik*. The latter film, shot partly on location in Tripoli, reprises the narrative of a young aristocratic woman (played by Cecyl Tryan) at the mercy of an evil Sheik, with the powerful Maciste in the role of a sailor who saves her honor, first by beating off fellow soldiers who try and molest her as she is being taken by force to North Africa, and then by rescuing her from the arms of the Sheik himself. Pagano is an imposing strongman – he bends iron and fells enemies without breaking a sweat – but one devoid of any lustful tendencies. He is a tender giant, ministering to the ill captain on board, and above all, he is the populist everyman. Clad in a sailor's undershirt for much of the film, the former dockworker's raw but benign masculinity stands out amidst the theatrical costumes and settings. As an icon of national manhood, Maciste is indeed "against the Sheik": not only the one in his film, who represents Oriental barbarism, but also the one played by Valentino, whose ambiguous sexuality and open appetites rendered him unfit to embody the Fascist vision of virility. As Giorgio Bertellini argues, Italian male stardom in this era always exists in an implicit relation to the Duce, and Pagano served as a model for Mussolini's own stylings of Italian masculinity, from the physical resemblances (strong jaw, intense eyes, imposing torso, balding heads), to the populist ethos, imperious gestures, and displays of strength and athleticism (Bertellini, 2005; Ricci, 2008; Landy, 2008; Reich, 2011).

In 1926, Valentino suddenly died, and while Twentieth-Century Fox launched a massive search in Italy for his replacement, Valentino's persona of the culturally conflicted Arab and female rescuer was taken on by newcomer Spada in *Kif Tebbi*. While the acting styles, plot, and shot sequences testify to the transnational nature of the Orientalist genre, *Kif Tebbi* may also be considered a transition to a new filmic era marked by the quest to convey a uniquely Italian colonial imaginary and sensibility. As we have seen, *Kif Tebbi* pays homage to two waves of Italian occupation (1911–12, 1921–1925) and anticipated a third, and it is not surprising that it was one of the first films to enjoy a subsidy from the Italian government Indeed, there is a politically-inflected shift in the cinematic intertext referenced by Spada's character, Ismail. Over the course of the film, as he decides to do his military duty, his masculine bearing becomes less that of Valentino than that of Mussolini, his Oriental softness exchanged for a harder manhood appropriate for war.

At the start of the film, Ismail is a man caught between two cultures. The son of a Tripolitanian notable, he has just returned from a transformative trip to Europe. Wearing an Italian suit and smoking a cigarette, he paces restlessly, at peace only in front of the altar to his continental journey which he has set up inside his father's compound. The camera lingers on the portrait of a European woman, the bottle of French cologne, the framed photograph of the Eiffel Tower, and the gramophone, which relate the loss of an amorous attachment back in Europe and Ismail's uncertain identification with his own culture. We see the impossible backwardness of his surroundings through the groupings of old men in white robes smoking from a hookah, through the servant who gapes at the gramophone, affirming his own primitivity, and through the tribal elders who gape at the warships depicted in Ismail's Italian magazine. What Ismail's "recollection objects" reference is not just nostalgia for Europe, but an experience of modernity that all Libyans can share by accepting the guide of the European colonizer who has traveled to their shores (Marks, 2000, p. 80). The disjunctions of time and space that come with cultural dislocation are most clearly evoked in one of the most interesting scenes of the film. Ismail flees from his oppressive home, riding his horse to a nearby desert dune. As he sits, lost in thought, embellished by his ornamental cape, a close-up channels for viewers the ghost of Valentino. Yet we quickly drift away from the Sheik, into Ismail's particular affective world, in which the desert is a prison rather than an exotic escape. A medium shot, in dull light and foreshortened perspective, depicts the landscape of empty dunes as oppressive, countering the conventional Saharan dramatics achieved in

Figure 1.2 Ismail dreams of Europe (Source: still *Kif tebbi,* 1928)

European colonial films through extreme long shots and chiaroscuro effects. This image is then overlaid with a horizon of possibility – the undulating sea – which is the gateway to a montage of image-recollections from Ismail's Italian sojourn. Busy construction sites, bridges, speeding trains and the blur of wheels in movement make the sands into a mirage of a mobile Italian modernity, with careful matching of perspectives in the transition from image to image lending a dream-like feeling. A caravan of camels marching by rudely interrupts this reverie. The innovative tracking shot of the camels' hooves in the sand evokes the rhythms of the desert, but it also conveys the disjuncture between Ismail's inner world and his immediate surroundings. The young Tripolitanian is a figure lost in translation, afflicted by a malady which only collaboration with the Italians will cure.

In reality, there are three models of culture in play here – Italian, Libyan, and Turkish – all of which are presented and contrasted through the lens of masculine values and behavior. The supreme standard of civilization in this Italian film is naturally European modernity, and here, as in *The Sheik,* it is associated with male self-control and the overcoming of Oriental lasciviousness. "When an Arab sees a woman he wants, he takes her," declaims Valentino, as Ahmed, in *The Sheik.* Spada's characterization of the Arab in *Kif Tebbi* rebukes this. His restrained gaze and body language, like his noble actions, offer an enlightened model of Arab manhood, to be contrasted both with the less civilized Rassim (rival tribal leader and hirsute "bad Arab" of the film) and with the backward Turks. Rassim is Ismail's direct antagonist and the representative of a Libya closed to European influences. He questions Ismail's masculinity, mocking him for "perfuming himself like a female" (to which Ismail replies that in Europe he has met "strong men who know how to bend iron and dominate the seas"). Yet it is the Turks, current masters of Libya, who are depicted as the true barbarians: they have no concept of justice; they maraud and plunder; they are carriers of a Muslim faith that brings out the worst Arab tendencies, and they stand for an uncontrollable and decadent part of the Mediterranean – the Levant – that must be reclaimed for Rome (Fuller, 2007, pp. 39–41).

Competition for the female nomad Mne brings out this confrontation between styles of manhood and civilization most clearly. Stalked by Rassim, Mne initially hides from Ismail, but she soon opens up to him, helped by his desexualized demeanor (he calls her "the laughing girl") and the intuition of her blind sister, Gamra, that he has pure intentions. The film does not neglect the play of gazes and allure of the veiled woman that form part of the appeal of this genre but the tone is playful rather than erotic. At their first meeting, Ismail gazes at her uncovered sandaled foot, but when she tracks his gaze and hastily withdraws her foot under her tunic they both laugh heartily. Camerini also defuses things by mocking the Orientalist trope of forbidden looking: when Rassim, who is plotting to kidnap Mne, is hanging about her tent, hoping for a glimpse of her, Mne whets his appetite by rustling the tent's opening, only to present him with a braying baby goat instead. Within this scheme, Rassim represents traditional "uncivilized" Arabic mores with respect to women, as in *The Sheik*, but it is the Turk who poses the greatest threat. After seizing Mne's caravan, a Turkish soldier spies the young woman, and from his perch on his horse, leers at her, leaving no doubt as to her fate if he takes her. His face, shot in close up is an ensemble of features (hooked nose, frizzy hair, beady eyes, lascivious expression) which evoke criminality and otherness, in its Levantine and later Semitic iterations. As a soldier, he is also a negative model of armed manhood – the Italian southern bandit-rapist, with attendant mustachioed and swarthy physicality – that had no place in Fascist Italy. The Turk, in this film, is more than the enemy in the struggle for Libya: he is a symbol of all that Italy must disavow and disallow in its refashioning of Italy and the Mediterranean as modern imperial spaces.

As against Rassim and the Turk, Ismail plays the role of savior, consonant with the conventions of Orientalist films. He challenges Rassim to a duel that results in the death of the latter, and hides Mne away in the home of an ally. Mne is the agent of his masculine redemption after his brush with the emasculating mores of the West, but also the foil for his portrait of the "good Arab" who offers an alternate model of colonial behavior, particularly with regard to relations with indigenous women. From 1912 onwards, the Italian colonial authorities had gone out of their way to assure the populations they subjugated that their women would be respected, only to look the other way when confronted with cases of rape and harassment. The emphasis on the mutual nature of the bond between Mne and Ismail in *Kif Tebbi* has its origins here, as well as in the conventions of screen romance: the particular mix of paternalism and passion displayed by Ismail is meant to offset the lustful and brutish behavior of both Rassim and the Turks. In their most intimate on-screen moment, the couple hug and kiss passionately. Spada's gaze and gestures here evoke Valentino in his exotic lover stance, but the film deviates from the fantasies of female slavery proffered by most Orientalist films in

Figure 1.3 Ismail as Leader (Source: still *Kif tebbi*, 1928)

offering viewers an ideal of romantic partnership. "Io ti appartengo e tu mi appartieni" (You belong to me and I belong to you), Mne murmurs to him as they embrace.

There is, of course, a political inflection to this face-off between Western and Oriental models of masculinity. Much of this war movie's dramatic tension comes from Ismail's transformation from a romantic estranged from his surroundings to tribal leader able to mobilize his men for battle. In a key scene, he is acclaimed as the new *capo* by Rassim's *mehalla*. Facing his exultant troops, who chant with raised rifles, he says gravely "I am proud to take command of you. We will leave as soon as possible!" Shot first in profile and then from a three-quarter angle, he is imperious in his ornamental cape. The visual and verbal referents for his persona are no longer Valentino, but Mussolini, who had visited Tripolitania the year before. Initially, Ismail's redemption is for Turkish benefit, as he does his duty and goes off to fight for the Turkish cause, but he soon falls into disfavor with the Ottomans for his philo-Italian sentiments and is given a death sentence. By the end of the film, Ismail has escaped from his prison in time to see the triumph of the Italians. Ismail will not become an exile, nor remain a moody misfit at home: under Italian rule, he will be able to reconcile his two worlds, placing his enlightened perspective to use as a leader and warrior. From his initial existential dilemma, born of rootlessness – "no longer Arab, but unable to be European," – the novel glossed it – Ismail becomes the perfect colonial intermediary (Zùccoli, 1923, p. 12). And although he is temporarily reunited with Mne, his new object of desire is the Italian flag, setting a precedent that will be respected in empire and military films for the duration of the regime.

Mne, too, has learned a lesson: wandering through the desert is a male privilege. Early in the film, in a long melodramatic sequence, her sister Gamra perished as they fled across the dunes after their caravan was seized by the Turks. Ismail's subsequent reclusion of Mne may have saved her from harm to her honor, but it also put an end to her nomadic existence, confining her indoors in the manner of the women of settled Muslim populations. When her mother arrives to take her back to her *cabila*, her response – "kif tebbi" (as you wish) – brings an order to the film's gender politics that matches the resolutions it proposes in the spatial and racial realms. By the end of the movie, both Ismail and Mne have been reterritorialized. The former is restored to his natural home and duties as tribal leader; the latter to her subordinate position within her own tribe; and with them, Tripolitania, now able to find its Roman heritage without the overlay of Levantine decadence. Even as it took Italians on a virtual tour of Tripolitania's exotic customs and locales, *Kif Tebbi* turned "Arab fatalism" into a justification for the mandate to submit and settle into the spaces and laws of familial and Fascist authority.

Looked at from the perspective of 1930s empire cinema, *Kif Tebbi* is notable for the violence it shows: not the mass battles of the Ethiopian War, with their deaths by cannons and airplanes, but two close-up killings, both the work of Ismail, to protect Mne's honor. As actual Fascist violence escalated, such scenes vanished from the screen, replaced by a strategy of keeping male protagonists "clean" by partitioning off brutalities to the anonymous hordes of the Italian army. Gone, too, would be the star's dilemma of whether to collaborate, although the male conflict between romantic passion and military duty will persist. These shifts in the treatment of colonial violence betray the burden faced by the Fascists: to represent the colonies as modern places "that showed the decisiveness of Fascist action in dealing with opposition to its rule" while denying Italian aggression (Burdett, 2007, p. 37). What could not be denied or screened out, though, were the displacements and temptations that came with expansion overseas, and empire films test the dictatorship's autarchic ambitions against the mobilities, cultural transfers, and interpersonal exchanges inherent to colonial conquest and war. As James Clifford reminds us, narratives of human location are constituted "as much by displacement as by stasis," and practices of displacement are constitutive of cultural meanings through the moments of identity and other differentiation they generate (Clifford, 1997, p. 2). Italian empire films make spectacle of these nomadic moments, even as their plots engineer the exile of nomadic characters. Moreover, as the Fascists recognized, mobility was also inherent to the institution of cinema, from the transnational circulations of texts, people, and capital that lie behind its productions, to the movements of desire it stages on screen and in the body of the spectator. With their recourse to exotic attractions and their international intertexts, empire films like *Kif Tebbi* thus reveal the contradictions of a Fascist filmic project that sought to mobilize the gaze and the emotions while stripping the cinema of its status as a space governed, like the Mediterranean, by an ethos and eros of *transito* (Bruno, 1993, pp. 52–7; Bruno, 2002).

Bibliography

Ahmida, A.A., 2005. *Forgotten Voices: Power And Agency In Colonial And Postcolonial Libya.* London and New York: Routledge.

Andall, J. and Duncan, D. eds., 2005. *Italian Colonialism: Legacy and Memory*. New York: Peter Lang.

Atkinson, D., 1999. Nomadic Strategies and Colonial Governance: Domination and Resistance in Cyrenaica, 1923–1932. In: J.P. Sharp, P. Routledge, C. Philo and R. Paddison, eds., 1999. *The Entanglements of Power: Geographies of Domination/Resistance*. London: Routledge, pp. 93–121.

Atkinson, D., 2007. Embodied Resistance, Italian Anxieties and the Place of the Nomad in Colonial Cyrenaica. In: L. Polezzi and C. Ross, eds., 2007. *In Corpore. Bodies in Post-Unification Italy*. Madison, NJ: Farleigh Dickinson, pp. 56–79.

Baldinetti, A., 2010. *The Origins of the Libyan Nation: Colonial Legacy, Exile, and the Emergence of a New Nation-State*. New York: Routledge.

Behdad, A., 1994. *Belated Travelers. Orientalism in an Age of Colonial Dissolution*. Durham, NC: Duke University Press.

Ben-Ghiat, R. and Fuller, M. eds., 2005. *Italian Colonialism*. New York: Palgrave.

Bertellini, G., 2005. Duce/Divo. Masculinity, Racial Identity, and Politics Among Italian-Americans in 1920s New York City. *Journal of Urban History*, 31(5), pp. 685–726.

Bertellini, G., 2010. The Atlantic Valentino: The "Inimitable Lover" as Racialized and Gendered Italian. In: D. Gabaccia and L. Baldassar, eds., 2010. *Intimacy and Italian Migration*. New York: Fordham University Press, pp. 37–48.

Bosworth, R., 1996. *Italy and the Wider World*. London and New York: Routledge.

Bruno, G., 1993. *Streetwalking on a Ruined Map. Cultural Theory and the Films of Elvira Notari*. Cambridge, MA: Harvard University Press.

Bruno, G., 2002. *Atlas of Emotion: Journeys in Art, Architecture and Film*. London: Verso.

Burdett, C., 2007. *Journeys Through Fascism. Italian Travel Writing Between the Wars*. New York: Berghahn.

Chambers, I., 2008. *Mediterranean Crossings. The Politics of an Interrupted Modernity*. Durham, NC: Duke University Press.

Clifford, J., 1997. *Routes. Travel and Translation in the late 20th Century*. Cambridge, MA: Harvard University Press.

Coletti, M., 2006. Il Cinema Coloniale tra Propaganda e Melò. In: O. Caldiron, ed. 2006. *Storia del Cinema Italiano*. Venice: Marsilio, pp. 354–62.

De Certeau, M., 1984. *The Practice of Everyday Life*. Berkeley: University of California Press.

Delueze, G. and Guattari, F., 1986. *Nomadology: The War Machine*. New York: Semiotexte.

Elena, L. ed., 1999. *Film d'Africa. Film Italiani Prima, Durante, e Dopo l'Avventura Coloniale*. Turin: Archivio Nazionale Cinematografico Della Resistenza.

Farassino, A., 2000. *Fuori di Set. Viaggi, Esplorazioni, Emigrazioni, Nomadismi*. Rome: Bulzoni.

Fuller, M., 2007. *Moderns Abroad: Architecture, Cities, and Italian Imperialism*. New York and London: Routledge.

Gabriel, T.H., 1988. Thoughts on Nomadic Aesthetics and the Black Independent Cinema: Traces of a Journey. In: C. Andrade-Watkins and M.B. Cham, eds., 1988. *Blackframes. Critical Perspectives on Black Independent Cinema*, Cambridge, MA: MIT Press, pp. 62–79.

Gili, J. and Brunetta, G. eds., 1990. *L'ora dell'Africa nel Cinema Italiano, 1911–1989*. Rovereto: Materiali di lavoro.

Graziani, R., 1932. *Cirenaica Pacificata*. Milan: Mondadori.

Hansen, M., 1986. Pleasure, Ambivalence, Identification: Valentino and Female Spectatorship. *Cinema Journal*, 25(4), pp. 6–32.

Hay, J., 1987. *Popular Film Culture in Fascist Italy*. Bloomington, IN: Indiana University Press.

Jerary, M., 2005. Damages Caused by Italian Fascist Colonization. In: R. Ben-Ghiat and M. Fuller, eds., 2005. *Italian Colonialism.* New York: Palgrave, pp. 203–8.

Kaplan, C., 1996. *Questions of Travel, Postmodern Discourses of Displacement.* Durham, NC: Duke University Press.

Labanca, N., 2002. *Oltremare. Storia dell'Espansione Coloniale Italiano.* Bologna: Mulino.

Landy, M., 2008. *Stardom Italian Style. Screen Performance and Personality in Italian Cinema.* Bloomington: Indiana University Press.

Marks, L.U., 2000. *The Skin of the Film. Intercultural Cinema, Embodiment and the Senses.* Durham, NC: Duke University Press.

Marks, L.U., 2006. Asphalt Nomadism. The New Desert in Arab Independent Cinema. In: M. Lefebvre, ed., 2006. *Landscape and Cinema.* New York: Routledge, pp. 125–48.

Martinelli, V., 1978. I Gastarbeiter fra le Due Guerre. *Bianco e Nero,* 39(3), pp. 3–93.

Miller, C., 1998. *Nationalists and Nomads. Essays on Francophone African Literature and Culture.* Chicago, IL: University of Chicago Press.

Nochlin, L., 1989. The Imaginary Orient. In: L. Nochlin, ed., 1989. *The Politics of Vision. Essays on Nineteenth-Century Art and Society.* New York: Harper & Row, pp. 33–59.

Palumbo, P. ed., 2003. *A Place in the Sun: Africa in Italian Colonial Culture from Post- Unification to the Present.* Berkeley: University of California Press.

Raybaud , A. and Scharfman, R., 1993. Nomadism between the Archaic and the Modern. *Yale French Studies,* 82(1), pp. 146 –57.

Reich, J., 2011. Slave to Fashion: Masculinity, Suits, and the Maciste Films of Italian Silent Cinema. In: A. Munich, ed., 2011. *Fashion in Film.* Bloomington, IN: Indiana University Press.

Ricci, R., 2008. *Cinema and Fascism: Italian Film and Society, 1922–1945.* Berkeley, CA: University of California Press.

Shohat, E., 2007. Gender and the Culture of Empire. In: M. Bernstein and G. Studlar, eds., 2007. *Visions of the East: Orientalism in Film.* New Brunswick, NJ: Rutgers University Press, pp. 19–68.

Studlar, G., 1989. Discourses of Gender and Ethnicity: The Construction and De(con)struction of Rudolph Valentino as Other. *Film Criticism,* 13(2), pp. 18–36.

Studlar, G., 1997. "Out-Salomeing Salome": Dance, the New Woman, and Fan magazine Orientalism. In: M. Bernstein and G. Studlar, eds., 2007. *Visions of the East: Orientalism in Film.* New Brunswick: Rutgers University Press, pp. 99–129.

Tamis, A.M., 2008. The Italian Colonial Cinema: Nationalism, Internationalism, and Notions of Alterity. Ph.D. Department of Italian Studies, New York University.

Zùccoli, L., 1923. *Kif Tebbi. Romanzo Africano.* Milano: Treves.

Filmography

Cabiria, 1914. [film] Directed by G. Pastrone. Italy: Itala Film.

L'esclave blanche, 1927. [film] Directed by A. Genina. Germany: Lothar Stark-Film.

Kif Tebbi, 1928. [film] Directed by M. Camerini. Italy: Società Italiana Cines.

Maciste contro lo sciecco, 1926. [film] Directed by M. Camerini. Italy: Fert Film.

Scipione l'Africano, 1936. [film] Directed by C. Gallone. Italy: ENIC.

The Sheik, 1921. [film] Directed by G. Melford. USA: Paramount Pictures.

La sperduta di Allah, 1929. [film] Directed by E. Guazzoni. Italy: Suprema Film.

Chapter 2

Blackface, faciality, and colony nostalgia in 1930s empire films

Julie Codell

In the 1930s, Hollywood made so many films about the British Empire that British directors and producers making empire films complained that Americans were taking all the good subjects. What are now called empire films,[1] films focusing on and heroizing the British Empire (see Ruth Ben-Ghiat's essay in this volume), were very popular on both sides of the Atlantic. In *Lives of a Bengal Lancer* (Hathaway, 1935) British actors played older British officers, and American actors played younger officers, metaphorically figuring the passing of the imperial "white man's burden" from Britain to America.[2]

Empire films contribute to postcolonial studies by offering both endorsement and self-reflection on nineteenth-century ideologies of empire, marking changes in these ideas by the 1930s. In this essay, I explore an important mode of colonial representation shared across British and American films: the use of blackface, a ritualized performance begun in America in the 1830s with performance characteristics beyond the "blacking up" of both black and white performers' skin. Blackface served a variety of functions in these films and could either reinforce imperial racial hierarchies or disrupt them. To underscore the functions of blackface in 1930s films, I merge theoretical analyses of blackface with Gilles Deleuze's and Felix Guattari's concept of "faciality" to suggest a distinct "blackfaciality" in empire films. I focus my analysis on on-screen encounters between a colonizer and a blackfaced colonized subject in several films: *Gunga Din* (Stevens, 1939); *Rhodes of Africa* (Viertel, 1936); *The Drum* (Korda, 1938); and *Sanders of the River* (Korda, 1935). Some encounters present fictionalized historical types (the English drummer boy in *The Drum*, the Thuggee cult[3] in *Gunga Din*, and the commissioner based on Robert Bowen, first British resident, in *Sanders*). Others fictionalize actual historical figures: Cecil Rhodes and Matabele Chief Lobengula never met.

Encounters, Mary Louise Pratt argues, are sites of human interactions' "ongoing relations," often inequitable, but permitting subtle resistance to colonial coercion by being open-ended, "interactive, improvisational" (Pratt, 1992, pp. 6–7). I argue that in these films' self-reflection on empire's changing history in the 1930s, blackface was deployed to contain the potential open-endedness Pratt considers inherent in colonial encounters. In some films, blackface resorted to an older racial code that encoded difference through parody and excess. But blackface could also permit deviating decodings in films to present the British Empire as the "good" empire in the face of rising fascism.

These films, however historical their narrative, were also in dialogue with colonial subjects' views of empire in the 1930s. For example, their representations of indigenous peoples, marked by blackened faces, offended Indian and African viewers. In the American film *Gunga Din,* the blackened Thuggee leader resembled Gandhi and the British film *The Drum* demonized a Muslim (blackfaced Canadian Raymond Massey); both films provoked riots in India (Chowdhry, 2000, pp. 57–192).[4] Both were set in the Northwest Province, responding to Italian and German criticism of Britain's harsh retaliation against resistance in Chittagong in the Northwest Province in 1930–1931 (Chowdhry, 2000, pp. 79–81; 136–8; Richards, 1984, pp. 47–57). US Senators also attacked the British incarceration of Indian nationalists. These criticisms, and the rise of Indian and African nationalism, exemplify "colonialism's moral delegitimation *before* its political demise" (Jaikumar, 2006, p. 2), as residual British imperial ideologies were exacerbated by international politics. Such awareness of these inflammatory issues affected the circulation and presentation of these films: to avoid offending colonial audiences, nude dancing African girls were censored by the Bombay Board of Film Censors, and scenes of black violence against whites and whites calling each other "bloody swine" were edited out for Indians (Jaikumar, 2006, p. 109).

Empire films uneasily embodied these conflicts in their uses of blackfaciality and ethnographic footage and, like all genres, self-reflexively critiqued their own conventions, particularly in their self-conscious assimilation of other genres, such as the Western and the melodrama. Priya Jaikumar divides empire films into romantic and realist subgenres, depending on their inflections of imperial projects and modes of address to spectators. In realist film, spectators are hailed as participants in heroic imperial projects through codes of uninterrupted narrative, continuity editing, naturalized racial hierarchies and unquestioned imperial ideology enhanced by specificity of place and time represented by maps, indigenous actors and local settings. By contrast, imperial romance presents multiple threats to empire, which, although eventually resolved, reveal a vulnerable empire. In romance, the colony becomes "a symbolic playground of the Englishman's passion, temptation, choice, victimization, transgression, and triumph during a period of declining political control," and its feminized, melodramatic protagonists become only part of empire's "network of meanings rather than its central structuring principle," unlike realist films' dominating protagonists (Jaikumar, 2006, pp. 144–5). I argue further that in realist films blackface sustains hierarchy by reiterating imperial ideologies through racial difference as a synecdoche of empire. In romance "blackened" figures acquire agency and authority, permitting limited and ambiguous improvisational encounters.

Blackface and faciality

Blackface "cross-dressing, in which one puts on the insignias of a race that stands in binary opposition to one's own" (Rogin, 1998, p. 30), appeared in the 1830s in the US with a complex class and racial symbolism tied to slavery and later to immigration. Its performance involved singing, dancing, wild gestures, colorful extravagant clothes, mask-like stereotypical "black" facial features, and Pidgin English, full of errors and malapropisms, all to lampoon blacks in minstrel shows.[5] By mid-century in Britain, it was deployed to represent colonized subjects. Children in blackface played Indians and Africans in imperial ceremonies throughout the empire.

In the interface between blackface and imperialism, Michael Pickering argues that the blackface mask was

> dependent upon a self-legitimating split between a civilised "Us" and an essentialised "primitive" "Them"... worked through cultural forms like minstrelsy to incorporate difference ... in a structure of cultural appropriation analogous to imperialism ... Where the white subject was sovereign, the black was ritualistically treated as its largely tamed opposite over which sentimental tears could be shed and frivolous laughter allowed... to produce a sense of "lesser breeds without the law" who were nevertheless always potentially eligible for recruitment to a Euro-defined category of the "human" provided they submit themselves to the beneficent rule of the West ... It was through this kind of incorporation of the idea of the black ... that minstrelsy, along with other cultural forms, provided an ideological basis for imperialist rule.
>
> (Pickering, 1997, p. 193)

Simon Featherstone argues that blackface was malleable and historically inflected in its meanings and allusions:

> an active network of transatlantic forms and performances that were energized by old complexities in slavery and emigration, new politics of emancipation, nationalism and imperialist activity, and by those intimate and complex reworkings of cultural meaning... blacking up remained, in Britain as in America, a politically fraught activity, and the black body that was produced a site of complex and disturbing struggles.
>
> (Featherstone, 1998, pp. 248–9)

Featherstone describes the "complex structure of pleasure" in minstrelsy's "white aesthetic" as a "contradictory politics of [racial] disavowal and voyeurism" (Featherstone, 1998, p. 241).

Yet, despite its mixed pleasures, the mask-like face in blackface performance remained a "disguise not identity," structured to fit "white space" (Featherstone, 1998, pp. 240–2), a fixed identity that Michael Rogin calls "the surplus symbolic value of blacks, the power to make African Americans represent something beside themselves" (Rogin, 1998. p. 14). Whites' appropriation of black identity meant that African Americans in minstrelsy performed demeaning stereotypes against themselves and for whites (Rogin, 1998, p. 21): Sambo was a perpetual child. Loyal, contented servant Tom served as a defense of slavery and segregation. Zip Coon, an abbreviation of raccoon, was easily frightened, idle, inarticulate, unhappy under servitude, but too lazy or cynical to resist (Bogle, 1989, pp. 3–18).

Blackface's racial cross-dressing both touched and parodied blacks, but was also about class for white working-class minstrelsy audiences who lived their whiteness precariously (Lott, 1993, p. 4). Blackface's proximity to and obsession with racial markings ambivalently celebrated and exploited the racial boundaries it crossed. Blackened whites made blackface "less a sign of absolute white power and control than of panic, anxiety, terror and pleasure," as cultural interactions also policed racial borders (Lott, 1993, p. 6). Thus, blackface was "less a *repetition* of power relations than a *signifier* for them – a distorted mirror, reflecting displacements, condensations, and discontinuities. Between blackface and its social field there exist lags, unevennesses, multiple determinations" (Lott, 1993, p. 8).

In colonial films, blackface was coded as alienation, racial difference, and exoticism, and its performance often foreshadowed characters' inevitable defeat. It fixed the colonial's mask-like face and read the body through performance – Pidgin English, obsequiousness, superstitiousness, and outlandish dress. Thus, blackface denied individual expression of, and communication by, colonized subjects: "Faces are not basically individual: they define zones of frequency or probability, delimit a field that neutralises in advance any expressions or connections unnamable to the appropriate significations" (Deleuze and Guattari, 1987, p. 168). Faciality forces "the flesh of the other into the machine of majoritarian subjectification and stratification ... the other's body is legislated against by the facial machine of the dominant" that in the end "proscribes the future of this minoritarian" (MacCormack, 2000).

In the reductive faciality system the face becomes the signifier of a person's humanity that is subject to territorialization that assures alienation from, rather than empathy toward, that individual. This system is

> a machine, constantly making and re-making its own significations and the subject it presents. The body is not coded or able to be read through the face ... in conformance with the face or expressed by the face. The face is not a natural extension of the flesh. Rather, the body is overcoded and annihilated through the system of the face ... This system creates a body that mimics the face as pure surface.
> (MacCormack, 2000)

The human face, in Deleuze's and Guattari's faciality, becomes an inhuman abstract system of signification, "enabling classification, knowledge, and control" and determining "what is passable and unpassable" (Loh, 2009, p. 345), or "unamenable," such as colonial resistance to imperial subjugation (Deleuze and Guattari, 1987, p. 186). Blackface turned into systemic blackfaciality enforced racial divisions and defined blacks as lampoonable, silly, ignorant, lazy, or happy under servitude. Yet in some films, it was a system meant to be overcome, as I argue below.

Blackfaciality in empire film encounters

In 1936 Ben Hecht and Charles MacArthur were hired to combine Rudyard Kipling's story *Soldiers Three* and his poem *Gunga Din* into a film staring British and Commonwealth expatriates Victor McLaglen, Cary Grant, and Douglas Fairbanks, Jr. Due to a shortage of "dark-skinned extras," hundreds of cast members stood on "revolving platforms that were operated by makeup artists armed with spray guns" of brown color (Harris, 1988, p. 133). But only untouchables, thugs and mahouts are blackfaced in the film. Blackface did not pretend to mimic any racial reality, but coded actors' bodies as evil or lower caste, blackening equally the defiant Thuggee leader (Eduardo Ciannelli) and his followers and the obsequious Din played by Sam Jaffe blackened from head to toe for the eponymous role. Loincloth and *chaddar* (cotton shawl), associated with Gandhi, were worn by both characters, too, although the Thuggee leader was Brahman, while Din was an untouchable. To appease Indian anger over the film, its original pre-title, which stated that the worship of the goddess Kali was "based on historical facts," was replaced with, "The supposed story is entirely fictitious." Publicity posters still emphasized the Thuggee cult, but Indian viewers saw "loyal" Din as a collaborator and the "evil" leader as a nationalist (Chowdhry, 2000, p. 160).

In the Thuggee temple, watching blackened Thuggee cultists assemble, Sergeant Archie Cutter (Cary Grant) furrows his brows, but Gunga Din is wide-eyed with teeth showing, a conventional blackface expression. The Thuggee leader, too, appears in this blackface pose (Figure 2.1). Later British officers taunt him about his "crystal ball" baldhead and call him "ape," terms of superstition and animality commonly applied to Blacks on both sides of the Atlantic. Yet, this anti-imperialist Thug sacrifices himself for his people, resonating with the Indian nationalism with which some Americans were sympathetic and anticipating Din's sacrifice, parallels which indicate the film's internal ambiguities.

Din ultimately gains agency by sacrificing himself for the regiment, receiving a military funeral. Racism (Din suffers verbal abuse) appears corrected and difference overcome through Din's posthumous military honors and British officers' compassion.

Figure 2.1 In the Thug temple: Gunga Din (Sam Jaffe) and Archie Cutter (Cary Grant); (Source: still *Gunga Din*, 1939)

But these honors also reward his minstrelsy. Blackfaciality marked his difference and then permitted it to be overcome by British munificence. Since in faciality the "demand for recognition risks assimilation" (MacCormack, 2000), Din's honors *must* be posthumous to avoid the assimilation implied by his increasing military agency and sacrifice.

Encounters in *The Drum* establish the possibility of good Indian-British relations in a film set in a province that had recently rebelled against Britain in 1930–1931. Prince Azim, played by the popular Indian child actor Sabu Dastagir,[6] is initially a bad boy shooting playfully at the British and lying about it, until fatherly Colonel Carruthers chastises him. The next colonizer-colonial encounter, between Azim and a Scottish drummer boy, is hostile. The drummer boy, Holder, starts to fight, and Azim's guards appear. Azim calls them off, asking Holder if they could be friends. Holder reluctantly acquiesces, acknowledging that indigenous aristocracy trumps physical force and even Britishness, and agrees to teach Azim to play the drum (Figure 2.2). This highly improvisational encounter, open-ended because it is between children, is paralleled by an encounter between Carruthers and the pro-British informant Mohammed Khan. This sequence is followed by treaty signing, then cuts to Azim drumming and asking Holder if he can someday wear a British uniform. In this romance film, Azim's identity is fluid and improvisational, perhaps because he is a child and an aristocrat and played by a popular actor.

Blackface here is subtextual. Sabu, often partially unclothed, but always extravagantly decorated and darker-skinned than appropriate for a Pathan prince, is feminized by soft lighting and backlighting and treated humorously. His feisty Zip Coon character

Figure 2.2 Prince Azim (Sabu) and Bill Holder (Desmond Tester) (Source: still *The Drum* (UK)/*Drums* (US), 1938)

is tamed into an advocate of empire, ruling under Indirect Rule.[7] Like Din, he saves the British, but unlike Din, he survives to become Britain's imperial partner, fittingly parented by Carruthers and his wife.

In romance (*Gunga Din, The Drum*), blackfaciality's differentiations are partially overcome as encounters become mutually transformative. In realist imperial films, blackface limits the improvisational open-endedness of encounters. In *Sanders of the River*, the idealized Sanders (Leslie Banks) controls Africa through sheer charisma. In Edward Wallace's Sanders novels, Sanders flogs and hangs Africans, portrayed as ever-warring cannibals. The film, instead, portrays a benevolent Sanders, "hater of lies" and "righter of wrongs," who treats empire like public school. Alexander Korda, believing the British Empire was a bulwark against fascism, intended a pro-empire film that would contradict his brother Zoltán's criticisms of empire.[8]

In his first encounter with Sanders in Sanders's office, Bosambo, played by the famous African-American singer, actor, and intellectual Paul Robeson, gives a thoroughly blackface performance, which Robeson later repudiated. The "sambo" in the character's name alludes to one of minstrelsy's stock characters, an ever-childlike character. Bosambo, a petty thief, has proclaimed himself king without Sanders's approval, the only legitimate way an African could become king. He appears near-naked in a leopard-skin loincloth while berated by Sanders (Figure 2.3). While being chastised, Bosambo grins sheepishly and looks downcast before three fully dressed Englishmen (Duberman, 1989, p. 179). He speaks Pidgin English, referring to the gospels as "Markey, Lukey, and Johnny." He wears excessively large jewelry, recalling the outlandish oversized clothing of minstrel performers, signaling his childish, feminized, narcissistic body.

Figure 2.3 Bosambo (Paul Robeson) in the office of Commissioner Sanders (Leslie Banks) (Source: still *Sanders of the River,* 1935)

In Sanders's office, Bosambo stands between maps of Africa and Nigeria (Figure 2.3), his large, athletic body territorialized as he agrees to Sanders's terms for kingship. Here empire transforms him from his combined identities as miscreant Zip Coon and childlike Sambo into obedient servant Tom (Dunn, 1996, p. 161), equally castrated and infantilized in all incarnations. His (and, by implication, all blacks') "nature" – lying, womanizing, and childish – requires Sanders's surveillance. The film was so demeaning that Robeson received criticism from the black public (Boyle and Bunie, 2001, p. 479). He claimed in defense that pro-imperial parts were added and scenes mitigating racism were cut without his knowledge.[9]

Blackface in these films reflects a resistance to rising Indian nationalism and to the anti-colonial Négritude evolving in the contexts of both the French colonies and New York's Harlem Renaissance. Robeson, active in the Harlem Renaissance community and sharing its pro-Africa views, starred in two British empire films. His athletic, football-player physique, brilliant intellect and star status could potentially disrupt imperial ideology by signifying black adult masculinity. But despite being a celebrity in Britain, he was described by the English press as typically "Negro" – smiling, childlike, deep-voiced and muscular (Boyle and Bunie, 2001, p. 301) – a stereotypical Tom as blackfaced in the press as in his film role, subsumed into blackfaciality's signification in which his identity as a Renaissance man (intellectual, musician, athlete, Rutgers University graduate) was subjugated to "the facial machine of the dominant" (MacCormack, 2000). Even Robeson himself held stereotypical views of Africans. On the set, asked by an Oxford-educated Ashanti prince about his leopard skin, Robeson retorted, "What do you wear in Africa? Tweeds?" The prince answered, "Yes, we do" (Boyle and Bunie, 2001, p. 299).

As Richard Dyer argues, white domination of the Other's body feminizes the black and is then used tautologically to justify white domination (Dyer, 1986, p. 6). Captured by a rival, Bosambo needs Sanders to save him. Although Bosambo fathers a son and defeats a rival, he is thoroughly territorialized and must sacrifice his "African" identity in order to be king: Sanders insists Bosambo marry only one wife, despite Bosambo's claims to be both Christian and Muslim, and promises to check up on him periodically. Robeson's blackface, enhanced by outlandish costumes and pidgin speech, is further inscribed by the feminization and infantilization of colonial subjects that function to "negate masculine sameness, a sameness so terrifying to the cultural position of the white masculine that only castration can provide the necessary disavowal" (Wiegman, 1992, p. 179).

However, Bosambo's character is not entirely naïve: not falling into the stereotype of the superstitious African, he readily recognizes that what Sanders calls "magic" is really a British spy network. This recognition suggests a moment of improvisational "acquiescence between the two men regarding the levels of implicit and explicit knowledge necessary to maintain the precarious balance of imperial power" (Jaikumar, 2006, p. 120). But his blackface performance telegraphs to the audience that he will ultimately succumb to white domination in marriage, religion, politics and periodical surveillance, despite being allowed to rule.

Robeson critiqued his blackfaciality in *Sanders* by playing a very different character in the romance *King Solomon's Mines* (Stevenson, 1937) as King Umbopa, who first appears in Western clothes among whites. By the time his true identity as a dispossessed African king emerges, he has already refused to act as a servant and later leads the whites through Africa, rejecting blackfaciality performance, language, and submission. Yet Robeson's presence could not defuse entirely the deployment of blackface to fix colonial identity.[10] In *Mines* Guyanese actor Robert Adams who played evil King Twala was outlandishly overdressed, and white actress Sydney Fairbrother in blackface portrayed the witch Gagool – both stereotypically evil characters.

Rhodes of Africa depicts an imaginary meeting between South Africa's Cecil Rhodes (Walter Huston) and Matabele Chief Lobengula (Ndaniso Kumala) in the Matabele kingdom to negotiate a treaty that would allow Britons to settle on Matabele land. The chief, speaking through a missionary translator, hysterically calls whites jackals and wolves. Clamoring warriors press against Rhodes's entourage, but the unflappable Rhodes convinces Lobengula to sign a contract, which the chief, unable to read English, turns upside down, appearing foolish. Lobengula signs it with a cross, a signature symbolizing ignorance. Throughout this encounter, Lobengula performs blackface, his excessive feathers like the loud clothes of minstrelsy, his face darker than his body, and his screaming and illiteracy recalling the Pidgin English and malapropisms of minstrel shows. This encounter echoes the Victorian evolutionary belief in the inevitable defeat of the dark races by the Europeans. Lobengula's blackface performance, like Bosambo's, foreshadows his defeat as an always already castrated object of demeaning humor. Later a feminized Lobengula weepingly berates himself for betraying his people, in contrast to the frenzied warriors, called savages in a text overlay, who now lead the tribe. Although the film is critical of Rhodes, criticism is expressed by British, not African, characters (Codell, 2007, pp. 254–66).

Blackface specularizes and systemizes difference through reenacted types: Bosambo, Azim, and Gunga Din become Toms, as critics in 1939 recognized (Jaher and King, 2008, p. 44). Thuggee leader and blackfaced Muslim rebel remain Zip Coons. While blackface confirms race's synecdochal relationship to empire in both subgenres, in realist films, "the more performance scripts identity, the more it serves power," whereas in romance, "the more the freedom to perform any role, the less subversion in the play" (Rogin, 1998, p. 34), as resistance is turned into friendship and loyalty. *Sanders* appears to be mixed, permitting Bosambo a conditional autonomy following his debasement.

An anomalous but revealing blackfaciality occurs in *The Sun Never Sets* (Lee, 1939). John Randolph (Douglas Fairbanks, Jr.) chooses a servant through a game in which African boys eat piles of white flour to find coins tossed into the flour. The first to get a coin becomes Randolph's servant, although the boy cannot keep the coin! The boy is re-named "Tuppence," his real name regarded as irrelevant. The boys are interchangeable; Randolph will "pick them often and fire them frequently." Humiliating themselves for a tuppence, these lampooned Africans' whitened faciality subjects them to the minstrelsy humor of a ghostly impersonal faciality that is "willingly" worn to efface any specificity of their interchangeable and disposable identities. Although encounters offer some escape from imperial order, as Pratt argues, the transformation of blackface into blackfaciality in this case serves to eliminate any possibilities of improvisational, open-ended encounters (Codell, 2011).

Colony nostalgia

Coded not just for fixing black identities but also for concomitant white anxieties, blackface marked unstable boundaries in colonial encounters. Rogin calls blackface in *Gone with the Wind* (1939), "plantation nostalgia," that served the audience's desire to experience an older order (1998, p. 41). In empire films, blackfaciality denotes what I call "colony nostalgia," a desire to return to a time when empire was considered unquestionably heroic. Blackfaciality in these films becomes a coded linguistic performance as described by Judith Butler: an utterance that constitutes identity as it is uttered, so that a statement constitutes or instantiates the object to which it refers in "performative utterances" (Butler, 1993, p. 95). We speak ourselves into being. Acts that "express" gender or race constitute the illusion of stable gender or racial – or imperial identity. Blackfaciality enacts what it names, to paraphrase Butler, and requires iteration to speak race as synecdochal of empire, while validating the British Empire as a good empire in implied contrast to fascism. In empire films at least, if not in the empire, blackfaciality performed stable imperial hierarchies and its redundancy uttered the colonized as subordinate and inferior forever.

Blackface in these films lacks the "spectacle" we find in Hollywood musicals, where performers blacken up before our eyes. In empire films we do not see agency but a projected Face – the composite re-reading of face, body, and landscape – in which, "it is not the individuality of the face that counts but the efficacy of the ciphering it makes possible ... This is an affair not of ideology but of economy and the organization of power" (Deleuze and Guattari, 1987, p. 194). Blackfaciality *emphatically* denies the individuality of the colonized face (even for well-known actors Robeson or Sabu) to suggest an economy of imperial rule at a time when empire was becoming suspect. By presenting a kinder, gentler empire (Sanders is called "father," and "civilizing" is the theme of *Stanley and Livingston* (King and Brower, 1939), the "willing" submission of colonial characters is incessantly naturalized by the repeated utterance/performance of blackfaciality.

For Deleuze and Guattari, faciality refuses to permit the wearer to communicate, to send a message about him/herself, but instead insists on the face's function to preorganize the world, to precede experience, deploying faciality's efficient, categorical clarity to limit meanings. Such facial coding, already inherent in film itself, rejects encounters' improvisation, preferring to contain a hierarchic colonial order in fiction, although, or because, this order was already unraveling in the empire. In romance, the strife of empire is acknowledged and requires the Other to help sustain it (Azim and Umbopa's Indirect Rule), but only after the Other is morally improved and while he is under constant surveillance.

Ethnography and blackfaciality

Ethnographic footage in empire films pits European modernity and technology against "primitive" Otherness. Empire films attempt to fuse different narrative temporalities (e.g., history, myth, biography) to construct an "imperial time" that appears unified by being rooted in the moment when colonizers' arrival announces a colony's "origin." In addition, ethnographic footage's "real" places make it "scientific," grounding colonial ideology in geographic place.

But such footage, usually presented only as documentary fragments, can interrupt imperial mythologies to expose temporal heterogeneity and discontinuity. Real indigenous people look into the camera, for example, while purportedly portraying pre-cinematic nineteenth-century "natives." These *modern* colonial subjects disrupt historical narratives and imperial origin myths by introducing colonized subjects gazing into the camera in a modern way, identifying themselves as actors, not as "primitives," and breaking the suture between spectators and fictional imperial protagonists. They convey the reality that their existence preceded European invasions to defy the imposition of imperial identities on them. Gazing into the camera and sometimes smiling into it, these actors overlay nineteenth-century imperialism with their own postcolonial modernity as living indigenous people. Returning their own ethnographic gaze, they address Western filmgoers directly and open up encounters' improvisational opportunities in real time.

Deleuze and Guattari include landscape in the faciality system. Landscapes in these empire films disrupt narrative by documenting real places. Yet landscape plays an even larger role in these films, whose studios spent large sums of money for "authentic" costumes and sets and to send second unit teams of filmmakers to Africa.[11] In *King Solomon's Mines*, drawn from Rider Haggard's popular Victorian novel, the film's publicity promised elaborate documentary footage, shots of the Valley of a Thousand Hills in Natal, South Africa, 4,000 natives beaded and bonneted in feathers, 12,000 arm bands, sharks teeth, tigers' claws, monkey's paws, Zulu ostrich feather headdresses, and an emu feather cape for King Umbopa. Zoltán Korda described frenzied Achioli tribal dances and exoticized Africans as "savages." One *Sanders* ad read: "A million mad savages fighting for one beautiful woman! Until three white comrades ALONE pitched into the fray and quelled the bloody revolt" (Dyer, 1986, p. 99), a completely incorrect description of the plot, but an indication of how important were racial difference and documentary-as-spectacle for the conception of empire films. For *Sanders*, 250 blacks were hired from Africa, Bristol, Liverpool, and Cardiff, and about twenty African languages were spoken on the set.[12] *The Illustrated London News* described the set's fifty thatched huts, imported shields, calabashes, spears, and other "authentic" items (Boyle and Bunie, 2001, p. 296). Ethnographic footage, dancers, ceremonies, and herds of wild animals attracted Robeson to the film (Holt, 2004, p. 147; Duberman, 1989. p. 179).

Ethnography could authenticate place and, by implication, validate ideology by marking difference, but it could also interrupt ideological messages. When stock footage of two natives on a hill in *Mines* also appears in *Rhodes*, "authenticity" is undermined. Real place becomes stock, reduced to a kind of faciality that disguises gaps in the presumed realism of place. Another gap is between *in situ* background and studio foreground. Robeson, filmed in the studio, is supposed to be in South Africa, but he is set against South African scenes, so blurry that the two sites remain clearly distinct in a ludicrously obvious disjunction. Even the imagined meeting between Rhodes and

Lobengula is disrupted by ethnography. African actors in the scene approach the camera in real time and look into it. When Rhodes offers a coin bearing Queen Victoria's image to Lobengula, the film cuts to African women smiling at/for the camera. Here modern Africans intervene in the imagined encounter, layering the film's temporalities with interventions of a present moment that contradict the imperial ideology of colonized people as unmodern.

Footage may deny spectators a transformative encounter with ethnographic Others by suppressing possibilities of "discovery, pleasure, interrogation, or shock," depriving "documentary of its own poetics ... by making those sequences perpetually subservient to an ideological vision regulated by the narrative sequences" (Jaikumar, 2006, p. 132). Depriving documentary of its poetics assures "that imperial realism refuses contact with its own historical moment, when divisions between colonizer and colonized were under attack" (Jaikumar, 2006, p. 133). Dyer sees the lack of suture as ideological:

> moments of song, dance, speech and stage presence are either inflected by the containing discourses as Savage Africa or else remain opaque, folkloric, touristic ... mysterious savagery ... This authentication enterprise also falls foul of being only empirically authentic – it lacks a concern with the paradigms through which one observes any empirical phenomenon. Not only are the "real" African elements left undefended from their immediate theatrical or filmic context, they have already been perceived through discourses on Africa that have labelled them primitive.
>
> (Dyer, 1986, p. 90)

For Dyer, decontextualized ethnography enters the fictional imperial discourse *by default*, having nowhere else to go discursively or ideologically. Certainly *Sanders*'s ethnography, unexplained and unintegrated into the narrative, became spectacle, deployed to authenticate the film's reality and endorse the narrative's veracity. Footage of migrating African herds seen from Sanders's plane epitomizes the "master-of-all-I-survey" bird's-eye view described by Pratt, a perspective that utters the surveying explorer/adventurer/conqueror's domination.

Yet there was much contemporary criticism of these films' ideologies, including a parody, *Old Bones of the River* (1938), which indicates that 1930s spectators did not necessarily accept a default position. Footage of rebuilt kraals, bare-breasted women working or dancing, children playing and artisans crafting could appear authentic, while excessive jewelry, heavily feathered warriors and soft shields appeared ludicrous. Among fake shields, oversized animal-teeth jewelry, overdone hairdos and patronizing scripts appear a few moments of a different reality of the Other at home or gazing back. Documentary is not unscripted here, of course, but these ethnographic fragments remain outside script, intertitles, plot, and characters to suggest realities in the *present* time beyond imperial narrative control, like the herds Sanders sees from his plane running unrestrainedly. Africans dance in the narrative because Sanders is away from Africa. Diegetically, they celebrate his departure, but perhaps they also anticipate Britain's departure, too. A glimpsed Africa, albeit brief and decontextualized, escapes the imperial gaze.

I suggest that ethnography could expose incoherences and gaps, that footage could be both authenticating and disrupting. Perhaps *because* it is not integrated, documentary highlights the narrative's, and perhaps empire's, fictional presentation of imperial history and colonized people. Dancing Achioli and migrating animals are startling, unsutured scopophilic pleasures, visually escaping the heavy-handed narrative and clumsy overlay of studio sets against *in situ* footage.

Blackfaciality contains encounters' open-endedness by reiterating the racial-colonial order in realism or by permitting limited improvisational exchanges in romance. As Homi Bhabha notes: "shifting positionalities will never seriously threaten the dominant power relations, for they exist to exercise them pleasurably and productively" (Bhabha, 1983, p. 205). Ethnographic footage likewise both opens and limits spectators' pleasurable encounters with the colonial Other, just as, Rogin asserts, blackface joined "structural domination to cultural desire" (Rogin, 1998, p. 12). Documentary footage glimpses colonial life and ceremony, reminiscent of the "cultural desire" aroused by *National Geographic,* for example, though footage also limits it by censorship or fragmentation, lest spectators enjoy unharnessed indigenous life too much. Ethnography offers a pleasurable escape into a momentary encounter with colonized subjects who – mask-less, black but not in blackface – return the ethnographic gaze of the Western audience, before being subsumed again into the narrative where blackfaciality, spectacle and colony nostalgia distracted audiences from the real imperial changes on the 1930s horizon.

Notes

1 Scholars writing on these films include Matthew Bernstein, Gaylyn Studlar, Melissa Thackway, Teshome Gabriel, John MacKenzie, among others. British Empire film makers include Hungarian refugee Alexander Korda, dubbed "the Kipling of the kinema," who produced a pro-empire trilogy on chivalric themes with brothers Zoltán and Vincent: *Sanders of the River* (1935), *The Drum* (1938) and *The Four Feathers* (1939). Producer Michael Balcon's more critical trilogy for Gaumont-British Corporation focused on imperial economics: *Rhodes of Africa* (1936), *The Great Barrier* (1936) and *King Solomon's Mines* (1937).

2 Rudyard Kipling's poem "The White Man's Burden" commemorated America's colonization of the Philippines.

3 Thug (from Sanskrit thag for conman or hoodlum) described individual criminals; Thuggee means gangs of robbers and murderers (often using strangulation) who preyed on travellers. The British believed they were a religious cult that worshipped Kali, goddess of change and associated with annihilation, but scholars are now sceptical about this.

4 That the Thuggee leader looked to some like Mussolini may reflect US ambiguities about India and empire.

5 Called minstrelsy, in these comic musical skits white and black performers wearing black make-up lampooned African Americans.

6 Son of an Indian elephant driver, Sabu (1924–1963) was a popular actor in empire films, first hired by documentary filmmaker Robert Flaherty for *Elephant Boy* (1937). He was originally offered the role of Gunga Din.

7 Policy whereby subsidized local leaders rule without armies and under British surveillance.

8 Alexander thought a British official would not shake an African's hand; Zoltán thought he would and won this point (Jaikumar, 2006, p. 110; Boyle and Bunie, 2001, p. 297).

9   He said this to a New York *Amsterdam News* reporter.
10 Other examples include *Tarzan, the Ape Man* (1932), in which a tribe of dwarfs are whites in blackface.
11 Barkas did location shooting for *Rhodes* and *King Solomon's Mines*. *Gunga Din* was shot in California and cut with documentary footage.
12 One London student Johnstone Kumau, later Jomo Kenyatta, was Kenya's independence leader (Boyle and Bunie, 2001, pp. 296–7).

Bibliography

Bhabha, H., 1983. Difference, Discrimination and the Discourse of Colonialism. In: F. Barker, P. Hulme, M. Iverson, and D. Loxley, eds., 1989. *The Politics of Theory*, ed., Colchester: University of Essex, pp. 194–211.

Bogle, D., 1989. *Toms, Coons, Mulattoes, Mammies, and Bucks*. New York: Continuum.

Boyle, S. T. and Bunie, A., 2001. *Paul Robeson: The Years of Promise and Achievement*. Amherst: University of Massachusetts Press.

Butler, J., 1993. *Bodies That Matter*. New York: Routledge.

Chowdhry, P., 2000. *Colonial India and the Making of Empire Cinema*. Manchester: Manchester University Press.

Codell, J., 2007. Imperial Masculinity, Mimicry and the New Woman in *Rhodes of Africa*. In: T. Barringer, G. Quilley, and D. Fordham, eds., 2007. *Art and the British Empire*. Manchester: Manchester University Press, pp. 254–66.

Codell, J., 2011. Domesticating Empire in the 1930s: Metropole, Colony, Family. In: L. Grieveson and C. MacCabe eds., *Empire and Film*, London: BFI/Palgrave Macmillan, pp. 189-203

Deleuze, G. and Guattari, F., 1987. *A Thousand Plateaus*. Translated from French by B. Massumi. Minneapolis: University of Minnesota Press.

Duberman, M. B., 1989. *Paul Robeson*. New York: Knopf.

Dunn, K., 1996. Lights ... Camera ... Africa, *African Studies Review*, 39(1), pp. 149–75.

Dyer, R., 1986. *Heavenly Bodies*. New York: St. Martin's Press.

Featherstone, S., 1998. The Blackface Atlantic. *Journal of Victorian Culture,* 3(2), pp. 234–51.

Harris, W. G., 1988. *Cary Grant*. New York: Doubleday.

Holt, J., 2004. A Dream Betrayed. In: J. Dorinson and W. Pencak, eds., 2004. *Paul Robeson*. Jefferson, NC: McFarland Press, pp. 145–51.

Jaher, F. C. and King. B. B., 2008. Hollywood's India. *Film and History*, 38(2), pp. 33–44.

Jaikumar, P., 2006. *Cinema at the End of Empire*. Durham, NC: Duke University Press.

Loh, M. H., 2009. Renaissance Faciality. *Oxford Art Journal,* 32(3), pp. 341–63.

Lott, E., 1993. *Love and Theft: Blackface Minstrelsy and the American Working Class*. New York: Oxford University Press.

MacCormack, P., 2000. Faciality. In: 4th European Feminist Research Conference. Bologna, Italy 18 September–1October 2000. Available at: http://orlando.women.it/cyberarchive/files/mac-cormack.htm [Accessed 06 December 2010].

Pickering, M., 1997. John Bull in Blackface. *Popular Music,* 16(2), pp. 181–201.

Pratt, M. L., 1992. *Imperial Eyes*. New York: Routledge.

Richards, J., 1984. *Visions of Yesterday*. London: Routledge and Kegan Paul.

Rogin, M., 1998. *Blackface, White Noise*. Berkeley: University of California Press.

Wiegman, R., 1992. Feminism, 'The Boyz,' and Other Matters. In: S. Cohan and I. Rae Hark, eds., 1992. *Screening the Male*. New York: Routledge, pp. 173–93.

Filmography

The Drum, 1938. [film] Directed by Z. Korda. United Kingdom: London Film Productions.

Elephant Boy, 1937. [film] Directed by R. Flaherty. United Kingdom: London Film Productions.

The Four Feathers, 1939. [film] Directed by Directed by Z. Korda. United Kingdom: London Film Productions.

Gone with the Wind, 1939. [film] Directed by V. Fleming. USA: Warner Brothers.

The Great Barrier, 1936. [film] Directed by M. Balcon. United Kingdom: Gaumont British Picture Corporation.

Gunga Din, 1939. [film] Directed by G. Stevens. USA: RKO Radio Pictures.

King Solomon's Mines, 1937. [film] Directed by R. Stevenson. United Kingdom: Gaumont British Picture Corporation.

Lives of a Bengal Lancer, 1935. [film] Directed by H. Hathaway. USA: Paramount Pictures.

Old Bones of the River, 1938. [film] Directed by M. Varnel. United Kingdom: Gainsborough Pictures.

Rhodes of Africa, 1936. [film] Directed by B. Viertel. United Kingdom: Gaumont British Picture Corporation.

Sanders of the River, 1935. [film] Directed by Z. Korda. United Kingdom: London Film Productions.

Stanley and Livingstone, 1939. [film] Directed by H. King and O. Brower. USA: Twentieth Century Fox Film Corporation.

Tarzan, the Ape Man, 1932. [film] Directed by W. S. van Dyke. USA: MGM.

The Sun Never Sets, 1939. [film] Directed by R. Lee. USA: Universal Pictures.

Chapter 3

The socialist historical film

Anikó Imre

Epic patriotism in a postcolonial perspective

It is hard to resist Michael the Brave, protagonist of the eponymous Romanian historical epic *Mihai Viteazul/Michael the Brave* (Nicolaescu, 1971). Mihai, a seventeenth-century Wallachian prince, played by star actor Amza Pellea, is handsome, earnest, and of course fearless. One cannot help rooting for him as he struggles to achieve his single goal: to unite the three principalities of Wallachia, Transylvania, and Moldavia within a Romania free of foreign oppression. We watch him lead his army through seven lavishly depicted heroic battles and stand his ground in no less heroic diplomatic encounters with European and Ottoman rulers. We feel for him as he sacrifices for the noble cause his desire for the woman he loves, his son, who dies in battle, and eventually his own life. One's heart soars when Mihai reunites Romania, but it breaks when his triumph proves ephemeral under imperial pressure and he is betrayed at the end of the film.

For me at least, it is hard to resist the particular pleasures of the socialist national historical epic, having been formatively influenced by the genre in my native Hungary. *Michael the Brave* evokes *Egri csillagok/The Stars of Eger* (Várkonyi, 1968), a film I saw many times in the theater and on TV, about the defense of the frontier fortress of Eger against Ottoman invaders by a heroic captain and his loyal fighters. The original novel on which the film was based, written by nineteenth-century novelist Géza Gárdonyi, was the first real novel I read, many of whose 800 or so pages reduced me to tears. Still, there is something counter-intuitive about my identification with *Michael the Brave* given that the film depicts the Hungarian Zsigmond Báthory, Prince of Transylvania, as a sniveling, two-faced coward. Clearly, this was a means of demonizing Hungarians as usurpers of Transylvania, a territory that had always belonged to the Romanian people in dictator Ceauşescu's history book. In the Hungarian history books I studied in school in the 1970s and 1980s, Transylvania had been a Hungarian territory until the peace treaties following World War I, and Báthory was more like Mihai: a brave, patriotic military commander and supreme diplomat. However, as I am watching *Michael the Brave*, this is just a passing thought in my mind. The film brings back memories of that curious swelling of patriotic excitement that fueled the socialist historical epic, and which renders the object of excitement – heroes and countries – of secondary import.

From a postsocialist vantage point, the heroes and countries appear nearly interchangeable. While the historical epic is an international genre with well-defined codes, the cycle of films it produced in the Soviet Empire in the 1960s–1980s carries a geopolitically and historically specific uniformity (Dobreva, 2011). The Hollywood codes of the genre are recognizable in the historical spectacles and political intrigues. But the Eastern European historical epic hinged on socialist regimes' strategic manipulation of popular nationalism in order to reinforce their own legitimacy against the waning credibility of Soviet internationalism in the 1960s. The turn to past historical epochs was also motivated by increasing competition with the contemporary attractions of Western consumer culture and the dissemination of television, which compelled socialist governments to provide their own home-grown propaganda edutainment.

My fascination with the genre returns me to the contradiction in my dual identification, the fact that the region-wide similarities of affect render the nationalistic address secondary: even though the primary goal of each film's history-weaving is to create national unity, the aesthetic, thematic and ideological overlaps among the films weave another, overarching regional pattern. This is a postcolonial pattern. It is my goal here to fold back the explicit patriotic messages of the films and uncover the unspoken postcolonial underpinnings of East European nationalisms within the historical epic. Using *Michael the Brave* and the Polish film *Janosik* (Passendorfer, 1974) as my case studies, I discuss how national historiographies obsessively return to imperial invasion as something against which national independence and sovereignty – always already assumed as a given – must be repeatedly established. The films in this cycle also share the central motif of small peripheral nations acting as the last line of defending European civilization against the Ottoman other. This motif puts the Soviet era in inevitable continuity with the Ottoman Empire, against which the inherent Europeanness of Eastern European nationalisms needs to be demonstrated. Only postcolonial discourses' interconnecting of power and representation, subjectivity and hybridity can explain how the region's nationalisms absorbed and mediated between two kinds of coloniality. Only a postcolonial framework can make visible the theoretical through line between the national specificity of these films, which was meant to reinforce official histories, and their regionally shared aesthetic pleasures and ideological contradictions. Let me elaborate on both the timeliness and difficulties of such a project.

I first encountered postcolonial studies in the early 1990s. Along with feminist theories, postcolonial scholarship opened up a defamiliarized view of my home region of Eastern Europe, newly rescued by neoliberal capitalism from the grips of socialism. At that time, I had been literally and figuratively trying to escape the visceral sense of what I could only describe as claustrophobia in my native Hungary by taking advantage of Western European study opportunities. Ironically, the very paradigms that I thought would lead me to a more spacious way of thinking and living, away from Eastern Europe, led me right back to the postsocialist terrain. Postcolonial and feminist theories both crystallized for me nationalism as the ultimate reason for my claustrophobia and offered first-class tools to make sense of my discontent. They helped me see the contours of a region-wide pattern of colonial resentment and defensiveness, which drew up impenetrable boundaries of gender, sexuality, and race-ethnicity around nations.

They made me articulate how this crippling psychological burden on populations was rendered unrecognizable in the guise of patriotic pride. They demystified the self-propelling histories of genetically and spiritually connected nation-families that I had taken for granted as the guiding narratives of my identity.

Reading Fanon, Césaire, Ahmad, Mannoni, Said, Bhabha, and later Spivak, Mohanty, Lorde, Anzaldúa, and others deconstructed the walls of patriotism and defamiliarized my burden of nationalism as a postcolonial formation. I dove into the personal-political project of telling the postcolonial story of Eastern European nationalism, starting with an essay that discussed the protagonists of Hungarian filmmaker István Szabó as "white men in white masks" (Imre, 1999) and continuing with my doctoral dissertation entirely devoted to a postcolonial and feminist reassessment of Eastern European cultures (Imre, 2002).

However, while my efforts to contribute to the difficult dialogue between Eastern European women and Western feminism fed into a growing conversation within an expanding academic and activist community, my attempts to bring together postcolonial and (post)socialist as related and mutually enriching terms were continually rebuffed. The resistance came from two places. On the one hand, postcolonial theories' concern with hybridity, subjectivity, and discursivity, which I valued so highly as deconstructive sticks with which to poke holes in East European nationalisms, turned out to be confined to the historical and racial territory marked out by Western European imperialism. Whenever I gave a talk or simply browsed the literature, it was clear that there is such a thing as a proper postcolonial scholar with a proper heritage and I was not one. The reactions ranged from quiet shunning to angry outbursts. Some of this was due to a rightful worry about the discursive dilution of postcoloniality and a compensatory effort to keep the field specific to the violent imperialism and racism of European empires. Some of it was no doubt disciplinary gatekeeping around an emerging academic field.

On the other hand, East European scholars were not too keen to be associated with the postcolonial either. It threatened self-contained national cultures and their unspoken racial scaffolding, the dual ethno-cultural heritage essential to claiming Europeanness and to self-protection against the realities of peripheral economic and political development. Even ten years ago, it seemed there were only a few, specialized places where Eastern Europe could be mentioned as a potential postcolonial location, and these places were far from the main current of postcolonial studies (see Imre, 2005). Discouraged by the double rejection, I turned elsewhere, to paradigms of globalization and transnationalism, which appeared more inclusive.

The fact that, in the 2011s, a chapter on the region would be a logical part of a collection on postcolonial cinemas signals a definite and welcome turning of the tide. The landscape has radically changed during my bitter absence from postcolonial studies. As I discuss in the next section, an entire, interdisciplinary field has grown out of the multiple cross-pollinations between Eastern European cultures and postcolonial studies. At least one important reason for this new scholarly crop must be that a new generation of hybrid intellectuals has entered the scene, who no longer see postcoloniality as an ideological threat to nationalism. The body of work now available bears out what I think is the greatest potential advantage of a postcolonial encounter with Eastern

Europe: its thorough and systematic interlacing of the experience of external oppression with internal repression; of the political-economic and the subjective-psychological experiences of colonialism. Conversely, Eastern Europe has much to contribute to postcolonial thinking in this regard, not despite but because of its oblique and complex participation in the racist and heterosexist paradigms of imperialism and colonization (as it has taken on the roles of both colonizer and colonized). Films and other audiovisual media have been crucial means of representation and mediation on these fronts. In the following, I first give a brief overview of the ways in which postcoloniality has been considered relevant for defamiliarizing Eastern European histories and cultures and how the inclusion of the region in the web of postcolonial possibilities enhances the web itself. Then I zoom in on the filmic output of the 1970s, when state socialist parties across the Soviet-controlled region tried to loosen their allegiance to Moscow and solidify their own legitimacy by rekindling popular nationalism through popular entertainment. I argue throughout that Eastern European nationalisms could function as primordial only at the expense of suppressing their constitutive colonial dynamic.

Eastern Europe's colonialities

The difficulty of thinking of Eastern Europe as postcolonial is certainly not the absence of relevant histories and features. On the contrary; there are multiple relevances, which present a crisscrossing, often contradictory pattern not easily mapped onto the history of Western European imperialism, which has determined the main signposts of postcolonial theorizing.

The most evident postcolonial register is the region's recent colonization by the Soviet Union following the end of World War II, when most of the states in question found themselves on the losing side. In most countries, this meant a full or partial military occupation coupled with more or less direct political control in the form of central ideological directives from Moscow, which permeated the working of every state institution. With the exception of Romania and Yugoslavia, led by "rogue" dictators Ceaușescu and Tito respectively, Russian was a required subject of the centralized curriculum in the satellite states from elementary school through college. Whether we can call Soviet domination colonization in the same way in each country concerned is open to debate given the tremendous diversity of experiences under Soviet rule (Owczarzak, 2009). Nevertheless, several authors point to the undeniable parallels between postsocialist and postcolonial states and states of mind. As David Kideckel argues (Kideckel, 2009), such states emerge from common conditions that are characterized by a sharp opposition between provincial and cosmopolitan cultures (see Verdery, 2002; Young, 2003); have imbalanced, distorted neoliberal economies (Bunce, 1999; Humphrey, 2002; Stark and Bruszt, 1998); struggle with democratization; fall prey to violent nationalisms (Appadurai, 1996, 2006); and have troubled relationships with past histories (Borneman, 1997; Comaroff and Comaroff, 2001; Petryna, 2002).

However, the relevance of postcolonial paradigms goes well beyond the recent history of the Soviet Empire. The hierarchical division between Eastern and Western

Europe harks back to the Enlightenment, which established Europe as the bedrock of rationality and democracy (Korek, 2007, p.15) and generated tropes that linked Eastern Europe with postcolonial Africa, Southeast Asia, and Latin America (Buchowski, 2006). Larry Wolff famously retraces the history of Eastern Europe as a discursive construct whose roots go back to two hundred years earlier than the Cold War and Churchill's infamous Iron Curtain speech (Wolff, 1994). While civilization was firmly tied to the West, Eastern Europe shifted to an imaginary location somewhere in between civilization and barbarism. Eastern Europe was the West's immediate and intermediary other. It was designated as a boundary marker, where Western Empires were protected from the invasion of uncivilized Eastern forces such as the Ottoman Turks. The borderland's mission to protect Western European civilization became deeply internalized in the course of the struggles for national independence in the 1840s. Eastern European nationalisms were thus formed in the West's image of the region, around a core of self-colonization. This colonial mimicry was perpetuated through a wish-fulfilling cultural assimilation that rested on the assumption of shared racial affinity with the West. Although Eastern European cultures did not directly participate in actual territorial imperialism, the hierarchical division between the two Europes qualifies as an imperial order sustained through mutually constituting Eastern and Western discourses (Verdery, 2002; Böröcz, 2001). In this sense, the Soviet Empire is just the latest phase in the history of imperial struggles over the territory, which has been multiply conquered, and where rulers and subjects often shifted roles. Milica Bakic-Hayden calls these intertwined historical memories of conquest and exclusion nesting orientalisms (Bakic-Hayden, 1995).

The fall of the Iron Curtain renewed the discursive hierarchy between East and West within the guise of neoliberal free market ideology. The majority of postsocialist populations have been designated the losers of capitalism, who are themselves to be blamed for their immobility and incapacity to adjust (Buchowski, 2006). A postcolonial analysis foregrounds the continued sense of inferiority and resentment within the nationalisms that fester beneath the official European rhetoric of a swift generational change that supposedly creates brand-new postsocialist citizens for whom democracy and market rationality are second nature (Sztompka, 2004).

The reality of the EU expansion, József Böröcz claims, is a continued division within the continent. Despite the EU's pledge to extend the four freedoms (of labor, capital, goods, and services) to all of its citizens, the hierarchy between the former imperial powers and the peripheral newcomers is unmistakable; unequal and unidirectional economic flows have characterized the privatization of postsocialist government assets. Tax incentives have been created to lure foreign direct investment, and new policies have allowed for siphoning off the national wealth of new member states. EU-based corporations are the most prominent investors while Eastern companies have very small investment portfolios. Negative stereotypes and discourses of backwardness and inferiority flourish, not despite, but because of the absence of a fully processed colonial history (see Imre and Bardan, 2011). Geopolitical power remains concentrated in the Western center, and technologies of Foucauldian governmentality are being deployed to normalize, standardize, and control the operation of postsocialist states. The EU's eastern expansion thus features and combines state coloniality with a civilizing mission that features low-level violence (Böröcz, 2001).

The colonial layers I have discussed are repressed in national histories, a repression enabled by the region's whiteness. But postcolonial thinking clearly shows that there is a continuity between the histories of nationhood and imperialism (Mbembe, 2008). The layers of postcoloniality that have been carefully edited out of state rhetoric and public discourses resurface in films whose aesthetic and affective address mixes entertainment with propaganda. The historical adventure genre, cultivated by all socialist governments in the 1960s–1980s, is one of the most prominent sites where the postcolonial premises of Eastern European nationalism are laid bare. As a cycle of films conceived to legitimate national sovereignty through film entertainment, it foregrounds the constant struggle between what Homi Bhabha famously calls the pedagogical versus the performative aspects of nationalism. He explains that the nation is produced as narration in a constant split between two different kinds of temporalities: the continuist, accumulative time of the pedagogical, and the reiterative, recursive strategy of the performative (Bhabha, 1994, p. 145). Rather than the homogeneous and horizontal view proposed by nationalist historiography, whose reference point is an unchanging "people," the "people" is in fact a complex rhetorical strategy of social reference repetitively produced and confirmed within a set of discourses.

> We then have a contested conceptual territory where the nation's people must be thought in double-time; the people are the historical "objects" of a nationalist pedagogy, giving the discourse an authority that is based on the pre-given or constituted historical origin in the past; the people are also the "subjects" of a process of signification that must erase any prior or originary presence of the nation-people to demonstrate the prodigious, living principles of the people as contemporaneity: as a sign of the present through which national life is redeemed and iterated as a reproductive process.
>
> (1994, p. 145)

The socialist historical epic foregrounds the paradox of this dual time of nationalism. The similarities of the genre across countries at the specific historical crossroads of weakening Soviet control and the increasing reach of Western-type media reveal the postcolonial insecurity of these nationalisms as the trace to be surmounted through compulsive repetition.

The socialist historical epic

The two films I discuss here exemplify the preoccupation with two key moments of the anti-imperial struggle that became repeatedly and performatively harnessed for validating national independence and Europeanness. *Mihai Viteazul* is one of many films dedicated to heroic resistance to the Ottoman invasion while *Janosik* takes place in the aftermath of the Rákóczi uprising against the Habsburgs in the early 1800s.

Mihai Viteazul is the most popular Romanian film of all time. Commissioned by Ceauşescu, it remains one of the most memorable achievements of nationalistic propaganda entertainment and was Romania's official Oscar entry for Best Foreign Language Film in 1971. The two-part epic loosely follows events between 1595 and 1601. The historical Mihai was a medieval prince who managed to unite the three principalities of Wallachia, Moldavia, and Transylvania for a few months in 1600. The film adheres to the spirit of history rather than to the facts, as the real Mihai was far from the brave liberator he is in the film (Jäckel, 2006, p. 78). Director Sergiu Nicolaescu was responsible only for delivering to the public the official ideas of national history. Released at the peak of the genre's popularity, the film was instrumental in forging a national unity among a majority of today's Romanians (Petrescu, 2003, p. 258). It is one of several films that dramatize the importance of Eastern borderlands stopping the barbaric Ottoman invasion and confirming Western Christianity and civilization. The best known of these are the Yugoslavian film *Boj na Kosovu/The Battle of Kosovo* (Sotra, 1989), the Bulgarian *Vreme na nasilie/Time of Violence* (Staikov, 1988) and the Albanian *Balada e Kurbinit/Ballad of Kurbini* (Çashku, 1990; Jäckel, 2006, p. 83). This motif is symptomatic of a nationalism rekindled from above by the Ceauşescu government and thus specific to East European state socialist culture, but it also reiterates the internalized marginality assigned to these nation-states within the enduring terms of the Enlightenment division of the continent. On the one hand, *Mihai* ostentatiously demonstrates colonial resistance to the Ottomans, eastern invaders of the past who no doubt stand as a reference to Soviet imperialism in the present. On the other hand, the internalized role of guardian against barbarian eastern forces inevitably involves national independence in an unacknowledged colonial identification with the West in the present. This interweaving dual dynamic – a sense of explicit superiority to the East and implicit inferiority to the West – was recognizable in the socialist epic across the specific historical narratives depicted.

The majority of historians have placed the actual formation of the Romanian nation between the 1848 struggles for independence and the 1918 creation of Greater Romania. But Greater Romania was a deeply fragmented polity. The effects of centuries of political separation presented a challenge to the newly enlarged state and its population's sense of national identity (Petrescu, 2003, p. 244). The sovereign nation-state was still being seen as unrealized during communism, which needed to be defended against the Soviet and Hungarian threat (2003, p. 246). After Romania abruptly switched sides to join the Allied forces towards the end of World War II in 1944, the Romanian delegation argued to Stalin that Romania should be able to annex Transylvania because of the short-lived union of Transylvania with Moldavia and Wallachia under Mihai Vietazul (2003, p. 249). Ceauşescu's predecessor, Gheorghe Gheorghiu-Dej, initiated a campaign to reinvigorate local traditions and facilitate the ethnic unity of the fragmented Romanian nation in the 1950s. This involved placing the Romanian party-state within the historical tradition of medieval principalities. Nationalism was thus not a dormant sentiment spontaneously awakened from the grassroots but a conscious political strategy managed from above, from which large groups classified as class enemies were excluded (Petrescu, 2009, p. 523). During 1965–1968, Ceauşescu's early years, the popular perception of the regime gradually improved as a result of its foreign policy of independence from Moscow and opening towards the West, as well as its domestic policies of relative economic and ideological relaxation. Ceauşescu positioned himself as a maverick who defied Soviet domination, and a man of the people fascinated with the heroic deeds of the rulers of medieval Romanian principalities (2009, p. 530). A host of grand historical epic films such as *Stefan cel Mare/Stephen the Great* (Dragan, 1974), *Mircea/Mircea the Old* (Nicolaescu, 1989) and of course *Michael the Brave* capitalized on the theme of heroic struggle for independence through setting up a parallel and continuity between medieval leaders fighting the Ottomans and supreme leader Ceauşescu fighting the Soviets. The thorniest element of these epic constructions was Transylvania, which has been claimed by both Hungary and Romania as the cradle of the respective nations.

In the 1970s, Ceauşescu turned to the construction of ancient roots in the Romanian nation's half-mythic Dacian-Roman origin story. *Mihai* was followed and preceded by several other generously funded historical superproductions directed by Nicolaescu, each dedicated to bringing to life a slice of Ceauşescu's mythic history. *Dacii/The Dacians* (Nicolaescu, 1967) was set in 87 AD, when the territory of Dacia was invaded by Imperial Rome. It reinterprets the genesis of Romania as the result of blending between Roman and Dacian peoples, confirming in filmic form the popular theory of Daco-Roman continuity, first popularized in the seventeenth century. Reviving this theory was a crucial strategy in making the claim to an essential linguistic-cultural affinity with Europe that reaches back to ancient times. It also displays the contradictory ease with which the Ceauşescu government – similar to other socialist regimes – picked and chose among different instances of imperial domination and mixing, rejecting some in order voluntarily to submit to others. On a more directly political plane, the theory of Daco-Roman continuity allowed Ceauşescu's government to assert ownership over Transylvania and dismiss the province's majority Hungarian population as usurpers.

The effectiveness of the historical epic in building a sense of ethnic national unity was also due to communist governments' calculated investment in the film industry and a thorough communication and educational infrastructure to disseminate propaganda disguised as entertainment. The 1950s saw the establishment of the Caragiale Institute of Theatre and Film (IATC), the Alexandru Sahia documentary and short film studio, and the Buftea Studios. Gheorghiu-Dej's increasingly anti-Moscow line was a success domestically. He made historical films required viewings for schoolchildren and workers (Jäckel, 2006, p. 81). Under Ceauşescu, filmmaking was an extension of his "independent foreign policy" and resulted in co-produced patriotic epics. Buftea Studios offered some of the best technical talent in the East and provided cheap labor and modern facilities to Western partners. *The Dacians* was a Romanian-French production and *Columna/The Column*, (Dragan, 1968), another "Daco-Roman" movie, was co-produced with West Germany (Jäckel, 2006, pp. 79–81).

Michael the Brave was planned to be a collaboration with Columbia Pictures. Sergiu Nicolaescu, who had demonstrated both his loyalty to the Ceauşescu regime and his flair for the historical spectacle, and who had already directed six films in Western collaboration, was commissioned to direct the film. Charlton Heston was supposed to be cast in the lead role, Richard Burton was to play Zsigmond Bathory, with Orson

Welles, Elizabeth Taylor, Laurence Harvey and Edward G. Robinson in other roles. But Ceauşescu objected to the heavy American involvement and eventually ordered that they use an all-Romanian cast. Director Nicolaescu, a good-looking man who often acted in his own films, was targeted for the role of Mihai. However, Nicolaescu wanted the charismatic Pellea to play Mihai, and he himself ended up in the role of Mihai's adversary, the Turkish Selim Pasa. The film took three years to complete and was shot in Austria, Turkey, and Romania. It was ultimately financed by the Romanian government but was distributed by Columbia, receiving the largest international distribution of any Romanian film.

Michael the Brave, then, exemplifies the key components of the success of the socialist historical epic in forging national unity despite its evident propaganda intentions. The acting talent, the simple script, and the magnificent period spectacle all played a role, but even more crucial was the regionally and geopolitically specific way in which the film – and the genre – straddled education and entertainment. The script corroborated the version of history propagated by the regime in history books, and was validated by Ceauşescu's official, co-opted historians. It also intertwined dual colonial legacies: a rejection of Eastern colonization through the parallel between the Ottoman Empire of the past and the Soviet Empire of the contemporary present, and, at the level of production and distribution, by Ceauşescu's Western-oriented cultural policies.

The Polish *Janosik* (1974), directed by Jerzy Passendorfer and based on the 1973 television series of the same title, has also enjoyed uninterrupted, cult popularity since its release. The film is about a Slovak outlaw with a Hungarian name variously rendered as Johannes, Georg, Janko, Janik, Janicek, Jasiek, Janosz, Janos, Juro and Durko (Rassloff, 2010). "Janosik" is a derivation of the Hungarian "János" with the Czech/Slovak -ik suffix attached (Vortruba, 2006). The historical Janosik moved across several fluid borders during his short life in the eighteenth century. Poems and novels written of his life are required reading in Slovak and Polish schools. His story has inspired ten films and TV series altogether in the Czech, Slovak, and Polish territories between 1929 and 2009.

Janosik exemplifies a type of national epic hero unlike the type of aristocratic leader immortalized in *Michael the Brave*: the outlaw. In the territory of the Habsburg Empire, which stretched across present-day Hungary, the Czech Republic, Slovakia, Poland, the Ukraine, Romania, Serbia, Croatia, and Slovenia, the late seventeenth and early eighteenth century was a time of peasant uprisings. The most successful of these was led by Hungarian magnate Ferencz Rákóczi II, Prince of Transylvania, the richest landlord in the Kingdom of Hungary. His military operations were mostly conducted in the borderland area between the Habsburg and the Ottoman Empires. Rákóczi, also funded by the French crown looking to overthrow Habsburg domination in Europe, recruited the emancipated peasant soldiers of North-Eastern Hungary called *hajdus* or *haiducs* to join him. With their help, he seized control of much of Hungary by 1703. After several battles and much negotiation, the uprising failed and the prince was forced into exile. The subsequent return of Habsburg domination turned him and his fighters almost instantly into folk heroes. Some of his men went into hiding in inscrutable border areas and sustained themselves by highway robbery. Although these outlaws were not discriminating as to whom they robbed – or murdered, in many cases – folk stories, songs and later nationalist writers elevated them to the status of justice warriors who carried on the legacy of the uprising by protecting the poor against the rich, many of whom were German-speaking foreigners.

Rákóczi and his outlaw followers were further revived and embraced in the region during the national revolutions of the 1840s. They were appropriated by socialist party authorities by the 1960s, when nationalism made its way back into the official rhetoric. For the socialist regimes of the 1960s, the Rákóczi uprising and the outlaw resistance in its aftermath were appropriately heroic, safely removed from the present in history, and not associated with bloody revolts, unlike nineteenth-century national revolutions, which were feared to carry the risk of igniting street demonstrations. The uprising's benefits also included a tale of unity and cooperation between peasants and the highest nobility. It was ideal for fortifying national consciousness, unimaginable under the earlier, forced internationalism of Stalinist crackdowns in the 1950s. At the same time, it provided a contained affective outlet through entertainment.

The nationalistic fandom that such films ignited was also anchored in the actors who played the leads. In Poland, Marek Pepereczko, who played Janosik in the film, was widely considered a hunk and converted many viewers first to the TV series then to the film. The film itself solicited nationalistic identification right from the opening title sequence, a widescreen shot evocative of Hollywood Westerns, showing the hero, in folk period costume, riding on horseback, to the tune of inspiring music. The film score took on a life of its own, mobilizing affective associations with freedom and social justice and generating a kind of socialist fandom at the interface of folk motifs and state-sanctioned high culture. Written by Jerzy Matuszkiewicz, a widely celebrated jazz musician and composer, the theme evokes Polish highland folk songs and infuses them with a sense of adventure and romance through the orchestration of flute, trumpet, and guitar.

The introductory visual themes evoke and encapsulate the oppressed poor's righteous fight against the rich. With the high mountains of the Tatras as backdrop, outdoor landscapes provide perfect hiding places and battle grounds for manly men, who resemble the heroic cowboys in Hollywood Westerns. These sites are not historically accurate to the Rákóczi uprising and its aftermath, however. The film moves the historical Janosik from his actual place of birth and life in the Slovak-Hungarian lower Tatras to an area in the Polish highlands that had been embraced by nationalist Polish intellectuals of the 1830s, and then again after the crushing of the anti-Russian Polish uprising in 1864, as the birthplace of ancestral Polish culture. Nationalist writers were fascinated with an ethnic group called the Gorale, a shepherd community in this border area who spoke their own Polish-Slovak dialect and originally migrated there from the Romanian region of the Carpathians. The Gorale were "discovered" and romanticized in nationalistic accounts as a group unspoiled by civilization and foreign influence. Literary accounts of outlaw heroes, including Janosik, were associated with the Gorale long before the film was made. The film thus gives its protagonist a highland accent, which instantly evokes a long history of popular nationalism (Rassloff, 2010).

The same loose historiography applies to the main characters. The historical Janosik was born in Terchova, present-day Slovakia, in 1688 and joined the anti-Habsburg kuruc insurgency under Rákóczi in 1707. He was imprisoned after its defeat. Once released, he organized a thirty-man outlaw band. This was an ethnically mixed band, which mostly consisted of Slovaks and a few Poles, and moved across the three borders that crisscrossed these difficult lands among the Ottoman Empire, the Habsburg Empire and the Kingdom of Poland: and, within the Habsburg Empire, across the Hungarian and Austrian borders. Band members were usually single young men from the fringes of rural society: shepherds, laid-off soldiers, deserters, smugglers, bondsmen on the run, servants, priests, and prisoners (Rassloff, 2010). Similar to most historical outlaws, they had little political investment and robbed townspeople and nobles without much discrimination. Janosik himself was finally captured, tortured, and hanged in 1713 (Rassloff, 2010). His martyrdom unleashed an astonishing career as a legend and literary raw material. Contrary to modern images of Janosik, the oldest representations were free of ethnic clash between Slovaks and Hungarians, and only had rare instances of conflict with German intruders. Janosik's actual trial proceedings do not reveal ethnic causes or tensions either. The majority of the band's actual victims were presumably Slovak (Vortruba, 2006).

The 1974 Polish film fuses the myth of the noble robber with a socialist-realist interpretation of class struggle. The film and the series established Janosik as a Polish national hero, subtly repositioning him in national history through the location, costumes, and set design, which suggested the late eighteenth and early nineteenth century as much as the early eighteenth century. The new ethnic contours of the noble robber in the Polish version are evident in the choice of his antagonist Bartos, a sneaky killer who is identified as a Slovak-Hungarian (Rassloff, 2010).

There is no other character who could embody the layers of nested orientalisms and colonial ambiguities better than Janosik. The legend's availability for deployment by several national narratives, its edutainment power, and its longevity derive precisely from its open-ended interlacing of historical fact, folk culture, and high literary treatments that are not only trans-regional but often trans-European in their construction. The kind of nationalism that the Janosik legend weaves around an improper, outlaw hero implies an unacknowledged embrace of a colonial, Western European construction of the Eastern peripheries as rebellious and wild, a kind of permanent Wild East where the laws of civil nation-states are subordinated to popular justice.

As two distinct versions of the patriotic socialist edutainment epic, *Michael the Brave* and *Janosik* demonstrate the difficulty of the region's categorization in terms of postcolonial theories. But this difficulty is precisely what makes the effort worthwhile. Rereading the histories of East European nationalisms crystallizes a hidden but constitutive colonial division within Europe that continues to be significant. This postcolonial thread reaches back to the Enlightenment and forward into the future of an emerging European Empire. Unlike official public discourses, which insist on the discursive and political contours of distinct nations, feature films and other media texts display the multiple overlaps among national histories. They visualize a regional map of hybridities that demystify the self-avowed sovereignty of Eastern European nation-states and nationalisms as protesting too much. Understanding Eastern European nationalisms as postcolonial is not merely a metaphorical expansion of postcolonial studies. It also throws into relief the continuing imperial underpinning of uneven development within and beyond Europe.

Bibliography

Appadurai, A., 1996. *Modernity at Large: Cultural Dimensions of Globalization*. Minneapolis: University of Minnesota Press.

Appadurai, A., 2006. *Fear of Small Numbers: An Essay on the Geography of Anger*. Durham, NC: Duke University Press.

Bakic-Hayden, M., 1995. Nesting Orientalisms: The Case of Former Yugoslavia. *Slavic Review*, 54(4), pp. 917–31.

Bhabha, H., 1994. DissemiNation: Time, Narrative and the Margins of the Modern Nation. In: H. Bhabha, ed., 1994. *The Location of Culture*. New York: Routledge, pp. 39–70.

Borneman, J., 1997. *Settling Accounts: Violence, Justice and Accountability in Postsocialist Europe*. Princeton, NJ: Princeton University Press.

Böröcz, J., 2001. Introduction: Empire and Coloniality in the "Eastern enlargement" of the European Union. In: J. Böröcz and M. Kovács, eds., 2001. *Empire's New Clothes: Unveiling EU-Enlargement*. Central Europe Review, pp. 4–50, [online] 5 March 2003. Available at: http://aei.pitt.edu/144/01/Empire.pdf [accessed 01 December 2010].

Buchowski, M., 2006. The Specter of Orientalism in Europe: From Exotic Other to Stigmatized Brother. *Anthropological Quarterly*, 79(3), pp. 463–82.

Bunce, V., 1999. The Political Economy of Postsocialism. *Slavic Review*, 58(4), pp. 756–93.

Comaroff, J. and Comaroff, J.L., 2001. Naturing the Nation: Aliens, Apocalypse and the Postcolonial State. *Journal of Southern African Studies*, (27)3, pp. 627–51.

Dobreva, N., 2011. East European Historical Epics: Genre Cinema and the Visualization of a Heroic National Past. Forthcoming. In: A. Imre, ed. *The Blackwell Companion to East European Cinemas*. New York: Wiley-Blackwell.

Humphrey, C., 2002. *The Unmaking of Soviet Life: Everyday Economies After Socialism*. Ithaca, NY: Cornell University Press.

Imre, A., 1999. White Man, White Masks: Mephisto Meets Venus. *Screen*, 40(4), pp. 405–22.

Imre, A., 2002. Allegories of Transition: Feminism and Postcolonial East European Cinemas. Ph.D. thesis, University of Washington.

Imre, A., 2005. Whiteness in Post-Socialist Eastern Europe: The Time of the Gypsies, the End of Race. In: A. López, ed. 2005. *Postcolonial Whiteness: A Critical Reader*. Albany: State University of New York Press, pp. 79–102.

Imre, A. and Bardan, A., 2011. Vampire Branding: Romania's Dark Destinations. Forthcoming. In: N. Kaneva, ed., *Nation Branding and Eastern Europe*. London: Routledge.

Jäckel, A., 2006. Mihai Viteazul/Michael the Brave, Sergiu Nicolaescu, Romania, 1970– 71. In: D. Iordanova, eds., 2006. *The Cinema of the Balkans*. London: Wallflower Press, pp. 75–86.

Kideckel, D.A., 2009. Citizenship Discourse, Globalization and Protest: A Postsocialist-Postcolonial Comparison. *Anthropology of East Europe Review*, 27(2), pp. 117–33.

Korek, J., 2007. Central and Eastern Europe from a Postcolonial Perspective. In: Korek, J., ed., 2007. *From Sovietology to Postcoloniality. Vol. 32*. Stockholm: Södertörn Academic Studies, pp. 32–45.

Mbembe, A., 2008. What is Postcolonial Thinking? Interview by O. Mongin, N. Lempereur, and J.L. Schlegel. *Eurozine*, [online] 9 January 2008. Available at: http://www.eurozine.com/articles/2008-01-09-mbembe-en.html [accessed 1 December 2010].

Owczarzak, J., 2009. Introduction: Postcolonial Studies and Postsocialism in Eastern Europe. *Focaal*, 53, pp. 3–19.

Petrescu, D., 2003. The Alluring Facet of Ceauşescu-ism: Nation-building and Identity Politics in Communist Romania, 1965-1989. *New Europe College Yearbook*, 11, pp. 241–72.

Petrescu, D., 2009. Building the Nation, Instrumentalizing Nationalism: Revisiting Romanian National-Communism, 1956–1989. *Nationalities Papers*, 37(4), pp. 523–44.

Petryna, A., 2002. *Life Exposed: Biological Citizens After Chernobyl*. Princeton, NJ: Princeton University Press.

Rassloff, J., 2010. Juraj Janosik. In: M. Cornis-Pope and J. Neubauer, eds. 2010., *History of the Literary Cultures of East-Central Europe: Junctures and Disjuncture in the 19th and 20th centuries. Volume 4: Types and Stereotypes*. Amsterdam: John Benjamins Publishing, pp. 441–56.

Stark, D. and L. Bruszt, 1998. *Postsocialist Pathways: Transforming Politics and Property in East Central Europe*. Cambridge: Cambridge University Press.

Sztompka, P., 2004. The Trauma of Social Change: A Case of Postcommunist Societies. In: J.C. Alexander, R. Eyerman, B. Giesen, N.J. Smelser. and P. Sztompka, eds., 2004. *Cultural Trauma and Collective Identity*. Berkeley: University of California Press, pp. 155–95.

Verdery, K., 2002. Whither Postsocialism? In: C. Hann, ed. 2002. *Postsocialism: Ideals, Ideologies and Practices in Eurasia*. London: Routledge, pp. 15–22.

Vortruba, M., 2006. Hang Him High: The Elevation of Janosik to an Ethnic Icon. *Slavic Review*, 65(1), pp. 24–44.

Wolff, L. 1994. *Inventing Eastern Europe: The Map of Civilization on the Mind of Enlightenment*. Stanford, CA: Stanford University Press.

Young, R. J. C., 2003. *Postcolonialism: A Very Short Introduction*. New York: Oxford University Press.

Filmography

Balada e Kurbinit, 1990. [film] Directed by K. Çashku. Albania: Albfilm.

Boj na Kosovu, 1989. [film] Directed by Z. Sotra. Yugoslavia: Centar Film and Radiotelevizija Beograd.

Columna, 1968. [film] Directed by M. Dragan. Romania: Studioul Cinematografic Bucuresti.

Dacii, 1967. [film] Directed by S. Nicolaescu. Romania: Romania Film.

Egri csillagok, 1968. [film] Directed by Z. Várkonyi. Hungary: Mafilm.

Janosik, 1974. [film] Directed by J. Passendorfer. Poland: Zespol Filmowy.

Mihai Viteazul, 1971. [film] Directed by S. Nicolaescu. Romania: Romania Film.

Mircea, 1989. [film] Directed by S. Nicolaescu. Romania: Casa de Filme Cinci.

Stefan cel Mare, 1974. [film] Directed by M. Dragan. Romania: Romania Film.

Vreme na nasilie, 1988. [film] Directed by L. Staikov. Bulgaria: Boyana Film.

Part II

Postcolonial cinemas
Unframing histories

Postcolonial time is that in which colonial experience appears, simultaneously, to be consigned to the past and, precisely, due to the modalities with which its "overcoming" comes about, to be installed at the centre of contemporary social experience.
(Sandro Mezzadra and Federico Rahola, 2006)

This section opens with a discussion of three films about two liberation movements and the complex, open-ended, transformations, sometimes referred to as "decolonization," that followed. The challenge of reconceptualizing imperial/colonial histories and geographies is fundamental to these cultural transformations. Not only stories and maps, but the ways in which the stories are told and the maps are drawn, become open questions. Hamish Ford frames Gillo Pontecorvo's *The Battle of Algiers* (1966), Ousmane Sembene's *Camp de Thiaroye* (1987), and Michael Haneke's *Chaché/Hidden* (2005) as the postcolonial history of a self/other dialectic that has unfolded through and since French colonialism. Such a history reconfigures not only the geography of maps, but also the psychic geography of characters. Cinema, with its visual specificity, its freedom to sculpt time and to shape space, its synesthetic appeal to multiple senses, and its privileging of movement over stasis, is particularly well-suited to subverting conventional frames and choreographing new histories.

In Med Hondo's *L'Algérienne de Dakar/The Algerian Woman of Dakar* (2004), overlapping forms of oppression – the political and religious imperialisms of France and Islam, the use of Senegalese soldiers by the French against the Algerian rebels, and the transnational patriarchalism that underlies the use of rape as a weapon of war – also call for an approach that "unframes" imperial chronologies, identities, and borders. Jude Akudinobi's discussion of Hondo's film explores forms of representation in which African subjects are no longer exotic ciphers and ornamental accessories to idealized constructions of European subjects (p. 78), although Hondo's "fraught frames" also include post-independence disillusionments. Making histories permeable to one another while denaturalizing imperial narratives opens the way for alternative versions of how communities are formed and sustained.

Mireille Rosello's essay on Philippe Faucon's *Dans la vie* (2007) foregrounds what she calls the "microprocesses" that take place in the background of, and out of synch with, national/imperial historiographies. In Faucon's postcolonial comedy, she observes how television images from the Israeli/Lebanese war add to the already complicated community identifications of two elderly women, one Muslim and one Jewish, who are both displaced Algerians living in Toulouse. The women's mutual misunderstandings, though, strengthen rather than rupture the bonds they need to form for their mutual well-being. Differences and miscommunications, the film suggests, catalyze transformative interactions. The very notion of community is, in this sense, "decolonized." Even the assumption that younger generations, free of the memories and habits of colonialism, will be the ones to initiate new dialogues and new visions of the past, is comically disrupted as Halima and wheelchair-bound Esther negotiate postcolonial senior citizenship.

Mariam Lam's essay on the postcolonial condition in "Indochinese" cinema, which involves recent productions from Vietnam, Cambodia, and Laos, analyzes how multiple histories coexist in tension in this region: the French colonial past, the recent American imperial presence, and a future geared towards global capitalism. Older formulations of national and "Third Cinema" need to be reframed in order to accommodate the multilayered colonial and imperial histories of these three nation-states. When no paradigm suffices to comprehend and contain the complexities and localizations of entangled histories, then "poor theory" could be an option (Abbas, 2010). "Poor theory" thinks through the relation between dislocated spaces and cultural practices, including cinema, where the margins are no longer safely located on the margins but have migrated elsewhere. By framing this relatively marginalized region of Asia as a polemically productive space where regionalism becomes a possible alternative to imperialist strategies, Lam explores how these tensions and layers are conveyed in recent films made by Vietnamese diasporic filmmaker Trân Anh Hùng (*The Scent of the Green Papaya*, 1993; *Cyclo*, 1995), who strategically negotiates colonial cultural influences; Cambodian director Rithy Pahn (*Rice People*, 1994), who presents a more historically engaged version of *annamité*, and Laotian filmmaker Anousone Sirisackda, who co-directed the Thailand-Laos blockbuster *Goodmorning, Luang Prabang/Sabaidee, Luang Prabang* (2008) in which filmmaking emerges as a tourism-driven cultural and economic venture.

Sandro Mezzadra and Federico Rahola, from whom we have taken our epigraph, adroitly capture the convolutions of postcolonial time. Unframing histories is not only about undoing established historical accounts and fixed geographies but also about rediscovering the regional, the minor histories and local spaces, made available through anachronisms and deterritorializations.

Bibliography

Abbas, A., 2010. Keynote Address, "Poor Theory" and Asian Cultural Practices. *International Conference on "Inter-Asian Connections II: Singapore."* National University of Singapore, December 10, 2010.

Mezzadra, S. and Rahola, F., 2006. The Postcolonial Condition: A Few Notes on the Quality of Historical Time in the Global Present. *Postcolonial Text*, 2, 1.

Chapter 4

From otherness "over there" to virtual presence

Camp de Thiaroye – The Battle of Algiers – Hidden

Hamish Ford

Europe is literally the creation of the third world ...

(Frantz Fanon, 2004)

A person is a person only because of other people.

(Xhosa proverb)[1]

This work originated in a fascination with *Caché/Hidden* (Haneke, 2005) for its portrayal of the present-day West as inhabiting a decidedly unreconciled postcolonial moment. Before addressing *Hidden* directly, the chapter ahead seeks to flesh out a select "back story" through two other films charting important moments in France's colonial history: *Camp de Thiaroye/The Camp at Thiaroye* (Sembene and Faty Sow, 1987) and *La Battaglia di Algeri/The Battle of Algiers* (Pontecorvo, 1966). The culmination of this process in *Hidden* presents thus-far suppressed memory, experience, and figuration of the colonial other now operating as a spectral and virtual presence *inside* the privileged Western subject. Across the films – played out between colonial, anticolonial, and postcolonial eras – I sketch the development of what Edward Said calls this subject's "imaginative geography and of the dramatic boundaries it draws" (1979, p. 73). The discussion ahead seeks to chart the spatial eroding of the demarcation between this figure and its colonial other to a point where a virtual image of the latter haunts the former from within.

Set in colonial Africa near the end of World War II and made four decades later, *Camp de Thiaroye* both renders a protean symbolic stirring of the anticolonial period that would explode following the Viet Minh's totemic eviction of the French from Indochina in 1954 at Dien Bien Phu, and points directly to today's complicated postcolonial situation. The film is not a "neutral" account but rather what Teshome H. Gabriel calls "a 'look back to the future,' necessarily dissident and partisan, wedded to constant change" (1989, p. 54). Popular with African audiences but first banned in France, *Thiaroye* subsumed centuries of colonial history through a close-up of a late, very particular and revealing moment. The film also looks forward to a postcolonial future – perhaps an idealistic one – from the messy reality of the late 1980s when the film itself was made. Through this historically palimpsestic lens, we can see the complex spatial staging of a shared but deeply unequal subject/other identity mechanism. The earliest of the three films, *The Battle of Algiers,* has been used by both liberation groups and the U.S. Pentagon for educational and training purposes. My analysis of this final "warning" to the colonial West at the apogee of its crisis, foregrounds the importance of space, not only to colonial power, but also to French and Western identity per se, in a showdown between subject and other. Haneke's *Hidden* brings the temporal and spatial dimensions of this composite story into the present, exploring how colonial history not only scars its original victims but permanently marks its heirs in an ambiguous and unstable postcolonial now, where the dialectical trauma of subject and other plays out in an interiorized and virtual image-world that uncannily resembles the "real" one.

In their settings, the selected films present colonial, anticolonial, and postcolonial moments respectively, as charted by three filmmakers' particular perspectives. Co-directed with a young Senegalese compatriot, *Thiaroye* features Ousmane Sembene's trademark rigorous critique of colonialism from the perspective of subaltern subjects via an unflinching gaze that romanticizes neither European nor African traditions and culture. Featuring prominent use of both Algerian and French figures, *Algiers* was based on an original autobiographical script by FLN (*Front de Liberation Nationale*) leader Saadi Yacef and directed by Italian Marxist filmmaker Gillo Pontecorvo, whose national and political background places him outside a clear colonizer/colonized distinction (though he has been accused of denying Saadi sufficient story credit). *Hidden* is the only film here entirely written and directed by a Western filmmaker, the pan-European figure of Michael Haneke (born in Germany, raised in Austria, since 1999 working mainly in France), and the only one concentrating on a European subject. Beyond their contextual origins and differences, the films resonate across colonial, anticolonial, and postcolonial eras as shot through with frequently radical – if very different – critique. The accumulated *histoire* they tell is not linear. In one sense this can be seen as tragic when it comes to the not yet fulfilled promise of a genuinely postcolonial world. But the films' telling of history as palimpsest[2] is also the key to their ongoing generative power in enabling us to make some sense of our pockmarked present. In what follows, subject and other agonistically interact and mutate upon the shifting spatial zones and proximities of the colonial, the anticolonial, and the postcolonial. This provocative drama concurrently plays out as historical-material reality, ideological script, and challenging figurative images.

Camp de Thiaroye

Camp de Thiaroye presents a historically-determined colonial space whose self-other binaries are disrupted, dramatically and historically, by its African protagonists. The narrative concerns a little-known military atrocity following the return to Africa in late November 1944 of a group of French colonial draftee troops known as *tirailleurs,* members of Charles de Gaulle's Free France forces. After risking their lives and their sanity fighting fascism in Europe, the men now await decommission behind barbed wire in a transit camp outside Dakar, Senegal. A standoff soon develops as the army denies

Figure 4.1 Arriving at a military camp back in Africa where local draftee colonial troops await decommission after fighting to free Europe from Nazism, infantryman Pays (a survivor of Buchenwald) becomes increasingly disturbed upon encountering barbed wire and surveillance towers (Source: still *Camp de Thiaroye*, 1987)

the soldiers the official local rate of exchange for their French francs. A growing sense of rebellion among the men is exacerbated when their commanding officers accuse them of having "stolen the money from corpses" in Europe. The army's position is both cruel and logical: to exchange the money at the official rate would signify that the Africans were equal to European soldiers, opening the symbolic door to the incursion of rights, associated with the "free" West, into colonial space. After the *tirailleurs* seize and hold a French colonel for ransom, they are told they will get their money in full. Instead, they are massacred in a 3 a.m. tank shelling – an attack, it becomes clear, that was approved by both the Colonial Minister and the Governor-General.

Far from simply inverting colonialism's binary system, the film does not dismiss Europe *tout court* either through chauvinist nationalism or folkloric primitivism – "hence, no dances, no hands beating drums, no colourful rituals" (Taylor, 1989, p. 107). The film's most complex character, Aloise Diatta (Ibrahima Sane), African Sergeant-Major of the *tirailleurs*, is clearly enamored of European culture and speaks not only excellent French but also English. While his love of European music and literature is by turns perplexing and reassuring to his French superiors, Diatta's more sophisticated (not to mention cross-cultural) knowledge – causing much applause at the film's African premiere (Diawara, 1992, p. 158) – also undermines the colonial self/other binary by parodically deflating military and intellectual hierarchies of race. Yet this cosmopolitan fluency (he also has a French wife) means neither that Diatta becomes an assimilated Western-allied African leader nor an emblematic figurehead for the Africans' immanent rebellion. Instead he pledges solidarity to their uprising – which, the rank-and-file soldiers inform him, voids military rank.

As this story develops, language demarcates the mutations of political space. The "pidgin" French used by the *tirailleurs*, which caused much amusement among the African audience at the premiere, was "first common among veterans of World War II," according to Manthia Diawara (1992, p. 157). This "broken" colonial language gains a deeper significance and power once the men vote to cease relying on Diatta's expert francophone erudition – though not before he has delivered a withering radical history lesson to the French officers. The men instead consciously choose to articulate their newly asserted agency in its authentically impure, protean idiom. This shift in linguistic agency works to solidify a radical formal strategy characteristic of Sembene's middle-period work, termed by Philip Rosen a "decentred collective narration," which is driven by plural rather than protagonistic action (1996, pp. 43–8).

While *Thiaroye* takes place entirely on the Africans' home continent, the space is clearly not "theirs." But, Diawara writes, having seen the German occupation, and having fought "ferociously to free France, they no longer see themselves as second-class citizens" (1992, p. 157). The men seem significantly transformed by their experiences in Europe, although not in a way that allows us to re-invoke a West/non-West delineation implying that "freedom" is learned in Europe, but rather in a way that demythologizes such oppositions.[3] The *tirailleurs* were used as dispensable frontline troops, the direct result of their subaltern position. Many of them were POWs, some surviving Nazi concentration camps. Yet while presented more sympathetically than the French in the film, the African soldiers are hardly more developed as characters than their French superior officers. Even the most classically developed African character, Diatta, retains an unreal air. Rather than a work of distinct individuals, this is a collective portrait of historical actors and symptoms.

Importantly, the French are represented not just as simple racist types but also by the liberal figure of Captain Raymond (Jean-Daniel Simon). Drawing upon Foucault's notion of "fellowships of discourse" in discussing Said's work, Wolfgang Iser describes "regulations of admittance" in which "the individual – for instance, the colonizer – is subjected to the power of discourse, but is simultaneously enabled to wield it" (2006, p. 175). The description characterizes Raymond's complex role as a subject both empowered and limited by colonial discourse. Upon seeking out Diatta in friendly conversation, the two men are dwarfed by the massive local baobab trees, amongst which Diatta had momemts earlier rejected local custom by walking away from a cousin whom his family, in his absence, had arranged for him to marry. When Raymond then expresses horror upon learning Diatta's village was razed by French forces in 1942, killing his parents, the Captain quickly explains it was a Vichy-era atrocity, to which Diatta replies that Gaullist and French fascist military behavior in Africa seem absolutely consistent with one another. "Nazism transformed the whole of Europe into a genuine colony," writes Frantz Fanon (2004, p. 57). But, following its defeat, European governments demanded reparations and the return of stolen property (ibid). The double standard, whereby violent domination of land and subjects in Europe is punished harshly while the same war victors who demand reparations in Europe retain their own brutal regimes in the colonies, is keenly felt here.

The complex and arbitrary politics of space during a world war are starkly revealed when Diatta goes for a drink at a brothel's courtyard bar in Dakar. First welcomed as an American soldier, he is revealed as a *local* "negro" by his request for Pernod and ordered to leave. Moments later Diatta is beaten up on the street by a U.S. soldier, an African-American, who later visits him at the camp whereupon the two share a friendly moment of trans-national black solidarity. Meanwhile, in the much more homogeneous cultural space of the Dakar military HQ, we see the truly cloistered nature of colonial agency played out. Such strict codification reaches its symbolic apogee in the film with the growing ostracism of Raymond by his fellow officers when he argues that France cannot "remake herself after the war by robbing the natives," especially those "who have fought in your place, gentlemen." Subsequently snubbed by his colleagues at the officers' bar and becoming the object of their suspicious glances through an open window, this partial "black sheep" liberal outsider literally has nowhere to go. When we do see him seek out Diatta (with whom he seems to have a good relationship) under the baobab trees, their differences on the matter of colonialism *per se* ends the conversation and drives Raymond back to the French Army base. The antecedent of today's more familiar liberal Western subject, whom we see in *Hidden*, is presented starkly in *Thiaroye* as trapped by the contradictions and disavowals of a prescribed role and inherited privilege, his notionally progressive personal attitudes notwithstanding.

Aesthetically distinct from the sequences in town, the film's primary *mise-en-scène* is the abstract, dusty space of the camp itself. Dominated by monochromatic light brown and yellow tones, Camp Thiaroye is set off from the similarly colored space surrounding it by barbed-wire fencing and surveillance towers manned by local African French Army soldiers. That the psychologically disturbed infantryman Pays (Sijiri Bakaba), a survivor of Buchenwald who now does not speak, remains unpersuaded that the men are no longer in "*the* camps" gives immediate and tragic expression to the continuity between colonialism and fascism for these Africans. After they take control of the space (in accordance with textbook military strategy, as Diatta reminds the hostaged French General), Pays takes it upon himself to climb a surveillance tower to stand guard in a powerful gesture of appropriation. However, the old nightmares return in force when he is awakened by the bright lights of approaching tanks and rushes to warn the skeptical men that the Germans are attacking, gesturing to his "souvenir" SS helmet. Dismissing the desperate Pays as now totally crazy, the *tirailleurs* return to their beds only to be mass-murdered, given the ultimate punishment for a very modest gesture of self-determination: claiming fair pay for deeply traumatic work far from home and taking control of a space that will in the future be acknowledged as at least in principle theirs.

The Battle of Algiers

The Battle of Algiers famously stages the protracted, apocalyptic breaking point of colonial power in its official phase. From the start, the film is characterized by a claustrophobic urban *mise-en-scène* in which we can see the lines delineating French self and Algerian other as both over-determined and yet also revealing a deeply intermeshed dialectical

Figure 4.2 Disguised FLN leaders escape French paratroopers into the labyrinthine folds of the Casbah – the constricted, intimate, vertiginous stage and epicentre for Algeria's anticolonial resistance (Source: still *Battle of Algiers*, 1966)

identity mechanism at work.[4] The film switches between two main spaces, first identified (by screen titles) and shown as interconnected in an overhead tracking shot: the French quarter, mainly the military command centre as well as cafés and environs, and the Algerian quarter known as the Casbah. As the paratroopers take charge of the city under Colonel Mathieu (Jean Martin), the military strives increasingly to separate the two realms, keeping the "dangerous" (Algerian) other – the FLN – from harming the "innocent" (Western) subject – the French civilian population – through strict border control, surveillance, bombings, and torture. In 1961 Fanon described the abject nature of such a spatially divided reality:

> The colonized's sector is a sector that crouches and cowers, a sector on its knees, a sector that is prostrate. It's a sector of niggers, a sector of towelheads. The gaze that the colonized subject casts at the colonist's sector is a look of lust, a look of envy.
>
> (2004, pp. 4–5)

The dividing line, featuring barbed wire and military checkpoints between Algerian and French space, breeds both paranoia and desire. (The latter is exploited by the FLN, which uses attractive women to smuggle and detonate bombs after they have been flirted with by French border guards and café denizens.) The military's would-be panoptical surveillance controls demarcations of space much better than it does the identities crossing the border every day as the military seek out the "terrorists." After Mathieu lectures the paratroopers and shows them hidden camera border footage in the elevated military headquarters above the city, he and his lieutenants map out the FLN's cell structure via diagrams that are gradually filled in with operatives' names.

Dominated by curving stairways that dissect ancient buildings, the labyrinthine space of the Casbah is the physical and mythic home to the FLN, hiding its leadership at a moment's notice thanks in equal measure to the architecture and to help from supporters. For the French military, the elusive nature of the enemy and the space that houses it embody both Western fantasies about the mysterious Orient and France's failure to possess – or, permanently to destroy – Algeria's heart. For all its superior technology and firepower, frequently on savage display, the military exudes a familiar colonial air of crisis and repressed psychic anger. Michael Vann describes Mathieu's men as "impotent once they leave the order and regularity of the French Quarter ... Seething with frustration, the French authorities realise the limits of their power" (2002, p. 189). Mathieu's paratroopers want violently to penetrate, control, and destroy, yet they also fear, the *prise de possession* of the Casbah and all it represents: the ultimate domain of the other. Hélène Cixous (who grew up in Algeria) describes the heated geography of this space. As "the oldest of Algeria's cities," the Casbah was "the most convoluted one, [with] the cascade of alleyways, the odours of urine and spices." She describes the "secret" of Algiers as

> the savage genitals, the antique femininity. Yes, the Casbah with its folds and its powerful and poor people, its hunger, its desires, its vaginality, for me it was always the clandestine and venerated genitals of the City of Algiers. And it suggested rape.
> (2003, cited in Reid, 2005, p. 94)

Eventually capturing or killing the FLN leadership, after blowing up their last safe house, Mathieu declares that the "the tapeworm" threatening Algeria is now dead. But the film's forceful concluding images of huge mass demonstrations two years later show the Casbah mythically impenetrable and impossible to placate.

While the film powerfully evokes the intimacy and violent erotics of colonialism's increasingly claustrophobic subject/other relation at its incendiary limit, as well as the organic *return* of "the tapeworm", binary delineation remains quite intact for the metropolitan subject back in France. Despite what we might assume was a common awareness of the Algerian situation, Leslie Hill writes that overall "the war in Algeria was of marginal interest to the majority of French citizens" (1992, p. 796). Such marginalization remained feasible since the trouble was kept "over there" across the water, helped by polite fictions circulated by politicians and mass media, and the banning of films seeking to properly broach the topic during the war. Spatial separation notwithstanding – indeed entirely congruent with its cause and effects – *Algiers* presents the colonial narrative of morality as completely breaking down.[5] In fact, the atrocities were not just occurring "over there." The long-suppressed October 1961 massacre of around 200 unarmed Algerian protesters by police in the heart of Paris (the elliptical history behind *Hidden*'s story) is the deeply submerged doubling of the atrocities shown in *Algiers*.[6] It would take four decades for this radically closer-to-home aspect of the story to become more widely known; Saadi and Pontecorvo's representation of what happened across the water at the peak of the war, although actually showing the FLN's initial defeat, was immediately banned in France.[7]

"As anticolonialism sweeps and indeed unifies the entire Oriental world," writes Said, "the Orientalist damns the whole business not only as a nuisance but as an insult to the Western democracies." The former colonial subjects are then deemed violent terrorists, their cultures "damned when 'we lose them' to communism or their unregenerate Oriental instincts ... The West is the spectator, the judge and jury, of every facet of Oriental behaviour" (1979, pp. 108–9). *Algiers* presents increasingly organized and empowered colonial subjects acting out a chilling encroachment upon Europe at its "vulnerable extremities", despite being hopelessly outgunned and quite literally trapped in what is technically – again – their own realm. The Algerians' mythic as much as operational epicenter remains their involuntary prison-like home within the maze-like folds of the Casbah. But despite repeatedly suffering deadly violation and apparently being at last brought to heel, the Casbah strikes back as *vagina dentata* – a vulnerable, alluring space with the hidden teeth to ultimately overthrow the colonial world as it stands.

Caché/Hidden

Hidden charts a limit point in the repressed, virtual interiorizing of colonialism's subject/other relation.[8] Rather than locating the "problem" outside metropolitan Europe, and presented from a subaltern perspective, *Hidden* instead forces us to see the contemporary state of the relationship from within a specific Western subject marked by historically enabled privilege and a guilt-laden fear of revenge. Ara Osterweil describes the contextual connection between *Algiers* and *Hidden*:

> As demonstrated by the riots that rocked Paris in November 2005, much remains unchanged in French society since 1971, when the ban on *Battle of Algiers* was lifted ... Haneke's exquisite excavation of the French-Algerian conflict as channelled through domestic nightmare heralds the return of the bitterly repressed.
>
> (2006, pp. 36, 38)

The perceived threat of this "return" of unresolved issues central to French colonial history, is refracted through an incident in our protagonist Georges Laurent's (Daniel Auteuil) childhood. Under pressure from his wife Anne (Juliette Binoche), Georges eventually confesses that he suspects who is "terrorizing" them with surveillance-style videos. As a boy he had selfishly sabotaged his parents' planned adoption of a young Algerian, Majid, whose mother and father – employees of Georges' family – were presumably killed in the October 1961 Paris massacre. His very reluctant articulation of this history both mirrors the suppression of its broader context in France and encourages viewers to interrogate their own national – and perhaps personal – historiographies, rather than to imbibe a didactic moral or political lesson.[9]

The key to *Hidden*'s insidious effect is that its primary audience is very likely situated in a similarly privileged first-world space broadly recognizable in the film itself. The cultural complicity rendered through the *mise-en-scène* of space and lifestyle, gesture and social manners, gradually increases the viewer's self-conscious discomfort as Georges

Figure 4.3 Postcolonial relations are played out in a banal yet privileged and virtual space when TV book show host Georges Laurent accuses a French Algerian of terrorizing his family with surveillance videos after the young man requests to discuss his father's suicide to which Georges was witness, and his unimpressive response recorded on video. (Source: still *Hidden*, 2005)

slowly develops into a devastating portrait of the Western subject positioning itself as "victim" of the feared and repressed former colonial other – despite possessing all the economic, political, and social advantage. This is most clearly played out when Majid's present-day teenage son (Walid Afkir), comes to see Georges at his workspace, an imposing if bland public broadcasting office building. The new-generation postcolonial other requests the chance to discuss his father's recent suicide, to which Georges was witness. Staged within the building's anonymous bathroom, which could be anywhere in the first world, the confrontation reveals the winner in this colonial-postcolonial story on the verge of violent rage, fueled by a paranoia that Said sees as the European subject's defining psychological response to the Arab other (1979, p. 72). Georges's bathroom rage is also a postcolonial staging of Fanon's reversal of the colonial explanation for the other's aggression and impoverished mental and moral faculties. "For Fanon," writes Joanne Sharp,

> it was colonialism that was regarded as psychopathological and violent, not the colonised. Thus, the negative character traits that were associated with the colonised (violence, hysteria, laziness ...) were interpreted by Fanon as conditions brought on by colonialism.

> (2009, pp. 127)

Throughout *Hidden*, the adult Majid (Maurice Bénichou) and his son retain a sense of alterity, remaining mysterious but unfailingly polite and not unimpressive. It is, rather, a forensic focus on the Western subject and its heritage that reveals neurosis, hysteria, mental laziness, moral dishonesty, and violence. Considered from this angle, Brigitte Peucker's description of Haneke's work takes on decidedly ethico-political and historical implications when she writes: "Sadomasochism is centrally present in most of Haneke's films" (2010, p. 143). It is within the space of the Western subject's state-run employment and media power, a properly anonymous incarnation of what Gilles Deleuze calls modern cinema's characteristic "any space whatevers" (1989, p. xi), that we are physically and culturally trapped.[10]

The question of the image and its virtual power is foregrounded not only by Georges's place of work and role as a TV literature show host but also through *Hidden*'s much commented-on formal reflexivity.[11] The film's opening shot presents a pleasantly light and airy Parisian side street in spring colors, an image that turns out to be a video being watched by Georges and Anne, whom we first meet as the voices of mystified viewers on the soundtrack. These not-yet on-screen characters are immediately allied with the audience as anxious viewers seeking to explain the voyeur-like footage and hermeneutically to decode its motivation and meaning. This initial congruence between diegetic and spectatorial subjects incorporates us into the film's perceptual, cultural, ethical, political, and interpretive vortex. As opposed to the comparatively transparent images of *Thiaroye* and *Algiers* (the subtly theatrical staging of the former and the gritty re-enactment style of the latter entailing more easily elided reflexive forms), here we watch the comfortable spaces of a recognizably privileged twenty-first-century modernity while also being forced to realize that such a film-world could be – and considering *Hidden*'s being shot on DV, in fact literally is – constituted by the screening of video. The film works to destroy not only our belief in representational space, but also the epistemological power to make distinctions between history's inscribed identities of self and other. Majid is seen as residing "within" Georges via the virtual power of dreams and/or repressed memories – even if, as the bathroom scene and the vastly different residences of the two men show, space remains clearly marked by historically resonant socio-economic power and access. The film charts the contrasting spaces of suburban Paris circa 2005 and the privileged subject's "interior." But both realms are accessed via the virtual, which fails to confirm the veracity of either the spaces we see or our primary subject.

The complex process and presence of virtuality when it comes to reconceiving space and identity are made strikingly apparent by the unresolved issue of who made the videos, but perhaps more importantly by the question of *how* they were possibly made. There is a curious, seldom mentioned problem here: the camera that must have shot the tapes does not appear to have been "hidden" at all, and the images' common frontal perspective and proscenium arch-style framing are indistinguishable from the long shots throughout *Hidden* itself. Beyond referencing "our" film's own manufacture, this suggestive emphasis on virtuality forces us to consider that such cameras themselves might be either so ubiquitous since September 11, 2001 that we do not notice them, or alternatively that they are in fact "nowhere." In the first scenario, Georges becomes entrapped by his own culture's security system – not perhaps the culprit its masters had in mind. In the second, no cameras are *needed* because we are watching "unedited footage" of a real, if suppressed, history that is interior to and aesthetically indistinguishable from Georges's context, while also entirely transcending it.

The film's final image, a frontally-framed shot of a school, is both benign and threatening in evoking the vertiginous threat of the virtual. This is perhaps the most epistemologically unaccounted for and hermeneutically open image in the film's codification of space as defined by the colonial inheritance of subject/other relations. The mysterious observer-inquirer roles played by the two sons throughout *Hidden* inflect our understanding of their optically and thematically ambiguous appearance here. Does this hint at a complicitous responsibility for the tapes and therefore a radical solidarity that opens up the chance for a new and reconciliatory future, as part of which the colonial subject's historical responsibility is fully acknowledged by its progeny? This would suggest that the promise of the postcolonial might indeed become a reality. Alternatively, we could be seeing in this image a grim, paranoid generational continuation of the subject/other dyad that works like the French-Algerian equivalent of what Thomas Elsaesser calls "negative symbiosis", grafting German and Jewish identities to their respective other (1996, pp. 203–6). Irrespective of how we read this very open last image, the viewer is left facing the ambiguous material, the atrocity and promise, of history's contemporary palimpsestic marks. Any genuinely "hopeful" reading of the final image needs to engage with at least the ghostly presence of an historically enforced identity mechanism uncomfortably, intimately – and always asymmetrically – shared between subject and other.

Discussing Antonio Negri and Michael Hardt's work on the possibilities for radical postcolonial democracy, Jacques Lezra writes:

> [W]ith the advent of globalization the encounter between "the European Self" and its colonized other is no longer necessarily to be described according to the logic (or the rhetoric) of reciprocal destruction ... That "counterviolence" is "reciprocal" does not mean, for instance, that you and I, or a colonizer and the colonized subject, do violence to each other, though this may be entailed in such relations, but rather than you and I recognize that our relation is a violent one.
>
> (2003, pp. 50–1)

Taken in concert with the cinematic back-history I have sketched, the affective and conceptual impact of *Hidden* becomes devastating in the last three shots of the film. Addressing this relationship at a potentially fork-in-the-road moment, these shots demarcate the slippage of space through which the self/other distinction plays out as an interior drama of repression and guilt, of mutual violence and dependence. This epistemologically and conceptually destabilizing affect is enabled through the reflexive, virtuality-enforcing use of video. In the first of these final shots, the privileged but anonymous domestic space of the Laurents' bedroom provides the *mise-en-scène* for a layered image of "cocooning" in which the self-styled victim of "blowback" closes heavy curtains after taking an afternoon sleeping pill, then disrobes and slips beneath the duvet. This is followed by what we assume is Georges's final flashback, memory, dream, or imagined image, a frontally framed proscenium arch composition (like the surveillance videos) showing the young Majid being forcibly carted off to an orphanage away from Georges's palatial childhood home. And finally, we are left with the quietly eerie and very hermeneutically open narrative/non-narrative double-image (depending on whether we detect the optically and conceptually obscure presence of the two sons in the frame) of a French public school in the afternoon. The layered use of space in *Hidden*'s concluding sequence – notionally exterior, though strongly suggesting an immanent "going in"; then more clearly interior and virtual (dream-like and very "filmic"); and finally, both real and entirely figurative – seals a first-world cinematic experience in which the former colonial other finds virtual expression inside the otherwise history-disavowing Western subject via an image form appropriated from a surveillance obsessed culture, making up a story – ultimately a "hopeful" one – so close to home that escape is no longer possible.

Conclusion

Said writes: "[R]esistance, far from being merely a reaction to imperialism, is an alternative way of conceiving human history" (1994, p. 215). What all three films I have addressed show in their very different ways is how resistance – physical, political, conceptual, psychological, aesthetic, and virtual – emerges through the figure of colonialism's other. Although the effects in the films are often radical, we do not see – just as with history itself – anything like hegemony's definitive overthrow. Rather a gradual and epic fight back forces face-to-face realization of each pole's mutual reliance for an ongoing sense of self, so long and intertwined has been this shared – though always grossly inequitable – history. The Xhosa proverb at the start of this chapter is thereby played out as materially grounded and ethically violent truth.

Camp de Thiaroye already stages a deconstruction of the self/other binary, played out upon its debased colonial stage. Here and in *The Battle of Algiers* the binary is subverted by way of resistance or negation emanating from the other, initially positioned as a spatially and conceptually distinct entity. While the first two films explicitly chart colonial history from an avowedly anticolonial perspective, they also allow us better to understand the confused postcolonial present. Further, they contain within their dialectical presentations of space and identity intimations of a genuinely postcolonial world. That the inevitably idealistic, or at least mythical, dimensions of such intimations may not match the world as we know it is less a reason to dismiss such films than to use their meditations to cast a renewed critical light on what passes for global relations today.

The biggest shift appears between the still "gritty" if deeply suggestive and figurative worlds shown in the first two films addressed in this chapter and the more overtly virtual presentation of *Hidden*, where the coordinates of space, identity, and politics are dissolved by the slippery reflexivity of the virtual and an appropriately subdued portrayal of contemporary life after colonialism's official end. Yet the preceding two films also prefigure this postcolonial in the way they play out as virtual events. In *Thiaroye* we can see the camp as a stage or screen, demarcated by symbolically loaded barbed wire fences and surveillance towers, on which a conflict of mythic proportions, more operatic than conventionally "realist", is enacted in close up. After taking control of the camp itself as they seek modest thanks for helping restore Europe's own hallowed freedom, the newly self-conscious African subjects are subsequently destroyed in the flames of French colonialism's own moral self-obliteration. In the context of their immediate material-historical reality, the men are atrociously "punished" for insubordination. From the film's own perspective four decades later, they are soldiers who have fought and died for a future still not yet fully achieved. With *Algiers*, virtuality is most clearly figured through the panoptical control the French authorities seek over the Casbah's inhabitants. While still vulnerable to violation and attack, by escaping full X-ray penetration, the Casbah becomes a realm of fantasy, hatred, and fear for the French, all the while gaining in imaginary power and ultimately immutable resistance. The most dangerous virtuality becomes that which (as in *Hidden*) negates epistemological domination.

Hidden updates rather than radically transcends the earlier films' presentations of space and identity as mutually inscribed central stages for the ongoing saga of colonialism's heritage. While historical reality's violence was unavoidable for the often-bloodied protagonists of the earlier films, here it is much more quietly situated in a way that allows the Western subject to claim ignorance. But that history still makes itself felt, forcing its way less from the outside world of Paris (which seems peaceful enough for now) than via the intimate and impossible-to-escape pathways of interiority and the virtual. Such a ground – unstable, vertiginous but absolutely hard in terms of palimpsestic historical force – is the most intransigent, because it operates both through and beyond the visual. By the time of the present day scenario enacted in *Hidden,* there is no longer a physically or indeed conceptually delineated rebellious other clearly to fight or contend with (Georges's disingenuous paranoia and that of the West since "September 11" notwithstanding). Haunted by the virtual presence of the other's mysteriously impassive, almost spectral figure, residing within a recognizable and banal reality, *Hidden*'s Western subject flails in the indecidabilities of what in *Thiaroye* and *Algiers* is a less obvious virtuality. This virtuality undermines colonial power in the on-screen world by disabling epistemological penetration; in the off-screen world, it mobilizes the medium of cinema to enact anti-colonial critiques that remain generatively essential for any imaginings of postcolonial futures.

Notes

1 As cited in Taylor (1989, p. 90).
2 See Waller (Chapter 10, this volume) for a discussion of how a palimpsestic presentation challenges linearity's enabling of self-aggrandizing and amnesiac national histories in the West (pp. 158–9).
3 Sembene describes the impact of witnessing Europeans at first hand as a World War Two soldier in Niger, with "those who considered themselves masters naked, in tears, some cowardly and ignorant. When a white soldier asked me to write a letter for him, it was a revelation – I thought all Europeans knew how to write. The war demystified the coloniser, the veil felled" (Sembene cited in Adenekan, 2007).
4 This is exemplified in the figure of Colonel Mathieu, who has been on both sides of the colonial fence as a former World War Two French resistance fighter and a veteran of France's Vietnamese loss. Hill writes of the colonel's whatever-it-takes policies that there is "far more complicity and agreement between Mathieu and his Algerian adversary than Mathieu and the liberal French and English-speaking press" (1992, p. 801).

5   Recalling Captain Raymond's liberalism in *Thiaroye*, well-known real life French-FLN mediator Germaine Tillion "wanted to show that torture was not the truth of the [French] Republic in the same way that the camps had been the truth of Nazi Germany," writes Donald Reid (2005, p. 105).
6   Haneke recalls that upon seeing a documentary about the massacre, he was shocked this could occur at the heart of civilized Europe (2005). The main surprise is that it happened "here."
7   When finally released in 1971, screenings were met with threats of violence, and a major TV network did not broadcast the film until 2004 (Reid, 2005, p. 98).
8   This final section devoted to *Hidden* explores in much more theoretically developed form some points first addressed in a review-style essay (Ford, 2006) on the film's significance following its success in Australia. Elsewhere framed within the very different context of film-philosophy discourse, the film is treated as part of a select group I address as exemplifying a "cinema of negativity" using Adorno's aesthetic theory (Ford, 2011).
9   Roy Grundmann writes that while Haneke from the start of his career "developed a keen eye for the problems of his own class, his work did not focus on class struggle, imperialism, or the oppression of third world countries" (2010, p. 3). With *Hidden* this dichotomy breaks down.
10 The seemingly "authorless" space typified by Georges's office building and bathroom also exhibits the neutrality claimed by state-funded media in its coverage of historical reality. But with the young French-Algerian clearly an outsider in this institutional hub – its well-appointed decor and clean surfaces, as well as actual purpose, indebted to centuries of Western global exploitation – such neutrality is invoked as a mythical veil for ongoing hegemony and dominance.
11 The role of virtuality as connected to a mediatized space is perhaps most clearly referenced in terms of production, by Georges's TV show itself, and consumption, by the Laurents's anthropologically appropriate domestic space combining viewing room, office, lounge, library, and dining area. The wraparound shelving features a then-large monitor that not only screens the video tapes but also emits live TV images from a troubled larger world (a news story about an Italian national's role in the U.S.-led "coalition's" occupation of Iraq), offering shards of a present-day narrative of empire and a contemporary Europe indecisive about its identity within a Western world dominated by the USA. It seems appropriate that although his own big screen relays the lie of a postcolonial present with links to the colonial-era cause of Georges's own problems, he pays no heed to what Osterweil calls these "shadowy images" that "cast the family's private drama of retribution in a more global light" (2006, p. 38).

Bibliography

Adenekan, S., 2007. Writer and African Film legend. *The New Black Magazine*, [online] 4 July. Available at: http://thenewblackmagazine.com/view.aspx?index=884 [Accessed 21 September 2010].

Deleuze, G., 1989. *Cinema 2: The Time-Image*. Translated from French by H. Tomlinson and R. Galeta. Minneapolis: University of Minnesota Press.

Diawara, M., 1992. *African Cinema: Politics and Culture*. Bloomington: Indiana University Press.

Elsaesser, T., 1996. *Fassbinder's Germany: History, Identity, Subject*. Amsterdam: Amsterdam University Press.

Fanon, F., 2004. *The Wretched of the Earth*. Translated from French by R. Philox. New York: Grove Press.

Ford, H., 2006. *Hidden*: A Film For Our Time. *RealTime*, October-November, 75, p. 18.

Ford, H., 2011. Broken Glass by the Road: Adorno and a Cinema of Negativity. In: H. Carel and G. Tuck, eds., 2011. *New Takes in Film and Philosophy*. London: Palgrave Macmillan, pp. 65–85.

Gabriel, T. H., 1989. Third Cinema as Guardian of Popular Memory. In: J. Pines and P.Willemen, eds., 1989. *Questions of Third Cinema*. London: BFI Publishing, pp. 53–64.

Grundmann, R., 2010. *A Companion to Michael Haneke*. New York: Wiley-Blackwell.

Haneke, M., 2005. Interview. *Hidden*. [DVD] London: Artificial Eye.

Hill, L., 1992. Filming Ghosts: French Cinema and the Algerian War. *Modern Fiction Studies*, 38(3), pp. 787–804.

Iser, W., 2006. *How to do Theory*. Malden, MA: Blackwell.

Lezra, J., 2003. Sade on Pontecorvo. *Discourse*, 25(3), pp. 48–75.

Osterweil, A., 2006. *Caché*. Cover story. *Film Quarterly*, 59(4), pp. 35–9.

Peucker, P., 2010. Games Haneke Plays: Reality and Performance. In: R. Grundmann, ed., 2010. *A Companion to Michael Haneke*. New York: Wiley-Blackwell, pp. 130–46.

Reid, D., 2005. Re-viewing *The Battle of Algiers* with Germaine Tillion. *History Workshop Journal*, 60(1), pp. 93–115.

Rosen, B., 1996. National, International and Narration in Ousmane Sembene's films. In: S. Perry, ed., 1996. *A Call to Action: The Films of Ousmane Sembene*. London: Praeger, pp. 27–55.

Said, E. W., 1979. *Orientalism*. New York: Vintage Books.

Said, E. W., 1994. *Culture and Imperialism*. New York: Vintage Books.

Sharp, J. P., 2009. *Geographies of Postcolonialism*. London: Sage.

Taylor, C., 1989. Black Cinema in the Post-Aesthetic Era. In: J. Pines and P. Willemen, eds., 1989. *Questions of Third Cinema*. London: BFI Publishing, pp. 90–110.

Vann, M. G., 2002. The Colonial Casbah on the Silver Screen. *Radical History Review*. 83, pp. 186–92.

Filmography

La Battaglia di Algeri/The Battle of Algiers, 1966. [film] Directed by G. Pontecorvo. Italy/Algeria: Igor Film.

Caché/Hidden, 2005. [film] Directed by M. Haneke. France/Austria/Germany/Italy/USA: Sony Pictures Classics.

Camp de Thiaroye/The Camp at Thiaroye, 1987. [film] Directed by O. Sembene and T. Faty Sow. Algeria/Senegal/Tunisia: SNPC, ENAPROC and SATPEC.

Chapter 5

Fraught frames

Fatima, L'Algérienne de Dakar and postcolonial quandaries

Jude G. Akudinobi

African cinema, insofar as it generally seeks exchanges between art and life, and has affinities with introspection and social critiques, has been an "instrumentalist" cinema in very distinct ways. Rather than blissful escapes from reality, African cinema, right from its inception, has favored critical engagements with it. Africans appropriated cinema as a cultural form with incisive features and expressive verve for social and political analysis. Hence, the screen becomes a ruminative site where, through their films' narratives, "issues of the day" and broader discourses are critically examined and worked through. This predilection has involved the search for forms of representation that consolidate political activism and cultural expression. It has also involved struggles for self-definition, positioning cinema in relation to the complex and shifting dynamics of society and establishing critical grammars of representation to articulate these dynamics (see, for instance, Malkmus and Armes, 1991; Diawara, 1992; Ukadike, 1995).

Also, at issue, is who the films represent. Who are the subjects of the films, and to whom are the films addressed? With respect to the latter, the impetus has been to reclaim and rework certain features of African cultures and experiences and, given Africa's depreciatory representations in dominant cinemas, extricate Africanness from the domain of the primitive and mythic. Put differently, cinema was construed by the African filmmakers as a novel platform for the national project of rebirth and reconstruction. Knowledge of the operations of ideology within representational practices exerted pressures which created unique trajectories of agency and self-awareness, making the nexus of self, community, and culture key to African filmmakers. Films became explorations of alternative frameworks for representation in which African cultures and peoples were no longer exotic ciphers and ornamental accessories to idealized Western constructions of selves. They also became platforms for radical social change and inspirational principles, though as Diawara (2010) has noted, within contemporary African film making, there is a growing tendency to explore narrative forms, aesthetic frameworks, and richer vocabularies with which to charge African realities with more expressive meanings.

With *Fatima, l'Algérienne de Dakar* (2004), Med Hondo calls for representational frameworks that speak of and to the post-independence disillusionments. Here, exploring the imaginative regeneration of African cultural precepts, posing aesthetic challenges to dominant representational forms and codes, and instituting bold frameworks for spectatorial positioning become critical components of his ideological project. Hondo, who has been described as *un cinéaste rebelle*, a rebel filmmaker, by Signaté (1994) situates the narrative dynamics of *Fatima* between history and cultural politics, exploring in particular how the former enters into new relations with the latter. Through snatches of experimental aesthetics, for example, he inserts the imagination as a possible tool for engaging history. As a tool, imagination creates spaces where history, memory, and lived experience are in critical dialogue. In the film, notably, repressed memories, marginalized voices, elided narratives, and circumscribed lives are used to explore systems of representation, ethnicity, gender, identity, and class. Thus, *Fatima* is about a tumultuous past as much as it is about a beleaguered African present of economic, political, religious, and cultural ferment.

In the film, the eponymous heroine, Fatima, under pressure from family members and the pervasive bigotry of her community, marries Souleyman, a Senegalese lieutenant in the French colonial army, who had raped her during the Algerian war of independence. With Abdelkader, her dark-skinned son from that tragic encounter, she receives a warm communal welcome in Dakar, Senegal, at the insistence of El Haj Fall, a kindly man esteemed in the community, who had sent his reluctant son back to Algeria to redeem his transgression and marry his "sister in Islam." Among those at the reception are two *tirailleurs*, ex-servicemen of the French colonial army, and El Haj Seck, alias Mister Double Dose. Years later, after the birth of other children, the budding domestic stability is disrupted when Souleyman is promoted to captain and invokes his religious and cultural prerogative to take a second wife. Supported by his mother, Aïssatou, Souleyman is pitted against Fatima and El Haj Fall. Aïssatou moves out and El Haj Fall welcomes Fatima and his grandchildren to his compound. To ensure her independence, El Haj Fall helps Fatima find employment in a restaurant owned by his friends, the Delgados. Home from her job, one night, Fatima and El Haj Fall, walk in on a drunken Souleyman, who citing love and Islam, has come to claim his wife and children. In the ensuing fray, Souleyman falls, hitting his head on an artifact in the courtyard. With Souleyman on his deathbed, surrounded by El Haj Fall, Fatima and children, a griot, whose exhortations opened the film, appears as a reflection in a mirror on the wall of the room, and closes the narrative without any indulgent catharsis.

Clearly, *Fatima* is not a formulaic narrative of betrayal and reconciliation. Hondo is careful not to make the ambivalent Souleyman's trip to ask for Fatima's hand in marriage a credible spiritual quest or expiatory venture. Hondo eschews sentimentalism by formulating exacting trans-historical, transcultural, and transnational frameworks for Fatima's experiences. Without question, Fatima is a courageous woman, and while the film could be read as a survivor's story, it is not about individual destiny *per se*. Through her, Hondo argues that the expectations of women's liberation, at the cusp of anti-colonial struggles, are yet to be fulfilled. Fatima's experiences are used to interrogate certain features of, and developments within, postcolonial Africa. While her tribulations are allegorical of the continent's, she is not a mythic figure steeped in a facile, epic narrative of "resistance." Hondo does not present a simplistic "life-and-times" narrative, and in inextricably weaving discourses of identity, gender, religion, nation, and belonging, he engages the ambiguities of historical memory and certain quandaries of post-colonial Africa.

Fatima, is also not a narrative of "homeland" and "exile." Even though the title transposes a national identity into a different geographical space, Fatima, under the guidance of El Haj Fall, receives full cultural citizenship in Dakar. By choosing a title in which difference reverberates and in constructing a transnational space in which to tell her story, Hondo pushes for a discourse of African identity beyond rigid national and cultural (b)orders. It is also remarkable that religion, marriage, family, and community, rather than Western judicial institutions, constitute the locus of negotiations for her eventual restitution. Further, even though the story begins on the larger canvas of history, the narrative shifts become more personal through the trope of journeys. For Souleyman, it began as a coerced journey of reconciliation, of coming-to-terms, and for Fatima, one of restoration. The significance of these journeys is allegorical of the continent's predicaments and history. Seen this way, *Fatima* is, arguably, a narrative about the dramas, dreams, and dilemmas of independence.

Through *Fatima*, Hondo, poses difficult questions like: What discursive values can we assign the history of anti-colonial struggles? Whose interests do the contemporary African ruling classes serve? Whatever happened to the dreams of a fair and equitable society? On whose terms and within what structures will new cultural formations in Africa spring? Definitive answers to the foregoing and other questions about the contours and trajectories of postcolonial Africa require much more sustained investigation, and are beyond the scope of this inquiry (see, Mbembe, 2001; and, Quayson, 2000, for instance). The issues and quandaries raised here are intended to be provocative, especially as they are intricately interwoven in the film.

Altered states

It is significant that Fatima's experiences were circumscribed by forces out of her control, especially war and rape. Wars usually involve the transgressing of boundaries: geographical, moral, and psychical. Often, too, wars engender breakdowns of law, order, and rationalities. The enemy is presented not only in material form, but as a threat to the definition and defense of selves, communities, and nations, may be conceptualized through abstract categories and ideologies, embedded in complex, semiotic codes beyond the *casus belli*. Whereas rape does not belong within the accepted classificatory systems of armaments, its pervasive manifestation as "an instrument of war," is often used to terrorize, demean, and extend the battlefront to bodies, usually those of women and children. By Souleyman's admission, rape was condoned by the French colonial army in Algeria as long as the culprits were discrete. Far from winning tangible assets, at least in shaping the outcome of wars, the libidinal investment in rape, with its play of power and control, constitutes a traumatic and symbolic conquest. Rape creates a violent libidinal economy whose currencies – violation, terrorization, and demoralization – perversely generate, in the perpetrators' minds, fantastical scenarios of subjugation over the abject enemy "Other." Thus, through rape, Fatima's body becomes a physical, psychological, and symbolic theater of war; worse, among some members of her natal community, her rape by an enemy and agent of the colonizing force throws identification with her into crisis insofar as her "honor" is ostensibly integral to their sense of wholeness and identity. While this ambivalent identification may derive from the residual feelings of loathsomeness against the colonizing force and other unpleasant experiences from the war that haunt their communal memory, what is called into question here are not just definitions of "honor." Hondo suggests that her community's ambivalence toward Fatima also carries repressed racist stereotypes and anxieties about black male sexuality. It is, therefore, significant that rape, an instance of deprecatory violation, sets and structures her paths to integration and redeemed (self) respect in Dakar. Strikingly, Hondo uses her rape to situate colonialism within the realm of trauma.

It is, thus, significant how Fatima, to borrow from Nnaemeka (1997), is inserted in the "politics of (m)othering"; more so, as motherhood in the nationalist imagination invites compelling identifications through which the nation imagines and "recognizes" itself as sovereign. Within this framework, women as symbols of nation, community, and "difference" are, quite often, encumbered with "a burden of identification" through which indulgent ideological fantasies are mobilized and contradictory discourses are repressed. With the latter, especially, "mother" as a figure of honor and virtue is desexualized and opened to the fluctuations and anxieties embedded within complex social and emotional dynamics. As a figure of besmirched "honor," Fatima's capacity to "reproduce" communal purity is seen as compromised: more so, as her abjection is tied to a system of identification and disavowal that construes her dutiful mothering as perverse. Hence, her father's objection, over an aunt's suggestion that she should have terminated the pregnancy, may be read as a political gesture of defiance of the cultural system that nullifies the humanity of such mothers and children. In framing the film through personal, familial, communal, national, and continental registers, Hondo highlights how her body and experiences become the loci of difficult discourses of transformation, in particular the involvement and sacrifices of women in anti-colonial struggles. In foregrounding the racism and xenophobia that institute hierarchies of belonging, through which she is inferiorized, Hondo argues that such pernicious dispositions perpetuate a blindness to the humanity of an "other." That the repressive Algerian Family Code became law in 1984, twenty-two years after independence, is telling (see, Salhi, 2003).

Her repositioning in Dakar as a wife and mother, forging a fulfilling life rather than suffering exilic ennui, takes a hilarious turn when some local women visit during her second pregnancy. Here, sexuality, "tradition" and religion inspire a performance of guises and subversive identities where libidinal fantasies offer temporary relief from the strictures of propriety. This scene is more than capricious game-playing by the women. Like a carnival, it constructs a space where the inhibitions of "tradition" and patriarchal strictures are inverted. If this scene hints at the possibilities of "liberation" it is even more significant that all adopt "respectable" postures and banter when El Haj Fall walks in. Whether their reactions are seen as prudent gestures of self-preservation or as an instance of the restrictive intrusions of patriarchy, the women's licentious jokes and bawdy revelry suggest ways of sneaking in what often is elided or "unspeakable." The women's capacity for fuller expressions of their subjectivities, while under wraps, so to speak, in their *boubous,* are still potent. In establishing a correspondence between desire, space, and gender roles, the scene disrupts the frame through which African women are, quite often, imagined as hopelessly oppressed. That their sense of freedom is figured more in terms of sororal bonding, maternity, and power is just as significant. Through this visit, Hondo presents another facet of Fatima's integration. Unlike her previous pregnancy, from rape, there is no ambivalence in this instance. So, in a way, the scene constitutes a restorative process.

New fronts

The griot's opening address to the camera, which establishes the film's narrative construction, abrogates the prohibition in dominant cinema against characters looking directly into the camera. Just as important, the spectator is invited to participate in and witness the unfolding scenarios. Hondo's griot, as muse, is not, to borrow from Huggan (2001), a "postcolonial exotic." Appearing intermittently in the film, he is imbued with evocative powers and charged with bridging narrative gaps as well as sensitizing the spectator, advising Africans against repressing historical memory as a way of transcending alienation and sundry postcolonial predicaments. As such, he is not just an experimentation with narrative forms. The gray-toned sequences as the film opens and closes, thematize memory. Overall, in creatively re-appropriating and repositioning African storytelling traditions, as well as exploring questions of authorship, Hondo, makes the case for a politicized, even revolutionary, film language. Through the griot, a repository of communal memory and chronicler of the times, Hondo self-reflexively establishes critical relationships with the film's diegetic world and inserts a discourse of alterity. It is notable, too, that the griot is positioned at the confluence of the film's thematic and formal concerns, and as a moral authority.

Similarly, a prescient madman, who comes out of the shadows of society, literally and figuratively adds a unique narrative dimension to the film. Like a detective, he holds the key through which certain puzzles in Senegalese history can be pieced together. He comes out of the margins of society, the latter generally predicated on "sanity," and his presence undermines the terms of belonging or worth in the society, the boundaries of "otherness" and difference. By resurrecting ostensibly buried or forgotten fragments of history, he manifests a "return of the repressed." His outbursts are directed at imaginary audiences, and by implication the spectators. His "intrusive appearances," which constitute unauthorized speech, critique official history and power relations. He points out that the pursuit of a just society, particularly as the quest depends upon the rule of law, transparency, and accountability, is still elusive. Critically, he charges the state with complicity in institutionalizing a murderous political culture, and poses moral challenges by speaking truth to power.

In a way, too, he could be read as metaphorical or symptomatic of the madness that has beset the society. That he, an outcast, is placed in a testimonial position by Hondo not only contests notions of "madness," but highlights how his exclusion has been integrated by the ruling elite into prevailing discourses of citizenship. That his outbursts provide counter discourses to the dominant political and social narrative of "nation" is just as important. As a figure erupting from the national unconscious, he occupies a liminal politicized space. Significantly, his outbursts are anchored to specific, volatile historical moments. He contests, for instance, accusations of treason in 1962 against Mamadou Dia, the first Senegalese Prime Minister. He also contests official accounts of the young, brilliant activist Omar Blondin Diop's ostensible suicide in 1973 at Senegal's notorious Gorée prison. Dia's radical vision for the emergent nation state, articulated in his acclaimed seminal work, *The African Nations and World Solidarity* (1961), was at odds with that of the erstwhile President Léopold Sédar Senghor's. (see, Busia, 1962; Ferkiss, 1962; J.G. St. Clair Drake, 1963; Whiteman, 2009). Omar Blondin Diop's eclectic involvement in the revolutionary ferment of 1968 in France, Senegalese oppositional politics, radical film cultures – appearing, for instance, in Jean Luc Godard's *La Chinoise* (1967), *One Plus One* (1968) and *Week End* (1967), Simon Hartog's *Soul in a White Room* (1968) – and his erudite review of Andy Warhol and Paul Morrissey's *Chelsea Girls* (1966) are equally distinctive for *Fatima*'s inter-textual references. Dia was sentenced to jail "in perpetuity" but granted amnesty in 1978, after prolonged incarceration (see, Whiteman 2009). Omar Blondin Diop's case, shrouded in contradictory official reports, remains without retributive justice. By juxtaposing colonial repression with Africa's own history of political repression, Hondo highlights deeply disturbing ironies. Also, through the madman, Hondo extends *Fatima*'s inter-textual reference to the Algerian war epic and *Palme d'Or* Winner, *Chronicle of the Years of Embers* (1975), where the director, Mohammed Lakhdar-Hamina, in a brilliant self-reflexive touch, plays a madman.

The inter-textual instances in the film are not mere narrative adornments. Dedicating the film to the memories of Ababacar Samb Makhram, Abdoulaye Doula Seck, Dibril Mambety, and Kateb Yacine, whose poetry Fatima's father reads, Hondo situates the film in a continuum of radical African cultural production. *Mein Bruder War Ein Fliegerman*, a poem about the Spanish Civil War – a moment of national crisis and the fight for rights – written by the antifascist, German playwright and theater director, Bertolt Brecht, is juxtaposed in the film's opening scenes with the Algerian struggles for independence. Brecht favored experimenting with dramatic form to instigate social change and make audiences active participants. Brecht's troubled history with Hollywood finds expressions in the film's experimental flourishes. Just as Omar Blondin Diop is exalted in a song, *Death of Omar Diop Blondin*, by the French rock group, Heldon, Cheikh Anta Diop, the radical historian, is proclaimed in a song by a Senegalese nightclub band. Elsewhere, pictures of the revolutionary icon, Ernesto "Che" Guevara, adorn the 1965 Afro-Asian Conference setting in Algiers, while his spirited denunciation of imperialism reverberates as Souleyman is led through the site's hallway. The conference, held just a few months before the Algerian coup of 1965 referenced in the film, adds profound ironies to Africa's postcolonial conundrums. The film is also suffused with the spirit and iconic presence of Frantz Fanon, a luminary of anti-colonial struggles and postcolonial studies, who denounced French colonialism in his works and through his involvement in the Algerian struggles for independence. In the film, Che and Fanon embody dynamic political dissent and radical intellectual modes of engaging colonial history. Further integrating the iconic with the cinematic is a poster of the

Figure 5.1 Fatima confronts Souleyman over decision to take a second wife (Source: still *Fatima, l'Algérienne de Dakar*, 2004; M.H. Films)

infamous 20 May 1942 French campaign, *Journée Nationale Nord-Africaine de Collect des Textiles*, through which Hondo critiques the expropriatory tangents and pernicious dynamics of colonial relations.

Put together, the foregoing instances highlight the intertextuality of postcolonial discourses. What we have, here, are elaborate interplays between the film and other discourses, aimed at fashioning critical registers with which to engage Africa's postcolonial quandaries. Hondo appears to suggest that an exclusive focus on Fatima's experience may not be adequate to engage the entanglements of postcolonial Africa. Hondo, however, is not concerned with resolving all postcolonial quandaries with the film. His interests lie more with appropriating Fatima's experiences as critical guides for exploring the ambiguities, institutions, and conditions of postcolonial Africa. The intertextual references allow for entries into, and struggles over, various meanings that may be more implicit than explicit. Situating Fatima's experiences in the broadest cultural, institutional, and historical contexts offers a richer framework for critical analysis of these categories and invites reflections on the relationship between seemingly disparate elements.

Conflicted relations

The film also explores the identities produced within and after conflicts. In this respect, Souleyman's paradoxical status as a colonized subject and colonizing agent stands out. Through Abdelkader, Hondo breaks down restrictive notions of family. By having the boy described early in the film as "a slave's son," "bastard," "son of a migrating crow," and "nigger," Hondo shows how the issue of one's origins is embedded in discourses of identity. Through him, Hondo also addresses the Maghreb's diffidence about their "Africanness." It is significant, in this respect, that Fatima is coerced into marrying Souleyman for family honor, social respectability, and to give Abdelkader "a name." In a critical scene, her son mistakes the portrait of Frantz Fanon in the household for his father's, wondering if "he will come." Wisely, his understanding maternal grandfather, El Haj Mamood, answers that Fanon was, "A brother come from far away, from Martinique, to help us fight in our war for liberation."

By putting identities at the narrative core, especially exploring the parameters of difference, Hondo opens up the contentious issue through showing areas of overlap, favoring heterogeneity rather than homogeneity. Also at issue here are people often excluded or marginalized, like Fatima, Abdelkader, and the madman. With them Hondo suggests that notions of a sacrosanct African identity are not just idealistic but reactionary to the trajectory and dynamics of contemporary Africa, as well as the ideals of Pan-Africanism. In Algeria, Abdelkader was seen as a figure of racial contamination and moral failure. As well, Fatima's mention of *Tamazigh* as a "Berber language" and her "first language," *a mother tongue*, in a romantic scene with Souleyman, speaks to the contentious politics of "heritage," "belonging," pluralism and identity in Algeria (see, Layachi, 2005). In pointing out Fatima's layered identities, particularly Amazigh (Berber) and Arabic, the Senegalese, Cape Verdean, and Spanish filiations of the Delgados, and Souleyman's extensive family heritage across West Africa cultures, Hondo contests the simplistic, nationalist notion that whittles down and projects the intrinsically multiple layers of identity into idealized, ostensibly iridescent, essences.

The constructed natures of identities are central to postcolonial theory where identities are often positioned at the confluence of histories and power relations and are never seen as absolute. Consistent with postcolonialist thinking, Abdelkader may be Hondo's way of proposing new forms of identities against the grids of racial and nationalist chauvinism. Representations of identity in early African cinema often emphasized discourses of "authenticity" to contest the self-imposed, colonialist project of reforming the "African." Not surprisingly, those representations were premised on the ostensibly intrinsic, and as such easily identifiable, constitutive elements of "Africanness." Often, too, they accentuated place, origins, and culture, looking back with a sense of loss and nostalgia. In *Fatima*, however, the idea of identities based on essences or immutable criteria is abrogated in favor of an approach that acknowledges the shifting dynamics of African cultural formations. Seen this way, *Fatima,* sets up transcultural spaces for the exploration of African identities beyond nation states, incorporating discourses of hybridity.

Hondo foregrounds the ideological charges, inconsistencies, and conflicted relations, rumbling at the core of the postcolonial African nation state in a sequence involving a farmers' protest. Insofar as the farmers note in various ways that they are still under the aegis of colonial and imperial interests rather than enjoying their much vaunted independence, the scene explores transformative platforms and establishes the critical relations between economic and political power. Concentrating on the impassioned interactions between the characters and the process of political engagement, the scene functions as both commentary and theater. As commentary, it calls attention to unequal relations of power in the postcolonial state. Its critique of bourgeois consumerism, predatory capitalism, and the political economy of globalization introduces class-consciousness and nudges spectators into contemplative rather than passive relationships with the narrative. Again recalling Brechtian theater, Hondo enlarges the narrative frame, and explores other spaces and standpoints for political action. As an audacious aesthetic intervention, like the scene where destitute children literally litter the street, Hondo poses questions about dominant codes of representation, championing critical relations between audiences and cinema that challenge spectatorial complacency.

Crucially, there is no spotlight on a leader or any instant "revolutionary" manifesto during the protest. Hondo appears more concerned with instigating democratic process and oppositional thinking. Even though El Haj Fall intervenes, at a certain point, it is more as a moderator. Interestingly, El Haj Fall indicts African leaders but "absolves" the Westerners, who in his view, are protecting their interests, and he encourages diversified agricultural production rather than the colonially induced single-crop economies, as a panacea. It is also very significant that the marginalized farmers get their own spaces, reclaim their own voices, and reaffirm their own stake in the nation state. Rather than being spoken to and spoken for, the subaltern, here, gets to speak. So, in proposing a critical rather than an acquiescent relationship to certain restrictive social realities of postcolonial Africa, Hondo is more concerned with radical forms of subjectivity.

The key here, for Hondo is that Africa's postcolonial quandaries must be situated in relation to its complex social and historical realities. From this standpoint, the masses can grasp certain crucial elements through which the individual and the community's position in the political economy of globalization may be more fruitfully understood. Plainly, the farmers are embroiled in attempts to make sense of the social and ideological riddles of postcolonial Africa.

In nationalist discourses, religion may be used to generate feelings of belonging, shared values, and "national character." The ostensible distinguishing markers are not just reserved for nations but used to assign individual moral worth. Insofar as religion is implicated in the constitution of certain codes of conduct, relations, and identities, reductionist shows of religiosity come under attack in the film. Not surprisingly, an aureate drive to build more mosques at the expense of social amenities and employment opportunities is subjected to a nuanced critique. Even though El Haj Fall's insistence that Souleyman redress his transgression by marrying Fatima is premised on moral principles derived from Islam and personal convictions, he is tolerant of the secular streak of a friend, Mister Double Dose. The narrative's moral tone is not, in other words, reducible to Islamic tenets. Hondo critiques the initiatives for more mosques, for example, on the grounds that grandiose displays are not effective indices of morality, and that hypocritical posturing is banal.

Hondo's film proposes new social relations not tied to affected shows of faith, which merely abet moral ambiguities, perpetuate blindness to the realities of poverty and need, and pose enormous challenges to building a just and equitable society. Religion, Hondo suggests, should not determine national character or even individual worth. Whereas religious fundamentalists see change in terms of corruption, especially of "timeless" spiritual values, Hondo argues for dialogues and standpoints which must

Figure 5.2 A grown Abdelkader at study, flanked by a picture of Frantz Fanon and poster of the discredited *Journée Nationale Nord-Africaine de Collect des Textiles* (Source: still *Fatima, l'Algérienne de Dakar*, 2004; M.H. Films)

include tolerance and commitment to civil liberties. He shows, moreover, that religions are often ensconced in complex ideological debates, social transformation, and gender politics (see Masud *et al.*, 2009). To disarm the racist barbs from some villagers against Fatima and Abdelkader, a considerate member counsels the recalcitrants thus: "Do not forget Bilal was black. Our Prophet, Peace be on Him, chose him as muezzin." Similarly, countering Souleyman's interest in a new wife, Fatima reminds him that The Prophet's daughter "demanded from Ali, her husband, never to take a second wife." In a related instance, El Haj reminds his resentful wife, Aïssatou, of their *own* monogamous marriage. Souleyman's chauvinistic interest in taking a second wife is shown to have more to do with libidinal gratification than with piety or need, and, in this sense, contradictory to the political ideals of the revolutionary struggles that begot and will sustain independence. So, in all, Hondo is not against religion but the political uses to which it may be put and the social pitfalls to which it may be vulnerable. Souleyman's egoistic longings for a second wife, under the pretext of religious prerogative, are used to highlight threats to marital security for women under polygamy and in religious cultures that accept divorce by repudiation. Here, Hondo extends the discourse of liberation by showing selfish and narrow interests as afflictions of the postcolonial elite.

Think again

Although Souleyman's death, a tragic accident, invites reflection, Hondo is careful not to make him a tragic victim, especially as he represents the emergent ruling class, preoccupied with social mobility, perks of power, and a covetousness that compromises the ideals of progress. His death symbolizes the rejection and obsolescence of an emergent post-independence bourgeoisie. Moreover, in signaling a shift in Fatima's position from one of subordination, justified by religion, within the marriage relationship to one that restores her full humanity, Souleyman's death challenges the power and social relations that favor the elite and sustain patriarchy. Insofar as the film is about engendering new cultural formations and social relations, and negotiating new national and cultural identities, Souleyman's death allows Fatima's fuller integration in Dakar.

Souleyman embodies a paradox for the postcolonial state insofar as he is mired in reactionary practices and interests that work against the common good. Seen this way, his death could be read as a narrative requirement for the film's ideological project, especially as Hondo eschews a pithy, cathartic, happily-ever-after framework. Through Souleyman's death, as decorated military officer, Hondo demythicizes heroism. Instructively, El Haj Fall introduces his ex-service *tirailleurs* friends to Fatima as people who "delivered Europe from the Nazi plague," describing their decorative ribbons as "candies one gives children" rather than insignia of recognition or honor. Also aware of colonial chicanery, a *tirailleur* decries their meager pensions noting, "Still we were in all the bloodbaths in Europe. For dying in trenches, then we were good French niggers. With our country's independence, we switch back to Senegalese savages and our pensions are frozen, 'crystallized.'" Aligned with Ousmane Sembene and Thierno Faty Sow's *Camp de Thiaroye* (1987) (see Hamish Ford in this volume), and Rachid Bouchareb's *Days of Glory/Indigènes* (2006), Hondo, here, asks: What becomes of "heroes" when the nationalist, mythic elements upon which their status is founded are shattered or at least put in doubt? Remarkably, the shockwaves generated by *Days of Glory* ruffled French political history and prodded the erstwhile French president, Jacques Chirac, into rescinding the odious pension policy.

While set across historical registers, *Fatima* is not framed within a facile dynamic of memory and recovery. The past is not gold-toned; instead, it is a dilemma (see Waller in this volume). Here, history is invoked in order to investigate what clues an obnoxious past may harbor for the conundrums of the present. The meanings and critical significance of the past are key to the film's narrative, and juxtapositions of fragments of that past, however mediated, are used to establish dialogues between history and allegory, especially with Fatima as the needle and thread through which swatches of individual and national histories are stitched together. Whereas historical films may focus on "defining moments" or national figures and, quite often, aspects of national myths, Hondo's focus on ordinary folks situates their struggles in the construction of the postcolonial nation-state. This is very important because the various struggles, and entangled processes under interrogation here become frameworks for reading the politics of liberation. In picking the founding moments of "nation," Hondo sets up a unique contextual framing for Fatima's story, and through the film's inter-textual tangents he suggests the complex ways that the relationship between narratives of "nation," necessarily involve intricate networks. Hence, Fatima's biography, deeply entangled in the birth of a nation, sets up alternative frameworks through which Hondo infuses his own readings of, and concerns about, grand "national" narratives or myths.

Representations of history, inevitably, involve creative engagements with the past. A historical film may engage popular memory critically, just as it could be positioned against "official" or dominant accounts of history. Hondo's film suggests that, given the inevitable gaps in, and ambiguities of, "official" history and popular memory, each must always be left open to revisions and reinterpretations. The film's immersion in history, however, is not about milestones *per se*. Rather, it is about how these milestones tell the stories of transformations within Africa. The film is concerned with how various changes in Africa create spaces for the construction and circulation of new identities. Hence, it shows that African identities, like other identities, are in constant flux and constructed between spaces, considerations, and dynamics that transcend national boundaries.

Conclusion

History has long been, for complex reasons, a battleground for ideas, ideologies, identities, and representations. Not surprisingly, *Fatima* has corollaries in Algerian cinema that, according to Austin (2010) go "against amnesia," and antecedents such as Youssef Chahine's *Jamila the Algerian* (1958), *The Battle of Algiers* (Gillo Pontercorvo, 1966), (see Hamish Ford in this volume), and its documentary reprise, *Gillo Pontercorvo's Return to Algiers* (1992). It also has affinities with Rachid Bouchareb's recent, *Outside the Law/Hors-la-loi* (2010). Assia Djebar's *Children of the New World*, which chronicles the experiences of Algerian women during the independence struggles and was published just before the country's emancipation, is noteworthy, too, as a literary precursor of Hondo's film.

Setting *Fatima* in the contexts of colonial history and the ruptures of the post-independence African nationalist imagination, Hondo creatively engages various prickly concerns. Reinterpreting colonial history was, following independence, seen as integral to (re)constructing the emergent nation-state. Accepting this challenge, Hondo chooses an extraordinary constellation of experiences, aesthetics, and themes through which to instigate a reappraisal of the terms, institutions, and discourses that frame Fatima's and, by extension, Africa's dilemmas. His ambition here, arguably, is not to find therapeutic closure but to illuminate the dizzying ranges of narratives, incongruities, and ambiguities that constitute the narrative economies of identities and histories. Not surprisingly, *The Battle of Algiers* and the Algerian war still excite vehemently polarized identifications (Caillé, 2007; Celli, 2004; Chanan, 2007; Harrison, 2007; Jeancolas, 2007).

Given the foregoing, the film's politically inspired aesthetic and narrative framework is inevitable, particularly as the epistemological frames and critical spans of Africa's postcolonial quandaries far exceed schematic categories of representation. Early in the film, for instance, the French colonial forces' raid, under Souleyman's captainship, causes unbridled terror and is marked by rampant executions. The hideousness of these raids is underscored later, through his voice-over, recalling their days on the battlefront when the creed was: "A living Arab is a possible *fellagha*. A dead Arab is a confirmed *fellagha*. If an Arab runs, he is also a *fellagha*; if he doesn't, he's smart: In both cases, shoot!"

The whispered arrest of El Haj Mamood's friend, Youssef, in Algiers, *after independence*, and panicked citizens scampering at the sight of soldiers some renegade youths call "watchdogs" indicate pervasive restiveness. The facts that Algeria was plunged into civil war from 1992 to 2004 and endured a nineteen-year state of emergency, abrogated only in February 2011, coupled with Smith's (2008) view that the erstwhile oppressed have become oppressors, are relevant here. From a different angle, Aïssatou's support of Souleyman's wishes to take a second wife with the argument that it was better than having concubines, and her accusations of exaggeration and disobedience against Fatima, mark her as a reactionary, partisan mother-in-law and saboteur of women's solidarity, and extends the preceding paradoxes to the "home front."

The humanist discourse at the core of *Fatima* has sexual and political violence as rhetorical reference points. As a war rape narrative, Fatima's experiences of violation, ostracism and stigmatization invite compassionate identifications with her. Souleyman's preceding recollection of the colonial army's operational creed hints at "crimes against humanity" much like the French soldier's question to his cynical squadron mates: "Guernica ring a bell? There are Guernicas everywhere." This reference to the German bombardment of Guernica, during the Spanish Civil War juxtaposes Basque nationalism, Algerian anti-colonial struggles, and issues of self-determination, with antifascist and anti-Nazi resistance. Here, too, Picasso's masterpiece, *Guernica*, inspired by the bombing, becomes a rich inter-text for Hondo's engagement of political violence.

Overall, *Fatima* delineates complexities arising from the past that have certain parallels in the present and invite engagement with the charged political and social dynamics of postcolonial Africa. In his engagement, Hondo is interested in articulating the various discourses around Fatima's experiences that accrue over time *and* across locations. Crucially, he extends the inquiry to the institutions, dispositions, and unspoken assumptions that imbue these discourses with exquisite significance.

Acknowledgments

I am deeply indebted to Obioma Nnaemeka, Med Hondo and Aboubakar Sanogo for their various "enabling acts." My profound appreciation goes to Margie Waller and Sandra Ponzanesi for their patience and support. To my mother, Ann O. Akudinobi, who went to eternal rest as this project was underway: respect and honor.

Bibliography

Austin, G., 2010. Against Amnesia: Representations of Memory in Algerian Cinema. *Journal of African Cinemas*, 2(1), pp. 27–35.

Busia, K.A., 1962. Book Review *The African Nations and World Solidarity* by M. Dia. *Annals of the American Academy of Political and Social Science*, 342, pp. 182–3.

Caillé, P., 2007. The Illegitimate Legitimacy of *The Battle of Algiers* in French Film Culture. *Interventions*, 9(3), pp. 371–88.

Celli, C., 2004. Gillo Pontecorvo's Return to Algiers. *Film Quarterly*, 58(2), pp. 49–52.

Chanan, M., 2007. Outsiders: The Battle of Algiers and Political Cinema. *Sight and Sound*, 17 (6), pp. 38–40.

Dia, M., 1961. *The African Nations and World Solidarity*. Translated from French by M. Cook. New York: Frederick A. Praeger.

Diawara, M., 1992. *African Cinema: Politics and Culture*. Bloomington, IN: Indiana University Press.

Diawara, M., 2010. *African Film: New Forms of Aesthetics and Politics*. New York: Prestel USA.

Djebar, A. 2005. *Children of the New World*. Translated from French by M. de Jager. New York: The Feminist Press at City University of New York.

Ferkiss, V.C., 1962. Book Review of *The African Nations and World Solidarity* by M. Dia. *The Western Political Quarterly*, 15(3), pp. 545–6.

Harrison, N., 2007. Pontecorvo's "Documentary" Aesthetics: *The Battle of Algiers* and the Battle of Algiers. *Interventions*, 9(3), pp. 388–404.

Huggan, G., 2001. *The Postcolonial Exotic: Marketing the Margins*. London and New York: Routledge.

Jeancolas, J.P., 2007. French Cinema and the Algerina War: Fifty Years Later. Translated from French by M. Tierney and C. Tarr. *Cineaste*, 33(1), pp. 44–6.

Layachi, A., 2005. The Berbers in Algeria: Politicization of Ethnicity and Ethicization of Politics. In: M. Shatzmiller, ed. 2005. *Nationalism and Minority Identities in Islamic Societies*. Montreal and Ithaca, NY: McGill-Queen's University Press. pp. 195–28.

Malkmus, L. and Armes, R., 1991. *Arab and African Film Making*. London and New Jersey: Zed Press.

Masud, M.K, Salvatore. A., and Van Bruinessen, M. eds., 2009. *Islam and Modernity: Key Issues and Debates*. Edinburgh: Edinburgh University Press.

Mbembe, A., 2001. *On the Postcolony*. Berkeley: University of California Press.

Nnaemeka, O., ed., 1997. *The Politics of (M)Othering: Womanhood, Identity, and Resistance in African Literature*. London and New York: Routledge.

Quayson, A., 2000. *Postcolonialism: Theory, Practice or Process*. Cambridge: Polity Press.

Salhi, Z.S., 2003. Algerian Women, Citizenship, and the "Family Code. *Gender and Development*, 11(3), pp. 27–35.

Signaté, I., 1994. *Un cinéaste rebelle: Med Hondo*. Paris: Présence Africaine.

Smith, W., 2008. From the Oppressed to Oppressors. *The American Scholar*, 77(4), pp. 109–16.

St. Clair Drake, J.G., 1963. Book Review of *The African Nations and World Solidarity* by M. Dia. *The Journal of Modern African Studies*, 1(1), March, pp. 112–13.

Ukadike, N.F., 1995. *Black African Cinema*. Berkeley: University of California Press.

Whiteman, K., 2009. Obituaries. Mamadou Dia: First Prime minister and Key Figure in the Politics of Senegal. *The Guardian*, 3 February, p. 30.

Filmography

Camp de Thiaroye, 1987. [film] Directed by O. Sembene and T. Faty Sow.Algeria/Senegal/Tunisia: SNPC, ENAPROC and SATPEC.

Chelsea Girls, 1966. [film] Directed by P. Morrissey and A. Warhol. USA: The Film-Makers"

Chronicle of the Years of Embers, 1975. [film] Directed by M. Lakhdar-Hamina. Algeria: O.N.C.I.C.

Fatima, l'Algérienne de Dakar, 2004. [film] Directed by M. Hondo. France: Canal France International, and M.H Films.

Gillo Pontercorvo's Return to Algiers, 1992. [film] directed by G. Pontercorvo. Italy: Mixer Documenti, RAI 2 Television. Orme s.r.l.

Hors-la-loi/Outside the Law, 2010. [film] Directed by R. Bouchareb. France: Tessalit Productions.

Indigènes/Days of Glory, 2006. [film] Directed by R. Bouchareb. France: Tessalit Productions.

Jamila the Algerian, 1958. [film] Directed by Y. Chahine. Egypt: Ideal-Titro.

La Battaglia di Algeri/The Battle of Algiers, 1966. [film] Directed by G. Pontecorvo. Italy/Algeria: Igor Film, and Casbah Films.

La Chinoise, 1967. [film] Directed by J.L. Godard. France: Anouchka Films.

One Plus One, 1968. [film] Directed by J.L. Godard. England: Cupid Productions..

Soul in a White Room, 1968. [film] Directed by S. Hartog. UK: LUX.

Week End, 1967. [film] Directed by J. L. Godard. France: Comacico.

Chapter 6

Postcolonial relationalities in Philippe Faucon's *Dans la vie*

Mireille Rosello

Morocco-born Philippe Faucon is one of the French directors whose films have regularly documented various aspects of France's postcolonial present and colonial past. He is particularly interested in the cultural consequences of France's presence in Algeria and in the ways in which the definition of Frenchness is currently changing as it intersects with competing narratives of ethnicity, gender, and national history.

His films often explore the daily micro-practices that develop within and between communities that are still perceived as minority, ethnic, or even foreign. Like most filmmakers of Maghrebi origin, Faucon focuses on the difficulties encountered by the members of families who do not necessarily agree on what it means to belong to a community that the majority of French people will view as an ethnic minority. Unlike the majority of so-called *Beur* or *banlieue* films however, Faucon's stories often revolve around female characters, and invite the viewer to consider minority ethnic communities from a different perspective. *Samia* (2000) foregrounds a young *Beurette* struggling to find her place within her family and within French society and *Dans la vie*, the film I focus on in this chapter, is about two elderly women whose complicated friendship asks interesting and new questions about the relationship between the individual and his or her community.

The attention to gender issues, however, is not the only element that makes *Dans la vie* an interesting new contribution to postcolonial cinema. In retrospect, a film like *Samia* can be added to an already rich collection of *film-banlieues* that tend to focus on similar and by-now canonical topics whereas *Dans la vie,* released in 2007 adopts a significantly different perspective. Although the film touches on issues already addressed in Faucon's previous work, it reflects the evolving stakes of the colonial debate. Not surprisingly, postcolonial films have dealt with issues linked to past and contemporary tragedies. Films, such as Bouchareb's *Indigènes,* that document the role of North African soldiers during WWII, or Michael Haneke's *Caché* (an exploration of the memory of October 1961), analyzed in this volume by Hamish Ford, suggest that the past haunts the immediate present. Postcolonial cinema also testifies to the social, cultural, economic disenfranchisement that continues to plague the sons and daughters, or rather now grandsons and granddaughters, of North African workers who emigrated to France after the Second World War.[1]

To the extent that the memory of colonialism revolves around topics such as slavery, colonial violence including the use of torture by the Republic, or the aftermath of past conflicts of decolonization, it is hardly surprising that works of art that address France's postcolonial present should focus on disturbing social phenomena and encourage outrage and/or a political reaction from the viewer. *Dans la vie*, however, provides us with a completely different frame of representation, and it modifies our perception of what is relevant or problematic in this context.

The main protagonists of *Dans la vie* are Esther and Halima.[2] Esther is Jewish, and she is disabled. Her son, a successful dentist cannot take care of her on his own and hires Halima to do so. Halima, a Muslim woman who lives in Toulon with her husband and daughter, is a nurse who also takes care of Esther. The tense but genuine bond that slowly develops between the two women is the result of an encounter between two individuals, but also between at least two communities. Moreover, the issue of what it means to belong to these communities and of how such communities are defined is constantly renegotiated within the film. *Dans la vie* combines the colonial past and the immediate transnational present. Both are equally crucial to the way in which the characters relate to each other, to their own communities, to that of others, and to France in general. On the one hand, the legacy of colonization cannot be underestimated: both women are originally from Oran and belong to the generation who lived through the Algerian war and resettled in France after independence. Yet, just as important is the immediate present. The fact that the film takes place during the 2006 war between Israel and Lebanon has direct repercussions on the relationship between Esther and Halima.

Dans la vie, which does its cultural work at the level of popular culture, echoes those theoretical discourses that have analyzed two distinct yet related and controversial sets of postcolonial issues: the relationship between the individual and his or her community on the one hand, and the analysis of cultural conflicts and of their resolution in a Western democracy. The film is a complex narrative that shies away neither from the staging of a Republican[3] or intra-community dissensus nor from optimistic fictional resolutions. *Dans la vie* practices a version of what Gerald Graff advocated as a solution to cultural wars: it "teaches conflicts" (1992). Here postcolonial cinema does not focus on rewriting history or on exposing the fraying of the social fabric in European society. Rather, the film helps us imagine a series of possible solutions to be added to our imaginary. It is a comedy that refuses any fatalistic connection between disagreement and violence, and invites the viewer to laugh at the regular misunderstandings triggered by the characters' struggles with their own contradictory definitions of what it means to belong and to act, either as docile insiders or rebellious subjects.

The France that Faucon's film represents is a country where very specific forms of debate about "communities," and especially ethnic or religious communities, have developed. Migrants of Maghrebi origin or their children or grandchildren are often assumed to function as groups whose cultural, religious, and social practices separate them from the imagined *Français de souche*'s[4] way of being French. When used in the plural, the French word "communautés" is presented as the opposite of the (French) Republic, and the public figures who have voiced their fears about the disintegration of a supposedly unified French identity often use the word "*communautarianisme*" as the name of a political error. At the risk of caricaturing their argument, they claim that "communautarianisme" endangers the French Republic as a whole and exacerbates conflicts among populations who live on French soil and share the public space. "Communautarianisme" is always pejorative and connotes sectarianism. It is what communities do wrong when they act as monolithic groups that defend their own interests or self-contained identities instead of embracing the values of an egalitarian, secular state whose goal is the integration of all individuals regardless of their origin. One of the most representative detractors of communautarianism is philosopher, historian, and political economist Pierre-André Taguieff who, in *La République Enlisée* suggests that communautarianisme is accompanied by "ethnocentrism or sociocentrism, and ... self-absorption, involving a strong sense of self-worth and a tendency to self-enclosure" (Taguieff, 2005, p. 71). Taguieff thus targets not only those communities whose members (allegedly) insist on exclusionary identity politics (presumably minority groups) but also intellectuals or politicians whose "postmodernist" tendencies (Taguieff, 2005, p. 72) lead them to privilege a utopian and vague openness to all forms of difference or otherness at the expense of social cohesion and real equality.

It may well be that such polarization between Republicanist views and communautarianists is an artificial opposition. Republicanists supposedly represent the most radical form of universalism (that forgets the problem of substituting a middle-class male man for the Universal Subject). Communautarists, on the other hand, are suspected of relativism and of imprisoning individuals within their communities. Yet, the nuances within each position are often lost in the debate. Those who argue for a different and subtler approach to a specifically French form of multiculturalism are not easily heard. In this context, the work of French sociologist Michel Wieviorka comes to mind. His analyses of secularism, racism, and social fragmentation strike a decidedly original chord and his voice has been noticed across the Atlantic as well as in France (Wieviorka, 1996, 2005, 2007; Wieviorka and Ohana, 2001). Naomi Schor, a North American literary and cultural analyst has called him as a "champion of multiculturalism" (Schor, 2001), but he might be more accurately described as one of the thinkers who wish to navigate *between* abstract universalism (too often appropriated by the dominant Western subject) and a cultural relativism that would reproduce, at the level of the community, the tyranny of a collective norm to which each individual is subjected (Wieviorka and Ohana, 2001). One of the quiet but remarkable achievements of *Dans la vie* is to contribute to the conversation on "communities" through a portrait of individuals who both strongly identify with a group and disagree about what exactly it means to be loyal to certain values, (regardless of whether these values are perceived as the norm that their own culture imposes or as their own dissident point of view within the group). Moreover, Faucon has chosen to explore the issue of community from a perspective that has also constituted a meeting point between Taguieff and Wieviorka. The story of the difficult yet ultimately fruitful relationship between a Jewish and a Muslim woman raises questions about the new manifestations of racism, or more specifically anti-Jewish and anti-Muslim sentiments in France. Both Taguieff and Wieviorka agree that anti-Semitism in France is on the rise but has taken new forms especially since the beginning of the second *intifada*. Wieviorka hesitates to adopt Taguieff's term of "Judeophobia" (Taguieff, 2002; Wieviorka, 2007, p. 68), but both scholars link recent forms of anti-Semitism to transnational issues, especially to the conflict between Israel and Palestine.[5]

The globalization of anti-Semitic discourses, however, is only one of the effects of the international situation and Muslims of North African origin are also affected by the changing of paradigms. French Muslims are now likely to be affected by what commentators call "Islamophobia," a global phenomenon that more or less coincides with the post 9/11 era. The right-wing identification of "Islam" as what causes cultural wars has slightly modified the definition of communities. In France, the emphasis on religion may not have been the most significant reflex during the 1980s and the 1990s when the themes of migration, integration, and naturalization were at the centre of political platforms. A specifically colonial and postcolonial reaction towards Algerian migrants is now combined with a blanket suspicion towards Muslims, regardless of their origin. In France in general, the possibility of tensions between dominant ethnic French people and migrants of North African origin or their children (the generation of *Beurs* and *Beurettes*) has certainly not disappeared, but what the film suggests is that old forms of ordinary racism are now combined with other configurations of conflict: *Dans la vie* shows that the relationship between French Jews and French Muslims has become more volatile and that the definition of "communities" has added transnational elements to a postcolonial foundation.

The way in which Faucon's film treats Muslim and Jewish communities and characters of Algerian origin thus invites the reader to be attentive to the significant absence of well-known postcolonial themes and the presence of new transnational issues. The moments when a given difference makes a difference, and when it does it not, introduce an element of surprise that reveals and slightly troubles our presuppositions.

A structuring absence is the figure of the stereotypical *Français de souche*. Esther and Salima are both quintessentially French, but radically different from the universal French citizen who continues to be imagined as secular and ethnically unmarked. Both women are religious and strongly attached to what may be described as their communities (Arabs and Jews). Yet, the way in which they deal, on a daily basis, with the present and the past (the history of the Algerian war as well as today's conflict in the Middle East) forces them to redefine the way in which they relate to their community: they take into account the pressures exerted by the norm but also articulate positions that outsiders to the group might otherwise not have been able to recognize as "Jewish" or "Muslim."

The constant effort at redefinition has a direct effect on the representation of the two women's relationship with the colonial past. It also explains another remarkable absence in the film. In *Dans la vie*, the spectator finds no trace of what postcolonial scholars have called the French "wars of memory" which are usually explained as the traumatic traces of a badly managed collective and national memory (Stora, 2007; Blanchard and Veyrat-Masson, 2008; Balibar, 2007). In Esther and Halima's fictive world, no "ethnicisation of memories" complicates and perpetuates the "colonial fracture" (Blanchard *et al.*, 2005).

L'ethnicisation des mémoires, c'est la fracture dans la fracture. Les groupes se battent entre eux: les Juifs contre les Arabes, les Arabes contre les noirs, les Noirs contre les Juifs, relégués, tous relégués dans les banlieues de l'histoire. Chaque groupe s'approprie une partie de l'histoire dans une surenchère victimaire absolument désolante.

(Cherki, 2008, p. 181)

[The ethnicization of memories is a fracture within the fracture. Communities fight each other: Jews against Arabs, Arabs against Blacks, Blacks against Jews, all relegated to the ghettoes of history. Each group appropriates one part of History through an absolutely lamentable bidding for the victim's position.][6]

Halima and Esther are not divided by the colonial past but by the immediate present. They share their Algerian origin as a point of commonality and sameness. The colonial past is a lived reality that they have in common as inhabitants of the same nation. Their perception, or rather the way in which the narrative encrypts them, is that they are from the *same* place, Oran, rather than members of colonial communities that found themselves separated by the war of Algeria and are now divided by the postcolonial fracture.

From this perspective, the fact that Esther is Jewish and that Salima is an Arab is a difference that does not make a difference. Both characters treasure the same memorial narrative of what Algeria was and still is for them: a place they loved and both miss. *Dans la vie* formulates a very specific version of "nostalgeria," the typically French phenomenon that is understood as a longing for an idealized (colonized) native Algeria. Both Esther and Halimi are extremely nostalgic. They share reminiscences and frequently allude to Algeria as a place that they miss, which has disappeared as a country of origin. Esther says to Halima, "On n'oubliera jamais, c'est dans notre tête" (We will never forget, it is in our mind), and the "*nous*" that she constructs unites them in their grief.

Visually, Algeria is present as a recurrent ghost that interrupts the narrative. Wherever she goes, Esther takes a book with her. It is an album of photographs of Algeria that she regularly looks at, while the camera forces, or invites us to share her focalizing gaze. Halima's and Esther's nostalgia, however, is both de-politicized (it has nothing to do with the former colonizers' assumption that colonial France had a positive influence on its overseas territories and that contemporary France should not be changed by its migrants), and re-politicized to the extent that the two women's sharing of their past modifies the traditional historical division between camps. Faucon would not have disoriented viewers if he had constructed a frame within which each of the women had adopted a specific history. Esther could have been portrayed as a "*pied-noir*," a Jewish *pied-noir*, who would have been alienated from rather than connected to her Algerian neighbor. He could have fictionalized the legacy of the border that was gradually and violently erected between Jews and Muslims when the French ruled in Algeria. From a specifically French historical perspective, the splitting of a Judeo-Arab community can be traced back to colonial policies that granted different privileges to colonized Jewish populations. In 1870, the famous "decret Crémieux" gave Algerian Jews French citizenship while Muslims were still under the constraints of the "indigénat code." The war of Independence continued to reinforce the wall between Arabs and

Jews as Esther Benbassa reminds us in an interview about Faucon's *Dans la vie*. Jews, she explains, were ironically perceived as allies of the colonizers by other colonized subjects and they were also treated like European "*rapatriés*" by the French when they left Algeria after the end of the war (Faucon, 2008). In *Dans la vie*, however, it is simply impossible (not only complicated) to map Esther and Halima onto the colonizer/colonized grid. The film presents us with an optimistic, almost utopian relationship between a Jewish and an Arab woman.

And yet, it is also impossible to reduce the characters to these categories and to interpret *Dans la vie* as an allegory of a reconciliation between two diasporic people. The film does not avoid what has become the most obvious potential source of conflict between French Jews and Arabs: the Palestinian issue. The post-Algerian independence community is now split according to the transnational and global binary logic that confuses Israel with Jews and Arabs with Palestinians. Contemporary history acts as a site of discord and potentially explosive identifications, but the way in which Faucon constructs this split is worth noting. The separation into two camps seeps into the plot through television. The television set, in Halima's living room, is an object that installs borders between the two women by implicitly inviting them to take sides. At the same time, the film is obviously not interested in providing us with much information about the Israel-Lebanon conflict itself. Television images are selected to point out that both Israeli and Palestinian civilians find themselves in the position of victims who elicit empathy. When Esther watches the news with Halima and her husband and hears that Israeli civilians have been killed by rockets, she leaves the room, acknowledging the emergence of a space from which she feels alienated. She later calls her son to ask him to pick her up. She cannot stay in the house anymore she says, asking whether he has watched the news and telling him that civilians in Israel have died. The statement is matter of fact, and the relationship between her desire to flee and her report is not articulated. Any attempt to do so would force her to recognize that the link between her two hosts and the death of Israelis is a construction that demands very abstract and arbitrary narratives of identification between Jews and Israel, between Muslims and Palestinians.

The film is keen on symmetry in that area. Just as Esther is affected by television coverage of what is happening in Israel, Halima gets visibly upset when journalists cover the attack on Lebanon. But once again, her anger is motivated by the spectacle of victims. The film never constructs any dialogue about the causes of the war, the historical reasons that led to the conflict, and it does not try to take sides or to express an ethical or political opinion. Television functions as a transnational foreign voice that intrudes into the house and interrupts the ambiguous fusion between the two women. A simplistic narrative of a split international space is inserted into a neighborhood where interpersonal relationships are much more complex and subtle. The way in which the transnational map is drawn not only separates the women according to borders within non-French territories (Palestine and Israel are portrayed as mortal enemies) but also demands that they organize their identity according to this binary. They must take sides.

Moreover, the war contaminates other types of identitarian markers or rather pushes some to the top of the ideological pecking order. All of a sudden, Esther identifies with

Israel because she is Jewish and Halima insults the TV because she identifies as a Muslim and therefore as a Palestinian when children are killed. Earlier conversations between the two friends suggest that they are aware of the fact that anti-Semitism is increasing in the French *banlieue,* and at least one scene shows that Halima's daughter must put up with racist remarks. But television programs reorganize these local issues through a transnational logic that structures the global community around the Palestinian-Israeli issue.

Nevertheless, *Dans la vie* also shows that characters are capable of interpreting the news, of choosing their channel, of refusing to adopt the narrative imposed on them. When Esther leaves the room, obviously affected by what she has just seen, Halima asks her husband to switch to a different program. Later, when she talks to her daughter about what happened in Palestine, she suggests that she finds it difficult to deal with the presence of Esther in the house. Her daughter, refusing to confuse Esther with Israeli politics, immediately points out that Esther has never planted a bomb. The identification between Israel and their guest is a narrative that does not have to be accepted at face value. The film shows this back and forth between the risk of splitting and the careful and time-consuming negotiations involved in disallowing that powerfully simplistic narrative. Television discourse may exacerbate conflicts and erect borders, but it is not capable of destroying the small chaotic networks of solidarities that the characters construct, day after day, in spite of, perhaps thanks to, the constant challenges that they meet in the process.

When the film focuses on micro-practices and specific moments of negotiation between the characters, the illusion that they belong to monolithic communities that overdetermine their choices and opinions cannot be sustained. The fact that Esther is Jewish and Halima Muslim does not result in predictable lists of sameness or difference. A series of scenes revolving around food, religion, hospitality and solidarity suggests new ways of imagining what happens when different communities, but also individuals who belong to those communities, disagree about what constitutes the right way to cook, the right way to eat, but most importantly, the right way to interact with people whose cuisine is different. What happens when Halima tries to cook for Esther implicitly redefines what it means to belong to a community. The film proposes a new way of thinking about how to live together, regardless of what individuals have in common.

What the two women share or not becomes spectacularly obvious when their relationship changes as a result of Esther's son's departure. When he leaves Toulon for one month for professional reasons, Halima offers to take his mother into her own home, which immediately complicates what could have remained a purely professional relationship between the two women. Private sphere and workspace are fused, and the contract and friendship between the two women become subject to daily transactions, negotiations, and conflicts. Daily practices (such as cooking, watching television, talking to neighbors) either to conform or interrupt collective identities, forcing subjects to acknowledge at which point their religion, cultural habits, or ethnicity are relevant or irrelevant. The most important question is no longer: "how should I relate to my Jewish/Muslim neighbor?" but rather "how does my neighbor relate to the fact that she is Jewish or Muslim (and what does this mean to me)?"

When Halima first talks to her husband about the possibility of taking Esther into their home for a month, he is not enthusiastic. His objections have to do with propriety, religion, and food: "What are people going to say? That we are mad. She does not eat like us. She does not have the same religion. We have nothing in common." What he emphasizes here is difference and a lack of commonality. The word "people" does not refer to any specific community, and yet it is clear that the only opinion that matters is that of "people" like him, the people to whom he belongs, not because he is "with" them but because he is like them. He does not know what Esther eats. All he knows is that it is different from what he is used to. He does not explore the difference and does not compare. He does not suggest, for example, that he is bothered by certain rituals. The existence of a difference is enough for him to draw the conclusion that cohabitation is undesirable.

His position, however, is not articulated as an individual preference or a personal opinion: his argument is that Esther's presence would be considered a form of madness by his community. Imagined people, who are not in the room and not in the frame, are invoked as the reason why he would rather not welcome Esther. As a character who is supposed to have internalized his community's standards and pressures, he presents the viewer with a strong narrative about the implausibility of such forms of cohabitation in contemporary France. The film seems at first to suggest that when "Arabs" in general and this man in particular envisage sharing a flat with "Jews," the parameters that they will use have to do with food and religion. From this point of view, from within that frame, his conclusion is: "we have nothing in common." He articulates an unwritten rule, a norm. Cohabitation, it is implied, is unreasonable unless people have the same religion and eat the same food. Although the husband is never directly involved in the preparation of meals, it is clear that he has a sense of what is proper: *convivere*, literally the act of eating together, functions as an invisible border that separates individuals according to ethnic and religious categories.[7] At first sight then, those who fear the effect of *communautarianisme* could (mis)use this scene as evidence that the national fabric has been eroded and replaced by intolerant subgroups. Communities are sectarian and their members believe that it would be mad for people who do not eat the same food to live together.

Remarkably, however, this recognizable form of *communitaurianisme* is precisely not described as emanating from a whole community (Muslims in general), but as the site of a struggle between two Muslim characters or at least a disagreement between two members of that community. The husband articulates a sort of abstract rule that his wife refuses to treat as a norm or as a relevant parameter. To his "people who do not eat the same food would be mad to live together," she opposes a different type of logic that the film, as a whole, proposes as the solution to his separatism. She does not argue in favor of a more universal form of tolerance or acceptance of otherness, but for specific forms of solidarity that involve a desire to explore differences, though her efforts are no guarantee that she can avoid misunderstandings, let alone overcome them. The scene during which husband and wife formulate divergent views about the relationship between sociability, food, and religion takes place in Halima's house and around the dinner table. They share a meal, which seems to confirm the man's hypothesis: cohabitation is possible because they eat the same thing. But the images tell a different story, emphasizing both togetherness and separation, showing that each character defends a different definition of conviviality and sociability.

At first the two characters are together on the screen. They have everything in common: food, language (they speak Arabic), and religion. The others are those who are on the other side of those borders (Jews, who mostly speak French in the film and who eat kosher). This composition is soon fragmented in interesting ways, complicating the spectator's sense of who is included and who excluded, who is the same and who is different. When the camera focuses on Halima, she is already double: a mirror behind her lets us see her back as well as her face. The husband, on the other hand, is against a wooden panel that underscores if not his solitude, at least his self-containment as a subject. Later, when Esther moves in, he will also be filmed several times as isolated by the two women's complicity. He lies alone in bed while they talk in Esther's bedroom, and he knocks on the closed door and asks if they are going to talk all night.

The visual separation between Halima and her husband reproduces the theoretical gap that opens between their two positions. Halima insists on what the two women share (in the sense of "have in common"), proposing a new community that is gradually mapped for her husband and the viewer. "But you know she comes from Algeria, like us. Mesquina, who is going to take care of her?"

Not only does Halima refuse to accept her husband's narrative of difference, but she also contests the notion that solidarity should only be extended to those who are like us. Esther's religion and food play no part in her argument. The reasons that she invokes to justify why solidarity is mandatory have to do with her own religion and sense of morality, not Esther's identity: Islam, she says, promises heaven to those who help others. The type of abstract community of solidarity that Halima is trying to outline for her husband is not based on shared religion, language or nationality but on what should be his own definition of what is right: one should take care of older relatives, and your own religion (not the other's) dictates the way you relate to your neighbor. Why they should "take care" of Esther, according to Halima, does not have to do with having the same religion but with practicing religion, one's religion, seriously. She is not telling her husband that she wants to take care of Esther either because Esther is the same or because she is different, but because regardless of difference or similarity, she is a person in need that one must take care of.

That said, and the confusion is interesting, she also emphasizes similarities by mobilizing a discourse of kinship and a kind of twoness in one. The scene ends with her words: "*Elle et moi, on est comme des sœurs*" [She and I, we are like sisters]. She names the type of relationship that has formed in terms of a family bond and not in terms of nation (we never know whether they are both French or not), ethnicity, or religion.

The parameters that Halima uses to construct the two women as sisters in one family are, therefore, just as arbitrary as those that her husband chooses. His "we have nothing in common" could have been justified by a reference to recent colonial history. In the scene when her husband uses food as a way to separate Esther from "us," Halima simply refuses to take this parameter into account as what creates or disallows practices of solidarity. Food is not constructed as a border. That difference makes no difference.

Figure 6.1 We are sisters (Source: still *Dans la vie*, 2007)

Elsewhere in the film, the issue of how different subjects treat the connection between food and religion is precisely explored.

As a caretaker, Halima chooses to find out what kind of difference culinary difference makes. The way in which she learns is just as important as what she learns, and here the film didactically presents Halima's process of discovery as a possible model for any French viewer. When she tries to prepare a meal for her new patient, at first an awkward silence grows between the two "sisters." We watch Halima talking to a few other characters but not to Esther about her hesitations about what is kosher and what is not. This is not because Halima resents the fact that she has to prepare special food, but because she does not know how to cook kosher, and she is so embarrassed by her lack of knowledge that she does not dare ask. Her desire to know the other, then, is accompanied by a sort of discretion that complicates the learning process but ultimately proves fruitful.

When Halima asks a butcher if he can explain to her what exactly "she" can eat, he graciously obliges, explaining that all the meat he sells is kosher. The butcher then immediately switches to Arabic and asks Halima where she is from. He is both the Jewish native informant and he a member of the undefined postcolonial community Esther and Halima are slowly constructing. The butcher's "where are you from?" is not the aggressive question of a national who wishes to relegate the other to the margins, but the "where are you from" which already suspects that there is something in common, that the customer and the butcher are part of a "we" that transcends the categories of nation, of religion, and even of language. The butcher, it turns out, is from Tunisia and when he finds out that Halima is from Oran, the conversation becomes very familiar. He flirts with her, offering to marry her or at least to invite her and her family (but not her husband) on his next vacation. The anthropological quest (what does Esther eat as a

Jew?) is successful, and the network of relationalities that makes up Halima's world has gained one more member and identified another national territory as both relevant and irrelevant. The butcher has been in Toulon for twenty years, and, like Halima, he is from the Maghreb. Their language is a mixture of French and Arabic and their conversation is a mixture of jokes and exchange of information about religion, food, and visits to Algeria or Tunisia. If there is a community in this case, it is a community based on a micro-project: Halima's wish to prepare a meal that Esther can eat. Its members are Jews and Muslim, men and women, friends and strangers, and symbolic relatives.

Yet, Halima's careful attempts to discover Esther's religious practice without admitting to her that she does not know how to prepare her food does not end in a simple erasure of differences. After going through so much trouble to buy kosher meat (i.e. after the director has proposed a "lesson" to the uninformed viewer), Halima prepares the meat she got from the butcher. The only problem is that she adds goat cheese to her meatballs. Esther immediately points out that she cannot eat the dish. Once again, the scene takes place around a table, around food. Halima, in a sense, fails because she has not accumulated enough knowledge to prepare a proper meal for her Jewish sister, but her mistake is productive because it gives her the opportunity to ask questions and get more accurate information from Esther herself. She learns that in this case, there is no difference between milk and cheese and that mixing dairy products and meat renders the food improper. This last scene is an emblematic vignette of the whole film: differences exist, the two "sisters" are not identical, nor are they incompatible. Their attempt at bridging differences is not always successful and even when it is, it is imperfect and sometimes leads to conflicts and incidents. The key to their friendship is based not on previous knowledge and a shared origin but on the constant renegotiating of their own relationship to categories of religion and secularism, nationality and ethnicity.

Dans la vie insists that the two women are both capable of identifying with a sub-national community but also that they are not imprisoned by their origin and identity. Of course, their independence is never guaranteed, and the film is not an apology for the self-contained individualistic subject who constructs him or herself autonomously. Relationality, on the other hand, takes many different forms and is not a substitute for identity. Halima constantly tries to find out what it means for Esther to be Jewish. Her husband, on the other hand, invokes Esther's Jewishness as a given, even though he does not know what her Jewishness really means to her. The community of neighbors makes the same assumptions. Halima makes it clear to her family that she intends to use the money that she is earning while taking care of Esther to go to Mecca with her husband. Some of her relatives and neighbors claim that her pilgrimage will not be acceptable because it will have been paid for with Jewish money. They see Esther as an interchangeable Jewish subject, who represents Jewishness or even Israel.

Halima and Esther themselves are not free from such paradigms, and their friendship is endangered whenever they cannot find a way of disidentifying while identifying at the same time. Their relationship is described as a form of interdependency that requires the constant re-invention of practices and discourses of solidarity.

The vulnerability of their bond comes from the fact that the basis for their solidarity is based neither on commonality nor on the appreciation of difference but on a constant re-negotiation of how they define their values within and on the margin of a globalized contemporary France. The film does not shy away from the representation of very specific gendered, ethnic, or class constellations. And the way in which the film constructs such categories maintains interesting and dialectical tensions between, on the one hand, the representation of daily practices (idiosyncratic private behaviors and supposedly a-political individual preferences), and on the other, an extremely general global discourse that is relayed by international media. While a certain type of transnational global discourse imposes a problematic frame of reference where issues of universalism and particularism predominate, a contrapuntal perspective emphasizes practices of solidarity or moments of friction that provide us with another discourse on the link between individual and collective memory and history.

Halima and Esther's relationship demonstrates the possibility of building forms of solidarity that do not involve a choice between differences and similarities. Sometimes they celebrate differences; sometimes, they look for similarities. And the fact that neither similarities nor differences are, per se, chosen as the basis of a certain form of commonality implies that the two women, without ever talking about it, refuse to be caught in an alternative between universalism and particularism. The film suggests instead that it may be possible to wish for the development of forms of solidarity and communities based on interdependency rather than commonalities, however they are defined.

Notes

1   In a chapter entitled "Droit de Cité or Apartheid," Balibar suggests that colonial heritage is responsible for a process of "recolonization," which carves the space of strangers-insiders within Europe. They can be integrated only as fake citizens whose contractual relationship with the state they may never negotiate for themselves (Balibar, 2004, p. 40).

2   On the way in which banlieue-films and beur cinema have gradually moved away from the figure of the banlieue youth and focused on the role of the long silenced and despised father, see Hargreaves 2000. *Dans la vie* is one of the rare systematic representations of mothers.

3   The definition of what it means to be "French," to live in a French Republican regime, is changing rapidly: traditional French universalism, directly inherited from the Enlightenment, is interpreted by conservative voices as promoting a form of social cohesion that is endangered rather than enriched by intra-national cultural differences. That view is clearly challenged by a whole current of thought (see Balibar, 2004; Noiriel, 2007), of which *Dans la vie* is an example. From that perspective, if there are tensions between a certain idea of the Republic and the expression of (religious, linguistic or cultural) differences, the solution should not consist in erasing the latter. I use "Republican" to signal the existence of a debate and "republicanism" to refer to those forces within French society that tend to resist certain forms of multiculturalism in the name of Republican ideals.

4   *Français de souche* refers to French citizens whose origin is assumed to have coincided with the borders of the nation state, but the fuzzy formulation hides a euphemism: a "*Français de souche*" is expected to be of European origin, i.e. white.

5   Wieviorka describes Taguieff's position as follows: "According to him, we have now entered a 'new' era of Judeophobia, characterized by an 'inexpiable' hatred of Israel, an 'absolute,' 'demonising' form of anti-Zionism with overtones of negationism and a world view censuring the convergence 'of the new anti-neoliberal leftism and the warriors of the radical Islamist movements'" (Wieviorka, 2007, p. 66).

6 Translations by the author.
7 But convivere is also the beginning of a larger form of "conviviality" that has recently been explored by Paul Gilroy in his study of postcolonial London. Gilroy celebrates the kind of cross-community encounters that may develop thanks to music (Gilroy, 2004).

Bibliography

Balibar, E., 2004. *We, the People of Europe? Reflections on Transnational Citizenship*. Translated from French by J. Swenson. Princeton, NJ: Princeton University Press.

Balibar, E., 2007. Nos sociétés doivent faire ensemble leur histoire commune. Interview by M.A. Ouarabi. *El Watan*, [online] 2 December 2007. Available at: http://www.algeria-watch.org/fr/article/pol/france/balibar_visite_sarkozy.htm [accessed 1 June 2010].

Blanchard, P., Bancel, N., and Lemaire, S., 2005. *La Fracture coloniale*. Paris: La Découverte.

Blanchard, P. and Veyrat-Masson, I., 2008. *Les Guerres de mémoire: la France et son histoire*. Paris: La Découverte.

Cherki, A., 2008. Confiscation des mémoires et empêchement des identifications plurielles. In: C. Coquio, ed., 2008. *Retours du colonial: disculpation et réhabilitation de l'histoire coloniale*. Nantes: l'Atlante, pp. 176–85.

Derrida, J., 1998. *Monolingualism of the Other or the Prosthesis of Origin*. Translated from French by P. Mensah. Stanford, CA: University of Stanford Press.

Faucon, P., 2008. *Dans la vie, film de Philippe Faucon*. Interview by E. Benbassa. *Le Monde de L'Education*, [online] 29 February 2008. Available at: http://www.ldh-toulon.net/spip.php?article2558 [accessed 20 December 2010].

Gilroy, P., 2004. *After Empire: Melancholia or Convivial Culture?* London and New York: Routledge.

Graff, G., 1992. *Beyond the Culture Wars: How Teaching the Conflicts Can Revitalize American Education*. New York: Norton and Co.

Hargreaves, A. 2000. Resuscitating the Father: New Cinematic Representations of the Maghrebi Minority in France, *Sites*, 4(2), pp. 343–51.

Huffer, L., 2006. Derrida's nostalgeria. In: P.M.E. Lorcin, ed., 2006. *Algeria and France, 1800–2000: Identity, Memory, Nostalgia*. Syracuse, NY: Syracuse University Press, pp. 228–46.

Levine, A.J.M. 2008. Mapping Beur Cinema in the New Millennium. *Journal of Film and Video*, 60(3–4), pp. 41–59.

Noiriel, G., 2007. *A quoi sert l'identité nationale*. Marseille: Agone.

Schor, N., 2001. The Crisis of French Universalism, *Yale French Studies*, 100, pp. 43–64.

Stora, B., 2007. *La Guerre des mémoires: la France face à son passé colonial*, (entretiens avec Thierry Leclère). Paris: Aube.

Taguieff, P.A., 2002. *La nouvelle judéophobie*. Paris: Mille et Une Nuits.

Taguieff, P.A., 2005. *La République enlisée*. Paris: Edition des Syrtes.

Wieviorka, M. ed., 1996. *Une société fragmentée? Le multiculturalisme en débat*. Paris: La Découverte.

Wieviorka, M. 2005. *La Différence: identités culturelles: enjeux, débats et politiques*. La Tour-d'Aigues: L'Aube.

Wieviorka, M., 2007. *The Lure of Anti-Semitism: Hatred of Jews in Present Day France*. Translated from French by K. Couper Lobel and A. Declerc. Leiden: Brill.

Wieviorka, M. and Ohana, J. eds., 2001. *La Différence Culturelle. Une Reformulation des Débats*. Paris: Ballan.

Filmography

Caché, 2005. [film] Directed by M. Haneke. USA: Sony Pictures Classics.
Dans la vie, 2007. [film] Directed by P. Faucon. France: arte France Cinéma.
Indigènes, 2006. [film] Directed by R. Bouchareb. France: Tessalit Productions.
Samia, 2000. [film] Directed by P. Faucon. France: Canal+.

Chapter 7

The postcolonial condition of "Indochinese" cinema from Việt Nam, Cambodia, and Laos

Mariam B. Lam

When we speak of hybridized national cinemas in postcolonial "Indochina," we invoke multiple war histories and resonant tensions between a French colonial past, a recent American imperial present, and a global cultural capitalist future. Understanding cultural production in the contemporary period also requires a postcolonial refashioning of approaches centered upon older formulations of "national cinema" and "Third Cinema," both internally fraught movements always already in contestation with one another. Most film scholarship on postcolonial Southeast Asia privileges the history of the French colonial period of *L'union indochinoise* – the French-governed "Indochinese Union" of the three nation-states of Việt Nam, Cambodia, and Laos. Today, provocative cultural production is taking shape in both France and peninsular Southeast Asia. How do younger, often colonial educated *auteurs* negotiate the currents of anti-colonial politics and state policing tendencies using their formal colonial aesthetic training and calling upon diverse cultural influences? How do current post-socialist and neoliberal circumstances both constrain cinematic activity and propel it into international waters and onto distant shores? What kinds of theoretical and methodological approaches are needed for analyzing the postcolonial lives and aesthetic layers embedded in these productions?

By investigating the work of several recognized filmmakers, including Vietnamese French director Trần Anh Hùng (*The Scent of Green Papaya, Cyclo, Vertical Ray of the Sun, I Come with the Rain,* and *Norwegian Wood*), French-educated Khmer feature and documentary director and screenwriter Rithy Panh (*Rice People, Un soir après la guerre/ One Evening After the War, S-21: The Khmer Rouge Killing Machine, Un barrage contre le Pacifique/The Sea Wall*), and Lao director Anousone Sirisackda (*A Father's Heart, Sabaidee Luang Prabang!*), this chapter will call attention to the cultural, aesthetic, political, and economic pressures on each director's creative ventures.

This chapter's argument is a simple one; the multiply-layered colonial and imperial histories of these three nation-states and this particular region as a whole impose certain constraints on the post-Cold War re-development of these national film industries, while they also allow unique innovations. I do not here mean to ignore the related East Asian, Soviet, South Asian, and other Southeast Asian colonial influences upon this geopolitical space. Instead, I intentionally choose to focus attention on "French Indochina's" present *site* of postcolonial re-development in order to magnify the shift from European colonialism to American-style global cultural imperialism.

Cultural critic Ackbar Abbas' current work on "poor theory" thinks through the relations between dislocated spaces and cultural practices including cinema, contemporary art, music, performance, and theory itself:

> "Poor Theory" is not the rejection of theory for "direct action"; nor is it simply the use of theory in defense of the poor and under-privileged. It starts with a perception of the inadequation, even incommensurability, of theory to practice; but instead of lamenting the inadequation, it looks for ways of arbitraging the incommensurability. This is where "poor theory" speaks to the concerns of "Inter-Asian Connections." As recent economic and cultural developments have suggested, "Asia" today is the name for a space where "progressive" and "retrograde" are fused and confused, where "anachronisms" are the order of the day, where the margins are no longer safely located on the margins, but have migrated elsewhere: a space where the local and specific have become dislocated.[1]

From Abbas's perspective, the oppositional politics at the foundation of Third Cinema are rendered moot. In our current climate of diasporic cultural educations, tertiary migrations, and information technology, the oppositional is always negotiated and the national always corrupt.[2] By extension, older notions of national cinema no longer hold up in the face of contemporary production, distribution, and circulation models or global audience receptions.

Abbas' further identification of "Asia" as a polemically productive space (gesturing toward military-industrial-academic cartographies carved out for WWII and Cold War purposes) also allows me to play with a revisionist historiography of this relatively marginalized region of Asia to perform a kind of geo-intellectual "affirmative action," if you will.[3] Asian postcolonial and cultural studies critics, including Kuan-Hsing Chen, Naoki Sakai, and Gayatri Gopinath, have in recent years considered regionalism as a possible alternative conceptual framing of anti-imperialist strategies.[4] Similarly, Walter Mignolo's older notion of "Latinidad" as it applies to the "idea of Latin America" as a now pervasive force pushing across the world and beyond area studies allows me to explore regional specificities and their simultaneous global resonances and implications (Mignolo, 1991 and 2000).

The late Martiniquan writer, scholar and critic Édouard Glissant flexed his regionalist notion of *antillanité* (i.e. shared Antillean and Caribbean creole histories and identities) in order to link it not only to African slave histories and European colonizers, but also to Indian and Chinese indentured servitude, indigenous groups within the Caribbean and across Latin America and North America, and plantation cultures in the American south (Glissant, 1997, 1999, and 2010). Glissant and other adherents of the *créolité* movement stressed the rejection of French postcolonial centrality by exploring the interconnections of subaltern histories and diverse spatialities and place-makings, and by questioning the linear historiographies of origins and languages. Glissant concluded with configurations of "composite cultures" that de-center any core-periphery positionalities by shifting emphasis away from the victors of colonial history and onto "the Other America," which includes shared subaltern colonial histories and territories.

Donald Pease has more recently proposed Glissant's work on "Other Americas" as a corrective to American exceptionalism (Pease, 2009). By combining these East/West *and* North/South regionalized anticolonial or postcolonial approaches, I perform what Édouard Glissant conjures up with his notion of "other Americas," diversely situating the proliferation of global south struggles within and across one Asian region.[5]

Peninsular Southeast Asia presents an ideal instance of Glissant's point. In the French literary and filmic canons, "Indochina," "Annam," and "Vietnam" are all terms for a *tabula rasa* on which to project a cultural imaginary of France's colonial capabilities, complexities, and complaints. In *Phantasmatic Indochina: French Colonial Ideology in Architecture, Film, and Literature*, Panivong Norindr (1997) examines "Indochina" as a geopolitically colonized space of French imperialism, which also served as a mythical, fictive, and imaginary, or "phantasmatic" construction of Southeast Asia. Norindr provides a useful starting point from which to highlight the "colonization of the mind" or cultural imagination that has taken place from the first half of the twentieth century to today in modern French aesthetic and cultural productions. I take these to include literature, adventure writing, travel narrative, anthropology, historiography, journalism, cinema, and other media.

Nicola Cooper's work extends Norindr's argument by examining the *mise-en-valeur* of cultural colonization in Indochina itself (2001). Cooper's contextualization of immigrant politics in France after the Second Indochina War allows me to recast certain interpretations of Vietnamese French auteur Trần Anh Hùng's cinematic works:

> By investing in these stereotypes, playing the part and adopting the persona desired and required by France, populations of Vietnamese origin have thus reinvented a strategy through which they may avoid excessive visibility, persecution and racism. A rejuvenated French paternalism, reminiscent of the nation's colonial attitude to indigenous Vietnamese, thus sets the terms for migrant inclusion to the ranks of France's bons immigrés. Continued submission is required.
>
> (Cooper, 2001, p. 293)

To achieve "Frenchness à venir," or a Frenchness to come, is to work toward mastery of French cultural codes and "to relate vertically to an ideal image of the French nation, not to find common ground with other immigrants who have embarked on this process of "becoming-French" (Lionnet and Shih, 2005, p. 2). Trần Anh Hùng's early Vietnamese films target both French and Vietnamese mainstream audiences, two dominant national cultures within which he is minoritized (as an immigrant and as a diasporic subject, respectively). He chooses select forms of subaltern representational visibility in relation to two nationalist receptions, rather than recognizing shared political aesthetic strategies between his work and that of other "minor transnationalisms," or other diasporic Indochinese filmic representations.

In the film *The Scent of Green Papaya*, Trần repeats the "model minoritization" of young Vietnamese women, deploying his own wife, actress Trần Nữ Yên Khê, to do so throughout his Việt Nam trilogy (*The Scent of Green Papaya*, 1993; *Cyclo*, 1995; and *Vertical Ray of the Sun*, 2000). In the first, an inquisitive peasant servant girl struggles within an upper-class Vietnamese family at the height of French colonial Indochina to become the new traditional Vietnamese-yet-modernizing Western wife, Mùi. Playing up what I will call the *annamité* of Asian *bons immigrés*, or benign diasporic model minorities within France's own national borders in order to differentiate them from France's malignant racialization of African, Caribbean, and Maghrebi immigrants, Trần Anh Hùng's films are set in Việt Nam but do not overtly address French colonialism. Trần's characters are good "annamités," or *les Annamités*. They appease traditional Vietnamese nationalist and contemporary postsocialist Vietnamese desires for a globally projected revitalized Vietnamese charm, at the same time that they satisfy mainstream French curiosity about its colonial subjects and novel compatriots. This epistemologically exploitative representational tactic is, in turn, projected by a postcolonial immigrant subject, Vietnamese French film director Trần, onto a socially weak caricature of Vietnamese femininity, the Mùi character.

In the years immediately leading up to Trần's emergence, both Régis Wargnier's 1991 film *Indochine* and Jean-Jacques Annaud's 1992 film *The Lover* – in which colonial historical, racial, and gender politics are mere plot devices compelling the romance plots between colonizer and colonized – meet with international box office success. These productions do not necessarily take French colonialism as central. Colonial practices and machinery function only as historical backdrop. In *The Scent of Green Papaya*, one likewise hears curfew sirens in the distance and the passing airplane from time to time as a reminder of the French colonial presence during a contentious political historical period. The gambling addicted Vietnamese patriarch sports a western-styled white suit, the hero is a colonial educated and classically trained pianist, and Mùi is infatuated with her discovery of rouge lipstick.

Within the repertoire of French cultural production, "Indochina" as subject and object, as form and content, has come to be associated with the inclusion of beautiful colonial dress, tropical locations, exoticized thespians, and colonial nostalgia. Trần's work is hailed as representative of the "new wave" in Vietnamese French stylistics, now free from the confines of depressing socialist realist Vietnamese war narratives and propagandistic military plots dominated by the U.S.'s imperial experience in Việt Nam. In the same way that experimental filmmakers are deemed *avant-garde*, *la francophonie*, or postcolonial Francophone production is also lauded as "avant-garde," because it appears to be addressing relevant contemporary social contexts with its treatment of subaltern cultural forms while employing "western" aesthetics and stylistic devices.

Does the French filmschool-trained, diasporic Vietnamese Trần Anh Hùng strategically negotiate these persistent colonial cultural influences, or does he just deploy them for mainstream French, mainstream Vietnamese, and global commercial "independent film" approbation? By comparison, Martin McLoone (2006, p. 10) has argued that Irish cinema is actually an "*arrière-garde* cinema." He argues that:

> a younger generation of small- and medium-budget films addressing the socio-economic developments that constitute the "Irish national"– including urbanization and consumerism, co-exists, today, with "first cinema" productions

that continue to reinscribe the myth of romantic rural Ireland, also sold as commodity kitsch.

For Francophone Vietnamese who choose to portray themselves on screen, each scene is a recollection of the traumatic colonial past whether or not French colonialism is depicted on screen. As Frantz Fanon has described the schizophrenia engendered by "blackness," these cultural producers also must be "doubly conscious" of their own desired self-representation and their imposed ethnic and racial identification through the "black veil" of a projected French colonial imaginary (DuBois, 1903). Such a "double consciousness" does not always lead to minority inferiority complexes as Fanon cautioned; they can lead instead to the more inclusive global perspective of postcolonial, multicultural, and transnational cultural political tactics.

Rather than treating these works as fashionable *avant-garde* aesthetic practice, I combine the cinematic oeuvres of Trần Anh Hùng, Rithy Panh, and Anousone Sirisackda under what I call l'*annamité*, or a convergence of filmmakers and other cultural producers who recognize the essentialization of Asian *bons immigrés* and reappropriate this essentialist reception strategically for their own personal political and professional advantage. In doing so, they reinvigorate the development of a Southeast Asian regional cultural alignment with Glissant's earlier notion of *la créolité*.

The limitation of the provocative theoretical work of both Norindr and Cooper lies in their filtering of works such as those of Trần primarily through the lens of French (post)coloniality without simultaneously recognizing the pressures of (post)coloniality in Việt Nam, Cambodia, and Laos that weigh on these postcolonial filmmakers.[6] It is not insignificant that Trần Anh Hùng's *The Scent of Green Papaya* and *Vertical Ray of the Sun* are the only two diasporic Vietnamese films that made their analytical way into the first book of Vietnamese film criticism published in English by the leading state film critic in Việt Nam, Ngô Phương Lan. Indeed, not even Trần Anh Hùng's film *Cyclo*, which was not released in Việt Nam due to political censorship concerns on both sides, made it into Ngô Phương Lan's *Modernity and Nationality in Vietnamese Cinema* (2007). The book's discussions of Vietnamese national cinema abide by familiar binary oppositions between tradition and modernity in socialist realist and post-renovation policy (Đổi Mới) films. The text includes brief interpretations of nearly a dozen films in the socialist realist vein, with nearly all filmmakers based in Hà Nội. After the end of the Vietnam War in 1975 and since the beginnings of film criticism in Việt Nam, the southern Vietnamese film industry has been popularly and academically dismissed as commercial by northern trained filmmakers and critics. It is only within recent years that foreign and diasporic film critics have focused any attention on the hotbed of film production taking place in Hồ Chí Minh City, or Sài Gòn, and Nha Trang. While the film industry itself is finding restored life in southern spaces and throughout the diaspora, a higher educational and aesthetic value is attributed to northern *auteurs*, as Hà Nội has continued to assert its post-1975 seat of power.

In their introduction to *Theorizing National Cinema*, Valentina Vitali and Paul Willemen, insist that it is important to distinguish cinema as both "an industry and as a cluster of cultural strategies" (2006, p. 2). Their work will be important throughout my argument as they consistently pinpoint the continued complications of international political economic shifts that weigh upon specific national cinema aesthetics. Trần's choice to de-politicize the French colonial and Vietnam War histories throughout his Việt Nam film trilogy served his greater desires to continue working and shooting in "the homeland," and to participate in Việt Nam's national cinematic re-development. Contemporary diasporic Vietnamese filmmakers from the U.S. and Australia, with films focusing on boat refugees fleeing the socialist state or those with the war as backdrop, have not done as well critically in Việt Nam.[7] These other thematic foci impede superficial transnational and international cultural reconciliations with their reminders of the state's own war atrocities. Trần has made a return on his strategic investments as the first diasporic Vietnamese *auteur* to break back into the Vietnamese film industry.

Trần's ability to break back in was due in part to his international box office success with *The Scent of Green Papaya*, as well as his relatively apolitical aesthetics and the quality of French technological production. He was invited several times to Hà Nội as a visiting instructor at the national Vietnamese film program funded in large part by the Ford Foundation. Trần's mentoring of now leading younger Vietnamese filmmakers Bùi Thạc Chuyên (*Night Run*, 2000; *Living in Fear*, 2005; and *Adrift*, 2009) and Phan Đăng Di (*Lotus*, 2005; *When I Am 20*, 2008; screenwriter for *Adrift*, 2009; and *Bi, Don't be Afraid*, 2010) secured his position as transnational friend to the postwar re-development of the Vietnamese film industry. He was instrumental in bringing the Vietnamese directors to the attention of Venice and Cannes Film Festival curators, as well as in putting them on the networking path of international festival circuits more generally. Việt Nam, like France, accepts its national(ist) subjects and friends selectively.

One friend in particular, the Ford Foundation, has, in fact, taken a major role in the development of the Vietnamese film industry, which now has a short film program as of 2003 run by TPD/VGA and headed by Bùi Thạc Chuyên. It also has an educational exchange program with the University of Southern California implemented in 2004, a short film library also established by TPD/VGA in 2005, a film studies program implemented by TPD/VGA in 2004, a film studies program at the University of Social Sciences and Humanities as of 2005, and a documentary cinema program in direction offered by Ateliers Varan as of 2004. These programs are all located in Hà Nội. From 2006–2009, the curricula and development were expanded as a result of further investments in the domestic industry by Ford, USC, TPD, Varan, AMPAS and others.[8] I raise Ford's heavy investment to foreshadow Priya Jaikumar's caution found in this collection's "Postface" of the dangers of allowing Western foundations and visual archives (the British Film Institute) to control a nation's filmic tradition (India).

Meanwhile, following Trần Anh Hùng's acceptance into the French mainstream art house film circuit and subsequently into the contemporary Vietnamese cinematic canon, Trần has focused his attention on conquering more mainstream audiences with the "neo-noir" psychological thriller *I Come with the Rain* (2009), starring international celebrities Josh Hartnett, Byung-hun Lee, Takuya Kimura and Shawn Yue, with action scenes set in Los Angeles, Mindanao-The Philippines, and Hong Kong. Most recently, he chose to adapt a 1987 novel by popular Japanese author Haruki Murakami, *Norwegian Wood* (2010), inspired by the Beatles song of the same name and starring a well-known

Japanese cast including Kenichi Matsuyama and Rinko Kikuchi, nominated for the Best Supporting Actress Oscar for her role in *Babel* (2006). I cite Trần's cinematic trajectory above, because historically film scholars:

> recounted the birth and growth of an industry that proliferated, radiating outwards from the heartlands of capital – a thrust forward, from "advanced" societies such as Western Europe and the United States to the periphery as an exemplary trajectory of modernization sweeping across the world. In this context, the film industry was metonym for the industrialization of culture and a metaphor for modernity itself, while the universal character of film language, presumed in spite of the striking diversity between different national film industries, helped to give cultural legitimacy to the economic dominance of some cinemas globally.
>
> (Vitalli and Willemen, 2006, p. 2)

This is the same political economic model of cultural imperialist cinematic expansion explicated by media scholars of globalization such as Toby Miller *et al.* in *Global Hollywood* (2001, 2008). However, here in the case of Trần Anh Hùng, we find an example of a subaltern cultural producer, however "corrupted," negotiating transnational and multivalent postcolonial pressures and impediments – manipulating them, in fact, in the service of his own global cultural aesthetic and commercial pursuits.[9]

From Trần Anh Hùng's deployment of de-politicized colonial nostalgia and family drama in the Vietnamese context, I move now to another French-trained filmmaker, Cambodian documentary and narrative feature film director Rithy Panh. The Khmer filmic portrayals of violence, retribution, and madness in Panh's *oeuvre* give me the opportunity to excavate the subaltern subjects in Cambodian postcolonial cinematic history through the lens of a more politically and historically engaged *auteur* of *l'annamité*.

Rithy Panh was born in 1964 in Phnom Penh, Cambodia. Imprisoned by the Khmer Rouge in 1975, he escaped in 1979 by fleeing to the Mairut refugee camp in Thailand, and then to Paris, where he studied at L'Institut des Hautes Études Cinématographiques. Panh's first narrative feature film *Les gens de la rizière/Rice People* (1994) was adapted from the 1966 novel *Ranjau Sepanjang Jalan/No Harvest But a Thorn* by Malaysian author Shahnon Ahmad. The film is set and filmed, not in Malaysia, but in the Cambodian village of Kamreang, in the Kien Svay and Boeung Thom areas of Kandal Province that lie on the banks of the Mekong River near Phnom Penh. It tells the story of a rural family in post-Khmer Rouge Cambodia as they struggle to bring in their rice crop. The film won critical acclaim at Cannes, the Toronto International Film Festival, and the Academy Awards, and put both Panh and Cambodia on the proverbial map.

Panh has explained in interviews that his grandparents were peasants and that his father was the first in the family to migrate to the city, though he took his children to visit the ancestral rural areas once a year. Panh remembered his grandparents and their neighbors as generous and sincere people and often wondered how some of those villagers came to be part of the lower ranking Khmer Rouge. He was already interested in re-piecing together this genocidal history as an "art objective" by exploring the people's

Figure 7.1 Crazed Om in her rice fields at the conclusion of the film (Source: still *Les Gens de la Rizière*, 1994)

memories of that time. However, having left Cambodia in 1979 as a stateless refugee, he could not return, so began to work on the stories of the refugees at Site 2 (Mairut) in Thailand.[10] There he met a woman named Yim Om who told him often of the "soul of the land" and of their "pregnant rice" with such a "poetic, ecological sense" and an imaginative sensitivity that she inspired Panh to make this film about life and death, about the gestures of nature and its precariousness, and about its incompatibilities with notions like private property (Panh, 1994).

The film follows a rice farming family made up of a father, mother, and seven daughters (deemed socially useless except for the eldest daughter, who is betrothed, and one of the younger daughters, who is able to attend school intermittently and is the only literate member of the entire family). Poeuv, the father dies slowly from an infected thorn wedged in his foot while plowing in the fields. They cannot afford proper medical care provided only in the distant city. Om, his wife, and the seven daughters must struggle to work the land and protect it from flooding, crabs, sparrows, and much more. Om cannot reconcile her own weakened gendered positionality in relation to the other village families and is gradually transformed into a madwoman in the attic. By the end of the film, widowed matriarch Om, played by veteran Khmer actress, Peng Phan, stares off into the distance and darkness of the night from the domestic cage in which she is imprisoned for her own sanity, and pleads, "I worked and I worked. I plowed with all my strength. I sowed, I replanted, I harvested. But it's all the same, I don't see anything. Where's my rice? Where's my rice?"

Some of the harvest has been paid to the city sanitarium to pay for Om's health care costs, some to pay off debts to the village families, some to the local chiefs, some presumably to the Khmer Rouge for allowing them to remain on their land, and some as dowry to the oldest daughter's betrothed. Panh masterfully weaves this tale of labor, loss, and madness as economically driven and socially enforced, without losing any of the rice farmers' humanity and dignity. Vitali and Willemen remind us that, "The functioning of cinema as an industry and a cultural practice in any of these territories is overdetermined by the institutions of the state – from censorship through to taxation and real estate policies – but the economic forces sustaining any given film do not necessarily mobilize the available narrative stock in the directions preferred by the state" (2006, p. 7).

It is perhaps for these reasons that Rithy Panh chose the Khmer Rouge's Tuol Sleng prison, referred to as S-21, as the site of *S-21: The Khmer Rouge Killing Machine* (2003), which reunites former prisoners (including the artist Vann Nath), and their former captors for a chilling and confrontational visual explication of Cambodia's violent history. This is not a history the state of Cambodia wants to remember; this film is not a tool of nationalist or global cultural reconciliation. In one exchange between ex-Rouge prison guard chief, Houy and ex-prisoner Nath, Houy recounts:

> We made up an activity of sabotage; we invented the evidence in order to execute a prisoner. There was no court to judge him. When the document was finished, he was taken to his death ... Each man has his own memory, each his own history. The aim was to break down their entire memory and make an act of treason out of it ... Today when I think about it, it was against the law. I'm ashamed of myself. But I don't think about it. When I think about that, I get a headache. So when someone comes to get me to go out to eat and drink, I get drunk, come home, go to sleep.
> (*S-21: The Khmer Rouge Killing Machine*, 2003)

Vann Nath responds,

> For me it's not like that. For me, each of our meetings is very painful. I don't really want to come to these meetings, because we're not here to tell pleasant stories. We only talk about this unbearable past, which we can't escape. I can't, anyway. I'm trying to understand what happened, to make sense of it. I want to understand it. We meet like this, but that doesn't mean it's a chance to cleanse ourselves of evil.
> (*S-21: The Khmer Rouge Killing Machine*, 2003)

History is not simply memorialized and covered over by new state developmental initiatives.

The S-21 Tuol Sleng prison is today a Genocide Museum and a global tourist attraction for the state. At the same time, international political action campaigns and non-governmental organizations are demanding legislation from United Nations tribunals to seek reparations for the vanquished and punishment and political justice against the perpetrators. Rithy Panh has said of this campaign,

> Passing judgment on the Khmer Rouge is essential. It means asserting the will of a state of law. No one can commit a genocide and get away with it. But justice is only

one stage in the process. The trial must be accompanied by an effort of memory to protect future generations.

He admits that his "way of carrying out [his] share of the work of remembrance is by talking and by providing a platform for the witnesses of the genocide, both victims and torturers" (Panh, 2003). My preference for Panh's more historically and politically engaged professional trajectory over Trân's more localized cinematic interventions moves us toward the goals of my larger theoretical project. Before making his most recent and most mainstream narrative film, *Un barrage contre le Pacifique/The Sea Wall* (2008), Panh released two more documentaries, a docudrama, *The Burnt Theatre/Les Artistes du Théâtre Brûlé* (2005), about the dilapidated state of Cambodia's former national theatre, and *Le papier ne peut pas envelopper la braise/Paper Cannot Wrap Up Embers* (2007) about prostitution, featured in Biarritz and Paris and winning awards in Shanghai.

Rithy Panh's adaptation of Marguerite Duras's 1950 novel, *The Sea Wall*, was a French, Cambodian, and Belgian co-production, starring Isabelle Huppert. It is set in French colonial Cambodia in 1931. A widow and her two children, Joseph (20) and Suzanne (16), eke out a settler colonial existence exploiting rice fields located close to the ocean's edge. Each year their crops are flooded, and their only hope of success lies in the construction of a seawall. The mother refuses to give up, battling corrupt colonial bureaucrats as well as the sea.

Panh says in his director's statement for the 2008 Toronto International Film Festival "beyond time and cultural differences" he feels a "particular and mysterious connection" with "Marguerite Duras' eye, a very typical oriental compassion, beyond the usual judgments and simplifications, an almost 'inner' outlook about my country and people, an eye that doesn't judge, an eye that says, 'We are all alike.'"[11] Panh explains his interest in the novel further in an extended interview:

> First of all, it's a novel I like immensely and which I kept under my pillow for years. I was attracted to the ideas present in the novel: the colonial theme, the sense of utopia, and how they worked together ... Generosity is not just about giving but it's also about not taking what is not yours ... My first contact with Marguerite Duras was through her screenplay for Alain Resnais' *Hiroshima Mon Amour*. Having just emerged myself from genocide, Alain Resnais' work on *Night and Fog* and *Hiroshima Mon Amour* really moved me. Resnais was the filmmaker who made me realize that filmmaking is a tool of expression I could use to express my own story ... First the two topics of the utopianism and the anti-colonialism ... Duras is one of the first novelists to have a clear anti-colonialist position. It's no coincidence that on a political level she is very close to the Communist party. But I have to be clear that I've experienced Communist regimes and they weren't that great. Oftentimes people confuse Communism with utopianism ... As for Michel Fessler, the co-writer ..., I hired him because he had lived in Africa when he was a child and I was intrigued that he had spent some time in the colonies. More correctly, they were no longer colonies but had been the French colonies. At the beginning I didn't want

him to write anything. I wanted him to accompany me on a trip to Cambodia to visit the scouted locations. I wanted him to listen to the sounds of Cambodia, the voices of the Cambodians, to discover the story of the people of *that* country. It was only after he went through that initiatory phase that we began the writing. (italics mine)

Panh continues that the film was "less about idyllic landscapes or love stories so I could emphasize the political side of Duras ... It's so important to hold onto that dream of solidarity, of sharing, of access to knowledge."

I cite the long interview passage above to highlight Panh's sense of a larger global network of postcolonial interconnectedness from Africa, France, and Cambodia. He intentionally creates a filmic family of shared postcolonial resonances, even casting professional and non-professional actors and actresses based on their own personal historical narrative accounts. He has asserted:

We don't realize it but in this era of amazing technologies many people nowadays don't have the rights to access images, not even the rights to create images themselves from their own histories. For filmmakers like me it's not only about making the movie, it's that each film you make is like a form of resistance. It's saying, "I am presenting to you my point of view of history." How many African films have you seen in Toronto this year? (Interviewer responds, "none.") But it's not only the Toronto International Film Festival. It's the whole system of how movies are made. The system is unfair. Commensurably, in the previous century it was the most-developed countries that mastered the reading of written works. In the century we live in now, the richest countries control every aspect of sound and image communication. The smaller countries are condemned to disappear in the digital flow. If there are no movies, festivals obviously can't show them. It's that the distributors don't want them. The producers don't want them. The television stations don't want them.

(Panh, 2008)

Practicing what he preaches, Panh created Bophana, an audio-visual resource center, in Phnom Penh, Cambodia. The center's namesake is the subject of one of his early docudramas, *Bophana: A Cambodian Tragedy*, about a young woman who was tortured and killed at S-21 prison. The center gathers images and sounds from all over the world and makes these resources accessible to all Cambodians. The center's staff provides professional training for young directors and film technicians. He realized that there was a need to make audio-visual memories available to Cambodians. The Bophana Center has been so successful that the center programmers decided to collaborate with, and give technological training to, the landlocked West African country of Burkina Faso. Panh comments with pride:

It's one of the first South-South collaborations. We're trying to share what we know in terms of image-making. After that we would like to do the same thing with Senegal, with Lebanon, or Rwanda. We're trying to create a network. What we want to claim is the right of access to images. We have the right to have access to memory. We're not asking for commercial rights – the rightholders can keep them – but, just the right to have access. In Cambodia we don't have the means of accessing our own images. For an African, it's easier to watch films from Brazilian television on Teleglobo than African films. If a people do not have the means of fabricating the sounds and images of their own history, they are doomed to disappear.

It is difficult to compare the personal political cinematic stakes and trajectories of Trần Anh Hùng and Rithy Panh without some level of judgment. However, oversimplifying the differences between their approaches to building up a local film culture may miss the larger point that:

> all too often the emphasis on the major-resistant mode of cultural practices denies the complex and multiple forms of cultural expressions of minorities and diasporic peoples and hides their micropractices of transnationality in their multiple, paradoxical, or even irreverent relations with the economic transnationalism of contemporary empires.
>
> (Lionnet and Shih, 2005, p.7)

But Ella Shohat and Robert Stam caution that,

> while the media can fashion spectators into atomized customers or self-entertaining monads, they can also construct identity and alternative affiliations ... Just as the media can exoticize and otherize cultures, they can also reflect and help catalyze multicultural affiliations and transnational identifications.
>
> (2003, p. 1)

While Panh's catalyzing nationalist filmic developmental work in Cambodia was intentional, Trần's initial role as a self-producing and self-entertaining monad is transformed by the Ford Foundation and transnational politics into an arbiter of Vietnamese film industry development. Tensions between local networks and international dynamics continually apply different pressures on postcolonial cultural producers.

To elaborate, unlike the more developed Southeast Asian nations (e.g. Singapore, Thailand), Việt Nam, Cambodia and Laos have been unusually slow to embody a collective regionalist disposition relative to ASEAN (the regional economic body that is the Association of South East Asian Nations) economic development and world cinematic circuits. The fissures and disjunctions created by French colonial lineages and the secret war by the U.S. against Cambodia and Laos have left these three nation-states at different stages in their current global economic dealings. Each country is therefore in a unique position with regard to its cultural arts and educational development. The three do, however, share in the same travel and tourism market goals. While tourism and cultural tourism may be only one of many economic investments making up Việt

Nam's gross national product (approximately US$244 billion in 2009), it stands as one of the biggest incomes for The People's Democratic Republic of Laos (approximately US$14 billion GNP in 2009).

As a whole, Laos has perhaps been the slowest in realizing its own national filmic aspirations, precisely as a result of its postcolonial and post-Cold War devastations. It has taken the coming of age of the postwar generation to bring about any resurgence of major cinematic activity in the metropoles of Vientiane and Luang Prabang. For a brief foray into the nascent Lao film industry, I focus on the work of Anousone Sirisackda, director of *A Father's Heart* (2007) and co-director of *Sabaidee, Luang Prabang/Good Morning, Luang Prabang* (2008). *A Father's Heart* was commissioned by international non-governmental organizations trying to stop the spread of the "bird flu" epidemic in Laos. It is a touching portrayal of the relationship between a father and daughter who raise chickens and of how they, along with their livestock-farming neighbors, must contend with such a massive blow to their livelihoods. Eighteen short YouTube clips comprise the film in its entirety and are available for free public access online.[12]

The Lao blockbuster, *Sabaidee, Luang Prabang!*, was the first Lao film with funding from the Lao government in the postwar period. In it, Anousone Sirisackda strategically placed shots of magnificent temples and ruins, song and dance by ethnic minority hill tribes, local wedding culture and line-dancing, making merit at temples, Laos Airlines, and lush landscapes and seascapes of Sri Pan Don, Pakse, and Vientiane throughout the film to give the film a touristic dimension. These scenes that encourage foreign visitors are what secure Anousone Sirisackda's state funding and coproduction. At the beautiful waterfalls along the Mekong River, we learn from our heroine guide that the French tried to destroy them because they impeded their colonial shipping lines. Some cross-cultural education takes place between the two protagonists when they arrive late for their return boat trip. She insists the boat's absence is their own fault and that the honest shipman will return, while her Lao-Aussie companion tells her she should not have paid the captain ahead of time because he now has no reason to come back for

Figure 7.2 At Tad Pha Suam Waterfalls in Pakse, Champasak Province, Mekong River, known as a hot spot for tourism in coffee, tea and ethnic minorities (Source: stills *Sabaidee, Luang Prabang*, 2008)

Figure 7.3 Main characters at Pha That Luang Temple in Vientiane (Source: still *Sabaidee, Luang Prabang*, 2008)

them. The boatman returns the next morning for the couple; the hero and the audience are both impressed by the honesty and conscientiousness of such a quaint people. In another scene, the heroine's girlfriend warns her that relationships with Western men do not last, while her precocious younger sister encourages the romance, leaving viewers to imagine their own possible international romance plots. The viewer also finds occasional scrolling of the warning, "Smoking and alcohol are bad for your health and other people's health," each time a scene includes cigarettes or beer, reminding the viewer that censorship and policing are still prevalent in this charming national culture that deserves much more exploration by foreign tourists and scholars alike.

Following the success of *Good Morning, Luang Prabang!*, the Thai co-director of *Good Morning, Luang Prabang!*, Sakchai Deenan, made a second film that forms a prequel of sorts to the Lao film, called *From Pakse with Love* (2010 – also known as *Sabaidee 2*).[13] The plot follows an actor/writer trying to sell his old-style art house screenplays to Thai film production companies. They decline, preferring newer topics. One of the man's previous funders rants, "Art house directors fail, get drunk, start again, not funders ... can you eat art? You cannot eat art." Nevertheless, after a long, windy, wide-angle journey to an ex producer's son's friend's wedding, which takes the protagonists through what appears to be the exact same terrain traversed in the first *Sabaidee,* the audience learns that this is a semi-biographical portrayal of the director's first visit to Laos, which convinced him to make the first *Sabaidee* and to work toward developing the local Lao film industry. We learn that Lao Anousone Sirisackda and Thai Sakchai Deenan, together with Lao-Aussie heartthrob Ananda Everingham and rising Lao starlet Khamly Philavong, combined forces and enlisted both the tourism industry and the Lao government in the production of *Good Morning, Luang Prabang*, again the first government-sponsored film since the war.

With the widespread Thai and Lao national and Asian regional popularity of these two films, the Lao film industry re-emerges as a tourism-driven cultural venture for The People's Democratic Republic of Laos. Anousone Sirisackda is now the President of Lao

Art Media based in Vientiane. Both directors continue to criss-cross the Thai-Lao border for film production ventures. Southeast Asian cinema bloggers have begun to include Laos in their postings. The first Vientianale International Film Festival took place in 2009, the first Luang Prabang Film Festival was founded the following year in 2010, and the United Nations in Lao PDR backed the "Rising Star" competition at the second Vientianale International Film Festival held from April 21–24, 2011 in Vientiane. The Rising Star competition for those aged sixteen years and under and took the theme, "We are the Future," called for submissions of two-minute films that must be shot on mobile phone cameras. The festival as a whole is supported by the Department of Cinema of the Ministry of Information and Culture, which would have been nearly unimaginable only two years earlier, and it is a free event that aims to entertain and educate audiences about the potential richness and diversity of Lao film culture by presenting feature films, documentaries, films for children, music videos, and short films.

These Laos filmmakers, their collaborators, and the Lao state itself, have learned the benefits and effects of Asian regional tourism from neighboring countries, from throughout upwardly mobile Southeast Asia, from wealthier East Asian middle class tour groups (Korean and Chinese, in particular), and from the West, all curious about the quaint, serene, and less developed developing countries. Vitali and Willemen (2006, p. 8) read Phil Rosen's notion of cinematic "textuality" as one that includes unifying mechanisms among the diverse strategies at work in any given text at the same time that it stands before the "inevitable impulse for semiotic dispersion":

> By projecting onto a geo-political configuration this understanding of textuality as a push and pull towards and against unity, Rosen can read "nationality" as "an inter-textual symptom," in the process allowing for the diversity of trajectories that necessarily must be at work in any given cinema or group of films if they are to be understood as an adjunct to the longer-term construction of national subjectivities.

Tourism is not only a stylistic theme and plot driver in these two Lao films. The production process, as well as the aesthetically and economically-driven contents of these two films, allow me to re-cast the notion of cinematic "intertextuality" as one that is not only metaphorical or figurative in its content, but one that is also deeply compelled by a political economic intertextual referential field composed of diverse commercial industries and nationalist developmental rhetorics. These Southeast Asian peninsular films and filmmakers are drawing upon and cross-referencing one another's economic developmental models and governmental initiatives, one another's celebrity cross-over market potentials, the land and aerial borders that connect them all to one another by inexpensive regional airlines and tourist vanpool corporations, and major East/West collaborations and North/South co-productions. Together they signal the emergent body of *l'annamité* cinema I have attempted to delineate.

The strategies laid out throughout this chapter, the genealogy of theoretical models sketched at the outset of this essay, and my own interpretative deployment of these re-processed postcolonial *annamité auteurs'* personal professional political trajectories, all combined, enact an academic and cultural industrial performance of "minor transnationalism" (Lionnet and Shih, 2005) or "methodological cubism" and "the deployment of multiple perspectives and grids" (Shohat and Stam, 2003, p. 2). I conclude with another simple assertion: the study of postcolonial cinemas today can only be undertaken earnestly with interdisciplinary and inter-theoretical (e.g. diasporic, transnational, critical areas studies and ethnic studies) approaches.

Notes

1 Keynote address by Ackbar Abbas, 2010. "'Poor Theory' and Asian Cultural Practices," International Conference on "Inter-Asian Connections II: Singapore." National University of Singapore, December 10, 2010.
2 See Stuart Hall's explanation of encoding and decoding, dominant readings, oppositional readings, and negotiated readings that make up interpretative models of representation (1973).
3 Lieve Spaas's 2000 book, *The Francophone Film: A Struggle for Identity*, covers seventeen different French colonial countries with no single mention of any Southeast Asian nation or Indochina.
4 See for example, Kuan-Hsing Chen, 2000.
5 I thank Tanya Rawal, whose University of California, Riverside – Comparative Literature dissertation on global southern spaces across India, Italy, and the American South inspired me to imagine a different theoretical trajectory for my second monograph project.
6 For diasporic subjects, they must negotiate postcolonial conditions in both "the metropole" and "the homeland." For scholarship that explores such transnational interstices, see Grossman and O'Brien (2007), Tolentino (2001), and Robson and Yee (2005).
7 Consider Vietnamese American Hàm Trần (*Journey from the Fall*, 2006) or Vietnamese Australian Khoa Đỗ (*Mother Fish*, 2010).
8 The information was made available in Michael DiGregorio's 2011 research paper presentation on his directorial role and the role of the Ford Foundation in the building of the Vietnamese national film educational curriculum and programming in Việt Nam at the annual Association for Asian Studies and joint conference of the International Convention of Asian Scholars (AAS-ICAS). Convention Center, Honolulu, HI, April 2. For more thorough descriptions of the complex and conflicted history of Vietnamese cinema, see my other articles, Lam, 2011a and Lam 2011b. The latter includes an extended history of the Ford Foundation's investment in Vietnamese cinema development.
9 One might be reminded of Soyoung Kim's work on South Korean 'cine-mania,' which centers on "the blockbuster, export-oriented strategies and the accompanying erasure of Korean women's voices as the film industry negotiates its modernisation in the context of a suffocating variant of nationalism in tension with the pressures of American globalisation."
10 Rithy Panh's documentary, *Site 2*, was released in 1989, five years before *Rice People*.
11 From Rithy Panh's Director's Statement, 2008, Thirty-third Toronto International Film Festival in an interview with Michael Guillén at the weblog, The Evening Class: http://theeveningclass.blogspot.com/2008/09/tiff08-un-barrage-contre-le-pacifique.html, posted September 21, 2008; accessed October 13, 2010. Panh went so far as to shoot the film on the actual plots of land that Duras' mother had purchased ...

> I really wanted to go to the actual historical place and from there go on with the fiction, much the way Marguerite Duras writes in her novels ... in fact, Madame Donnadieu's project was not such a utopia because nowadays in that actual field that she was trying to exploit, generations later the production in that rice field has doubled, tripled, over the rest of the neighboring fields.

12 Anousone Sirisackda's film *A Father's Heart*, 2007, is available for screening at Blogbaker weblog: http://www.activeboard.com/forum.spark?aBID=98894&p=3&topicID=14110181, posted November 4, 2007; accessed October 15, 2010.

13 I extend my gratitude to Kannikar Sartraproong for her simultaneous translations of both films.

Bibliography

Abbas, A., 2010. Keynote Address, 'Poor Theory' and Asian Cultural Practices. *International Conference on "Inter-Asian Connections II: Singapore."* National University of Singapore, December 10.

Chen, K.H., 2000. *Asia as Method: Toward Deimperialization*. Durham, NC: Duke University Press.

Cooper, N., 2001. *France in Indochina: Colonial Encounters*. Oxford: Berg Publishers.

DiGregorio, M., 2011. Research paper presentation on his directorial role and the role of the Ford Foundation in the building of the Vietnamese national film educational curriculum and programming in Việt Nam. *Annual Conference of the Association for Asian Studies and Joint Conference of the International Convention of Asian Scholars (AAS-ICAS)*. Convention Center, Honolulu, HI, April 2.

DuBois, W.E.B., 1996. *The Souls of Black Folk* (originally published in 1903). New York: Penguin Classics.

Glissant, É., 1997. *Poetics of Relation*. Ann Arbor: University of Michigan Press.

Glissant, É., 1999. *Caribbean Discourses: Selected Essays*. Charlottesville: University of Virginia Press.

Glissant, É., 2010. *Poetic Intention*. Beacon, NY: Nightboat Books/UPNE.

Grossman, A. and O'Brien, Á. eds., 2007. *Projecting Migration: Transcultural Documentary Practice*. London: Wallflower Press.

Hall, S., 1973. *Encoding and Decoding in the Television Discourse*. Birmingham: Centre for Contemporary Cultural Studies.

Kim, S., 1998. '*Cine-Mania*' or Cinephilia: Film Festivals and the Identity Question. *UTS Review: Cultural Studies and New Writing* 4(2), pp. 174–87.

Kim, S., 2006. From *cine-mania* to blockbusters and trans- cinema: reflections on recent South Korean cinema. In: V. Vitali and P. Willemen, eds. 2006. *Theorising National Cinema*. UK: British Film Institute, pp. 186–201.

Lam, M.B., 2011a. "Circumventing Channels: Indie Filmmaking in Post-Socialist Việt Nam and Beyond. In: M. Ingawanij and B. McKay, eds. Forthcoming 2011. *Independent Cinemas in Contemporary Southeast Asia*. New York: Cornell University Press,.

Lam, M.B., 2011b. Việt Nam's Growing Pains: Cultural Education and Transnational Politics. In: S. Laderman and E. Martini, eds. *Vietnam and "Vietnam" Since 1975: Transnational Legacies of the Second Indochina War*. Durham, NC: Duke University Press, pp. 1–19.

Lionnet, F. and Shih, S. eds., 2005. *Minor Transnationalism*. Durham, NC: Duke University Press.

Mignolo, W.D., 1991. *The Idea of Latin America*. London: Wiley-Blackwell.

Mignolo, W.D., 2000. *Local Histories/Global Designs: Coloniality, Subaltern Knowledges and Border Thinking*. Princeton, NJ: Princeton University Press.

Miller, T. 2001. *Global Hollywood*. London: British Film Institute

Miller, T., Govil, N., McMurria, J., Maxwell, R. and Wang, T. eds., 2008. *Global Hollywood 2*. London: BFI.

McLoone, M., 2006. National Cinema in Ireland. In: V. Vitali and P. Willemen, eds. 2006. *Theorising National Cinema*. UK: British Film Institute, pp. 88–99.

Ngô, P.L., 2007. *Modernity and Nationality in Vietnamese Cinema*. Yogyakarta, Indonesia: NAFF, JETPAC and GalangPress.

Norindr, P., 1997. *Phantasmatic Indochina: French Colonial Ideology in Architecture, Film, and Literature*. Durham, NC: Duke University Press.

Panh, Rithy, 1994. Interview. *Les gens de la rizière* [DVD], Distributed from Chicago: Facets Video.

Panh, Rithy, 2008. Director's Statement, Thirty-third Toronto International Film Festival. Interviewed by M. Guillén *The Evening Class* [online] 21 September 2008. Available at: http://theeveningclass.blogspot.com/2008/09/tiff08-un-barrage-contre-le-pacifique.html, [accessed 13 October 2010].

Pease, D.E., 2009. *The New American Exceptionalism*. Minneapolis: University of Minnesota Press.

Robson, K. and Yee, J. eds., 2005. *France and Indochina: Cultural Representations*. New York: Lexington Books.

Shohat, E. and Stam, R., eds., 2003. *Multiculturalism, Postcoloniality, and Transnational Media*. New Brunswick: Rutgers University Press.

Spaas, L., 2000. *The Francophone Film: A Struggle for Identity*. Manchester: Manchester University Press.

Tolentino, R.B., 2001. *National/Transnational: Subject Formation and Media In and On the Philippines*. Manila, PI: Ateneo de Manila UP.

Vitali, V. and Willemen, P. eds., 2006. *Theorising National Cinema*. UK: British Film Institute.

Filmography

A Father's Heart, 2007. [Film] Directed by A. Sirisackda. Thailand/Laos: UNICEF, Lao Media, Nahico, Japan.

Adrift/Chơi vơi, 2009. [Film] Directed by Bùi T.Ch. Vietnam/France: Vietnam Feature Film Studios and Acrobates Films.

Babel, 2006. [Film] Directed by A.G. Iñárritu. France/USA/Mexico: Paramount Pictures.

Bi, Don't be Afraid/Bi, đừng sợ, 2010. [Film] Directed by Phan Đ.D. Vietnam/France/Germany: Acrobates Film, arte France Cinéma, Sudest-Dongnam.

Cyclo/ Xích Lô, 1995. [Film] Directed by Trần A.H. Vietnam/France/HongKong: Canal+, Centre National de la Cinématographie (CNC), Cofimage 5.

From Pakse with Love (also known as *Sabaidee 2*), 2010. [DVD] Directed by S. Deenan. Thailand/Laos: BMG.

Hiroshima Mon Amour, 1959. [Film] Directed by A. Resnais. France/Japan: Argos Films, Como Films, Daiei Studios.

I Come with the Rain, 2009. [Film] Directed by Trần A.H. France/HK/Ireland/Spain/UK: Central Films, Lumière International, TF1 International.

Indochine/L'Indochine, 1991. [Film] Directed by R. Wargnier. France: Paradis Films, La Générale d'Imags, Bac Films.

Journey from the Fall/Vượt Sóng, 2006. [Film] Directed by H. Trần. USA: A Fire in the Lake, Old Photo Films.

Let the Boat Break its Back, Let the Junk Break Open/Que la barque se brise, que la jonque s'entrouvre, 2001. [TV Program] French Television, 2001.

Living in Fear/Sống trong sợ hãi, 2005. [Film] Directed by Bùi T.Ch. Vietnam: Vietnam Feature Film Studios.

Lotus/Sen, 2005. [Short Film] Directed by Phan Đ.D. Vietnam: Hanoi Academy of Film and Theatre.

Mother Fish/Cá mẹ, 2010. [Film] Directed by K. Đỗ. Australia: Imaginefly.

Night and Fog, 1955. [Film] Directed by A. Resnais. France: Argos Films.

Night Run/Cuốc xe đêm, 2000. [Short Film] Directed by Bùi T.Ch. Vietnam: Hanoi Academy of Film and Theatre.

Norwegian Wood, 2010. [Film] Directed by Trần A.H. Japan: Asmik Ace Entertainment, Fuji Television Network, Toho Company.

One Evening After the War/Un soir après la guerre, 1998. [Film] Directed by R. Panh. France/Cambodia: Compagnie Méditerranéenne de Cinéma, JBA Production, La Sept Cinéma.

Paper Cannot Wrap Up Embers/Le papier ne peut pas envelopper la braise, 2007. [Film] Directed by R. Panh. France: Catherine Dussart Productions (CDP), Institut National de l'Audiovisuel (INA), France 3 (FR 3).

Rice People/Neak Sre/Les gens de la rizière, 1994. [Film] Directed by R. Panh. Cambodia/France/Switzerland/Germany: JBA, La Sept Cinéma, Thelma Film AG.

S-21: The Khmer Rouge Killing Machine/S-21, la machine de mort Khmère rouge, 2003. [Film] Directed by R. Panh. Cambodia/France: Institut National de l'Audiovisuel (INA), arte France Cinéma.

Sabaidee Luang Prabang!/ Good Morning, Luang Prabang, 2008. [Film] Directed by A. Sirisackda and S.Deenan. Thailand/Laos: Lao Art Media and Spata.

The Burnt Theatre/Les Artistes du Théâtre Brûlé, 2005. [Film] Directed by R. Panh. Cambodia/France: Catherine Dussart Productions (CDP), arte France Cinéma.

The Land of the Wandering Souls/La terre des âmes errantes, 2000. [Film] Directed by R. Panh. France: Institut National de l'Audiovisuel (INA), La Sept-Arte.

The Lover/L'amant, 1992. [Film] Directed by J.J. Annaud. France/UK/Vietnam: Films A2, Giai Phong Film Studio, Renn Productions.

The People of Angkor/Les Gens d'Ankor, 2003. [Film] Directed by R. Panh. France: Institut National de l'Audiovisuel (INA).

The Scent of Green Papaya/ Mùi đu đủ xanh, 1993. [Film] Directed by Trần A.H. France/Vietnam: Lazennec Films, SFP Cinema, La, La Sept Cinéma.

The Sea Wall/Un barrage contre le Pacifique, 2008. [Film] Directed by R. Panh. France/Cambodia/Belgium: Catherine Dussart Productions (CDP), Studio 37, France 2 Cinéma.

Vertical Ray of the Sun/Mùa hè chiều thẳng đứng, 2000, [Film] Directed by Trần A.H. Vietnam/France/Germany: Canal+, Hang Phim Truyen, Lazennec Films.

When I Am 20/Khi tôi 20, 2008. [Short Film] Directed by Phan Đ.D. Vietnam: Hanoi Academy of Film and Theatre.

Part III

Postcolonial cinemas
Postcolonial aesthetics

> Without relations of difference, no representation could occur. But what is then
> constituted within representation is always open to being deferred, staggered, serialized.
> (Stuart Hall, 1996, p. 215)

As noted by Stuart Hall, representations are never the mirror of society but a contested
space open to infinite deferral, repetition, and reappraisal. In order to operate in so
many dimensions and on so many levels, postcolonial cinema has engaged profoundly
with the conventions and resources of film language. The essays in this section discuss
the highly original strategies that filmmakers have deployed in their projections of the
multiple temporalities and spatialities of the postcolonial imaginary. Paolo de Medeiros
notes the shipwrecks, journals, unburied bodies, and ruins that figure the simultaneity
of past and present in the three Lusophone films he discusses in his chapter. These films
share concerns with how a damaged present, upon which the future must be built,
might relate to the remains of past violence. This is a visionary cinema, he argues, that
looks toward the open sea, rather than to armed conflict, as a source of identity and
community in the wake of the disaster that the nation-state has turned out to be. These
films are ghost stories in which characters can merge with one another or disappear
without a trace. Plots take other unconventional turns that exemplify the difference
between the exclusionary linear narratives of nation and empire and the inclusive,
porous narrativity of postcolonial historiography. The remarkable imagery of these
films signifies symbolically and allegorically rather than consolidating any one version
of "reality" – most surprisingly perhaps in the instance of *Angola, saudades de quem te
ama* (Pakleppa, 2005), which is a documentary!

Sabine Doran discusses Raul Ruiz's postcolonial aesthetics as a "tactile turn," which
subverts the dominance of vision in knowledge systems of the West. The use of touch
rather than vision to interpret experience creates different relationalities, weaving
networks of connection rather than isolating moments of identification or antagonism.
A postcolonial manifesto could be composed around what Doran calls Ruiz's "aesthetics
of intrusion," whereby margins, peripheries, and frames resist the hegemonizing imperial
gaze both aesthetically and politically. In her analysis of Ruiz's *Three Crowns of the Sailor*
(1983), which, like the Lusophone films Medeiros discusses, is an allegorical ghost

story, Doran shows how the film's framing weaves foreground and background together, avoiding any "central conflict" and creating instead a nonexclusionary, nomadic network of relation. The film is thereby able to bring the earliest trajectories of Viking expansion and depredation into proximity with such seemingly disjunct pheneomena as slavery, prostitution, European imperialism, South American military dictatorships, and the Cold War.

In her chapter focusing on Italian director Maurizio Nichetti's historical fantasy *Luna e l'altra* (1996), Marguerite Waller finds the film an imaginative response to both the relative absence of reflection on the fascist Italian colonial era in post-war Italy and the rise of neofascist agendas in the 1990s. Like Hamish Ford and Sabine Doran, she discovers a redirection of the gaze from the composition of images within frames to the frames themselves and to the spaces that can be opened up between frames. The film increasingly interweaves the aesthetics of the ephemeral, nomadic circus with the tired forms of entertainment and education associated with state and commercial media and formal schooling. Allegorically satirizing Italy's right wing secessionist Northern League and neofascist political parties, Silvio Berlusconi's media monopoly, and the colonial exploitation of both Southern Italians and Africans, Nichetti's film, Waller argues, proposes a postcolonial imaginary that thoroughly metamorphoses both our understanding of the film image and national paradigms of community, gender, history, citizenship, selfhood, and most of all "the real."

Concluding this section, Sandra Ponzanesi links the aesthetics of postcolonial cinema with questions of intermedial translation and adaptation. This involves not only reflecting upon the role of the culture industry on the appropriation and commercialization of "postcolonial literature" for cinematic audiences, but also on the postcolonial aesthetics that emerges in the interaction between text and film. In this act of translation and transposition the postcolonial message can become diluted, defused, or lost, or it may be accentuated, emphasized, even created. The latter happens in Gurinder Chadha's transposition of Jane Austin's classic *Pride and Prejudice* (1813) into the postcolonially inflected *Bride and Prejudice* (2004). The successful translation of the postcolonial dimension from the semiotic realm of literature into the visual and sensorial coding of cinema may also occur. A perfect symbiosis, Ponzanesi argues, is found in Shirin Neshat's *Women Without Men*, an adaptation of the novel by the same name written by Shahrnush Parsipur. The magical realism of the novel is transposed into a film of stunningly poetic force, making the two art forms resonate with each other in a respectful and complementary way, realizing a postcolonial feminist intervention in different media that together reach a wider audience.

Bibliography

Hall, S., 1996. Cultural Identity and Cinematic Representations. In: H. A. Baker, M. Diawara, R. H. Lindeborg, eds. 1996. *Black British Cultural Studies: A Reader*. Chicago: The University of Chicago Press, pp. 210–20.

Chapter 8

Spectral postcoloniality

Lusophone postcolonial film and the imaginary of the nation

Paulo de Medeiros

Le schème de l'État-nation s'est ainsi multiplié dans le monde. Il n'en est résulté que des désastres.

(Glissant and Chamoiseau, 2009, p. 3)

Lusophone postcolonial film has been credited as being "a small but vital contribution to the extant history of sub-Saharan and world cinema" (Andrade-Watkins, 1995, p. 194). Yet it remains one of the least studied cinemas in general, something that has much to do with the conditions of civil war in Angola and Mozambique, with the lack of a strong tradition of Portuguese colonial film, and with the relative strangeness of the language and historical context, at least in comparison to, say, French postcolonial cinema. The brief, historicizing essay by Claire Andrade-Watkins, originally published in 1995, remains the basic starting point for anyone interested in Lusophone postcolonial film, just as the scattered comments one finds throughout Nwachukwu Frank Ukadike's *Black African Cinema* (1994) have not lost any of their original significance.[1] Without any pretensions either to historical coverage, or to updating those studies, my focus in this essay is what I call postcolonial spectrality in four very recent Lusophone postcolonial films: *O testamento do senhor Napumoceno/Testamento*, directed by Francisco Manso, (1997), focused on Cape Verde; *A costa dos murmúrios/The Murmuring Coast*, directed by Margarida Cardoso (2004) focused on the end of the colonial war in Mozambique; *Angola, saudades de quem te ama/Angola, Saudades from the One who Loves You*, directed by Richard Pakleppa (2005) covering post-civil war reality in Angola; and *Sleepwalking Land* directed by Teresa Prata (2007), focused on the civil war in Mozambique. These four films present postcoloniality as foremost a form of spectrality. A comparative analysis of the four makes clearer how important issues revolving around specters and other ruins are and how these relate to the respective national imaginaries. I include not only productions focused on the two nations that endured civil war immediately after the struggle for independence, but also one film dealing with a former Portuguese colony, Cape Verde, that traditionally placed itself in-between Europe and Africa, and one film directed primarily at Portugal. These films avoid any easy co-optation by nationalist projects and preclude the fallacious opposition between metropolis and colony.

Even as Lusophone postcolonial films are very much concerned with reflecting on their respective national communities, they can and should be seen also as transnational, as they are always co-productions drawing on a number of African and European resources. Thus, *Angola, saudades de quem te ama* was funded by a consortium that included South African and Dutch institutions; *Sleepwalking Land* drew on German and other Northern European as well as Portuguese resources. *A costa dos murmúrios* was co-produced with the German ZDF/ARTE and *Testamento* (as the DVD is titled) relied on Cape Verdean, Portuguese, French, and Belgian resources. Furthermore, their directors or the cast, are all in a sense also transnational, reflecting the realities of both colonial and postcolonial dislocations.

By comparing the representations of spectral postcoloniality in these four films, I do not intend to subsume them, or the nations they represent and construct, under one heading. The postcolonial realities of Portugal and its former colonies are far more complex than that, just as the films themselves have many other important elements that I must leave out of this discussion. Nonetheless, all four emphasize certain elements that not only problematize, but seriously question the concept of nation along postcolonial lines. One might be tempted to view them as "accented" in the sense suggested by Hamid Naficy (2001), and indeed all of the filmmakers under consideration could be regarded as exilic and transnational: Francisco Manso is a Portuguese director but *Testamento* was shot in Cape Verde: its cast comes from Cape Verde, Brazil, and Portugal; the film is a co-production of Cape Verde, Portugal, Brazil, France, and Belgium; and the fact that it is available at all is due in great part to its USA distributor. Margarida Cardoso is Portuguese but grew up in Mozambique and Teresa Prata, also Portuguese, grew up in both Mozambique and Brazil. Richard Pakleppa is not Angolan but Namibian and works in South Africa. Nonetheless, there are also significant differences between these films and the ones studied by Naficy. None of these four films engages, or is concerned with, exile even though they are all very much concerned with questions of dislocation and the possibility or impossibility of community building. Likewise, in all four films the notion of the nation, however important, has to be understood from a transnational perspective and within the framework of postcoloniality. In a sense too, they are forceful, ghostly, and haunting illustrations of what Glissant and Chamoiseau refer to as the general production of disaster out of the concept of the nation-state (2009).

There is no romanticization of the national in any of these films: *A costa dos murmúrios* reveals openly the fissures between Portugal and Africa as much as it shows the impossibility of thinking Portugal without also thinking of its relation to Africa. *O Testamento do senhor Napumoceno*, for its part, also lays open Cape Verde's in-between role as well as its Atlantic reach to the United States, one of the several destinations for Cape Verdean emigrants. And even if both *Sleepwalking Land* and *Angola, saudades de quem te ama* appear much more centered on their respective countries, the first keeps pointing to the sea, the Indian Ocean, as a way out and as a source of identity, and the latter shows how Angola has become firmly entangled on global, neo-colonial, market conditions.

War and memory

Saying that war is a common denominator for Lusophone postcolonial film might simply be stating the obvious, and yet it is an inescapable feature that cannot be ignored. Three of the African nations that were colonized by Portugal – Angola, Mozambique, and Guinea-Bissau – had to undergo grueling colonial wars that lasted over a decade, and after independence both Angola and Mozambique were devastated by almost uninterrupted civil wars lasting even longer. Indeed, although Angola and Mozambique became independent in 1975, it is only since 1992 that peace has returned to Mozambique, and in the case of Angola, only since 2002. Guinea-Bissau also had civil war, in 1998 and 1999, but obviously on a different temporal scale. Cape Verde, however, even if it knew the political repression of the *Estado Novo* – the Portuguese dictatorship that lasted from 1928 to 1974 – was never directly involved in armed struggle. That, I think, also explains why *Testamento* in some ways is a very different film from the other three under analysis. War is not a concern in *Testamento*, and even the change of government and the achievement of independence seems to be secondary as the film emphasizes much more a sort of continuum between colonial structures and those that followed it that have much more to do with class structure and patriarchal rule than with ideological issues. But in the other three films, war assumes center stage even when it has ceased. *Testamento* encompasses both the time before independence and the period immediately following it; *A costa dos murmúrios* revolves around the colonial war in Mozambique and especially as it was nearing its end in 1973; the action in *Sleepwalking Land* all takes place in Mozambique as well while the civil war was raging (1977–1992); and *Angola, saudades de quem te ama* focuses on the period almost immediately after the end of civil war in Angola (2002), as the film was started in 2003. War can be said to constitute an inescapable and haunting condition for the films' reflection on national identity, and one of the key elements that constitute the spectral postcoloniality the films enact.

Colonial hauntings

One could look at spectrality as having simply to do with ghosts and indeed, several of the films do relate, if not directly to ghosts, at least to the voices of the dead: *Testamento* is based on the reading of a will, and *Sleepwalking Land* is largely based on the reading of the found letters of a dead man. But the ghosts that matter are not, or not just, those. Rather, what is at stake is the conceptualization of a form of postcoloniality that is haunted, by colonialism of course, but also by the irruption into the present of those forces from the past that condition the possibilities for any future development of the polities in question, be it the new African nations or the old colonizing one. As is well known, Jacques Derrida's exploration of the concepts of the specter and of hauntology (1994) revolved to a great extent around the figure of Marx and of Marxism as an ideology, just as it also provided an exemplary reading of *Hamlet*. But it should not be forgotten that at the beginning of his reflections Derrida places the name of Chris Hani, the leader of the South African Communist Party, murdered in 1993, already invoking a connection with the problematics of colonialism and postcolonialism. Much of Derrida's argument can, indeed should, be transposed to a consideration of postcoloniality and its representations. In a sense, that is what Pheng Cheah does in his extensive elaboration of Derrida's hauntology for an understanding of postcolonial nations in Southeast Asia (1999). My views of Lusophone postcolonial film are inflected both by Derrida's concepts and by their further elaboration by Cheah and others, who specifically link them with questions of sovereignty, nationalism, and postcolonialism. One specific issue that I would like to highlight is the problematic relationship between postcoloniality and images of the nation, an issue that is already to some extent adumbrated in Derrida's own views, but that has become ever more pressing as globalization intensifies.[2]

Nation and violence

Sleepwalking Land exemplifies the conflict between postcoloniality and any idea of the nation, perhaps because of the fact that its plot line falls within the time frame of the civil war in Mozambique. Even though the narrative strategy of the film, based on the homonymous novel by Mia Couto (1992, 2006), is complex, its plot can be simply summarized: a young orphan boy, Muidinga (Nick Lauro Teresa) and an old man, Tuahir (Aladino Jasse) are fleeing from a refugee camp and come across a just burned bus, with charred bodies still sitting inside, that they decide to use as their home. Next to the bus, lying on the grass, they find the body of a man and a suitcase containing his notebooks. The two try to find their way to the sea and yet keep walking in circles so that they always return to the bus. The boy reads in the notebooks that the dead man had been looking for a boy to return him to his mother. The boy who is reading identifies completely with the missing boy which makes the old man angry. As the film develops the two stories do indeed merge and Muidinga becomes Gaspar, the boy the dead man, Kindzu (Hélio Fumo) had been searching for. Driven by despair at not finding a road that would lead them to the sea the young boy starts digging by the bus and water spurts out, quickly forming a large river that takes the bus with it to the sea.

Even though war dominates all action in the film, viewers get only two scenes directly involving the actions of the armed gangs responsible for much of the destruction. The first shows youths who clearly take a sadistic delight in the rape and murder of the bus occupants, making clear the liberties of the violence. The second, a story in Kindzu's notebooks, shows a group of men in some kind of uniform raiding one of the refugee camps to round up all the young boys they find and force them to join them. As Unicef reports, Renamo, the main opponent of the ruling Frelimo, had at least 10,000 child soldiers, "some as young as six years old" (Unicef, 1996).[3] It is important to note that not only is war never romanticized, it is shown to be devoid of any purpose beyond the random exercise of violence against others. There is no sense of any heroic struggle to build a community. Indeed, representations of community are limited to defenseless refugee camps. It is perhaps not surprising that the two main characters, Muidinga and Tuahir, want to escape into the sea. The image of the nation presented by the film is bitterly marked by the past – the boy continually seeks to find answers to his questions about what happened before –and its projection into the future renounces any traditional notion of territory, embracing a much larger utopian space, that of the Indian Ocean, as the only source of community.

The focus on the Indian Ocean has to be understood in terms of the colonial past in which Goa – the remnant of Portugal's ambitions in India – was always as much, or even more, significant for Mozambique than the European metropolis. But it also signals a shift away from the more obvious colonial and neo-colonial interests of Portugal. Indeed, one of the significant aspects of the imagination of the nation in this as well as in the other films, with the obvious exception of *A costa dos murmúrios*, is how transnational and relational it is beyond any attachment to the former colonizing metropolis. In *Angola, saudades de quem te ama*, it is China that appears as global link and in the case of *Testamento*, the United States of America. Any links in that film to Portugal are either mildly nostalgic, such as the Christmas foods imported before independence, or phantasmatic, such as the references to Portuguese literature. And in *Angola, saudades de quem te ama*, the few references to the former colonial power are either the ruins of the colonial buildings or a park with statues. None of the films can be seen as national allegories even if they do have moments, scenes, and even characters that function as such. The distinction is important, not so much because of the failings of a concept such as national allegory, at least as formulated by Fredric Jameson (1986),[4] but because of its possible importance to our understanding of how cultural production in general, and Lusophone postcolonial film in particular, negotiate a negative, or even bankrupt, ideological construct. This is as much an issue for Portugal as it is for the new independent states because both the restoration of democratic rule in Portugal in 1974 and the immediate decolonization can be said to have their roots in the exhaustion brought on by over a decade of colonial wars, and the final toppling of the fascist regime

Figure 8.1 Napumocemo and Adélia walk by a shipwreck (Source: still *Testamento*, 1997)

with its teleology of the nation as specially chosen civilizational agent. After 1974, Portugal had to reinvent itself as a European nation, even if it was to be spared the devastation of the civil wars that took over Angola and Mozambique.

Shipwreck and hauntology

One of the most recognizable and haunting images of these films is the shipwreck. Always already linked to the imperial and colonial enterprise, the shipwreck, either literally or in one of its iterations as ruin, also functions symptomatically as a figure for a spectral postcoloniality and as a form of national allegory. In *Testamento*, one of the crucial scenes – and a way in which the film goes beyond the novel by the same title (Almeida, 1991, 2004) – takes place in front of the wreck of a ship that has been stranded. It is in front of it that we see the love blossom between Mr. Napumoceno and Adélia – a young woman who appears as suddenly as she disappears from his life. It is a doomed, impossible, and crazy love affair between the old man and the young woman but one which is cast precisely in terms of a national allegory to which the abandoned ship serves as necessary background. The film and the novel's plot unfold via the reading of Napumoceno's testament. Set in a time frame before and just after independence, the plot allows one to follow the development of Napumoceno from a poor, uneducated boy to a successful businessman with a fascination for the United States and some mild political ambitions.

In *Sleepwalking Land* the burned bus that becomes a temporary home to Muidinga and Tuahir is a wreck that becomes a sort of ship as it floats and is carried by the river waters towards the ocean. In a sense it is like the toy Muidinga pushes in front of him

Figure 8.2 Muidinga and Tuahir have reached the Indian Ocean in the burnt-out bus. (Source: still *Sleepwalking Land*, 2007)

most of the time, a sort of sailboat on wheels made out of debris. This could be seen perhaps as a poor substitute for real shipwrecks, but it is no more phantasmatic as the boats left half-sunk around the diverse ports of the former Portuguese colonies. Furthermore, once it reaches the Ocean it passes by a real wreck, that of an abandoned cargo ship. A woman is living on board, having decided never to return to the land where she was first raped and then terrorized by her own community after she gave birth to a mulatto child, whom she is forced to abandon. She is the mother of the boy Kinzdu searches for, and, in Muidinga's imagination, becomes his own mother. The ship is ironically and symbolically named *Moby Dick*, a name the boy, Muidinga, seems impossibly to remember when he (mis)names a young goat he finds *Mody Dick* (sic). And one should not forget the "ghost" trains Tuhair "sees" because he used to work at a train station. There is no melancholic nostalgia associated with such memories as they are rather used to signal that positive elements of the past that have been obliterated by war, such as regular work and modern travel, will return once the war is over. Not quite a figure, even symbolic, of a shipwreck, those imaginary trains are certainly as spectral as the burned bus, the toy, and the abandoned freighter.

A costa dos murmúrios depends on the figure of the shipwreck as a memory of imperialism. Floating bottles of methyl alcohol drift ashore and are mistakenly drunk by many Africans who then die. Like them the corpse of the young Portuguese soldier – the husband of Evita, the main character and narrator – also drifts to shore and is dimly seen on the beach towards the conclusion of the film. But, significantly, the film never shows any actual shipwrecks since its action unfolds during the last years of the colonial war in Mozambique. The narrative structure of the film, based on an acclaimed novel by Lídia Jorge of the same title (1988), is highly complex, involving a recollection by Eva of what she had experienced as a young woman (Evita), newly-married to her student companion, who was drafted to serve in the Portuguese army to fight in Mozambique.[5] The film, like the novel, stages a problematization of traditional history through memory that sharply criticizes and deconstructs official narratives of the nation and relates the events of the colonial war, specifically as experienced by women, in present-day Portugal, decades after the return to democracy and decolonization. As much a working out of the individual and collective trauma of the war, as a bitter and biting critique of simple imaginations of the nation, the novel was one of the first to allow for any form of public discussion – however limited – of the colonial war. The film, by Margarida Cardoso, not only renewed those concerns, and extended discussion to a much larger circle of people beyond intellectuals, but also showed how contemporary the issue of the colonial war, and indeed of imperialism and colonialism in general, are for any conceptualization of Portugal as a nation. The shipwrecks in *A costa dos murmúrios* – the title itself already invokes a ghostly assembly of murmurs at the coast – are the shipwrecks of the Invincible Armada that sailed from Lisbon on 28 May 1588 when Portugal had temporarily come under the Spanish Crown and Philip II of Spain had decided to try to defeat the English. It is in front of a huge painting depicting that ill-fated, disastrous, enterprise that we see a blind captain of the Portuguese army delivering a lecture on the immortality of the Portuguese nation to the assembled military and their families who were staying in the hotel *Stella*

Maris, converted to the official residence of the Portuguese soldiers and their families. The acrid symbolism of that scene is inescapable as it reveals not only a continuity of imperial folly that is made evident through the actual physical blindness of the speaker, but also denounces and denies any teleological greatness to the Portuguese nation. The figure of the shipwreck in *A costa dos murmúrios* becomes doubly spectral, referring at once to the coming crumbling of Portuguese imperial pretensions and to its own past subordination. All of Portugal's national imaginary is effectively questioned and rendered as not only blind and misguided but fundamentally phantasmatic.

"The time is out of joint" (*Hamlet*, Act I, scene v). That last sentence of Hamlet's after his encounter with the ghost of his father, would be an apt description of this scene in *A costa dos murmúrios*. Derrida uses it as a means to start his reflections in *Specters of Marx* (1994), and returns to it several times, most noticeably when addressing the state of world-affairs and European democracies (Chapter 3). But it is equally descriptive of *Angola, saudades de quem te ama*, a documentary portraying fragments of daily life in Angola in the aftermath of the civil war. The film depicts all sorts of ruins, from the shelled out buildings, to the abandoned tanks, to the literal shipwrecks in Luanda's harbor, but one merits special attention for its multiplicity of meanings. The scene is part of a segment in which we follow several beautiful young models as they are being photographed for some advertising campaign, and it is doubly staged as it were, for the both the photographer and the film camera, in front of the hull of a shipwreck, hauntingly named not Moby Dick but Karl Marx, rusting away by the beach. Although the film as a whole eschews allegorizing, that shipwreck is a strong, even bitter, allegory of the nation and of the dashed hopes of emancipatory ideologies that have almost destroyed the entire country.[6] Another image stands out as the camera reveals a semi-abandoned park with large colonial statues of a couple. As children play near the statues,

Figure 8.3 Haunted shipwrecks and stranded ideologies (Source: still *Angola, saudades de quem te ama*, 2005)

a young girl who climbs the statue of the woman places herself as if she were being carried by the statue. It is impossible to determine to what extent this image might have been staged, but ultimately it does not matter since it signifies more as an allegory than as a representation of reality. The image of the small child holding on to the larger-than-life female statue is another spectral national allegory of both a melancholy, orphaned future and a petrified past, which has become a figure for absence while still being very much present.

Gender politics

An ambivalence of a different sort permeates the representation of the young fashion models. On the one hand they can be said to embody a different, affluent, cosmopolitan, sophisticated, and desirable nation, an image of the nation that is as much at odds with the overwhelming reality of poverty and devastation, as it is proof of a postcolonial commodification within the networks of global capitalism. As the BBC recently (2009) reports, while at least 60 per cent of Angolans subsist on less than two dollars a day, Luanda has become the most expensive city in the world.

At first sight one could think that the film itself becomes an accomplice in such a strategy of commodification as it focuses on the "exotic" beauty of the models. However, even if some of that certainly is at play, the film also tries to give them a voice so that their opinions, the realization for instance, that solidarity has vanished from Luanda, or that their own lives are at odds with the luxury they represent, somewhat counterbalances the inevitable consumerist and voyeuristic gaze. But only somewhat. The documentary remains from beginning to end mesmerized with the group of young boys who live in the streets and try to earn some money from washing cars, barely subsisting on a floury mixture hastily cooked on the pavement, and by sniffing and sucking on gasoline-soaked rags. Indeed, in all of these films, with the exception of *A costa dos murmúrios*, one can fairly say that traditional gender roles prevail and are never questioned, even when it is a woman who, in *Sleepwalking Land*, draws the balance and affirms that those who suffer the most in times of war are not those who fight, but the women and children. The emphasis in *Sleepwalking Land* is on the story of the old man and the young boy as they try to reach the sea and on Kindzu and the notebooks he left behind when he was shot. Not surprisingly, *Testamento* is the most conservative of them all, whether one thinks about the opening images of the women crying over the death of Napumoceno, upon whom they are dependent, or Napumoceno's infatuation with Adélia and his inability to imagine love except as ownership. Adélia, however, is not an allegory of the nation. If she stands for something it could be said that she represents freedom, the political freedom brought on by independence, a freedom which Napumoceno in his old age cannot quite grasp, and whose disappearance can be said to drive him into the demented state in which he quickly dies.

Sleepwalking Land also shows how patriarchal society operates, while at the same time avoiding the sexist approach of *Testamento*. In one scene an old, and to all intents and purposes, deranged, woman, the widow of a Portuguese property owner, remains in her ruined house. Kindzu seeks help from her in finding the boy, Gaspar.

Obviously not in any sense an allegory of the nation, this character, nonetheless, serves to represent the past and how it lingers in the present. In her concern to care for her "children" – who are nonexistent, we realize, when the camera shows her addressing empty space or reaching for a quickly disappearing animal – some of the tragedy of colonialism is reenacted.

Of the four films, only *A costa dos murmúrios* attempts a different approach to gender issues. Eva, or Evita, continually problematizes and deconstructs gender relations with respect to both the nation and colonialism. Already as a young woman she is the principal force contesting the logic of the war, as it is explained to her by her husband's immediate superior, Captain Forza Leal (Adriano Luz), and the position of women in it, focusing on their daily experiences and what they must endure, be it improper medical conditions or domestic violence. The 1988 novel by Lídia Jorge, already made all of this abundantly clear, and the 2004 film by Margarida Cardoso can be said to take it one step further. One scene, out of many, can be selected to illustrate: When Evita (Beatriz Batarda) and her husband, together with the Captain and his wife, Helena (Monica Calle), go looking for entertainment and realize that the bar at the beach is closed, the men decide randomly to shoot and kill flamingos. It is an extremely violent scene that both represents and displaces the cruelty and sadism of the war that is going on. The film makes the link to violence directed at women extremely clear by showing Evita, who is wearing a dress printed with bird figures, cringing with every shot that is heard. The film, released in 2004, addresses Portuguese society with a call for reflection on the colonial wars – on how they still shape the imagination of the nation in the present and how their trauma has not been addressed in any significant way. It is also as a reminder of the seriousness of domestic violence that keeps increasing in Portugal.[7]

Their differences notwithstanding, all four films represent postcoloniality as spectral and as affecting, however variously, both the former colonized countries as well as the former metropolis. They also deploy several metadiscursive strategies that contribute to such a representation. In the case of *Angola, saudades de quem te ama*, this is carried out mostly by the focus on the activities of the fashion photographers as the film creates a *mise-en-abîme* effect in which the film camera both duplicates and expands on the photographer's camera. Going beyond the limited purpose of the fashion photographer's image production, allowing the models to present their own views on their work and the discrepancies between the world of glamour and their daily lives, the film sets up a specular relationship that is complicit with, but also denounces the objectification and commodification involved in those scenes. By explicitly setting itself up as a collection of fragments, the film manages to avoid falling into a totalizing representation of the nation. In the other three films, all of them fictional and based on acclaimed novels, the metadiscursive strategies get more complex. Even aside from issues relating to the adaptation or transposition of literary texts into film and the necessary changes carried out in that process, substituting filmic protocols for the textual ones, it is noteworthy that all three rely on texts within texts in order to problematize reality and its representations. Thus, in *Testamento* it is the reading of Napumoceno's will, both the legal document he wrote, and the audio tapes he left to his illegitimate daughter, that allows for the narrative to unfold and for the film to conflate scenes from the past with the diegetic present. And similarly, in *Sleepwalking Land*, what allows for a merger between the two seemingly separate narratives, that of Muidinga and Tuahir in their search for the Indian Ocean and of Kindzu in his search for Gaspar, are the notebooks left in the suitcase of the dead Kindzu, which Muidinga reads aloud at night before he and Tuahir fall asleep. The conflation of the recent past and the immediate present thus enacted also allows the identities of Muidinga and Gaspar to merge, at least in the boy's imagination, so that he can insist on remembering and not yielding to despair.

Remembrance

The emphasis on remembering is yet another link among the four films. In *A costa dos murmúrios* remembering is catalyzed by metadiscursive means and is central to our understanding of the film. Indeed, both novel and film are reenactments of memory against the grain of historical amnesia. The film appears to simplify somewhat the novel's double structure – a brief narrative, titled "The Locusts," which represents the official view of the events leading to the death of Evita's husband, and then the rest of the novel, which is an act of deconstructive remembering that exposes the fallacy of the official, sanitized, version of historical events. The film transposes that complexity into its own grammar, and continuously intercalates elements from the initial narrative with the more fully developed one. At the same time, it also reflects on its condition as filmic representation of reality by starting with the use of seemingly documentary footage from the 1970s, showing the arrival of passengers from Lisbon at Lourenço Marques, as the capital of Mozambique was then known.[8] As with the little girl embracing the huge statue in *Angola, saudades de quem te ama*, what is at stake is not the authenticity of such scenes, nor whether they were staged or not, but their effect. By providing a documentary-like start to her fictional film, Margarida Cardoso, who until then had only produced documentaries, immediately invites the viewer to reflect on common assumptions about veracity and representation.[9]

Lusophone postcolonial film, in all of its variety, represents a powerful reflection on the recent past, including the extreme violence that characterized the transition from the colonial to a postcolonial era, as crucial to the conceptualization of a different future.

Notes

1 Although this situation may be about to change – for instance, the description of a new book by Fernando Arenas on *Lusophone Africa: Beyond Independence* (2011) refers to a cinema among other cultural artifacts – at present the tendency is still to ignore Lusophone African cinema altogether.

2 The discussion of Derrida's reflections in *Specters of Marx* has been very extensive. The essays collected in *Ghostly Demarcations* (Sprinker, 1999) are arguably the most important point of departure, and personally, Cristopher Prendergast's "Derrida's Hamlet" (2005) remains fundamental. I have previously developed some related arguments focusing on the question of postcolonial identities as haunted and spectral (Medeiros, 2005).

3 See the on-line Unicef report *The State of the World's Children* 1996 (accessed 06 December 2010). And also K. B. Wilson's "Cults of Violence and Counter-Violence in Mozambique" (1992) that analyzes the way in which violence was systematized in the Mozambican civil war: "A fundamental position of this paper is that Renamo's violence is not a peripheral aberration, reflecting for example poor military discipline, but is on the contrary one of Renamo's central operational tools and has been elaborated for this purpose to become virtually a 'cult'" (531).

4 Since Jameson published his essay on "Third-World Literature in the Era of Multinational Capitalism" in 1986, reactions have been largely critical as his overarching claim that all Third-World literature would be a national allegory obviously leads to reduction. However, see also Imre Szeman's "Who's Afraid of National Allegory? Jameson, Literary Criticism, Globalization" (2001).

5 Lídia Jorge's 1988 novel was one of the best and most critically acclaimed literary representations of the colonial wars. It was translated and published in English in 1995 and Margarida Cardoso's film (2004) has rekindled attention to it. Mark Sabine has recently completed an essay on the film and the issue of nostalgia (2010) and I am grateful for his having let me have an advance version of it.

6 Estimates indicate half a million dead, 100,000 amputees, and approximately 2 million displaced people. See for instance the brief report from Agence France Presse (2000) available at the Global Policy Forum site, the report prepared by the U.S. Bureau of Citizenship and Immigration Services (2000), or Victoria Brittain's *Death of Dignity: Angola's Civil War* (1998).

7 For 2007 the RTP news service reported approximately 22,000 registered crimes of domestic violence and a continued rise in relation to past years (RTP, 2008). See also the detailed report prepared by Filipa Alvim, *Mulheres (In)Visíveis* for Amnesty International (2005).

8 Mark Sabine makes reference to this footage and, relying on information provided by the director, Margarida Cardoso, comments on its provenance as a domestic film and its subsequent manipulation so as to resemble archival documentary footage (Sabine, 2010).

9 Included in her filmography is the important and often-cited *Kuxa Kanema* (2003) on the use of cinema and television by the state to construct a certain idea of the nation. Reviewer Phil Hall writes, "this is one of the finest films about filmmaking ever created. Rarely has any film-related documentary presented its subjects with such skill, maturity, and intelligence" (2004).

Bibliography

Agence France Presse, 2000. Angola's 25 Years of Civil War. *Global Policy Forum*, [online] 9 November, 2000. Available at: http://www.globalpolicy.org/component/content/article/202/41480.html [accessed 10 December 2010].Almeida, G., 1991. *O Testamento do Senhor Napumoceno da Silva Araújo*. Lisboa: Caminho.

Almeida, G., 2004. *The Last Testament and Will of Senhor da Silva Araújo*. Translated from Portuguese by S.F. Glazer. New York: New Directions.

Alvim, F., 2005. Mulheres (In)Visíveis. Relatório da Campanha "Acabar com a Violência sobre as Mulheres". *Amnistia Internacional Portugal*, [online] 2005. Available at: http://www.amnistia-internacional.pt/dmdocuments/Relatorio_das_Mulheres.pdf [accessed 10 December 2010].

Andrade-Watkins, C., 1995. Portuguese African Cinema: Historical and Contemporay Perspectives. In: K.W. Harrow, ed. 1999. *African Cinema: Postcolonial and Feminist Readings*. Trentham, NJ: Africa World Press, pp. 177–200.

Arenas, F., 2011. *Lusophone Africa: Beyond Independence*. Minneapolis: University of Minnesota Press.

Brittain, V., 1998. *Death of Dignity: Angola's Civil War*. London: Pluto Press.

Cheah, P., 1999. Spectral Nationality: The Living on [Sur-Vie] of the Postcolonial Nation in Neocolonial Globalization. *Boundary 2*, 26(3), pp. 225–52.

Couto, M., 1992. *Terra Sonâmbula*. Lisboa: Caminho.

Couto, M., 2006. *Sleepwalking Land*. Translated from Portuguese by D. Brookshaw. London: Serpent's Tail.

Derrida, J., 1994. *Specters of Marx: The State of the Debt, the Work of Mourning, and the New International*. Translated from French by P. Kamuf. New York: Routledge.

Glissant, É. and Chamoiseau, P., 2009. *Quand les Murs Tombent: L'Identité Nationale Hors-la-Loi?* Paris: Éditions Galaade, Institut du Tout-Monde.

Hall, P., 2004. Review of *Kuxa Kanema: The Birth of Film*. *Film Threat*, [online] 22 April 2004. Available at: http://www.filmthreat.com/reviews/6009 [accessed 10 December 2010].

Jameson, F., 1986. Third-World Literature in the Era of Multinational Capitalism, *Social Text*, 15, pp. 65–88.

Jorge, L., 1988. *A costa dos murmúrios*. Lisboa: D. Quixote.

Jorge, L.,1995. *The Murmuring Coast*. Translated from Portuguese by N. Costa and R.W. Sousa. Minneapolis: The University of Minnesota Press.

BBC, 2009. Luanda Priciest city for "expats." *BBC News*, [online] 11 June 2009. Available at: http://news.bbc.co.uk/2/hi/business/8094873.stm [accessed 10 December 2010].

Medeiros, P., 2005. Re-Constructing, Re-Membering Postcolonial Selves. In: H.C. Buescu, and J.F. Duarte, eds., 2005. *Stories and Portraits of the Self*. Amsterdam: Rodopi. pp. 37–50.

Naficy, H., 2001. *An Accented Cinema: Exilic and Diasporic Filmmaking*. Princeton, NJ: Princeton University Press.

Prendergast, C., 2005. Derrida's *Hamlet*. *SubStance*, 34(1), pp. 44–7.

RTP., 2008. Violência Doméstica em Portugal Aumenta Quase Seis por Cento, [online] 13 March 2008. Available at: http://ww1.rtp.pt/noticias/index.php?article=332930&visual=26 [accessed 10 December 2010].

Sabine, M., 2010. Killing (and) Nostalgia: Testimony and the Image of Empire in Margarida Cardoso's *A costa dos murmúrios*. In: C. DeMaria, and D. MacDonald, eds., 2010. *The Genres of Post-Conflict Testimony*. Nottingham: Critical, Cultural and Communications Pres, pp. 249–76.

Sprinker, M. ed., 1999. *Ghostly Demarcations: A Symposium on Jacques Derrida's Specters of Marx*. London: Verso.

Szeman, I., 2001. Who's Afraid of National Allegory? Jameson, Literary Criticism, Globalization. *The South Atlantic Quarterly*, 100(3), pp. 803–27.

Unicef, 1996. *The State of the World's Children 1996*, [online] 1996. Available at: http:// http://www.unicef.org/sowc96/ [accessed 6 December 2010].

Ukadike, N.F., 1994. *Black African Cinema*. Berkeley: University of California Press.

United States Bureau of Citizenship and Immigration Services, 2000. *Angola: Current Political and Human Rights Conditions in Angola*, [online] 4 December 2000. Available at: http://www.unhcr.org/refworld/docid/3dedf3204.html [accessed 10 December 2010].

Wilson, K.B., 1992. Cults of Violence and Counter-Violence in Mozambique. *Journal of Southern African Studies*, Special issue: Political Violence in Southern Africa, Vol. 18(3), pp. 527–82.

Filmography

A costa dos murmúrios/The Murmuring Coast, 2004. [DVD] Directed by M. Cardoso. Portugal: Atalanta Filmes.

Angola, saudades de quem te ama/Angola: Saudades from the One Who Loves You, 2005. [DVD] Directed by R. Pakleppa. Angola: Luna Films.

Kuxa Kanema: The Birth of Cinema in Mozambique, 2003. [DVD] Directed by M. Cardoso. Portugal: Lapsus/Filmes do Tejo.

O Testamento do senhor Napumoceno/Testamento, 1997. [DVD] Directed by F. Manso. USA: Spia Media.

Sleepwalking Land, 2007. [DVD] Directed by T. Prata. England: HB Films.

Chapter 9

The aesthetics of postcolonial cinema in Raul Ruiz's *Three Crowns of the Sailor*

Sabine Doran

An important moment in postcolonial aesthetics occurred in the 1930s, when a group of artists organized a counter-exhibition to the official *Exposition Coloniale Internationale* in 1931. These artists, Surrealists for the most part, had made common cause with Marxists, who "could regard each other as political allies" (Larsen, 1998) in their opposition to French imperialist policies. The gist of the Surrealists' critique lay in the idea that vision was a force of domination in Western cultures, a problem that called for an aesthetic response.[1] As Adam Jolles (2006) remarks, this moment had important repercussion in contemporary critical discourse:

> Preliminary evidence suggests that at the very least the Communist avant-garde perceived a way out of the artistic impasse caused by imperialism by making art that was meant to be anything but looked at. It would be work that would by necessity require an entirely different analytic and descriptive vocabulary – one that could bring to life the fetishistic, totemic, idolatrous, and/or ritualistic aspects of these objects (to name just a few of the obvious relevant categories). Perhaps the recent reemergence of this vocabulary in contemporary critical discourse points to the surrealists' belated success in reorienting Western aesthetic practice.[2]

Jolles describes this shift in postcolonial aesthetics as a "tactile turn," which attempts to subvert and reorient the dominance of the Western gaze. More recently, this tactile turn has become influential in postcolonial cinema, particularly in regards to what one could call "haptic cinema," to adapt Martine Beugnet's term "haptic visuality," which she describes as "a mode of visual perception akin to the sense of touch, where the eye, sensitized to the image's concrete appearance, becomes responsive to qualities usually made out through skin contact" (Beugnet, 2007, p. 66).[3] However, within a broader framework of an epistemology that uses touch rather than vision as a model of knowledge and sensory experience, I seek to focus in this essay on the relational power of touch, that is, touch as a force that creates and weaves networks of connections, a "sensing body in movement" (Manning, 2007, p. xiii), rather than a moment of identification. In other words, it is a matter of perpetual dynamic of interconnecting bodies and elements, a dynamic that also plays a central role in the Surrealists' technique of combining disparate images through techniques such as automatic writing (*écriture automatique*).

One of the modern directors to take up the Surrealist cause, Chilean-cum-French director Raul Ruiz, brings together in his multifaceted *oeuvre* a Surrealist aesthetic and a political perspective under the aegis of postcoloniality. Born in Chile in 1941, Ruiz has made more than 100 short and feature-length films over the course of forty years. Forced to leave his home country during the Pinochet dictatorship, Ruiz moved to France in 1973, where he earned a reputation as an important, if idiosyncratic, filmmaker. Ian Christie observes that "Ruiz has devised a rhetoric or rather a play between rhetorics, which allows him to speak in terms recognizable to Europeans, without either wholly accepting their culture or betraying his own" (cited in King 1990, p. 181). Though perhaps best known for the films he directed in the late 1990s, *Trois vies et une seule Mort/ Three Lives and Only One Death* (1996), *Généalogies d'un crime/Genealogies of a Crime* (1997), *Le temps retrouvé/Time Regained* (1999), and *Fils de deux mères ou la comédie d'innocence/Son of Two Mothers or The Comedy of Innocence* (2000), his earlier films are considered masterpieces of independent or art-house cinema, including what some see as his magnum opus, *Les trois couronnes du matelot/Three Crowns of the Sailor* (1983).

Michael Richardson (2006, p. 163) describes Ruiz as a "heretical surrealist," who "uses surrealist devices that are not against surrealism but outside of it." Through their use of Surrealist décor and devices, Ruiz's films open up a historical dimension within the Surrealists' reorientation of the gaze. Particularly in *Three Crowns of the Sailor*, which could be considered Ruiz's postcolonial manifesto, the Surrealist-inspired tactile dimension engenders what one could call an "aesthetics of intrusion." This is one among many different tendencies in postcolonial cinema,[4] in which a reflection on margins and marginality, framing, and the periphery constitute a resistance that is at once aesthetic and political.

In *Three Crowns of the Sailor*, Ruiz dramatizes margins as a haptic space, as texture and interconnectedness, through movements of intrusion; for as Douglas Morrey observes, "if the image offers itself to a kind of touching, then it intrudes upon vision, or vice versa – the boundaries between subject and object of perception are challenged" (2008, p. iii). Ruiz's attempt in *Three Crowns of the Sailor* to challenge the boundaries of perception is based on an insistence on margins and their linking power, creating networks and frameworks that are contiguous with each other rather than organized by a central vision.

In his *Poetics of Cinema*, Ruiz theorizes his aesthetic practice as part of his critique of what he calls "central conflict theory." He describes the central conflict thus: "someone wants something and someone else doesn't want them to have it"; the subsequent story is then "arranged around this central conflict" (1995, p. 11). What is lost in a cinema based on a central conflict is access to a "photographic unconscious," which Ruiz understands as a "corpus of signs capable of conspiring against visual conventions" (1995, p. 32).

Indeed, Ruiz's excessive network of references and styles is tied together in *Three Crowns of the Sailor* by the combinatory power of signs, letters, and numbers, through which the margins are sculpted, as it were. By dramatizing margins and marginality, Ruiz evacuates the center; in its stead, ornamental frameworks expose patterns and formations as ongoing structures. This procedure is reminiscent of Sergei Eisenstein's commentary on *¡Que viva Mexico!* (1931), when he asserts that, through the "images of the ornamental decomposing of faces and heads" we "enter" the process of creation itself (cited in King, 1990, p. 36). Similarly, Ruiz exposes through the framing of close-ups of body-parts the dialectical process of composition (creating structures, alphabets, and geometrical formations) and decomposition, revealing, formally as well as figuratively, liminal states between life and death, here and there, past and future. However, in their liminality, these states escape the "real-world poverty" (Stam, 2000, p. 95) which also manifests itself in a poverty of style, as Glauber Rocha insists in "Aesthetics of Hunger" (cited in Stam, 2000, p. 95). Instead, the excessiveness of Ruiz's style is rather a manifestation of a richly layered network of times and places.

Cartographies of displacement

Based on the Chilean myth of the *Funchalense* (one of the "mariner legends of the southern Chilean coast" [Pick, 1987, p. 48]), a ghost ship where a living soul is joined by specters of the past, Ruiz's *Three Crowns of the Sailor* follows the narrative model of the *Arabian Nights*, thus reviving the fluidity of storytelling, despite the film's fragmented form. The plot, like the visual style of the film, is surrealistic and thus defies logical explanation. The film begins in an unspecified port city of Poland. A student named Tadeusz murders his professor, without any apparent motive. While attempting to escape the city, he meets a drunken sailor who promises him a place on his ship if he agrees to listen to the sailor's story to give him three Danish crowns. The narration shifts to the sailor's point of view as he tells his story, which is presented in color, replacing the black and white cinematography of the opening. However, the sailor's story will be regularly interrupted by the frame narrative with the student (in black and white). The sailor recounts how he was recruited by a "blind man," warning him never to take money without getting something in return. The theme of exchange is one of the recurring motifs of the film, a motif that has deadly consequences, for the blind man will be killed right after his encounter with the sailor. The journey on the ship named *Funchalense* brings the sailor to the tropics of the Southern Hemisphere, to the seaports of Dakar, Singapore, and Tangier. During each shore leave, the sailor attempts to acquire a kind of surrogate family, starting with his encounter with a child prostitute (whom he will refer to as his "wife"), a black man in Greece (a father figure), and a young boy in Singapore (like a son). At the end of the film, the captain of the ship asks for the return of the money he had lent the sailor. After the sailor finishes his tale, the student kills him and takes his place on the *Funchalense*.

The circular structure of the film dispenses with the notion of a central conflict. Instead, the theatricality of framing brings the margins to life, especially since the leading figures in the film are marginal figures themselves, or "circular nomads" – in the words of Édouard Glissant (1997, p. 12)[5] – who belong, as the lady on board ship points out, to the *Lumpenproletariat*. In Marxian terms, the *Lumpenproletariat* are not proto-revolutionaries, like the proletariat, but are obedient to authority: prostitutes, the homeless, vagabonds, sailors, those who live at the margins of society and thus at the margins of the revolution. Ruiz, who is known for avoiding reductionist political views, obliquely evokes various contemporary political struggles for independence and self-determination through the cartography of the places the *Funchalense* visits in the Southern and Eastern Hemispheres, all of which were former colonies: the port city of Valparaiso in Chile (independent from Spain since 1810, but under military rule after the Pinochet coup in 1973); the seaport of Buenaventura, the main port of Colombia (after its independence still plagued by a history of drug trafficking, violence, and the presence of guerrilla and paramilitary groups); the seaport of Dakar, Senegal (which gained independence from France in 1960); Tangier (which attained full sovereignty with the rest of Morocco in 1956); Singapore in Southeast Asia (which gained independence from Britain in 1965); and the port city of Gdansk in Poland (where the famous Solidarity movement started in the 1970s, which, with its international impact, anticipated the end of the Cold War). Ruiz seems to point to the Polish Solidarity movement as a framework for his postcolonial aesthetics, for Poland is where the framing story takes place.

As the sailor enters the ship, he has to point to a series of destinations on a map, which, in their randomness, expose the sense of displacement characteristic of Ruiz's cinematography.[6] In *Three Crowns of the Sailor*, what is seen also needs to be read. The ship *Funchalense* functions as an allegory of cinematic cartography, mapping the spaces between the living and the dead through legends, storylines, and numerical (monetary) systems. The pact between the student and the sailor – exchanging stories and a place on the *Funchalense* for three Danish crowns – though not political per se, nevertheless has political overtones. Interwoven bodies are on the move in a virtual "hyperspace" where aspirations to independence and self-determination, characteristic of the politics of the time, are subverted according to Ruiz's critique of "central conflict" (Ruiz, 1995, p. 89). The virtual presence of ancestors shifts the focus towards a political unconscious and its liberation through stories from and about the past. Indeed, what seems to characterize Ruiz's aesthetics of intrusion is the emphasis on the power of a perpetual movement that resists reduction to stable identities, locatable in either a past or a present, a center or a margin.

A relational movement between past and future is realized in a haptic cinematography based on the weaving of letters. Using storytelling as a way to reconnect with the lives of the dead, the film creates a kind of postcolonial consciousness that enacts a change in power relationships and thus revives a past prior to the intrusion of colonial powers.

The opening shot of the film is a close-up of a pen writing, and we encounter the pen again on the *Funchalense*, where the captain's main occupation is to literally embroider the letters of a cryptic text into a cloth. Each sailor will embody or be embodied by a letter, which is tattooed on his skin. The letter of the film's protagonist turns out to be the letter A, which he embodies even before it is inscribed on his body. His body performs the letter in close-ups of his legs forming the shape of an A. Ruiz's cinema thus seems to introduce itself as a texture, woven as it is out of close-ups of body parts, which become the warp and woof of an affective strategy of intrusion.[7]

"Everything around is always contaminated," states the sailor in one of the film's more self-reflexive lines. His peers on board the *Funchalense* conclude: "Only one thing is pure: Our Lady, the sea, and some alcohol." The purity of the fluid elements of ocean and alcohol, together with a ghost-like surrogate mother (to whom the sailors go for comfort and advice) on board the ship, all three essential for maintaining life on board, are thus contrasted with the contamination that Ruiz presents as a perpetually present framing condition. Ruiz thus replaces the dialectics of center and margin, with an ongoing process of contamination that establishes networks of relationships. Contamination is to be understood in Félix Guattari's sense, as opposition to forms of representation.[8] It is a force, an intrusive process. Mimetic relationships are replaced by bodies caught in circular movements, through their coming and going, intruding on and being intruded upon by life and death. They do not represent, but embody forces, dynamics, both abstract and concrete, signifying the transgression of borders that haunt an ordered world. The specters of the past in *Three Crowns of the Sailor* are both figurative and abstract, emblematic of the shift in postcolonial aesthetics towards embodied structures, rhythms, and counter-rhythms. These specters destabilize internal scene linkages, while "opening the shots up to freer, diachronic relations across the entire film," as Adrian Martin (2006) remarks concerning Claire Denis's aesthetics. Thus an aesthetic of intrusion in postcolonial film means a shift towards film's inner life, which is not tied to a strictly linear unfolding. The circular repetition of intrusive patterns form a desubjectivized lyric fluidity. Ruiz's postcolonial aesthetics thus dramatizes a perpetual movement of intrusion through still moments in which sculpted letters, numerical combinations, as well as cartographies are exposed as frameworks,[9] open to be entered. These sculpted still moments mark the transitional points of a circular dynamic, which, in its circularity, is also an aspect of Ruiz's aesthetics of intrusion.

Sculpting the margins

Throughout *Three Crowns of the Sailor*, the sailor remains a nameless and marginal figure; it is through his encounters that a network of stories is woven. A texture is created, framed through body parts, sculpting the margins and their intrusion, as the opening shot of the first story-segment shows.

The first shot inside the frame story is a close-up in color of the sailor's legs shot from the back and forming the outline of the letter A. The inner horizontal line of the letter A is constituted by a distant queue of people waiting to emigrate, as their luggage indicates. Thus the political crisis is framed from a distance and yet is at the same time part of the framework. The close-up of the legs juxtaposed to the waiting people in deep focus is emphasized, self-reflexively, by the voice-over that tells us that he himself is waiting, looking for a job as a sailor.

In a corresponding shot, the shoreline on the other side of the bay forms a horizontal line in deep focus, framed again from the back of the sailor's legs, thus forming the letter A once more. Enframing first a line of people and then the shoreline, Ruiz creates correspondences between people and landscapes, land and water, here and there, at a standstill and yet also in movement. The framing legs of the A interweave liminal states of waiting (time) and shoreline (space), intertwining them with the sailor. These interstitial elements are thus both figurative and abstract. The exteriority intrudes upon interiority and vice versa, making the frame kinetic, so that paradoxically, although the legs are stationary, they are intertwined with (as well as the body's means of) movement.[10] However, Ruiz's deep focus functions differently here than in films like *Citizen Kane* by Orson Welles (a director who had a great influence on Ruiz). Instead of liberating the spectator, as André Bazin famously asserted in his analysis of Welles's and Renoir's use of the technique, Ruiz's deep focus creates a field of interwoven textures that force the spectator to intrude.

The movement of intrusion into the framework belongs to Ruiz's "politics of magic" (to use Michael Denning's phrase) (2004, p.185), meaning that the cinematic apparatus itself is exposed, displaying its deceptive as well as its seductive powers. Just as Welles in *Citizen Kane* used various camera and staging techniques to expose and deconstruct fascist aesthetics (in particular those techniques pioneered by Leni Riefenstahl in *Triumph of the Will*), Ruiz constructs a postcolonial aesthetics that resists the center-margin dynamic – the "central conflict" – focusing instead on invading the margins through a dialectic of close-up and deep focus. The combination of visual flatness and depth creates a haptic cinema,[11] instigating the intruding movement in deep focus and weaving the texture of the film in a back and forth movement. Corresponding to a dialectic of intruding and being intruded upon, the weaving movement itself is thus the characteristic artistic feature of Ruiz's aesthetic of intrusion. Combinations of disparate elements form patterns, rhythms, ordering systems, and thus self-perpetuating abstract structures, always in movement, always evacuating the center (and central conflict).

By perpetually drawing attention to the instability of the framework through striking combinations of disparate elements,[12] Ruiz harks back to the Baroque *ars combinatoria* in an attempt to transform the "internal logic" of events. As he writes in *Poetics of Cinema*:

> We must also change the internal logic of the events shown, and modify the very way in which fictional spaces are put together ... I should like to propose an open structure based on *ars combinatoria*. A system of multiple stories, overlapping according to certain established rules.
>
> (Ruiz, 1995, p. 88)

The internal logic of decolonization is thus approached through forms of doubling and multiplication, such as the doubling of places where independence movements are at work. The technique of doubling is crucial for the liberation of fiction from its attachment to truth, leading to what Thomas Elsaesser (2005, p. 253), in an essay on Ruiz, calls "a total skepticism about cinema's supposed realism." Instead, the postcolonial, as the most privileged case of doubling, is always moving between two places, and, most importantly in Ruiz's cinematography, two times, divided by borders between the past and the future, the pre- and the postcolonial. However, the contamination of borders in space (between states) and in time (moving back to the past and forward into the future) forces us to rethink the boundaries of the body. Bodies in *Three Crowns of the Sailor* are telling stories even as they are part of the stories being told. The film could be described as a *mise-en-abîme* of storytelling, the repeated incarnation of the letter A creating a Chinese box narrative structure: stories within stories within stories.

The power of fiction

Discussing the cinema of Pierre Perrault, John Cassavetes, and Jean Rouch, Gilles Deleuze describes a break that he locates in the 1960s with the notion that a fiction is penetrated by truth. The emphasis, he says, shifted to "the pure and simple story-telling function" of characters from "opposing realities," such as indigenous people, or "the poor," who tear the filmmaker out of his dominant reality:

> What cinema must grasp is not the identity of a character, whether real or fictional, through his objective and subjective aspects. It is the becoming of the real character when he himself starts to "make fiction," when he enters into the "the flagrant offence of making up legends" and so contributes to the invention of his people.
>
> (Deleuze, 1989, p. 145)

With reference to Rouch's films in particular, Deleuze points out that when the characters in *cinéma vérité* cross borders between reality and fiction they thereby cease to be either real or fictional; they are rather invented as "real" characters. Truth is not to be found or reproduced, for cinema "becomes creator and producer of truth," as Deleuze (1989, p. 146) writes.[13] The creative act of storytelling derives its force through the power of the false, which Ruiz exposes in moments of betrayal. In *Three Crowns of the Sailor*, it is the Tiresias figure of the film, the "blind man," who is producing truth through the metamorphic power of the false. Tellingly, the blind man is called "*traitre*" (traitor) by his murderers, because he told the five men searching for work that the ship *Funchalense* had just arrived, though it was common knowledge that the ship had been gone for a week. As the camera reveals, the word "traitor" is written on the sole of the blind man's foot, apparently in his own blood, though he claims it is just paint (Figure 9.1).

We find out, however, that when the sailor walks back into the harbor, he sees the *Funchalense* there, just as the blind man had said. Thus the blind man reorients the story through his own story-telling, allegorizing the creative power of the false that produces truth through its own conjuring.

Betrayal, indeed, becomes the driving force in Ruiz's *Three Crowns of the Sailor*, intruding perpetually, and thus displacing notions of truth-value. Through a Nietzschean turn towards the power of the false, the notion of truth itself is displaced by a past that is constantly intruding. The sense of intrusion is made most literal in the central scene of the film, the bordello scene.

Liminal spaces

On the sailor's way to the bordello, walking along the waterfront, along the line between water and land, constantly shifting camera positions introduce the theme of shifting vantage points, creating a sense of destabilization in liminal spaces. The motif of shifting on a line in movement is repeated in the opening of the bordello scene, in which a series of prostitutes introduce themselves with their strengths and weaknesses, each time

Figure 9.1 The death of the Blind Man (Source: still *Three Crowns of the Sailor,* 1983)

opening up different perspectives on erotic love. Moving and shifting points of view are then brought to a standstill in a close-up of a female leg, arranged (in combination with the leg of a chair) in the shape of the letter A – the most often discussed framing shot of the film (Figure 9.2); this time it is the sailor who is framed in deep focus, far removed at the other end of the room.

Deep focus here, in the image of the legs, prefigures the physical act of intrusion by interweaving movement and stasis. The dialectical movement continues by opposing the exposition of the woman's flesh (made literal, visually, by juxtaposing an image of meat on a barbecue with the close-up of a female leg) to the child prostitute, called Virgin Mary, whom the sailor ends up choosing, The sailor notices her while she is reading behind a curtain, as she introduces herself in a monologue. This prefigures the form of their engagement, which unfolds through stories and songs rather than through physical love.

The beginning of their encounter is shown through yellow filters. As they stroll outside, surrounded by kids throwing paper airplanes into the air, the vertical line between rising and falling that characterizes the movement of the paper projectiles prefigures the visual geometry of the room where the prostitute takes the sailor. The encounter between the sailor and "Virgin Mary" (whom the sailor will subsequently refer to as his wife) is thus framed by the warm yellow of sunlight outside, in contrast to the blue coldness at the end of the scene, when the prostitute gets paid and counts the money she received.

It is through the complementary colors of yellow and blue that the space itself is involved in a dynamic of expanding and contracting, thereby conjoining the stories of the sailor and the prostitute as complementary stories. The relation between the

Figure 9.2 Bordello scene (Source: still *Three Crowns of the Sailor*, 1983)

complementary colors of yellow and blue has often been thematized in modern art, forming what Eugene Chevreul called a "simultaneous contrast," in which complementary colors intensify each other – a phenomenon that became of central significance in the works of artists as different as Vincent van Gogh (*Starry Night*) and Kandinsky. The pattern of yellow and blue in Ruiz's bordello scene acts as an intensifier as we focus on the exchange of money (seen through blue filter), which the camera shows from a high angle. Money links the dead and the living in each of the subsequent scenes, since it is money that the sailor borrows from the captain, accumulating debt, in order to pay for the relationships (the surrogate family) that the sailor establishes during his shore leaves. By accumulating debt instead of capital, Ruiz, through this character, establishes a counter-force to capital accumulation and thus counters the essential drive of what he characterized in *Poetics of Cinema* as "central conflict theory." Instead, the negative force of debt ensures perpetual movements towards the margins of society, both economically as well as spiritually.

In *Three Crowns of the Sailor*, money is part of Ruiz's *ars combinatoria*,[14] relating the dead to the living, for the prostitute also has to pay off her late father's debt, just as the sailor will be forced to pay back the money he borrowed from the captain of the ghost ship. Thus the specters of the past keep intruding through the force of debt. The motif of being indebted to the past is here not a nostalgic one, but is rather represented as the abstract force of currencies, expanding in networks across borders and contracting towards transitional points.

The ultimate transitional points of *eros* and *thanatos* are most closely intertwined through the stories that are told. As the prostitute tells her story, she stands next to her coffin, in which she keeps her most valuable possessions. Her father had bought the coffin when she was mortally ill as a child. After her unexpected recovery, she decided to keep it. The vacillation between life and death is explored from a bird's-eye perspective, along vertical lines. The dolls that hang from the ceiling of the prostitute's room, with their illuminated eyes, create a liminal space between birth (children) and death (coffin). However, the liminal space is not only dramatized, but becomes a space in movement, constantly shifting, embodying movement itself, downwards, towards the coffin, and subsequently towards the counting of money. It is a dynamic in which the intrusion of death and money almost functions as a magnetic field, for it links those who are in need and ties them up in deathly cycles. Currencies thus create networks of relationships, which are not based on subjective experiences, but rather on abstract patterns and networks around the exchange of money. These patterns evoke global political and economical forces at work, without, however, having them take center stage. Instead they remain mere potentialities.

Especially in its bringing together of the tactile with the erotic, and in its focus on disparate body parts, this scene suggests direct parallels to the Surrealists' turn to sculpture, through which sculpture became redefined as a combinatory practice. For example, disparate body parts that are mechanically connected through ball joints, suggesting the potential for endless recombination, are characteristic of Surrealist sculptures such as Hannah Höch's *The Sweet One* (1926). Similarly, in Ruiz's film, friction is created through opposing elements of death and life, and further emphasized through the automata-like appearance of the dolls with illuminated eyes, half-dead and half-alive, also a preferred surrealist object (as in Duchamp or in Dalí's *Bust of a Woman*, 1933). However, in contrast to the Surrealists' interest in the psychoanalytical pleasure principle (a shifting between promising and thwarting pleasure), or the Freudian death drive, Ruiz's cinematography is not based on sensations of desire or pleasure. Instead, subjectivity is subsumed by patterns of movements, reappearances, sensory forces through which a texture is woven, which continually intrudes from the margins. Instead of fetishes and ritualistic objects, there are currencies creating networks, conjoining the Global South with Eastern Europe through the exchange of the enigmatic three Danish crowns.

Geographically, the origin of these crowns seems to point to the Scandinavian history of the Vikings and their early trajectories eastward and southward. The period of Viking expansion (and intrusion) might thus be evoked as a historic reference to early colonialism. The relational power of currencies, letters, and numbers relates bodies in movement to a cartography of countries in transition (Poland, Senegal, Chile, Colombia) – all postcolonial settings – which the sailor enters through the exchange of money. The often violent history of postcolonial settings is framed by the Polish fight for independence, achieved by the Solidarity movement that started in the seaport of Gdansk. Borders become embodied virtualities, expanding through the exchange of currencies, while at the same time contracting towards the three Danish coins (pointing to a virtual origin of postcolonialism) in a movement that is perceived foremost as a tactile sensation, creating a sense of bodies in movement (as networks and relational matrices).

Race and color

In a film that is based on fragmented images of bodies and lives, fluidity and circularity are important counter-forces to achieve narrative cohesion. Ruiz establishes cohesion by using primary colors (yellow, blue, and red filters) and circular camera movements, characteristic of the black and white scenes, where the encounter between student and sailor is presented. At the end of the sailor's journey, the storylines are folded into one another. In the last scene, which can be considered the pendant to the bordello scene in its use of color filter, a red filter exposes a transitional moment of violence, which renews life on the *Funchalense*. As in the bordello scene, which opened with a shot of candles on an altar and continued the theme of illumination through the dolls' light-emitting eyes, the use of color filters is again introduced through candlelight: the student lights the candles in the house of the murdered professor, to which he returns together with the sailor, in order to retrieve the promised three Danish crowns. In this scene, the cryptic letters that haunted the sailor in the form of tattoos on the crew of the *Funchalense* reappear written in blood on the wall, shot through a red filter. Shortly after, when the student hands the promised coins to the sailor, the scene is presented through a red filter again, and this time the source of the blood on the wall is revealed – it is from the murdered professor. The correlation between professor and letters remains enigmatic, as enigmatic as the word "traitor," also written in blood, on the foot of the "blind man" in the opening scene of the sailor's journey. What links the blind man to the professor, structurally speaking, is their role as messengers. They transmit a message that points to the "ship of dead," which is what the *Funchalense* in fact is in indigenous Chilean legends. Writing with the blood of the dead (the blind man, the professor) creates a structural frame, for in each case death results in the continuation of life on the *Funchalense*. The murder of the blind man leads the sailor to the ship, just as the murder of the professor leads the student to the ship. The exchange of money is inextricably bound to the inscription of letters. Both appear tinted in red at the end, when the student gives the three coins to the sailor. Framed now by the faces of statues (as opposed to legs embodying movement), the spill-over of color into the black and white frame-story of student and sailor announces a shift of perspective on the narrative level. The narrator/sailor has to accomplish the "abominable task" of killing the sailor/ narrator after the exchange of the three crowns.

Color filters intensify turning points. The black and white frame is itself thematized, however, in the murder of the sailor, for his face turns black when he is pushed into a heap of coal. He literally becomes a "black" man, like his late "father," for whom he had borrowed the three Danish crowns that are costing him his life at this point. Color intrudes here again, now touching upon the postcolonial theme of race. The sailor had met his (black) father-figure, a doctor dressed in a white suit, on a beach in Dakar, a transatlantic seaport and Senegal's capital. When he offered his father money, the black man threw it into the air, saying that his story was too long to be told; all that he needed were the enigmatic three Danish crowns (which appear to point back to the Vikings). The connection between the black doctor dressed in a white suit and his relationship to a Danish currency maps out a cartography of colonialism connecting Africa with Europe.

As a modification of bell hooks's formula of resistance from the margins (2000), an aesthetics of intrusion not only circumvents the binary notions of center and margin, but also recombines them as relational rather than hierarchical. Instead of a drama of "central conflicts" between margin and center, the margins are valorized in their own right, and the center's intrusions lead nowhere. The sailor points to the specificity of a vertiginous space and a virtual time, which Ruiz enframes as a centerless centrifugal force.

Notes

1 Panivong Norindr (1996) critiques the Surrealist counter-exposition, contending that, although it opposed imperialist aims, it ended up perpetuating the French nostalgia for places like Indochina. However, in this essay, Surrealist imagery will be of less concern than Surrealist montage techniques, which, as I will argue, represent an attempt to decolonize the imagery of the Chilean people in Ruiz's cinema.

2 This article was part of a special issue on "Surrealism and its Others."

3 See also Laura Marks (2000), although she prefers the term "intercultural cinema" to "postcolonial cinema" for her project.

4 In his analysis of Claire Denis's film *Chocolat* (1988), Frank Leinen (2003, p. 47) points to the replacement of dichotomist postcolonial thinking in Denis's cinematography with "a postcolonial consciousness which takes multiple perspectives and its discourse critical." For the notion of an aesthetics of intrusion, this shift towards a "postcolonial consciousness" is crucial, for intrusion is not directed against a central power or figure, but rather creates sensations of alertness.

5 Glissant (1997, p. 12) writes: "Circular nomadism is a not-intolerant form of an impossible settlement."

6 As Tom Conley observes in his *Cartographic Cinema* (2007, p. 207), cinema and cartography share many of the same traits; both require "complex modes of decipherment."

7 In Chapter 6 of this volume, Mireille Rosello points to the "transnational voice that intrudes" in Philippe Faucon's *Dans la vie* through television, and thus creates "chaotic networks of solidarity," which are also characteristic of the intruding forces in Ruiz.

8 For Guattari (1995, p. 92), the aesthetic event of a powerful artwork is viral in its effect, being known "not through representation, but through affective contamination."

9 Also Marguerite Waller suggests with respect to Nichetti's "postcolonial circus" a tendency in postcolonial cinema to reorganize temporal and spatial structures through repetitive forms such as patterns, maps, and framing techniques (see Chapter 10 of this volume).

10 Rosello (Chapter 6 of this volume) and Waller (Chapter 10 of this volume) also analyze the use of framing techniques as a characteristic artistic device in postcolonial cinema, for it thematizes the question of shifting perspectives.

11 Laura Marks (2002, p. 8) points out that Antonia Lant used the term "haptical cinema" to describe the dialectic between visual flatness and depth exploited in early films.

12 Historically, Ruiz's framing technique in *Three Crowns of the Sailor* shows interesting parallels to Wiene's use of framing techniques in *The Cabinet of Dr Caligari*; for the ghost ship *Funchalense* also offers in Ruiz's cinematography the framework for a reflection on cinema as a "ghostly machine." Dietrich Scheunemann (2003, p. 151) discusses framing devices in Caligari as a reflection on the fundamental features of the cinematic medium.

13 Deleuze discusses Rouch's "ethnofictions" as well as Welles's cinematography of forgery (as in *F for Fake* or *The Lady of Shanghai*) in the context of cinema's falsifying power and the notion of the artist as the creator of truth (which is crucial for Ruiz's cinematography). See also Ronald Bogue (2003, p. 150).

14 "In ars combinatoria," Ruiz (1995, p. 79) states, echoing a writer such as Jorge Luis Borges, "nothing is truly arbitrary, for the combinations inevitably produce meaning."

Bibliography

Beugnet, M., 2007. *Cinema and Sensation: French Film and the Art of Transgression*, Edinburgh: Edinburgh University Press.

Bogue, R., 2003. *Deleuze on Cinema*. New York and London: Routledge.

Conley, T., 2007. *Cartographic Cinema*. Minneapolis: University of Minnesota Press.

Deleuze, G., 1989. *Cinema 2 The Time-Image*. Translated from French by H. Tomlinson and R. Galeta. Minneapolis: University of Minnesota Press.

Denning, M., 2004. The Politics of Magic: Orson Welles's Allegories of Anti-Fascism. In: J Naremore, ed., 2004. *Orson Welles's Citizen Kane: A Casebook*, Oxford: Oxford University Press, pp. 185–216.

Elsaesser, T., 2005. Raoul Ruiz's Hypothèse du Tableau Volé. In: T. Elsaesser, ed., 2005. *European Cinema: Face to Face with Hollywood*. Amsterdam: Amsterdam University Press, pp. 251–4.

Glissant, É., 1997. *Poetics of Relation*. Translated from French by B. Wing. Ann Arbor: University of Michigan Press.

Guattari, F., 1995. *Chaosmosis: An Ethico Aesthetic Paradigm*. Translated from French by P. Bains and J. Pefanis. Sidney: Power Publications.

hooks, b., 2000. *Feminist Theory: From Margin to Center*. Cambridge, MA: South End Press.

Jolles, A., 2006. The Tactile Turn: Envisioning a Postcolonial Aesthetic in France. *Yale French Studies*, 109, pp. 17–38.

King, J., 1990. *Magical Reels: A History of Cinema in Latin America*. London: Verso.

Larsen, N., 1998. Preselective Affinities: Surrealism and Marxism in Latin America. *Cultural Logic*, 2(1) [online] 1998. Available at: http://clogic.eserver.org/2-1/larsen.html. [Accessed 25 October 2010].

Leinen, F., 2003. The Discovery of Otherness. In G. Rings and R. Morqou-Tamosunas, eds., 2003. *European Cinema: Inside Out. Images of the Self and the Other in Postcolonial European film*. Heidelberg: Universitaetsverlag, pp. 45–61.

Manning, E., 2007. *Politics of Touch: Sense, Movement, Sovereignty*. Minneapolis: University of Minnesota Press.

Marks, L., 2000. *The Skin of the Film: Intercultural Cinema, Embodiment and the Senses*. Durham, NC: Duke University Press,.

Marks, L., 2002. *Touch: Sensuous Theory and Multisensory Media*. Minneapolis: University of Minnesota Press, 2002.

Martin, A., 2006. A Ticket to Ride: Claire Denis and the Cinema of the Body. *Screening the Past*, 29 [online] 27 November 2006. Available at: http://www.latrobe.edu.au/screeningthepast/20/claire-denis.html. [Accessed 26 October 2010].

Morrey, D., 2008. Claire Denis and Jean-Luc Nancy, *Film-Philosophy*, 12 (1), pp. 10–30.

Mudimbe, Y.V., 1988. *The Invention of Africa*. Bloomington: Indiana University Press.

Nancy, J-L., 2008. The Intruder. In: J.L. Nancy, ed., 2008. *Corpus*. Translated from French by R.R. Rand. New York: Fordham University Press, pp. 161–70.

Norindr, P., 1996. *Phantasmatic Indochina: French Colonial Ideology: Architecture, Film, and Literature*. Durham, NC: Duke University Press.

Pick, Z., 1987. The Dialectical Wanderings of Exile, *Screen*, 30(4), pp. 48–64.

Richardson, M., 2006. *Surrealism and Cinema*. New York: Berg.

Ruiz, R., 1995. *Poetics of Cinema*. Translated from French by B. Holmes. Paris: Dis Voir.

Scheunemann, D., 2003. Once More on Wiene's *The Cabinet of Dr. Caligari*. In: D. Scheunemann, ed. 2003. *Expressionist Film: New Perspectives*, ed. Rochester: Camden House, pp. 125–56

Stam, R. 2000. *Film Theory: An Introduction*. Oxford: Blackwell Publishing.

Filmography

Chocolat, 1988 [film] Directed by C. Denis. France: Caroline Productions.

Citizen Kane, 1941. [film] Directed by O. Welles. USA: Mercury Productions.

F for Fake, 1973. [film] Directed by O. Welles. France: Janus Film.

Fils de deux mères ou la comédie d'innocence, 2000. [film] Directed by R. Ruiz. France: Canal+.

Généalogies d'un crime, 1997. [film] Directed by R. Ruiz. France: Madragoa Films.

The Lady of Shanghai, 1947. [film] Directed by O. Welles. USA: Columbia Pictures Corporation.

Le temps retrouvé, 1999. [film] Directed by R. Ruiz. France: Gemini Films.

Triumph des Willens, 1935 [film] Directed by L. Riefenstahl. Germany: Leni-Riefenstahl Produktion.

Les trois couronnes du matelot, 1983. [film] Directed by R. Ruiz. France: Film A2.

Trois vies et une seule mort, 1996. [film] Directed by R. Ruiz. France: Gemini Films.

¡Que viva Mexico!, 1931. [film] Directed by S.M. Eisenstein. USA: The Mexican Picture Trust.

Chapter 10

The postcolonial circus
Maurizio Nichetti's *Luna e l'altra*

Marguerite Waller

What is happening to the world lies, at the moment, just outside the realm of common human understanding. It is the writers, the poets, the artists, the singers, the filmmakers who can make the connections, who can find ways of bringing it into the realm of common understanding.

(Arundhati Roy, 2001, p. 32)

Theorizing the postcolonial

In the Call for Papers for the 2011 Convention of the Modern Language Association (2010), postcolonial theorists Shu-mei Shih and Panivong Norindr crisply state the epistemological problem confronted by the postcolonial theoretician/scholar: "No two postcolonial conditions are alike." They then call for participants to address one or both of two questions: "Can there still be grounds for 'postcolonial studies'?" and "If not, what would comparative postcolonial theory look like?" Italian film director/ clown Maurizio Nichetti proleptically responded to both these questions in an aesthetically and metaphysically postcolonial comedy, *Luna e l'altra* (1996), which appeared during a surge of anti-immigrant, neofascist political activity following the fall of the Berlin Wall, the demise of the Italian Communist Party, and the expansion of neoliberal economic practices by international financial and trade institutions. Scholars of Italian colonialism and its aftermath have pointed out that one of the singularities of this history is the relative absence of public reflection on the colonial era. The military defeat that brought Italian colonialism to an end after World War II pre-empted anti-colonial movements in the colonies and in Italy itself, while post-war restrictions on access to colonial archives, as well as reluctance to dwell on the nation's defeat, discouraged intellectual analysis. Pasquale Verdicchio has argued that a similar amnesia surrounds the violence with which southern Italy was subjugated by the North during "unification" (Ben-Ghiat and Fuller, 2008, pp. 1–3; Verdicchio, 1997b). Although Nichetti's films do not conspicuously present themselves as *cinema politico italiano*, the comedic signifying strategies of *Luna e l'altra* are precisely calibrated to the task of opening up a postcolonial space in which the subjugated knowledges of colonization galvanize a new cultural imaginary.[1]

Baroque relation

The specific, local situation to which the Milan-based Nichetti appears to be responding with *Luna e l'altra* is the emergence of two new political parties in Italy. Umberto Bossi's anti-Southern, anti-immigrant, xenophobic, secessionist *Lega Nord* (Northern League) won the mayoral election in Milan in 1993 and went on to become part of center-right-wing media mogul and alleged sexual predator Silvio Berlusconi's ruling coalition in 1994 (Andrews, 2005). Gianfranco Fini, who openly embraced Benito Mussolini's legacy in the early 1990s, making several explicit declarations in favor of fascism, later formed and became president of the *Alleanza Nazionale* (National Alliance) party, which combined elements of the *Movimento Sociale Italiano* (MSI), the direct descendent of Mussolini's fascists, and the scandal-ridden Christian Democrats (Andrews, 2005, p. 18). Fini became Berlusconi's Deputy Prime Minister in 2001, instigating the violent police action against those protesting against the 2001 Genoa summit of the G8.[2] Bossi and Fini, though they did not get along with each other, co-authored the notorious Bossi-Fini law (first enacted in 2002), the most punitive anti-immigration legislation in Europe (Andrews, 2005, pp. 62–4; Parati, 2005, pp. 149–52, 154–6).

Significantly, in responding to the rise of new fascisms and xenophobias, Nichetti sets the narrative of *Luna e l'altra* in the drab periphery of a northern Italian city during the postwar doldrums of 1955. Indeed, Nichetti, his cinematographer, and his costume designer went to great lengths to make not only the clothing, hairstyles, and furnishings of the characters, but also the look and feel of the film itself, authentically mid-1950s (Nichetti, 1996a). This literal authenticity, though, serves to accentuate the film's simultaneous evocation of the 1990s, in the form of a school principal and vice principal who clearly caricature Bossi and Fini, a young African Italian circus performer and his very cute camel, evoking immigration from both North and sub-Saharan Africa, and a television set – alluding to Berlusconi's media empire – being watched fixedly, though it shows only a static test pattern, by a group of circus performers who wonder whether they need to embrace this medium in order to bolster their failing box office returns. The film includes several other politically resonant temporal frames, as well: the height of Italy's colonial era, evoked with a brief recreation of a shot from Jean Vigo's anti-fascist school film *Zéro de conduite* (1933), the Second World War years, indexed and allegorized by an unexploded German bomb buried on the grounds of the fascist-run school, and the "economic miracle" of the 1960s, potently referenced in *Luna's* final sequence, which, like the final sequence of Fellini's *8½* (1963), takes place in a circus ring.

These frames, though, are presented neither chronologically nor developmentally. The term "baroque" as used by Caribbean postcolonial poet and theorist Édouard Glissant (1997) to describe a postcolonial "poetics of relation," more aptly characterizes how the temporal layering of the film operates. Simply put, Nichetti's film layers temporalities in a way that allows them to interact figuratively. Taking Glissant's cue, one could compare Nichetti's baroque to the ways in which each level of sculptures and paintings in a Bernini chapel, for example, produces its own patterns of prefiguration and fulfillment, while the vertically palimpsestic structure of the chapel also creates a spatio-temporal context in which its different temporalities interact with one another. In the process of interacting vertically as well as horizontally, images and events become charged with multiple figural possiblities, fluidly contextualizing one another in the imagination of the spectator. A kind of spatialized temporality – the temporality of the spectator's contemplation – is the indispensable enabler of this process (Alei, 2008). Any moment or image can provide an opening into this figural dimension, as the freeze frames at the end of the film, to which I will return, underscore. In Bernini's case, this figural dimension has a theological charge, whereas Nichetti's baroque, figured within the film by the itinerant circus, is closer to the nomadic subjectivity of Gilles Deleuze and Félix Guattari (1987). In either case, the relationships are not determined by the figures, but rather the figures emerge contingently, produced by their figural relations.[3]

A narrow door

It is Nichetti himself, as a post-World War II subject born in 1948, who would have been an elementary school student in the mid-1950s. He has speculated in another film, *Stefano quante storie* (1993), about the randomness of his having found his way from a conventional bourgeois background, via the political ferment of the late 1960s and early 1970s, to theater, animation, performance, and film directing while some of his contemporaries became policemen or teachers, and others, seemingly indistinguishable from the first group and from himself, languish in prison or have died because of their anti-establishment activism. Beginning with *Ratataplan* (1979) he has directed and starred in a series of brilliant politico-philosophical comedies, featuring a clown persona reminiscent of Keaton, Chaplin, and Tati that allows him to play with the "quivering ontologies" (Marciniak, 2006) produced by crossing borders of all kinds, including that between one decade and another (*Ho fatto Splash*, 1980) or between outer space and earth (*Domani si balla*, 1982). By contrast, in *Ladri di saponette/The Icicle Thief* (1989), Nichetti, parodying himself, becomes the victim of a porous corporate mediascape in which the co-presence of spaces, genres, and temporalities in the virtual landscape of the television screen threatens to reduce all signification to the level of a soap commercial (Waller, 1997).

In other words, Nichetti does not arrive at the threshold of a postcolonial imaginary with no previous experience of the conceptual and aesthetic challenges confronting the bourgeois, Western subject who desires access to another metaphysics. Graziella Parati, advocate and scholar of immigrant culture in Italy, writes persuasively about a "narrow door" offered by Italy's late twentieth-century immigrants that potentially "opens European/Italian tradition to nonwestern traditions" (1997, p. 175). Parati and others have found the presence in their midst of immigrant workers, families, writers, artists, and intellectuals transformative of their understanding of "Italian" history, geography, and culture (Clò, 2003; Lombardi-Diop, 2010; Matteo and Bellucci 1999; Matteo, 2001). What comes into view, she argues, is a dimension that is not "extra" national, as in *extracomunitari* (an Italian term for undocumented immigrants), but rather "inter-national" – "both within the margins of the nation space and in the boundaries *in-between* nations and peoples" (1997, p. 175, citing Homi Bhabha, 1990, p. 4). If we inflect the first part of Parati's formulation with the work of Japanese postcolonial theorist Naoki Sakai (1997; 2006), who has exhaustively questioned the use of terms like "modern" and "nonwestern" insofar as they reinscribe the colonial division of the world into "the West and the Rest," the emphasis would fall on the *encounters* that take place in the spaces between, interactions that develop (only) when trajectories and subjectivities are not fixed taxonomically within chronologies, positions, and identities, regardless of their provenance. Like Parati, Nichetti also invokes the nonWest and the nonNorth, but, also like Parati, Nichetti presents these spatial "others" discursively rather than geographically, as occurring in any context where the colonizing "West" and/or "North" are also being reproduced.[4]

A homophonic guide to sameness and difference

Even before the film begins, the title of *Luna e l'altra* presents spectators with a *mise-en-abyme* of de-essentializing word play. *Luna*, the Italian word for moon, may also be heard as *l'una*, meaning "the one." Thus "Luna," the moon, can also be, or can be at the same time, both *l'una* (the one) and *l'altra* (the other). When, even more loosely, the reader/viewer ignores the spacing of the letters and looks or listens for other homophonic possibilities, *altra* metamorphoses into *al tra*, translatable as "to the between," becoming a different kind of entity altogether – something like a gateway, or perhaps a door, "to the between."

Thinking about the moon as seen from earth, a recurring image in the film, we receive further hints about where the film might take its audience philosophically, politically, and aesthetically. We often think of the moon's light as simply secondary, a reflection of sun. But the appearance of this familiar heavenly body may also present itself in less hierarchical terms. Its several apparent shapes are, after all, as much the product of shadow as of light. Moreover, the shapes of the moon, except when it is full, are the result of *our* situated and simultaneous gaze at both the illuminated and the unilluminated sides. From a less terracentric perspective the light of the moon and its appearance of cycles are even more purely relational, created by the intersection of the sun's light by a moving material object, the moon, which in turn revolves around another material object, the earth, which is also in motion both around its own axis and around the sun. Images of the moon work somewhat analogously to cinema, in fact, where, in a darkened room, the materialities of celluloid and movie screen together transform the light coming from a projector into patterns that appear to be meaningful. Nichetti's film supports all of these readings, not only of the moon, but of pattern in general – whether historical, political, social, or cultural.[5]

Colonizers colonized

The film opens with the sound of marching feet and a voice barking "*sinistra ... sinistra*" (left ... left), followed on the soundtrack by a fanfare and a performance of the Italian national anthem. (Like Luna/*l'una*, *sinistra* here playfully undercuts the univocality of "*Il Canto degli Italiani*.") An aerial master shot reveals a school ceremony during which a bronze bust of a young woman is unveiled by two small boys. The accompanying eulogy, dedicating the bust to the *ricordo perpetuo* (perpetual memory) of Maestra Luna di Capua, imparts the distressing information that the young woman in question has sacrificed her life to save the lives of her students and colleagues. A close-up of the bust fades into a close-up of Luna's living form, and the film embarks on what at first seems to be a posthumous flashback to the events that have led up to this solemn commemoration. The film's narrative does not, however, return to the ending presented at its beginning. On his web page, Nichetti (1996b) provocatively wrote at the time of the film's release, "Before discovering the hidden secret in the heroic death of the *maestra* (teacher), we will have to run through the images of the entire film, images that are, however, only shadows chasing one another on a white screen." (translation mine). History and memory are presented as mysterious rather than explanatory.

Two classroom scenes, one a geography class on Africa and the other a lesson on varieties of ordnance, including the unexploded German bomb still buried somewhere on the school grounds, evoke Italy's complicated geopolitical history as both colonizer – in Africa, Albania, the Dodecanese, and Croatia – and (perhaps more ambiguously) colonized – first by its Nazi ally after the fall of Mussolini, and then, arguably, by the postwar U.S. occupation (which continues to this day in the form of large and growing military bases). Both dimensions of Italian colonial history soon migrate to the film's characters and their interactions. As the recently-arrived circus is being set up, two boys, the dark-skinned one with the camel and his lighter companion (the bearded lady's son), are duly enrolled in Luna's school, much to the annoyance of its racist administrators. Assigned to Luna's classroom, the boys are disruptive, though not without cause since Luna immediately confiscates a magic lantern they have stolen from the circus's Russian magician. Literally executing Luna's command to get down from the windowsill, the second boy leaps out of the classroom window onto the roof, motivating Nichetti's recreation of an iconic shot from Jean Vigo's classic anarchist film, *Zéro de conduite/ Zero for Conduct* (1993), in which students bombard their parents and teachers from the apex of the school's roof on Founder's Day. This nod to Vigo situates Luna herself in the role of colonizer as well as colonized, replicating the pattern of colonizations by and of the Italian nation-state on the level of her own professional life. Shamelessly exploited and sexually objectified by both the principal and the vice principal, she nevertheless enforces the militaristic discipline of the school *vis-à-vis* her students. Even on the most intimate level, at home, in a sunless basement apartment, surrounded by hostile, anti-Southern neighbors, she and her father repeat the colonizer/colonized dynamic. The straight-laced Luna and her father, a macho, housework-averse, singing Neapolitan, play a Grand Guignol of alternating oppressions of, and rebellions against, one another.

The dustbin of history

The school *bidello* (janitor/concierge), Angelo Franchini, a Keatonesque clown figure, played by Nichetti himself, is neither a colonizer nor, as a clown, a successfully colonized subject. Angelo is shyly and deeply in love with Luna whose strenuous efforts to perform the role of proper schoolteacher prevent her from reciprocating, or even noticing, his affections. Angelo also plays flute in a band of graying World War II Communist *partigiani* who play the old partisan anthems, *Bandiera rossa* and *Bella ciao*, at the funerals of comrades. This is the same band that plays the *national* anthem at the commemoration ceremony, a discovery that subtly extends the play on *sinistra* in the film's opening shot. The apparently obvious reference made by the decrepitude of the band members to the demise of Italian Communism after the fall of the Berlin Wall is interestingly complicated by a second intertextual reference to one of the classic prewar films of European political cinema. Playing the flute while dressed in his *bidello* uniform, the figure of Angelo comically recalls the tragic French aristocrat, Capitaine de Boeldieu, in Jean Renoir's *La grande illusion* (1937). De Boeldieu, an anachronism in the context of World War I's mass killing and trench warfare, sacrifices his life while playing a piccolo to distract German prison guards from the escape of two of his fellow, less aristocratic (one working class and one Jewish), prisoners of war. Angelo, the flute-playing janitor, will not be called upon to sacrifice his life, but by the end of the film he has surrendered both his uniform and his flute in order to perform in the circus (wearing a turban and harem pants). If Italian working-class social identities and left-wing politics are destined for the dustbin of history, as the Renoir reference suggests, then the dustbin may be where the action is.

A dark and stormy night

Having brought the purloined lantern home with her, Luna is sleeping fitfully when a bolt of lightening from one of the film's several violent storms activates the strange device. Luna's shadow separates itself from her body and goes its own way the next morning, while Luna, not realizing she has lost her shadow, goes to work. Identical in appearance to Luna, once she has washed off some residual duskiness, but relishing her freedom from Luna's repressed and repressive *persona*, the shadow Luna thrills Signor di Capua by reverting to Neapolitan dialect and showering him with affection. By the end of the day, having taken up residence in the local bordello, she confronts Luna with her decision to leave town with the circus. To make this plan work though, Ombretta (literally "Little Shadow" but also connoting shady or disreputable) must revitalize the circus, particularly following the debacle of the Russian magician's attempt to continue his shadow act without the magic lantern, an attempt that involves Angelo in a disturbing performance of black face.[6] As Ombretta first finds them, the performers in Nichetti's circus acknowledge that their program is outdated and momentarily entertain the idea that television – not so subtly referencing media mogul-turned-Prime Minister Silvio Berlusconi – might be the solution. A sequence showing the static test pattern of the state network (*RAI – Radiotelevisione Italiana*), fixing its audience's unswerving gaze on a claustrophobically tiny screen, telegraphs in an instant the difference between the nationalist/neofascist and the figural/palimpsestic gaze. Even the profit-oriented circus managers dismiss this petrification of body and spirit, opening the way for Ombretta to propose a new act, which turns out to involve a radical transformation of the Russian's magic lantern routine and to require the collaboration of the local proletarian, Angelo.

Before this Gramscian North/South alliance can be realized, though, the toxic, intersecting phallocentrisms of Nazism/fascism, nationalism/colonialism, and sexism/racism, which infuse all the sites in the film – school, home, butcher's shop, bordello, and even the circus itself – must be dealt with. A concatenation of events, culminating in the explosion of the German bomb, carries the film to its revelation of the secret of the heroic death of the *maestra*. The death of Luna/Ombretta's father, to which I will return below, initiates these transformations. In its aftermath, Ombretta impersonates Luna at the school's Arbor Day ceremony during which the vice principal (the Fini caricature) accidentally unearths the buried German bomb. As everyone else backs away in terror, Ombretta picks up the phallic projectile and carries it out of the schoolyard into a sidewalk urinal. A tremendous explosion, lavishly photographed and taking up considerable screen time, blows up the urinal – that quotidian signifier of masculine entitlement – and appears to blow up Ombretta as well. The explosion, though, leaves her unscathed since she is "just a shadow," and she decides to reunite with Luna on condition that Luna abandon her dreary career as a schoolteacher and (under cover of her "heroic death") join Angelo in the circus. The closing sequence of the film is set in the circus ring where Luna and Angelo perform a new version, more radical that their first one, of the alliance between the laboring classes of North and South envisioned by Gramsci in *The Southern Question* (Gramsci, 1995).

You can't get there from here

The process of making something "happen" epistemologically, though, cannot be represented. (The chaos of the storms and the explosion figures this unmappability in the film.) Moving marginalized subjects to center stage is more complicated than, say, putting the two circus boys on the bandstand during the Arbor Day ceremony, as the film quickly acknowledges. When the bomb is unearthed directly in front of them, their position on stage puts them in great danger. Becoming visible within the episteme that decrees one's absence and invisibility can have lethal consequences. How, then, does the film move (itself and its audience) from the "repressed inquietude" of the "obsolete but arrogant, modernist, xenophobic, colonial, misogynist, patriarchal, nation-state" (Sakai, 1997, pp. 165–6) toward a nonpatriarchal, "postcolonial" something/somewhere else? The witty, wicked, lightning-fast editing, the surreal dash of animation, the iconographic complexity of each shot, and the luminous physicality of the acting, particularly that of Iaia Forte's Luna/Ombretta, create a seductive web of cinematic pleasures that allow the film to make its metaphysical moves without the spectator being aware, on a "conscious" level, of what is "happening." The process of making something "happen" epistemologically can occur, in fact, only if spectators are not engaged in the kind of "knowing" that reinscribes a sense of mastery, but are rather, as Walter Benjamin theorized, being entertained in a state of "distraction" (1969, pp. 240–1).

An example of how Nichetti's spectators are nudged to activate the figures in his baroque chapel will bring us closer to the "secret" alluded to on his website. A clap of thunder interrupts what seemed to be a plot we were following concerning a butcher,

Tito, who is also the conductor of the band of musical *partigiani* with whom Angelo plays. Tito owns the local bordello, which he encourages the band members to visit after rehearsals in the butcher shop. After one rehearsal, Tito goes to visit the wife of one of the musicians, while the musician is visiting his bordello.[7] Suddenly the window frame behind the bed where Tito and the wife are about to have sex is entered by the head and two humps of a camel, while on the soundtrack the thunder is backed by a vaguely Middle Eastern musical theme and the sound of rain. The first of several storms in the film, the downpour also heralds a turn in the way we consume and interpret its images. The shot of the camel from inside the bedroom is followed by an exterior shot, of a procession of circus trucks arriving in the city, whose axis intersects at a ninety-degree angle with the axis of the bedroom shot. Using the "accidental" (rather than narratively motivated) intersection of the bedroom window and the camel as its switch point, the film departs on a new narrative track involving the circus. The disconnection between the two narratives redirects our attention to the space opened up between them. Shifting the gaze of the spectator from the composition of images within frames (our gaze is cut off just as we are about to see some sex!) to the procession or flow of images, figured by the Fellinian circus procession, the film constructs a different kind of audio-visual experience.[8] What begin to come into view are the edges of scenes and the spaces between them. Here, specifically, our attention is drawn to the contrast between Tito and the two tiny men and bearded woman who direct the circus through the night-time streets of the city. The non-normative circus characters, illuminated by jagged lightning bolts outside, mark a limit to the heteronormative sex/gender system, paradoxically exemplified by the "normal" adulterous couple. The camel will go on to exercise a charmingly disjunctive visual effect throughout the film, particularly when it is tethered outside the school – ground zero for the inculcation of the nationalist geography and historiography that occlude colonial violence, both epistemic and empirical, and its consequences for both colonizers and colonized. The camel's incongruity in the school yard draws attention to the historical and cultural connections between Italy and Africa, particularly when an old, half-submerged military mess kit, from which the camel has been drinking muddy water, is mistaken by the vice principal for the German *bomba*.

The postcolonial circus

The epistemological and aesthetic paradigm of the circus, synecdochally present on the school grounds, becomes an interestingly "dangerous" supplement to the paradigms of both epistemological and social organization promulgated by the state through its educational and entertainment systems (Derrida, 1976, pp. 141–64). As a nonhierarchical, nonnarrative series of performances, each with its own genealogy, the circus suggests intriguing alternatives to exclusionary party politics, nationalist geography and historiography, and binary constructions of self and other that only perpetuate the phallocentrism of power politics (Trinh, 1997, p. 417). Visually, the big top in the film resembles a soft-sided, glowing flying saucer resting lightly on the ground under the full moon. Within such an itinerant, ephemeral, inclusive space, circus performances become interrelated with one another through many processes: among them, the way the acts are sequenced, the collaboration and cohabitation of transnational performers in a community whose collective personality emerges and changes with the times and the places in which they perform, and, not least, the different ways in which each spectator interrelates the non-narrative sequence of performances and the unique angle of vision from which s/he does so. In what way does this community not, in fact, mirror the communities of spectators for which it performs? Or to put it differently, is the circus banished to the realm of the carnivalesque or even the extraterrestrial *because* it images the originary, nonbinary, generative workings of difference in the creation of community, an image that threatens the hegemony of dominant power relations? (See Rosello, this volume.) Concerning identities and power relations, postcolonial filmmaker and theorist Trinh Minh-ha writes:

> To raise the question of identity is to reopen the discussion on the self/other relationship in its enactment of power relations . . . In such a concept the other is almost unavoidably either opposed to the self or submitted to the self's dominance. It is always condemned to remain in its shadow while making attempts at being its equal.
>
> (1997, p. 415)

The *bordello*, located somewhere between the school and the circus, offers a "safe," commodified version of the circus paradigm, suggesting that the *desire* for more polymorphous social relations persists, though its satisfaction is available only in a very circumscribed way and only to adult males (virtually all the adult males in the community from across the political spectrum frequent Tito's bordello) and at the expense of both sex workers and wives. The bordello works something like a drug, or perhaps like a utility, maintaining (for the men) a dependable access to nonhegemonic subjectivities and interactions, which are, however, always already recuperated within the capitalist/patriarchal/colonial economics of both money and desire that permit them this access. What would it take to move out of this closed circuit and travel the rest of the way from *bordello* to circus?

With the arrival of the circus in the city, authority figures begin to experience difficulty, as does linear narrative. Characters and the narratives they think they are a part of begin to appear tangential to each other, regardless of which ones are, for the moment, in the foreground. Even Tito, who seems to cover all the bases as musician/ butcher/ communist/capitalist/comrade/cuckolder, is displaced when he tries to grope Ombretta, commodifying her in accord with his roles as butcher and bordello owner as a *bel pezzo di carne* (nice piece of meat). With a powerful knee to the groin and a slap with a slab of his own meat, the previously unnoticed shadow of the subaltern female relegates *him* to the shadows of extradiegesis.

Luna/Ombretta's father also disappears, though not without pathos. In the warmth of his daughter's (Ombretta's) affection, Signor di Capua regains his Neapolitan *brio*, venturing out of the apartment to celebrate her artistic triumph in the circus with a visit to the *bordello*. Ombretta, meanwhile, has successfully instructed Angelo in the arts of mutual seduction. The reconciliation of father and daughter is unsustainable, as this asymmetry in their sex lives suggests. Ombretta's desire is no more compatible with Signor di Capua's *machismo* than it is with her employers' *fascismo*. Furthermore, if, as Pasquale Verdicchio argues, the "unification" of Italy is really an alibi for the North's conquest and colonization of the South (1997a, pp.1–2; 21–51), the restored position for which Signor di Capua yearns is itself a colonized position. The southern macho is actually a good fit with northern fascism, as the electoral success of Fini's party in the South has demonstrated. But Ombretta, the shadow, has come into her own because she has broken with the hierarchical system of identity formation that made her secondary to Luna and Luna subordinate to the men in her life. During one of Ombretta's and Angelo's performances, the shadow of Ombretta's father suddenly enters the circus tent, approaches and embraces Ombretta, and ascends upward, giving a little goodbye wave. Bedlam erupts meanwhile at the *bordello*, as the camera reveals the frozen form of Signor di Capua, sitting in a bathtub silenced by a heart-attack with a great smile on his face. The static *cliché* of Neapolitan *machismo* cannot survive the flow of desires, the acknowledgment of, and pleasure in, the others' pleasure, that Signor di Capua, even with his stereotypical performances, was part of. His *trans-figuration* – his ability to figure across different frames – allows him to join other figures that might enter or exit at any time, but no longer to dominate Luna. In the wake of his loss, the rift between Luna and Ombretta begins to mend.

Lunar eclipse

Where, when, and who are we, Sakai asks, once we have exposed spatio-temporally orienting terms like "Western" and "modern" as artifacts of colonialism (1997, p. 166)? The double staging of the passing away of Signor di Capua, as experienced in the bordello and at the circus, acknowledges this knotty question, which has haunted deconstructive, queer, border, and postcolonial theory, both conceptually and affectively. The film's climax and dénouement take up the question of what becomes of the secondary – the subordinate, subjugated, occluded, colonized – figures in the absence of the master terms – the father, the center, the logos, the phallus, the West, the modern, the metropole, the nation. In a *tour-de-force* mirror sequence, the film returns to the riddle of how the secondary becomes the primary (*Luna/l'una*) and how to think about the "other" (*l'altra/l'al tra*) of this "one."

In an intricately choreographed scene between Luna and Ombretta that follows Signor di Capua's death/trans-figuration, the relative ontological status of the shadow world and what we take for the empirical, material, phenomenological world is first reversed and then rendered moot – not really the question after all. An establishing shot of the two figures in Ombretta's circus dressing room frames Luna standing screen right (apparently) in relation to her seated *doppelganger*, Ombretta, screen left. Ombretta's reflection is seen in her dressing table mirror. However, as Luna approaches Ombretta, their apparent positions are reversed. The whole screen, in effect, reveals itself to be a mirror (or mirror image) when the figure of Luna is suddenly eclipsed by her own movement into the room toward Ombretta. What Ombretta's double image now reveals is that the frame within the frame (the mirror within the mirror) has created an optical illusion of foreground and background, center and margin, mirror image and material body. In other words, the edges or borders form the picture at least as fundamentally as the picture determines the edges/borders. Gilles Deleuze, writing about a new breed of cinematic images and the desire that is necessary for their birth, refers to their mental rather than phenomenological ground:

> we no longer know what is imaginary or real, physical or mental . . . not because they are confused, but because we do not have to know and there is no longer even a place from which to ask. It is as if the real and the imaginary were running after each other, as if each was being reflected in the other, around a point of indiscernability.
> (1989, p. 7)

Not everyone is as excited as Deleuze by the prospect of this abolition of the real/imaginary distinction, however, nor does achieving it on paper or on film address the power relations at stake.

Epistemic panic

I borrow the term "panic" in the sense elaborated by Eve Sedgwick in her discussion of "homosexual panic" in *Epistemology of the Closet*. She describes a defensive reaction to a "male definitional crisis," suffered by an individual who is uncertain about his sexual identity. It is the whole system, though, that enables this "individual" panic by denying the possibility of definitional uncertainty, an uncertainty that can be triggered as easily by interaction with women as with men, as Sedgwick points out (1990, pp. 20; 177; 198). By analogy, those identities most grounded in and supported by nationalist/colonialist epistemology are likely to have a defensive reaction to the multiple definitional crises they suffer when those "others" against which they define themselves cross the line, when "aliens" become residents and even citizens. *Quando c'era lui,* (When *he* [Mussolini] was in power), splutters the principal of Luna's school, "camels stayed in Africa."

The circus performance of Luna/Ombretta and Angelo at the end of the film addresses this panic by means of a refiguring of bodies and shadows. In earlier performances, Ombretta changed shape behind a scrim while Angelo performed in front of it. But Luna/Ombretta and Angelo appear *together*, first as shadows behind the scrim, and then, as they step out to take their bows, as full color, three-dimensional live-action figures. Their "emergence from the shadows," a familiar enlightenment-inflected trope for the acknowledgement of subaltern and clandestine subjects, is, however, quickly ironized by the antics of two more figures, a new pair of shadows, who sneak onto the stage Luna/Ombretta and Angelo have just vacated to wave and bow to an implied audience in some other space, tangential to the live-action space. When the twin couples finally acknowledge each other across the now porous border marked by the scrim, they transform the conventional hierarchy of bodies and shadows.

Figure 10.1 Refiguring bodies and shadows (Source: still *Luna e l'altra*, 1996)

The ground that belongs to no one

Trinh Minh-ha writes "Interdependency [. . .] consists of creating a ground that belongs to no one, not even to the creator" (1997, p. 418). The move from one couple to two couples at the end of *Luna e l'altra* is as surprising as the camel's head was in the bedroom window and just seismic cinematically. The film enacts, through miraculously unpretentious and efficient imagery, the impact of desiring the removal of, or removing the desire for, terms and principles of domination. Not only do the spaces that can be accessed via the careful deconstruction of binary oppositions not disappear, these spaces proliferate. Sakai and Solomon's "postcolonial" description of the same situation that induces epistemic panic from within the "Western" episteme is that knowledge increases as a result of "replacing the sovereignty of bodies of knowledge with the sociality of knowledgeable bodies" (2006, p. 18). These interactions involve not only polymorphous interpersonal possibilities, but also unforeseeable interconceptual possibilities (Waller, 2005). Among and between conceptual systems, if they are not imagined in terms of self-enclosed, homogeneous "cultures," a space of heterogeneity that enables community *because* it belongs to no one opens up.

Two freeze-frames at the end of the film emerge as a novel trope for the precariousness of the Euclidean spaces, proscenium framings, and linear temporalities of exclusionary national geographies, historiographies, and politics. First the live action couple is frozen, overwritten with the film's title, and darkened. A beat later the shadow couple follows the first couple through the freeze frame into darkness – the same fecund cinematic darkness, I have argued elsewhere, into which Fellini sends his cast of characters from the circus ring at the end of *8 ½* (Waller, 2011). Produced by reprinting a single frame – in temporal terms 1/24 of a second – as many times as are necessary to make up the desired length of the shot, the freeze frame expands the image of a split second to become itself the edge or frame of the temporal continuum out of which it was taken.

It enacts the potential of any split second, in any conceptual dimension (literal, figural, physical, mental) to take on this framing power and, conversely, the ephemerality of any such frame.

Nichetti generalizes the epistemic, aesthetic, and affective power of this editing "secret," playing upon the dialectical theory and practice of montage elaborated by his revolutionary Russian predecessors, Sergei Eisenstein, Lev Kuleshov, and others (hence the Russian magician with the magic lantern). For the early Soviet filmmakers, the power of editing had to do with moving spectators from literal, referential readings of images to a conceptual level where new forms of thought and perception could take shape (Eisenstein, 1977, p. 238). But the goal of this leap into "montage understanding," as Eisenstein writes in his influential essay, "Dickens, Griffith, and the Film Today," is to create a new realism, which entails the projection of a new overarching unity. Cinematic montage, which was to extend synaesthetically through all "elements, parts, and details of film-work," should combine to achieve "an organic embodiment of a single idea or conception" (p. 255). The "whole screen image" was to pass into a new "unity." By *doubling* and *sequencing* freeze frames, Nichetti refuses unity, even a dialectical version of unity, as a goal. Neither freeze frame frames the other; it is the space of *interaction* between framings that emerges as originary, allowing the translucent scrim to serve as the point of connection rather than the line of exclusion between figures and their shadows. The move from one couple to two allows *both* couples, not to merge but to interact, and then to make way for more others (names of the film's cast and crew, in this case). Drawn contingently into each other's place and time, the freeze frames create yet one more, and the most consequential yet, "space between."

Notes

1 My reading of *Luna e l'altra* as a postcolonial film is pervasively indebted to the work of both Aine O'Healy (2007, 2009) and Derek Duncan (2008, 2010) on Italy's postcolonial cinema and to Millicent Marcus's *After Fellini: National Cinema in the Postmodern Age* (2002).

2 One protester was killed, and hundreds arrested. Detained protesters, according to author and eye-witness Geoff Andrews, were forced to sing Fascist songs (2005, p. 13).

3 Deleuze and Guattari use the pollination of an orchid by a wasp to exemplify the contingent deterritorializations and reterritorializations (wasp becomes orchid; orchid becomes wasp) of rhizomatic relations (1987, p. 10).

4 I am indebted to Tanya Rawal's treatment of the discursive production of "the global South" across many literary and cinematic sites in her M.A. thesis What Arbitrary Assignments! Revising the Global South and Engendering Community (2010).

5 Cristina Lombardi-Diop points out that the poems dedicated to the moon and its philosophical underpinnings by Romantic poet Giacomo Leopardi are also likely subtexts of the film (2010).

6 See Codell in this volume for an analysis of the racial politics of blackface.

7 The sex work of the women in "left-wing" Tito's bordello ironically figures capitalism in one of its most condensed forms. The labor power of the women is not only exploited to produce commodities; they are themselves the commodities produced.

8 Nichetti's relationship to Fellini is relevant to my argument, but this fascinating topic exceeds the scope of this essay.

Bibliography

Alei, P., 2008. Class lecture on Bernini's Chigi Chapel. U.C. Rome Study Center. Rome, Italy. April 22, 2008.

Andrews, G., 2005. *Not a Normal Country: Italy after Berlusconi*. London: Pluto Press.

Benjamin, W., 1969 [1936]. The Work of Art in an Age of Mechanical Reproduction. Translated from German by H. Zohn. In: H. Arendt. ed., 1969. *Illuminations*. New York: Schocken Books, pp. 217–51.

Ben-Ghiat, R. and Fuller, M., eds., 2008. *Italian Colonialism*. New York: Palgrave Macmillan.

Clò, C. 2003. Italy in the world and the world in Italy: Tracing alternative cultural trajectories. Ph.D. thesis University of California, San Diego.

Deleuze, G., 1989. *Cinema 2: The Time-Image*. Translated from French by H. Tomlinson and R. Galeta. Minneapolis: University of Minnesota Press.

Deleuze, G. and Guattari, F., 1987. *A Thousand Plateaus: Capitalism and Schizophrenia*. Translated from French by B. Massumi. Minneapolis: University of Minnesota Press.

Derrida, J., 1976. *Of Grammatology*. Translated from French by G. Spivak. Baltimore, MD: The Johns Hopkins University Press.

Duncan, D., 2008. Italy's Postcolonial Cinema and its Histories of Representation. *Italian Studies*. 63.2.

Duncan, D., 2010. With J. Andall. Hybridity in Italian Colonial and Postcolonial Culture. In *National Belongings: Hybridity in Colonial and Postcolonial Cultures*. Oxford: Peter Lang, pp. 195–214.

Eisenstein, S., 1977 [1949]. *Film Form: Essays in Film Theory*. Translated from Russian and ed. by J. Leyda. 1977. New York: Harcourt, Brace, Jovanovich.

Glissant, É., 1997. *Poetics of Relation*. Translated from French by B. Wing. Ann Arbor: The University of Michigan Press.

Gramsci, A., 1995. *The Southern Question*. Translated from Italian and introduced by P. Verdicchio. West Lafayette, IN: Bordighera, Inc. Purdue University.

Lombardi-Diop, C., 2010. Discussion of Leopardi's poems dedicated to the moon and its philosophical implications. [email] (Personal communication, 26 April 2010).

Marciniak, K., 2006. *Alienhood: Citizenship, Exile, and the Logic of Difference*. Minneapolis: University of Minnesota Press.

Marcus, M. 2002. *After Fellini: National Cinema in the Postmodern Age*. Baltimore, MD and London: The Johns Hopkins University Press.

Matteo, S., ed., 2001. *ItaliAfrica: Bridging Continents and Cultures*. Stony Brook, NY: Forum Italicum Publishing.

Matteo, S. and Bellucci, S., eds., 1999. *Africa Italia: Due continenti si avviciniano*. Santarcangelo di Romagna: Fara Editore.

Nichetti, M., 1996a. Discussion about Nichetti's films. [Conversation] (Personal communication, Milan, Italy, 4 July 1996).

Nichetti, M., 1996b. Pagina ufficiali dell'artista. [online] 1996. Available at: http://www.nichetti. it/ [Accessed 3 March 2003].

Norindr, P. and Shih, S., 2010. Call for convention paper proposals, *Modern Language Association*. [online] 2010. Available at: http://www.mla.org/cfp [Accessed 16 March 2010].

O'Healy, Á., 2007. Border Traffic: Reimagining the Voyage to Italy. In: K. Marciniak, A. Imre, and Á. O'Healy eds., *Transnational Feminism in Film and Media*. New York and Basingstoke: Palgrave Macmillan, pp. 37–52.

O'Healy, Á., 2009. *[Non] è una Somala*: Deconstructing African Femininity in Italian Film. *The Italianist*. 29, 275–98.

Parati, G., 1997. Strangers in Paradise: Foreigners and Shadows in Italian Literature. In: B. Allen and M. Russo, eds., 1997. *Revisioning Italy: National Identity and Global Culture.* Minneapolis: University of Minnesota Press, pp. 169–90.

Parati, G., 2005. *Migration Italy: The Art of Talking Back in a Destination Culture.* Toronto: University of Toronto Press.

Rawal, T., 2010. What Arbitrary Assignments! Revising the Global South and Engendering Community, unpublished M.A. thesis. University of California, Riverside.

Roy, A., *Power Politics.* 2001 Cambridge, MA: South End.

Sakai, N., 1997. Modernity and its Critique: The Problem of Universalism and Particularism. In: Sakai, N. ed. *Translation and Subjectivity: On "Japan" and Cultural Nationalism.* Minneapolis: University of Minnesota Press, pp. 153–76.

Sakai, N. and Solomon, J., 2006. Introduction: Addressing the Multitude of Foreigners, Echoing Foucault. In: Sakai, N. and Solomon, J., eds. 2006. *Translation, Biopolitics, Colonial Difference.* Hong Kong: Hong Kong University Press, pp. 1–35.

Sedgwick, E., 1990. *Epistemology of the Closet.* Berkeley: University of California Press.

Trinh, M., 1997 [1988]. Not You/Like You: Postcolonial Women and the Interlocking Questions of Identity and Difference. In: McClintock, A., Mufti, A. and Shohat, E. eds., 1997. *Dangerous Liaisons: Gender, Nation, and Postcolonial Perspectives.* Minneapolis and London: University of Minnesota Press, pp. 415–19.

Verdicchio, P., 1997a. *Bound by Distance: Rethinking Nationalism Through the Italian Diaspora.* Madison, NJ: Fairleigh Dickinson University Press.

Verdicchio, P., 1997b. The Preclusion of Postcolonial Discourse in Southern Italy. In: Allen, B. and Russo, M. eds., 1997. *Revisioning Italy: National Identity and Global Culture.* Minneapolis: University of Minnesota Press, pp. 191–212.

Waller, M., 1997. Decolonizing the Screen: From *Ladri di biciclette* to *Ladri di saponette.* In: Allen, B. and Russo, M. eds., 1997. *Revisioning Italy: National Identity and Global Culture.* Minneapolis: University of Minnesota Press, pp. 253–74.

Waller, M., 2005. "One Voice Kills Both Our Voices": "First World" Feminism and Transcultural Feminist Engagment. In: Waller, M. and Marcos, S. eds., 2005. *Dialogue and Difference: Feminisms Challenge Globalization.* New York: Palgrave Macmillan, pp. 113–42.

Waller, M., 2011. The Postcolonial Circus: Fellini and Nichetti. Unpublished paper presented on the panel "Circus Thoughts" at the Annual Convention of the Modern Language Association, Los Angeles, CA.

Filmography

8½, 1963. [film] Directed by F. Fellini. Italy: Cineriz.

Domani si balla, 1982. [film] Directed by M. Nichetti. Italy: Vides Cinematografica.

Ho fatto Splash, 1980. [film] Directed by M. Nichetti. Italy: Vides Cinematografica.

La grande illusion, 1937. [film] Directed by J. Renoir. France: RAC.

Ladri di saponette, 1989. [film] Directed by M. Nichetti. Italy: Bambú Cinema e TV.

Luna e l'altra, 1996. [film] Directed by M. Nichetti. Italy: Bambú Cinema e TV.

Ratataplan, 1979. [film] Directed by M. Nichetti. Italy: Vides Cinematografica.

Stefano quante storie, 1993. [film] Directed by M. Nichetti. Italy: Bambú Cinema e TV.

Zéro de conduite, 1933. [film] Directed by J. Vigo. France: Franfilmdis.

Chapter 11

Postcolonial adaptations
Gained and lost in translation

Sandra Ponzanesi

Since the beginning of cinema as a new art form, literature and film have inspired, antagonized, rivaled, and remediated one another.[1] The debate on literature and film is, in fact, as old as film itself. How does postcoloniality reframe and reinterpret this long-standing debate between literature and film? After a brief survey of the complex field of adaptation studies, I turn to an analysis and comparison of two postcolonial adaptations made by diasporic female filmmakers: *Bride and Prejudice* directed by Gurinder Chadha, based on Jane Austen's classic *Pride and Prejudice*, and *Women Without Men* directed by Shirin Neshat, based on the novel of the same title by Shahrnush Parsipur. Using these two examples of postcolonial adaptation, I will suggest that the intersection of cinematic adaptation and postcolonial cinema offers a particularly dense nexus from which to explore issues of postcolonial critique and its complex links to the cultural industry. This marriage of adaptation and postcolonial critique is, in fact, not always successful. In the transposition of semiotic codes, languages, genres, audiences, and markets something is as often lost as gained in translation.

The field of adaptation theory: 50 years beyond

The debate within adaptation studies has always revolved around a set of issues: should the film be faithful to the novel or should it be considered as a different medium with its own cinematographic conventions and system of representation? Either the value of literature must be defended against the cannibalization and vulgarization of cinema, or cinema has now redeemed itself from being a sub-art, a parasite on literature.[2] Adaptation studies and its technical aspects have undergone a complex development which unfortunately I cannot pursue here.[3] Nonetheless, for the sake of clarity, we can identify three main waves. The first wave, the *essentialist* one, dates back to 1957 with the publication of George Bluestone's seminal book *Novels into Film*. It is marked by the question of fidelity issues, and it is based on the unquestioned superiority of the novel over film. The prestige of the culture remains superior to that of film, which is seen as commercial and ultimately a devaluation of the original. This essentialist approach emphasized the disjunction between the two media, setting them up as rivals and emphasizing what novels can do that films cannot.

The second wave is the *structuralist* one, based on the assumption of equality between the two media and heavily influenced by the work of Gérard Genette (1982), Roland Barthes (1977), and Seymour Chatman (1978). This approach sees narrative (the language of literature and the language of movies) as composed of functions and all signifying practices as part of a shared sign system. This allows for a leveling of the hierarchy between the literary and the filmic. Narrative is a common denominator, but there are differences between the two semiotic systems that allow for the transferability of certain items and the untransferability of others.

The third is the *poststructuralist, feminist, postcolonial* wave to which this essay contributes. This strand considers the contextual and material conditions through which movies can be realized – for example, the socio-cultural contexts, the economic aspect of the cultural industry and the distribution system, and the questions of reception and evaluation – beyond Western and patriarchal mainstream paradigms. This last stream of adaptation studies concerns the breaking down of boundaries between literature and film, high culture and low culture, original and copy, while emphasizing the performative and transformative interactions between the two media. It acknowledges wider cultural implications and employs different disciplinary approaches such as cultural studies and feminist postcolonial theory. Adaptation is understood as "remediation," a translation of a text from one medium to another. Adaptation can then be seen as the reformatting and transcoding of the novel (Bolter and Grusin, 2000).

It is precisely this intermedial, intertextual, and contextual understanding of adaptation that has fostered a revival in adaptation studies, which ranges from Linda Hutcheon's argument that all texts are hypertexts (2006) to new media perspectives from which all texts appear remediated, reformatted, and transcoded. In place of the text/film dichotomy, new media studies proposes a paradigm of convergence (Jenkins, 2006).[4]

This notion of convergence is ripe for theoretical and methodological development, which also includes the undoing of the dominant Western paradigm (Stam, 2004; Pauwels, 2007). But despite these recent shifts, the postcolonial lens is rarely applied in adaptation studies. Such an intervention, I believe, has important implications for the fields of both adaptation theory and postcolonial cinema.

Postcolonial film adaptations

Postcolonial studies become relevant to the third wave of adaptation studies when the binarism between novel and film gives way to questions of translation, remediation, and contextualization. A quick survey of adaptations associated with colonial histories and postcolonial transitions serves to highlight adaptation's postcolonial potential. I will briefly distinguish four possible categories of postcolonial adaptations and then move on to a close analysis of two case studies that instantiate two of these categories.

My first category is the *adaptation of empire or colonial novels* such as *A Passage to India,* directed by David Lean, 1984, based on E.M. Foster's novel of the same name, or *Out of Africa,* directed by Sidney Pollock, 1985, based on the memoirs of Karen Blixen. The list could be much longer. This category comprises film adaptations that are fairly faithful to the source and as such do not undermine its colonial and conservative message.

The second category is the *adaptation of classics* with a view to correcting and complementing them, seeing them through a postcolonial lens, which offers a new understanding, context, and analysis of power relations not previously made visible. The 1999 adaptation of *Mansfield Park* directed by Patricia Rozema, for example, envisions Jane Austen's novel through the postcolonial critique of Edward Said, foregrounding Caribbean slavery, which in the novel is largely left in the background. A more light-hearted adaptation in this category is Gurinder Chadha's *Bride and Prejudice* (analyzed later in this essay), a tongue-in-cheek adaptation of Jane Austen's classic and often-adapted novel *Pride and Prejudice*, which recontextualizes in a modern frame and in a postcolonial/global setting, the war between the sexes in relation to the operation of capital within a patriarchal state.

A third category is the *adaptation of postcolonial texts* transposed into film by the Western cultural industry adapted either by Hollywood or by major European ventures. Here the question of big corporations or mainstream production houses is relevant as they tend to assimilate the novel into a mainstream cinematic discourse. Whether the critical edge of a postcolonial novel is maintained through its adaptation or whether different rules of the game come into play becomes the question. *The English Patient* (1992), written by Booker Prize winner Michael Ondaatje and adapted into a movie by Anthony Minghella (1996), has gained certain notoriety in this regard. The film is a case of postcolonial "defusion" as it displaces the postcolonial focus of the novel (which foregrounds the role of Kip – an Indian sapper in the British army – as corrective to European centered history writing) in favor of orientalist tropes, inspired, no doubt, by its corporate producers who had a Western target audience in mind (Morgan, 1998; Huggan, 2001, 115–17; Ponzanesi, 2008).

The fourth and last category of adaptation I would like to focus on here is that of *postcolonial adaptation* in the fullest sense. I refer to postcolonial films adapted from postcolonial novels by filmmakers who often work in the interstitial modes of production described by Hamid Naficy (2000). Often several national co-productions and partners are involved in making these new forms of transnational cinema possible and available for distribution. Art-house audiences may be envisioned as the viewers, and the filmmakers allow their diasporic and exilic positions to influence the aesthetic and stylistic characteristics of these adaptations. This category would include transnational adaptations that are more or less widely distributed, such as *Earth* (1998), directed by the Indian Canadian resident Deepa Mehta, based on Bhapsi Sidhwa's novel on partition, *Cracking India* (1992). Also in this category would be Shirin Neshat's *Women Without Men* (2009), based on the novel by the same title by Shahrnush Parsipur (analyzed later in this article).

Bride and Prejudice: from feminist cult to postcolonial flick

Jane Austen is one of the most adapted literary writers of all time. Her many novels, including *Pride and Prejudice, Sense and Sensibility, Emma, Mansfield Park, Persuasion,* and *Northanger Abbey* (whose first editions appeared between 1811 and 1818) have been adapted into BBC television series and films of differing impact, ranging from very faithful adaptations to more creative and autonomous ones, namely *Clueless* (1995), directed by Amy Hecklerling, a very modern adaptation of *Emma*.

Jane Austen has also been an inspirational model for literary rewrites, the most famous case being *Bridget Jones's Diary* (1996) in which the author, Helen Fielding, admittedly borrowed, or literally stole, much of her plot and many of her characters from *Pride and Prejudice* (1813), which might be considered the mother of all "chick lit" texts. The connection to chick culture should be clarified here, since it is a major commercial phenomenon. Subject to both biting criticism and the adoration of its fans, the *chickerati*, chick lit raises the question of whether it is market driven or representative of a form of feminist empowerment. It is written by women and for women and addresses women's careers, sexualities, and desires (Whelehan, 2005; Smith, 2008; Radner, 2011), and is thereby linked to recent debates over Third Wave feminism in relation to postfeminism (Genz, 2006; Snyder, 2008).

Given this context, it is not surprising that Gurinder Chadha's adaptation flourished. The market surrounding Jane Austen was booming as Austen became a feminist icon for both the chickerati and the adaptation industry. The film could also rely on the transhistorical and transcultural value of the novel for the Indian subcontinent. Emerging issues of feminism in India are still linked to traditional issues of courtship and arranged marriages, which therefore require a "postcolonial" requalification of these new feminist entanglements. By tapping into the popularity of the Bollywood industry and giving a postcolonial flavor to the war between the sexes – by transposing early nineteenth-century British class tensions into twenty-first-century cross-cultural relations – Chadha transposes Jane Austen into a modern, global dimension that appeals to diverse audiences: Jane Austen fans, chickerati, Bollywood buffs, world cinema experts, radical chic cosmopolitans and so forth, blending successful commercial strategies with mildly subversive narratives.

This kind of adaptation exemplifies the second category highlighted above (the adaptation of Western classics with a view to revising, revisiting, and rewriting their scope) where the original source has lost its primacy.

The film, released in 2004, was, in fact, received both with high accolades and raised eyebrows. Jane Austen's fans were irritated by the transposition of this canonical novel into the bombastic popular genre of the Bollywood masala film. Bollywood fans, on the other hand, found the film far too imitative of Hollywood musicals, and therefore not Bollywood enough. Chadha maintained, however, that Jane Austen's novels are a perfect fit for a Bollywood-style film as the focus on money and marriage, false pride and false nobility is still so pertinent to contemporary India (Wray, 2005).

Bride and Prejudice is a tongue-in-cheek parody of the historical costume drama. On a superficial level, as one reviewer writes, "East meets West" with the English novel of manners saga being transformed into Bollywood spectacle, replacing corsets with saris, the Bennets with Bakshis, and pianos with bhangra beats (Adarsh, 2004). However, on a deeper level, it is also a celebration of postcolonial hybridity in which the mimicry of the high-culture novel is allied with the celebration of India's rising status as a global partner. While Elizabeth is replaced by Lalita, played by the megastar

Figure 11.1 Lalita and Marc engage in an awkward cross-cultural encounter on a wedding dance floor in Amritsar (Source: still *Bride and Prejudice*, 2004)

Aishwarya Rai, the dark Byronic Darcy is replaced by a rather confused American Darcy who knows nothing about the complexity of caste, class, or gender in India outside the money frame.

Suchitra Marthur points out that postcolonial subversion is enacted in Chadha's film at the level of style as well as content:

> If the adaptation of fiction into film is seen as an activity of translation, of a semiotic shift from one language to another, then *Bride and Prejudice* can be seen to enact this translation at two levels: the obvious translation of the language of the novel into the language of the film, and the more complex translation of Western high culture into the idiom of Indian popular culture.
>
> (Mathur, 2007, p. 2)

Gurinder Chadha can be considered a South Asian diasporic filmmaker who proudly appropriates the many legacies her postcolonial condition offers her. Born in Kenya to Punjabi parents she moved to the UK at the age of four and grew up in Southall, London. She made her film debut with the short TV documentary *I'm British But ...* (1990) and won critical acclaim with her wonderful first feature film *Bhaji on the Beach* (1993). With her riveting *Bend it Like Beckham* (2002) she broke out internationally, something that has allowed her to trade on her credentials to make her own Hindi Movie. External to Bollywood, she has made an experimental and courageous crossover film, a kind of Hollywood/Bollywood modern romance.

In India, however, the film was a commercial flop. *The Hindu* wrote that it was naïve and poorly scripted, using gloss and glamor to camouflage weaknesses in the narrative and style (Bhaskaran, 2004). Notwithstanding these critiques, I would argue that *Bride and Prejudice* is the result of a postcolonial fusion. It asserts the transnational and transhistorical validity of Jane Austen's text yet also affirms the rise of a popular cultural industry, Bollywood. Bollywood produces more films annually than Hollywood, and speaks not only to Indians in India and the diaspora but also to transnational audiences at large, starting to claim a level of critical respectability at international film festivals.

Priya Jaikumar writes that the epithet "Bollywood" is a parodic and cheeky echo of the Hollywood industry, a mimicry that is both a response and a dismissal (Jaikumar, 2003, p. 25). *Bride and Prejudice*, though, refuses to fit into clear-cut East-West binarisms such as Britain-India or a Hollywood-Bollywood face off. Instead it blends cinematic traditions, which include Indian diasporic art house films such as *Monsoon Wedding*, directed by Mira Nair, 2001 (analyzed in this volume by Batra and Rice). *Bride and Prejudice* obviously benefited from the way paved by Nair who successfully combines the Bollywood sub-genre of the wedding films with the more critical perspectives that address issues of gender, race, ethnicity, and class. However, Gudha chose to combine it with the patriotic family romance, typical of the conservative Bollywood revivals of the 1990s such as *Dilwale Dulhania Le Jayenge* (Aditya Chopra, 1995), *Pardes* (Subhash Ghai, 1997), or *Kabhi Khushi Kabhie Gham* (Karan Johar, 2001).

As Martur writes, to present Aishwarya Rai as a modern Westernized heroine is something of an oxymoron within Bollywood conventions, where actresses in mainstream films play the demure, sari-clad conventional Indian heroine who is unscathed by anti-national and Western influences (Mathur, 2007). This is underscored by Guerracino who writes that Chadha's character appears to draw heavily on Western models of feminine behavior as an ideal for the diasporic woman. Lalita is less a reminder of Bollywood divas than of Western chick culture icons such as Bridget Jones and Carrie Bradshaw, who model the young metropolitan woman who has to negotiate between femininity and self-empowerment. However, in *Bride and Prejudice* emancipation and femininity are harmonized through a mixed marriage to a Western white guy, offering Western audiences the spectacle of domesticated alterity. This resolution represents an assimilationist rather than a feminist multiculturalism (Guerracino, 2009, pp. 380–1). The gender politics in *Bride and Prejudice* remain problematic. In the end Lalita, despite being a headstrong, feisty, and highly articulate heroine, remains the object of exchange between competing systems of capitalist patriarchy.

Chadha shares neither Trinh T. Minh-ha's experimental take, nor the outspoken political and feminist stance of other diasporic South Asian female directors such as Deepa Mehta and Mira Nair. Her films are a celebration of popular culture, where there are no clear borders between East and West, or, for women, between tradition and modernity. There is just a sustained ironic take on mainstream cultural assumptions and established genres. Chadha does not opt for imitation with a critical difference but for a "transmogrification," in Salman Rushdie's sense, an ambivalent mimicry, where the old blends in with the new to make a new creation which stands outside both. In this way, Chadha offers Western audiences an experience of cultural alterity which is unthreatening and easily assimilable, while addressing the undercurrent of inequalities that are, however, left unchallenged and untransformed. It is therefore not just a question of "incommensurability" between the cinematic discourses of Bollywood and Hollywood, and their different audience expectations, but also of "untranslatability" between the proposed models of feminine emancipation. While both models pertain to global consumer culture, they are actualized in different systems that Chadha's film is not always successful or persuasive in putting in relation to one another.

Can, then, *Bride and Prejudice* be read as a successful postcolonial adaptation that manages to make an intervention into Jane Austen's text by adding mimicry as a strategy that undoes both the colonial authority of classic texts and the patriarchal and neo-conservative trend of most Bollywood formula films? The replacement of gender politics based in 1813 with a shallow postcolonial hybridity fails to expose the mechanism of the global marketplace and happily pays lip service to its rules. Chadha's postcolonial pastiche, in its postmodern indeterminacy, is not up to the task of postcolonial critique, which addresses, resists, and reverses the legacies and novelties of both old and new forms of imperialism.

Postcolonial utopia: Women Without Men

Women Without Men is an acclaimed film made by the famous international photographer Shirin Neshat. Though this is her first feature film, Neshat is not new to filmmaking. Her short films about the life and experience of Iranian women have traveled widely, and the topic covered in two video installations *Mahdokht* (2004) and *Zarin* (2005) preceded the film. *Women Without Men* is based on Shahrnush Parsipur's novel by the same name. It was published in 1989 but banned in Iran, which eventually forced its writer into a life of exile in the United States. The book was first translated into English in 1992, and a second translation in 2004, with a preface by Persis M. Karim, received a considerable amount of attention. The novel is an outspoken feminist text, and therefore subject to censorship and a problematic reception in her country. The film chooses to focus on the theme of the 1953 coup and the large mass protest it caused, as the unifying background of the four women's stories. In 1953 a British and CIA-backed coup toppled the democratically elected government of the charismatic leader Mohammad Mossadegh, who had nationalized the oil industry in Iran, to reinstate the more Western lenient Shah Reza Pahlavi. The event resonates, though it is placed at a safer historical distance, with the recent political tensions in Iran, where a political uprising and mass protest have followed the 2009 presidential election.

In order to create the atmosphere of Teheran in the 1950s, Neshat filmed in Casablanca because she, like Parsipur, is *persona non grata* in Iran. The film creates the right atmosphere with the clever use of both diffused light and saturated colors and Neshat used local people to recreate the scenes of street demonstrations. The cast was highly international, as were the producers, and the film was a truly transnational collaboration.

As an example of postcolonial adaptation, this film (which falls under the fourth category of postcolonial adaptation in the full sense) is interesting for several reasons: it is written and adapted by two Iranian women living in exile, and it therefore focuses on issues related to Muslim women, while, at the same time, it also reaches transnational audiences addressing transnational themes such as love, sexuality, creativity, and freedom. It is a rather faithful adaptation, which, despite tying up a few of the novel's loose ends and detours, manages to convey the novel's bold narrative magic realism through stylized, powerfully poetic visuals. The film emphasizes the political content along with the feminist in order to convey the linkages between colonial legacies and postcolonial realities.

The novel was banned because it deals very outspokenly with taboo issues surrounding the female body and sexuality, such as virginity, menopause, honor killing, rape, multiple wives, divorce, and suicide. These are all issues that the government denounces as being imposed by Western feminism. They are therefore considered antithetical to loyalty to Iran and its national values. Neshat avoids many of the more contested feminist issues opting for a more linear narrative, which blends in with the powerfully aesthetic photography of cinematographer Martin Gschlacht in which the impact of still images is given priority over plot and narrative flow.

In order to understand the richness of this adaptation it might be useful briefly to outline the artistic careers of both the author and the director of *Women Without Men*, two unconventional and extremely successful artists. Neshat left Iran just before the Islamic revolution (1979) and the fall of the Shah. Her subsequent visits to Iran after the revolution led to the creation of a body of work that launched her artistic career. She achieved international renown for her brilliant portraits of veiled women which she overlaid with Persian calligraphy. This series of mostly black and white images, entitled "Women of Allah," was created between 1993–1997 and investigates the role of the Muslim woman and the feminine body in relation to violence during the revolution. She used Persian poetry and calligraphy to examine concepts such as martyrdom, the space of exile, and the issues of identity and femininity. As a result of these stylized pictures, where the Persian cultural references are opaque to non-Persian-speaking Western viewers, she was accused of using neo-orientalistic images for the pleasure and consumption of Western audiences. However, what she is trying to portray in her photography, and in her more recent work as a video artist, is the impossibility of dialogue among cultures, or between men and women. She creates a stark contrast between veiling and unveiling, the sacred and the profane, the prophetic and the poetic, homeland and exile, religion and violence. She paradoxically expresses seduction in sadness, and violence in serenity.[5] Males are seen through the female gaze and, though covered and forbidden, the female body is resurrected. In her video art Neshat often emphasizes the complexity of the theme of opposition in Muslim societies by showing two or more coordinated films concurrently on separate screens opposite one another, creating stark visual contrasts through such motifs as light and dark, black and white, male and female, voice and silence.[6] Her most recent short films are *Mahdokht* (2004) about a virgin obsessed with fertility who decides to plant herself as a tree, and *Zarin* (2005) which was shot in Morocco and chronicles the breakdown of a young woman who has been working as a prostitute. The latter two installations were a clear step towards Neshat's debut film, *Women Without Men*, which was six years in the making. The collaboration between these two exiled women is an interesting one, and the writer even appears in the film as a brothel madam.

Shahrnush Parsipur was an acclaimed writer in Iran. She studied sociology in Teheran and became fascinated with the Chinese language and civilization, which she studied at the Sorbonne in Paris from 1976 to 1980. In 1980, with the publication of several of her stories, Parsipur received considerable attention in Teheran literary circles. Her second novel was *Touba and the Meaning of Night* (Touba va ma'na-ye Shab 1989), which Parsipur wrote after spending four years and seven months in prison. In 1989 she published a short novel, again consisting of connected stories, called *Women without Men* (Zanan Bedun-e Mardan), an obvious take on Hemingway's short stories *Men Without Women*. In the mid-1990s, the government upped the pressure on the author in an attempt to persuade her to stop this kind of writing. As a result, in 1994 Parsipur went into exile in the United States, where she continued her writing, though she felt isolated from her community. The translation of her work into English and the adaptation of her work by Shirin Neshat brought her international fame.

The novel describes the life and experiences of five characters who end up in an enchanted garden, an abandoned orchard, to avoid the repression of patriarchy, religion, and the political regime. Their stories are separate yet intertwined in interesting ways in order to depict women of different class, status, age, and relationships with men. Mahdokht (from a previous video by Neshat), is a crazy woman obsessed with virginity, who, unable to find her way around sexuality, decides to plant herself as a tree. The tree with its attempt to sprout roots and have branches is a new feminist figuration of becoming (Deleuze and Guattari, 2004), an alternative space where women can be without men and act in accordance with their talents and nature. The other women are the traditional and religious Faizeh, and her friend Munis. Munis dies twice in the novel – she is first killed by her brother, to then come back to life as a mind reading ghost, yet a ghost that is physically real enough to be raped, and to become after her suicide a fervent communist activist. Farrokhlaqa, called Fakhri in the film, is the middle-aged, upper-class, cosmopolitan, Westernized woman who buys the enchanted garden. Zarrinkolah, renamed Zarin in the film (also from a previous video installation by Neshat), is a stunningly powerful character. This is emphasized through the skills of Hungarian actress, Orsolya Tóth, whose performance creates an unforgettably haunting character whose torment and torture are rendered through painstakingly beautiful visual references to Orientalism and its decadent representations of the East. Zarin is anorexic, and her painful skinniness stands in stark contrast to the voluptuous connotations of prostitution and sexuality. The images of the brothel (with Parsipur herself playing the madam), and of the Hamam where Zarin scrubs herself until she bleeds in order to cleanse herself of the taint of her countless clients, are reminiscent of Said's figures of Orientalism (making visual intertextual reference to the paintings of Jean-Léon Gérôme and Jean Auguste Dominique Ingres), and deconstruct those figures, as well, undoing beauty through pain and interrupting voyeuristic pleasure through visual disturbance.

This kind of adaptation differs from that of *Bride and Prejudice* analyzed above. The collaboration between these two artists runs deep and alters the spaces of both feminist critique and film studies, as well as that of postcolonial cinematography. The film is indeed a rather faithful adaptation of the novel, in the sense that it rarely deviates from its content, characters, and plot, though several details, which could be relevant, do depart from the original. Despite the incommensurability of the two different semiotic

Figure 11.2 Zarin in *Women Without Men* subverts orientalistic references interrupting visual pleasure and voyeuristic perspectives (Source: still *Women Without Men*, 2009)

systems, the verbal and the visual, these two artists mingle the semiotic codes of both in their work. Neshat's work is highly allegorical and poetic, and despite its emphasis on silence and slowness, it speaks volumes. Parsipur's style is rather concise and precise, with quick and incisive dialogues, but at the same time it is highly symbolic and visual, if a challenge to superficial adaptation.

Consider, for example, the following lines from the novel:

> In the mid-spring the tree in her body exploded. The explosion was not sudden, but rather came slowly. It was as if all the parts of her wanted to separate from each other. The parts of her body separated slowly, groaning. In an eternal metamorphosis the parts of Mahdokht separated from each other. She was in pain, and felt like she was giving birth ... Finally it was finished. The tree had turned completely into seeds. A mountain of seeds. A strong wind blew the seeds of Mahdokht into the water. Mahdokht traveled with the water. She traveled all over the world.
>
> (p. 122)

It is not surprising that Neshat decided to film all the characters described by Parsipur exept Mahdokht, who is the most challenging character to represent visually, and a character with whom it might be difficult for an international audience, not always interested in magical or surrealist representations, to engage. This specific kind of magic realism is characteristic not only of Persian written culture but also of the new Iranian cinema, which beautifully conveys both a material and, at the same time, oneiric engagement with reality. Though not part of this wave of New Iranian cinema,[7] Neshat's unique style renders Parsipur's magic explicit with its use of visual, allegorical images that lead to a fantastic and poetic world.[8] Whereas Parsipur creates realism through magic, Neshat opts for the utopian vision of possible worlds which do not yet exist, but could. Neshat has a Tarkovskian touch, entrenched in silence and spirituality, and deeply esoteric, but with something of Buñuel's sober surrealism.[9]

The process of adaptation actually reinforces the dialogue between text and film. Published in 1989, the novel made a postcolonial statement at a time when relations between the West and Iran were highly charged. It was the year Ayatollah Khomeini issued a Fatwa against Salman Rushdie for his *Satanic Verses*, published in 1988. The world was polarized on the issue of freedom of speech and the creative license that could be taken in addressing the issue of Islam. This controversy uncannily anticipated 9/11 and the subsequent clash of civilizations which perpetuated, as Said had written in *Orientalism*, the stereotypes about the feared Muslim other and Islam's oppression of women kept under lock and key. Postcolonialism here becomes a larger term that encompasses new forms of oppression and resistance, and also more complex forms of interrelations among structures of domination. The detection or invention of forms of agency and subjectivity becomes more difficult and requires new skills and tools. The world depicted by Parsipur is a rich kaleidoscope of female voices that defy authoritarianism and religious indoctrination. As such, they are not simply subaltern voices incapable of asserting their rights. The escape to the garden constitutes a form of utopia, a way of constructing alternative worlds, where subjectivity is not dependent on patriarchal relationships with men or society, particularly society under a repressive political regime that responds to invisible international orders, diffusing neo-colonialism with Westernization and liberalization of dress.

The garden is a long-standing trope for feminist genealogy where women establish their own concept of territoriality and where heterogeneity and intimacy can co-exist. Caren Kaplan has already studied the concept of the Garden in a book by the expatriate Caribbean writer Michelle Cliff, *Claiming an Identity they Taught me to Despise* (1980). Cliff's garden is a piece of land where she can find her identity and rest, not an enclosed space but a fluid terrain. Kaplan concludes:

> This is a new terrain, a new location, in feminist poetics. Not as a room of one's own, not a fully public or collective self, not a domestic realm – it's a space in the imagination which allows for the inside, the outside, and the liminal element in between.
>
> (Kaplan, 1987, p. 197)

The garden in Parsipur is a place of temporary exile, outside the city of Teheran, abandoned and in need of new inhabitants. Mahdokht, the woman tree, finally manages to sprout her roots and fill her branches with leaves thanks to the nurturing milk of Zarrinkolah, the prostitute now married to the good gardener, who has given birth after a nine-month pregnancy to a white lily, becoming herself almost as transparent as light. This ultimate metaphorical and allegorical interpretation of sisterhood, of abolishing the boundaries between body and nature, nature and culture, is attested to by Mahdokht's becoming a tree, and Zarin rising into smoke. Neshat simplifies many of these complex narratives and poetic twists but also opts for an open ending in which the garden is perceived as a positive utopian space where all the women bond and are reborn. Apart from Zarin, who dies in the end, becoming the most virgin and martyr-like figure (she is found floating Ophelia-like in a beautiful pool in the heart of the garden), all the other

Figure 11.3 The garden in *Women Without Men* is an enchanted but also a material location of rebirth (Source: still *Women Without Men*, 2009)

women continue their life in the garden. In the final scene the soldiers storm in and sit at the dinner table, signaling the end of an era. In this ironic scene Fakhri's guests stand around the table becoming passive viewers of a historical process, as the soldiers devour sumptuous food (Bresheeth, 2010).

Both the novel and the film have been banned in Iran and circulate underground, creating a conspiracy of resistance and freedom outside national boundaries.[10] Neshat wanted this film to demonstrate that democracy and the fight for it are not something imported from the West but internal to Iran. The film is dedicated to the Constitutional revolution of 1908 (which was the first democratic movement that limited the power of the shah) and is an indirect homage to the Green Revolution (2009–2010) protest against the disputed victory of Iranian president Mahmoud Ahmadinejad over opposition candidate Hossein Mousavi. Protests in support of Mousavi took place in Iran's major cities and around the world. When *Women Without Men* premiered in Venice (winner of the Silver Lion 2009), the entire cast walked the red carpet either dressed in green or wearing green scarves to connect the legacy of the past with the events of the present. By setting the film in 1953 in an era of political transition, the film succeeds in haunting the present by depicting the earlier period as one of stunning beauty and intellectual fervor. The film also showcases a period in which questions of nationalism, internationalization, and cosmopolitanism played a crucial role. As the claws of old imperial powers such as Britain were slowly transferred to the new empire, the US, and politics was conducted at the international level through the CIA, Iran has attempted a politics of nationalization and autonomy based on the Soviet model which contrasted with the liberal capitalist imperatives of the West. Later, after the fall of the monarchy in 1979 and the advent of theocracy in Iran following the Islamic revolution, a new religious regime, also with transnational dimensions, claimed the politics, public spaces, and spirit of the Iranian people. Resistance to the regime has taken on different forms in order to avoid censorship, imprisonment, and the death penalty. It is not a coincidence that the two artists mirroring each other, Parsipur and Neshat, opted for a life in exile, or outside Iran, in order to convey the possible reality of an Iran in transition, where women suffer but also feature as the driving force of change. In a certain way the film is more nuanced and less openly provocative than the novel. Yet the novel is, at times, more suggestive, poetic, and esoteric than the film. The specificity of the two different semiotic systems does not limit the potential and autonomous impact of either the novel or the film. Yet the two art forms resonate with each other in a respectful and complementary way that is different from the relationship of the other postcolonial adaptation I discussed above with its novelistic source.

Conclusions

This chapter has attempted to survey the rich history of adaptation studies and make a link between it and with the field of postcolonial cinema studies. The idea of postcolonial adaptations has different accents and meanings according to its context: reference to the source text as postcolonial or to the final result as a film which makes a postcolonial intervention. The two examples presented here analyze the work of two female diasporic filmmakers, the first engaging with a Western feminist classic, and the other with a modern feminist classic from Iran. *Bride and Prejudice* succeeds in creating a hybrid cinematic form, a crossover cinema that celebrates Bollywood while also adapting its formulaic conventions for Western audiences, and in this respect it is an interesting postcolonial adaptation. However, its superimposition of gloss and glamour upon a more elaborate transnational critique of gender, class, and caste results in an entertainment product that loses its critical edge, leaving it no more than a postcolonial flick. *Women Without Men,* by contrast, is the result of a complex and laborious international production, which visually does justice to the challenges of the novel, suspended between magic realism and a harsh critique of patriarchy, politics, and neocolonial regimes. The result is a splendid postcolonial adaptation in the fullest sense that operates independently from the novel but at the same reinforces its feminist postcolonial intervention, not least by reaching wider audiences and receiving international acclaim.

Notes

1 In Timothy Corrigan (1999, p 2) we read that: thirty percent of films made today derive from novels, eighty percent of bestsellers are turned into movies and three-quarters of Awards for Best Pictures are Adaptations
2 Despite existing for over fifty years, the field of adaptation studies still struggles to acquire scholarly recognition and respectability as it considered unsophisticated, undertheorized, and too incoherent. One of the accusations is that the field of adaptation studies goes no further than dealing with case studies, the close reading of novel transposition into films in terms of fidelity or betrayals, and that most of these case studies deal with adaptation of Western literature. However, it is often seen as a necessary evil to keep literary departments alive by seducing younger generations with the iconicity of the visual to remediate literature and keep classic authors such as William Shakespeare, Jane Austen or E.M. Forster high in the multimodal patterns of learning and teaching satisfaction rate. (For a survey of the field of adaptation theory see the work of Deborah Cartmell and Imelda Whelehan, 1999,

2007; Tim Corrigan, 1999; Dudley Andrew, 2002; Kamilla Elliott, 2003; Linda Hutcheon, 2006; Brian McFarlane, 1996; Simone Murrey, 2008; Robert Stam 2004; Robert Stam and Alessandra Raengo, 2004, 2005; Timothy Leitch, 2007; James Naremore, 2000).

3 Geoffrey Wagner (1975) proposes three broad categories which help us to get away from the dominant concept of fidelity: *transposition* (which means minimum apparent interference); *commentary* (which implies that the original is altered and the filmmaker can give a different interpretation to the original) and *analogy* (which is a considerable departure from the original in order to make a different art from.)

4 In *Convergence Culture* Jenkins discusses that new media will not simply replace old media, but will learn to interact with it in a complex relationship that he calls "convergence culture."

5 For some critical references to the work of Neshat see: Hamid Dadashi (2002) and Iftikhar Dadi (2008).

6 Neshat's recognition became more international in 1999 when she won the International Award at the XLVIII Biennial of Venice with *Turbulent* (1998), a critique of logos which shows women not being allowed to perform in public, and *Rapture* (1999), two screens opposite one another, in black and white portraying men closed off in a fortress and women moving towards the sea. She also made *Fervor* (2000), *Passage* (2001) with the music by Philip Glass, *Soliloquy* (1999) and *Pulse* (2001).

7 The New Wave movement in Iranian cinema includes the works of Abbas Kiarostami, Mohsen Makhmalbaf, Samira Makhmalbaf, and Jafar Panahi among others.

8 Shohini Chaudhuri and Howard Finn write that New Iranian Cinema has intrigued both critics and audiences for their use of ambiguous and epiphanic images. They prefer to explore these images as "open images," in order to understand them not just as referencing the cultural and political climate of Iran but also for their aesthetic particularity: the repressed political dimension returns within the ostensibly apolitical aesthetic forms of the open image (2006, p. 163).

9 In an interview Neshat named several directors who can be seen as her inspirational models. She mentions Eastern European and Russian directors, for whom symbolism and melancholy are major drivers. For example Andrei Tarkovsky, Ingmar Bergman, Aki Kaurismaki, Jim Jarmush, Roy Andersson, Lars von Trier, and Krzysztof Kieslowski. Their films are all highly stylized and have in common the ironic take along with the restrained emotional expression which convey profound pain.

10 However, it is important to remember that resistance and alternative production are also internal to Iran and not possible only in exile. See Saba Mahmood's critique of Iranian writers in exile who reproduce pernicious Orientalist tropes of victimhood and oppression (2008).

Bibliography

Adarsh, T., 2004. Movie Review "Balle Balle! From Amritsar to L.A. *Bollywood Hungama* [online] 8 October 2004. Available at: <http://www.bollywoodhungama.com/movies/review/7211/index.html> [accessed 18 January 2011].

Andrew, D., 2002. Adaptation. In: J. Naremore, ed. 2002. *Film Adaptation*. New Brunswick, NJ: Rutgers University Press.

Austen, J., 2002. *Pride and Prejudice* (First Edition 1813). London: Penguin Classics.

Barthes, R., 1977. *Image-Music-Text*. Translated from French by S. Heath. New York: Hill & Wang.

Bhaskaran, G., 2004. Classic made trivial. *The Hindu* [online] 15 October 2004. Available at: http://www.hinduonnet.com/thehindu/fr/2004/10/15/stories/2004101502220100.htm [accessed 19 January 2011].

Bluestone, G., 1957. *Novels into Film*, Baltimore, MD: Johns Hopkins University Press.

Bolter, D. and Grusin R., 2000. *Remediation. Understanding New Media*. Cambridge, MA: MiT Press.

Bresheeth, H., 2010. Shirin Neshat's Women Without Men. *Third Text*, 24(6): pp. 754– 8.

Cartmell, D. and Whelehan, I. eds., 1999. *Adaptations. From Text to Screen, Screen to Text*. London: Routledge.

Cartmell, D. and Whelehan, I. eds., 2007. *The Cambridge Companion to Literature on Screen*. Cambridge: Cambridge University Press.

Chatman, S., 1978. *Story and Discourse. Narrative Structure in Fiction and Film*. Ithaca, NY, Cornell University Press.

Chaudhuri, S. and Finn, H., 2006. The Open Image. Poetic Realism and the New Iranian Cinema. In: C. Grant and A. Kuhn, eds., 2006., *Screening World Cinema*. London: Routledge.

Cliff, M. 1980. *Claiming an Identity They Taught Me to Despise*. London: Persephone.

Corrigan, T. 1999., *Film and Literature. An Introduction and Reader*. Upper Saddle River, NJ: Prentice Hall.

Dadashi, H., 2002. Bordercrossings: Shirin Neshat's Body of Evidence. In: G. Verzotti, ed. 2002. *Shirin Neshat*. Rivoli-Torino: Charta, pp. 36–59.

Dadi, I., 2008. Shirin Neshat's Photographs as Postcolonial Allegories. *Signs. Journal of Women in Culture and Society*, 43(1), pp. 125–50.

Deleuze, G. and Guattari, F., 2004. *A Thousand Plateaus. Capitalism and Schizophrenia*. Translated from French by B. Massumi. London: Continuum.

Elliott, K., 2003. *Rethinking the Novel/Film Debate*. Cambridge: Cambridge University Press.

Fielding, H., 1996. *Bridget Jones's Diary*. London: Picador.

Genette, G., 1982. *Palimpsestes*. Paris: Seuil.

Genz, S., 2006. Third Way/ve. The Politics of Postfeminism. *Feminist Theory*, 7(3), pp. 333–53.

Guerracino, S., 2009. Musical Contact Zones in Gurinder Chadha's Cinema. *European Journal of Women's Studies*, 16(4), pp. 373–90.

Huggan, G., 2001. *The Postcolonial Exotic. Marketing the Margins*. New York and London: Routledge.

Hutcheon, L., 2006. *A Theory of Adaptation*. London and New York: Routledge.

Jaikumar, P., 2003. Bollywood Spectaculars. *World Literature Today*, 77(3–4), pp. 24–9.

Jenkins, H., 2006. *Convergence Culture: Where Old and New Media Collide*. New York: New York University Press.

Kaplan, C., 1987. Deterritorializations. The Rewriting of Home and Exile in Western Feminist Discourse. In: *Cultural Criticism*, 6, pp. 187–98.

Leitch, T., 2007. *Film Adaptation and Its Discontents: From Gone with the Wind to The Passion of the Christ*. Baltimore, MD: Johns Hopkins University Press.

Mahmood, S., 2008. Feminism, Democracy and Empire: Islam and the War on Terror. In: J. Wallach Scott, ed., 2008. *Women's Studies on the Edge*. Durham, NC and London, Duke University Press, pp. 81–114.

Mathur, S., 2007. From British "Pride" to Indian "Bride." Mapping the Contours of a Globalised (Post?)Colonialism. *M/C. A Journal of Media and Culture*, 10(2). [online] May 2007. Available at: http://journal.media-culture.org.au/0705/06- mathur.php [accessed 18 January 2011].

McFarlane, B., 1996. *Novel to Film. An Introduction to the Theory of Adaptation*. Oxford: Clarendon Press.

Morgan, M. M., 1998. *The English Patient*: From Fiction to Reel. *Alif: Journal of Comparative Poetics*, 18, pp. 159–73.

Murrey, S., 2008. Materializing Adaptation Theory: The Adaptation Industry. *Literature/Film Quarterly*, 36(1), pp. 4–20.

Naficy, H., 2000. *An Accented Cinema. Exilic and Diasporic FilmMaking*. Princeton: Princeton University Press.

Naremore, J. ed., 2000. *Film Adaptation*. New Brunswick, NJ: Rutgers University Press.

Parsipur, S., 2004. *Women without Men. A Modern Novel of Iran* (Zanan Bedun-e Mardan, 1989). Translated from Persian by J. Sharlet and K. Talattof. New York: The Feminist Press.

Parsipur, S., 2007. *Touba and the Meaning of Night* (Touba va ma'na-ye Shab 1989). Translated from Persian by H. Houshmand and K. Talattof. London: Marion Boyars.

Pauwels, R.M., 2007. *Indian Literature and Popular Cinema. Recasting Classics*. London and New York: Routledge.

Ponzanesi, S., 2008. Diaspora in Time: Michael Ondaatje's *The English Patient*. In: M. Shackleton, ed. 2008. *Diasporic Literature and Theory – Where Now?* Newcastle upon Tyne: Cambridge Scholars Publishing, pp. 120–37.

Radner, H., 2011. *Neo-Feminist Cinema. Girly Films, Chick Flicks and Consumer Culture*. New York: Routledge.

Rushdie, S., 1988. *The Satanic Verses*. London: Viking Press.

Said, S., 1978. *Orientalism*. London: Vintage Books.

Said, S., 1993. *Culture and Imperialism*. London: Vintage Books.

Smith, C., 2008. *Cosmopolitan Culture and Consumerism in Chick Lit*. London: Routledge.

Snyder, C.R., 2008. What Is Third-Wave Feminism? A New Directions Essay. *Signs: Journal of Women in Culture and Society*, 34(1), pp. 175–96.

Stam, R., 2004. *Literature Through Film. Realism, Magic and the Art of Adaptation*. Oxford: Blackwell.

Stam, R. and Raengo, A. eds., 2004. *A Companion to Literature and Film*. Oxford: Blackwell.

Stam, R. and Raengo, A. eds., 2005. *Literature and Film. A Guide to the Theory and Practice of Adaptation*. Oxford: Blackwell.

Wagner, G., 1975. *The Novel and Cinema*. Rutherford, NJ: Fairleigh Dickinson University Press.

Whelehan, I., 2005. *The Feminist Bestseller*. Basingstoke: Palgrave Macmillan.

Wray, J., 2005. Gurinder Chadha Talks Bride and Prejudice. *Movie News* [online] 7 February 2005. Available at: http://www.monstersandcritics.com/movies/news/article_4163.php/ Gurinder_Chadha_Talks_Bride_and_Prejudice [accessed 18 January 2011].

Filmography

Bend it Like Beckham, 2002. [film] Directed by G. Chadha. USA: Kintop Pictures.

Bhaji on the Beach, 1993. [film] Directed by G. Chadha. England: Channel Four Films.

Bride and Prejudice, 2004. [film] Directed by G. Chadha. London: Pathé Pictures International.

Clueless, 1995. [film] Directed by A. Hecklerling. USA: Paramount.

Dilwale Dulhania Le Jayenge, 1995. [film] Directed by A. Chopra. India: Yash Raj Films.

Earth, 1998. [film] Directed by D, Mehta. India: Cracking the Earth Films Inc.

English Patient, The, 1996. [film] Directed by A. Minghella. USA: Miramax.

I'm British But ..., 1990. [TV documentary] Directed by G. Chadha. England: British Film Institute (BFI).

Kabhi Khushi Kabhie Gham, 2001. [film] Directed by K. Johar. India: Dharma Productions.

Mahdokht, 2004. [short film] Directed by S. Neshat. France: Coproduction office.

Mansfield Park, 1999. [film] Directed by P. Rozema. England: Arts Council of England.

Monsoon Wedding, 2001. [film] Directed by M. Nair. United States: IFC Productions.
Out of Africa, 1985. [film] Directed by S. Pollack. USA: Mirage Enterprises.
Pardes, 1997. [film] Directed by S. Ghai. India: Mukta Arts.
Passage to India, A 1984. [film] Directed by D. Lean. England: EMI Films.
Women Without Men, 2009. [film] Directed by S. Neshat. Germany: Essential Filmproduktion.
Zarin, 2005. [short film] Directed by S. Neshat. Germany: Essential Filmproduktion.

Part IV

Postcolonial cinemas and globalization

[T]here is growing evidence that the consumption of the mass media throughout the world often provokes resistance, irony, selectivity, and, in general, agency ...

(Appadurai, 1996, p. 7)

Postcolonial cinemas exist in conflict, complicity and synergy with the dynamics of globalization. This is in part because the production and distribution of cinema in general, and postcolonial cinemas in particular, are dependent upon transnational forms of financing and exhibition. But it is also because postcolonial cinemas reflect upon many of the phenomena intensified by globalization, such as migration, refugees, diasporas, "terrorist" violence, environmental degradation, and financial crisis.

Meanwhile, the roles and technologies of cinema have changed rapidly during the last decades, and, as Arjun Appadurai writes, both mass migration and electronic mediation have altered the ways in which our imaginations operate. Subjects and images circulate concurrently, and "neither images nor viewers fit into circuits or audiences that are easily bound within local, national, or regional spaces" (1996, p. 4). Therefore, as our epigraph suggests, mass media encourage not only hegemony but also resistance and alternative forms of agency.

The engagement of postcolonial cinemas with globalization is also a reminder that the "colonial" is never really over and that neo-colonial power relationships reemerge within globalization. The postcolonial optic engages globalization, while maintaining a focus on alternative experiences and marginalized traditions, emphasizing agency, as Appudurai suggests, in the midst of corporate capital's seeming hegemony.

Shohini Chaudhuri illustrates how the strategies of Orientalism are being redeployed in contemporary discourses on terror, marking "others" as "unpeople," who are the modern equivalent of the savages of colonial days, excluded from systems of justice and rights. The aftermath of the September 11, 2001 attacks seems to have given new life to old colonial stereotypes and prejudices, which are being reinforced by neo-imperial repressive measures used in the name of democracy. Through a postcolonial reading of *Children of Men* (Cuarón, 2006), which is set in the dystopian future of 2027, Chaudhuri deciphers the covert workings of contemporary neo-imperial sovereignty, as it dehumanizes the West's others in networks of prisons for "terrorists" and detention centers for refugees (Chaudhuri, p. 204). The film, she argues, locates agency among these immigrants, refugees, illegals, and detainees (recalling the figures of immigrants and of Angelo the janitor in Waller's discussion of *Luna e l'altra*) who, in the film, hold the key to the continuation of human life.

The other contributors to this section discuss how filmmakers and their cinematic productions have managed, against great odds, to circumvent dominant commercial forces and move from marginal positions to the attention of global spectators. In their article on Mira Nair's *Monsoon Wedding* Kanika Batra and Richard Rice read this highly acclaimed international film as a convergence of mediascapes, soundscapes, and ideologies in a space between the local and the global. It mixes transnational feminist cinema with the popular Bollywood subgenre of the wedding film. The chapter focuses on a "transcoded audiologic," whereby technologies are remediated in everyday urban India while coexisting and being integrated with more traditional rituals and traditions. Bollywood is one of many forms of entertainment remediated by the film, but it should be highlighted that the Bollywood film industry produces more films per year than Hollywood. Even though it has not been taken seriously until recently by Western cinema critics, it has now permeated the realms of popular and diasporic culture to such an extent that it can no longer be thought of as outside the discourses of global and postcolonial cinema.

Digital technologies have multiplied and diversified both audiences, and the means of production, and distribution. Cultural exchange can bypass state censorship in certain cases, as well as Hollywood production values. In her chapter on Nollywood, Claudia Hoffmann explains how the booming Nigerian video-industry has flourished thanks to new accessible, and in a way "poor," means of production – the digital video. The use of low-cost cinematic tools, nonprofessional actors, and venues accessible to all, realizes many of Third Cinema's aspirations, although Nollywood is not devoted to the creation of a traditional political cinema like that of Francophone African cinema, but to entertainment. Thus Nollywood has not been taken seriously as a cinematic form, both because of its unglossy production values and the speed with which films are churned out. This does not mean that Nollywood is not meaningful, and even political, for its consumers who are spread across Africa and the many Nigerian communities in the diaspora. Nollywood benefits, in fact, from a means of distribution that does not rely on Western financial systems or even critical approval. Its wide appeal and ability to reach African audiences by talking about everyday life, religion, and the effects of globalization on local communities testify to the success of a cinema that is postcolonial in its subversion, circumvention, and renegotiation of many global networks of power and control.

Reference

Appadurai, A., 1996. *Modernity at Large. Cultural Dimensions of Globalization.* Minneapolis: University of Minnesota Press.

Chapter 12

Unpeople

Postcolonial reflections on terror, torture and detention in *Children of Men*

Shohini Chaudhuri

The year is 2027. After eighteen years of global infertility, the civilian infrastructure has broken down. Britain has turned into a totalitarian state based on mass surveillance and total closure of its borders. Immigrants are herded into cages and mistreated. At a detention center, an atrocity exhibition reminiscent of events at Abu Ghraib prison and Guantánamo Bay unfurls. Such are the scenarios posed in the science-fiction dystopia of *Children of Men* (Alfonso Cuarón, 2006), drawing connections among immigration debates, heightened state surveillance, the invasion of Iraq, and the US/UK "War on Terror," where torture is routine practice. For Slavoj Žižek, its apocalyptic future is a critique of present-day realities in which "the true focus of the film is there in the background" (Žižek, 2007). In this essay, I argue that *Children of Men* uses its science-fiction genre conventions and reportage-like camera style to portray a history of the neo-imperial politics of the present. Situating my analysis within a postcolonial critique of sovereign power, the state of exception, and its biopolitics, I focus upon how the film enables us to read the oppressive power dynamics of some of the darker aspects of today's global realities. First, I will explain what is postcolonial about my reading of this film, establishing parallels between discourses of Orientalism and contemporary discourses of terror and security, which provide the film with its social and political contexts. Then, I will move on to a close analysis, using the critical tools of postcolonial theory to explore the film's fictional portrayal of recent policies and its imagery of terror, torture, and detention.

This essay characterizes *Children of Men* as a postcolonial film on the basis of its aesthetic and political strategies which portray Britain as a postcolonial space, highlighting the legacy of imperialistic ways of thinking and behaving, including forms of racism and xenophobia reawakened by post-9/11 discourses of terrorism and illegal immigration. In mainstream Western discourse, terrorism is implicitly defined as "unjustified acts against First World populations" (Butler, 2004, p. 13). A postcolonial perspective (as I will deploy the term here) investigates the historical continuities between the imperial past and present-day violence, thus allowing a shift of focus onto the terror perpetrated by the sovereign power of the state. This essay therefore deals with the terror which sovereign (neo-)colonial power inflicts upon its victims, which is experienced by them as a violent, corporeal force. In other words, I am concerned with the biopolitics[1] of sovereign power from a postcolonial standpoint, as well as with the power asymmetries of the world-system and forms of racial oppression emerging in the global hinterland of "War on Terror" jails, detention centers, and border controls.

Influenced by Edward Said's notion of "Orientalism" (1991) (the distorted ideas about the Orient and its inhabitants that serve to justify the West's military and economic objectives) and his insights in *From Oslo to Iraq and the Roadmap* (2004), my essay also draws upon the work of investigative writers, including Mark Curtis's *Unpeople: Britain's Secret Human Rights Abuses*, from which I derive my title. The term "unpeople" designates "those whose lives are deemed worthless, expendable in the pursuit of power and commercial gain" (Curtis, 2004, p. 2). According to Curtis, they "are the modern equivalent of the 'savages' of colonial days, who could be mown down by British guns in virtual secrecy, or else in circumstances where the perpetrators were hailed as the upholders of civilization" (Curtis, 2004, p. 2). Particularly important for laying bare the rule of terror waged by states, Said's writings on the Palestinian-Israeli conflict highlight how the state's repressive measures are presented in the media as a legitimate response to or reprisal for terrorism, exploiting Orientalist fears of the "Other." This creates a *trompe l'oeil* effect that diverts attention from the conflict's historical origins within the state's own violence. While the terrorist threat may be real, the argument made here is that states often use terrorism as a cover for pursuing their own interests, amplifying the threat in order to introduce repressive measures. I also deploy the philosopher Giorgio Agamben's concept of "bare life" – life stripped of value and political status, and reduced to its biological basis (Agamben, 1995). As will be seen in the following discussion, Orientalist notions of Otherness can also be used to legitimate drastic measures that deprive subjects of their rights and reduce them to "bare life," as well as to solicit the population's consent towards illiberal policies.

In Britain and the US, such policies were initiated under the emergency aegis of the "War on Terror." The US administration determined that it was engaging in "a new kind of war" with a new type of enemy, which gave then President George W. Bush enhanced powers to imprison any suspects on whatever grounds (Danner, 2004, p. 84). In November 2001, he signed an order for the "indefinite detention" and trial by "military commission" of foreign terrorist suspects, exempting them from legal principles and rules of evidence that apply under US criminal law and under international law (Danner, 2004, p. 79). The CIA's "extraordinary rendition" program was expanded to enable Al Qaeda and other terrorist suspects to be arrested, clandestinely abducted, and transported to Guantánamo Bay and other prisons in a global network, which included Abu Ghraib, prison cells at US military bases, and CIA "black sites." Removed from the scrutiny of international monitors, detainees have been subjected to torture by military and civilian interrogators and by the agencies of other governments renowned for poor human rights records. This offshoring of torture (including the use of local contractors) has a neo-colonial dimension, following a historical pattern of exploiting "extra-territorial sites where prisoners are detained and tortured at the pleasure of sovereign power" and where colonial powers can exert their authority without customary legal restraints (Gregory, 2010, p. 84).

War on Terror suspects have been labeled "unlawful combatants" and "detainees" in order to remove them from the safeguards of the Geneva Conventions for prisoners-of-war – a strategy that, Agamben remarks, "radically erases any legal status of the individual, thus producing a legally unnameable and unclassifiable being" (Agamben, 2005, p. 3). Such a process of "judicial othering" (Gregory, 2010, p. 84) defines the prisoners as lesser humans, as unpeople. Just as the amorphous phrase "War on Terror" justifies a war without end, so "indefinite detention" has an expedient indeterminacy, which includes an absence of legal regulation as well as a lack of temporal specificity; Agamben compares it to "the legal situation of the Jews in the Nazi *Lager* [Nazi camps], who, along with their citizenship, had lost every legal identity" (Agamben, 2005, p. 4). Moreover, as Judith Butler has pointed out, the indefinite detention of foreign terrorist suspects "makes use of an ethnic frame of reference for conceiving who will be human and who will not," leading to "heighten[ed] racialized ways of looking and judging in the name of national security" (Butler, 2004, p. xv; 36). It has engendered a situation of widespread social panic and white paranoia in which, in Said's words, "the public is kept on tenterhooks by repeated red or orange alerts, people are encouraged to inform law enforcement authorities of 'suspicious' behaviour, and thousands of Muslims, Arabs, and South Asians have been detained ... on suspicion" (Said, 2004, pp. 221–2). A tide of Islamophobia has swept through Western societies – a fear of the Oriental Other provoked by state discourses about security and by media stereotyping. The US and UK governments have enfolded the invasion and occupation of Afghanistan and Iraq into "the War on Terror," the retributive logic of which is the unleashing of Western sovereign power against the Other. Said asserted that the wars in Afghanistan and Iraq have shown that the US comports itself in the Middle East in a way similar to that of Britain and France in their colonial era (Said, 2004, p. 222). While the imperial character of the occupation is clear from the US/UK coalition's rhetoric of bringing democracy and modernity to the Middle East as the self-appointed agents of "progress," what I seek to emphasize here are the neo-colonial deployments of sovereign power that attempt to rule by force outside the constraints of international law. This has had enormous implications. Not only the populations of Afghanistan and Iraq, but countless others have been reduced to the status of unpeople.

This process can also be seen at work in Britain, the setting of *Children of Men*. The verdict of Labour Prime Minister Tony Blair that "9/11 changes everything" heralded a huge incursion on civil liberties on the domestic front. Within this ideological climate, the government planned to introduce biometric identity cards (which would contain biometric data such as fingerprints or DNA sequences) linked to a national database. Although the plans have (for the time being) been abandoned, they would have enabled continuous monitoring of citizens – supposedly to prevent crime, terrorism, and illegal immigration. Mass surveillance in Britain, which includes phone tapping, interception of emails, bugging, and an extensive closed circuit television network, has already gained "the worst record ... among the so-called democratic world" (Jenkins, 2008, p. 29). These measures (many of them already permitted by the 2000 Regulation of Investigatory Powers Act, and subsequently extended by Home Secretary David Blunkett in 2003) are justified on the grounds of the War on Terror and need for greater security; but, as Simon Jenkins has remarked, they are "not countering terror but promoting it" (Jenkins, 2008, p. 29). Providing the excuse that "the innocent need not fear," they create a desire for self-protection that implants terror in the majority of the population, while activating traditional forms of racism in the belief that only "others" – the Muslims, Arabs, Asians and Blacks – will be affected.

Conflating the discourse of terrorism with discourses of "illegal" immigration and crime, the government and media have incited public fear of terrorists, immigrants, and asylum seekers. Tabloid newspapers abound with alarmist images of "bogus" asylum seekers, welfare scroungers and economic migrants (as if the desire for an economically better life were somehow a despicable goal) and persistently deploy the rhetoric of "floods" and "invasions" by immigrants. Within the European Union, policies of economic liberalization aim to allow the free flow of capital, goods, services, and people; however, those who lack the requisite citizenship status are denied entry and encounter the "Fortress Europe" or "Fortress Britain" mentality of border controls. For those who believe Britain to be over-populated, asylum seekers are perceived as a major threat, and in the post-9/11 climate they are profiled as potential terrorists. In 2003, Tony Blair proposed a new set of stringent measures designed to halve asylum applications within months (Blair, 2003). These included a greater use of detention centers and enlarging the list of countries from which asylum claims would be assumed to be "unfounded." The word "refugee" designates people fleeing from persecution or calamity and, in fact, under the 1951 United Nations Refugee Convention they are entitled to seek safety in other countries. However, in contemporary political discourse, the term evokes a less sympathetic reaction. Likewise, the label "asylum seeker," which came into popular usage in the 1990s, has the pejorative connotation of a person whose claim to refugee status has not yet been certified, producing the "non-status" of a certain group of unpeople.[2] The deportation of asylum seekers is often carried out by force and "in secret, well away from public scrutiny," thus utilizing fear "as a political tool to gain the nation's complicity, and ... commit harsh injustices that might otherwise be challenged publicly as breaches of human rights" (Ware, 2010, p. 105).

The state of exception

This slippage between discourses of asylum and those of terrorism and national security is precisely what *Children of Men* explores, as well as the erosion of civil liberties in the self-proclaimed heartlands of freedom, Britain and the US. As signaled by newspaper headlines like "Britain is slithering down the road towards a police state" which accompanied Jenkins's article, the repressive measures introduced by the governments in the post-9/11 climate of fear suggest there is a certain threshold between democracy and totalitarianism. This threshold is what Agamben has called a "state of exception," in which government powers are expanded, international laws are suspended, and subjects are stripped of their customary political rights. For Agamben, the term refers to a "consistent set of legal phenomena" that work to suspend the juridical order, and that "has today reached its maximum worldwide deployment" (Agamben, 2005, pp. 4, 87). Much debate arising from Agamben's work has focused on the state of exception as a space beyond the law – Guantánamo Bay and other sites as "black holes" in which anything is possible. It is more accurate to say that governments have "captured the legal process" for their own "political ends" (Curtis, 2004, p. 32). Disregarding international law, while simultaneously purporting to apply it, this is sovereign power acting with a neo-colonial violence.

The state of exception is exemplified in the post-Orwellian dystopia of *Children of Men*, a thinly disguised future version of Tony Blair's Britain. Its plot concerns a cynical and apathetic bureaucrat, Theo Faron (Clive Owen), who becomes embroiled against his will with a resistance movement known as the Fishes in their attempt to smuggle a miraculously pregnant black refugee, Kee (Clare-Hope Ashitey), across the border to the Human Project, a secret organization seeking a cure for infertility. In the *mise-en-scène*, the grey and grimy streets of London are only slightly defamiliarized, filled with rickshaws (a displaced signifier of Britain's former empire, now a common sight in the metropolis) and ubiquitous video screens appealing to the public to spy on each other and report suspicious activity (see Figure 12.1). The setting's similarity to our present makes more credible the film's science-fiction genre device of extrapolating contemporary trends and warning of the grim, totalitarian future that awaits Britain. To apply a postcolonial perspective, if the present can re-appear in the future, so can the past re-emerge in the present: the film thus calls upon its audience to reflect upon the repercussions of policies of the past within the present as well as their implications for the future.

Typically for science fiction, *Children of Men* deploys binaries to depict the social hierarchies that divide its narrative world.[3] The most obvious binary here is that of civilization and barbarity. Empires have historically consolidated their claims to legitimacy through such binaries, producing ideological narratives of belonging and exclusion that define the self against an imagined attack from racial, political, and religious Others. In the film, the response to fears of mass immigration has been to

Figure 12.1 Children of Men portrays an only slightly defamiliarized London, grey, polluted and filled with rickshaws (Source: still *Children of Men*, 2006)

declare all foreigners "illegal." State propaganda presents Britain as the last bastion of order, characterizing the rest of the world as a state of chaos: "only Britain soldiers on." Nonetheless, its citizens dwell in a state of civil war. Barred windows divide train passengers from the disorder raging outside, and the countryside is full of outlaws lying in ambush. Right from the outset, a state of terror and emergency is portrayed when a bomb explodes near a café in central London, evoking the 7/7 bombings that happened in the capital.[4] The suddenness of the attack is emphasized by the film's use of off-screen space: with a deafening thud, the blast rips apart a shop façade, causing smoke, debris, and the screaming wounded to spill out onto the street from the edge of the frame. The newspapers ascribe the bomb to the Fishes, who campaign for equal rights for every immigrant, while the Fishes claim that the government itself planted the bomb.

In Žižek's reading of the film, the references to an oppressive social reality are made in the background, through the "paradox of anamorphosis," not through a direct political parable (Žižek, 2007). This is a technique that, elsewhere, by way of Lacan's *Four Fundamental Concepts* and Hans Holbein's painting *The Ambassadors* (in which the skull at the subjects' feet is anamorphotically distorted), Žižek refers to as "looking awry" (Žižek, 1995, p. 90). In *Children of Men*, he claims,

> If you look at the thing too directly, at the oppressive social dimension, you don't see it. You can see it in an oblique way only if it remains in the background ... It's not really that all this infertility and so on is just a pretext for, I don't know, the hero's inner journey from this apathetic anti-hero mode to more active engagement and so on. No ... This fate of the individual here remains a kind of prism through which you see the background even more sharply.
>
> (Žižek, 2007)

In order for this to work, Žižek maintains, the background must remain as background. However, as Zahid Chaudhary has pointed out in his reading of the film, background objects become part of the foreground, as the camera continually refocuses its attentions (Chaudhary, 2009, p. 82). For this reason, I emphasize the film's reportage-like hand-held camera style which, with its long shots, long takes, whip pans and other frenetic movements into off-screen space, is highly suited to its raids into a history of the present. The pseudo-documentary style makes the camera appear as if it is recording events by chance, in real time. This generates a hyperrealism that encourages us to suspend our disbelief but also makes what it shows of the present within the future, or the past within the present, more difficult to disavow.

The dynamics of foreground and background in *Children of Men* also subvert the colonial legacy of Western film narrative in which the white hero typically has "the lion's share of time, resolution, safety and closure" (Goldberg, 2007, p. 44). According to this paradigm, the white hero inhabits the narrative foreground and embodies a universal Western subjectivity, appropriating the power to speak and act for others, while historical events are placed in the background, populated by the vulnerable and often-disposable bodies of racialized Others, the latter's suffering "absorb[ing] the threat of such pain from (white) western bodies" (Goldberg, 2007, p. 59). The tendency to submerge these characters in the background diminishes the extent to which the spectator is encouraged to care for them. In *Children of Men*, by contrast, there is one storyline privileging the foreground characters, and another in the background to which the camera is constantly drawn and which it provokes us to reflect upon. The stereotypical implications of the central story in which the white male protagonist, Theo, rescues a black woman are also undercut by a subversive narrative strategy in which the white protagonists – many of them played by major stars – die one by one: first Theo's ex-wife and leader of the Fishes, Julian (played by Julianne Moore), then his friend Jasper (Michael Caine), and finally Theo himself (Clive Owen). The film, moreover, makes us care for those in the background, who are reduced to the status of unpeople and bare life. A pivotal moment, as will be seen, is when Miriam (Pam Ferris) a white character from the foreground story, enters the background, making foreground and background merge. The identification becomes not just an empathy with one fictional character but, potentially, a more pluralistic identification based on a shared vulnerability. While the apathetic protagonist Theo demonstrates a shocking ability to switch off from the atrocities taking place around him, standing in for our collective denial of the implications of recent policies, the camera's reportage-style, allows it to raid the background, provoking a change in the audience's awareness. The film's political and aesthetic strategies here exemplify what Sabine Doran, in her essay in this volume, calls an "aesthetics of intrusion," which she identifies as characteristic of postcolonial cinema, (re)focusing on the margins and peripheries and thereby challenging dominant perceptions.

In an early scene, Theo disembarks on a railway platform lined with the cages of illegal immigrants destined for imprisonment and detention simply because they lack requisite identity cards and transit papers. An image of mass deportation reminiscent of *Night and Fog* (Resnais, 1955), which portrayed the role of railways in the Nazis' "Final Solution," the scene juxtaposes persecution in the past and in the present, exposing the brutal implications of immigration policy. In the cages scene, while the white European majority shows how political discourses of security and asylum deprive *all* of us of our rights and potentially reduce us to bare life, the complaints of a German-speaking woman about being locked in a cage with a black man act as a reminder of the racial markers that make some more susceptible than others to these measures.

Later, the camera moves with Theo as he walks past police in riot gear and cages of immigrants of mixed ethnicities. As he exits the frame, the camera rushes into the depths of the scene, unsteadily wending past a queue of people about to be placed into cages, some of them desperately holding up their passports. As screams are heard overhead, the camera tilts up to capture possessions being thrown out of a block of high-rise flats. The scene depicts the eviction, displacement, and dispossession of immigrants who are robbed of their identity as they are herded into cages and moved around like freight. It works both as another echo of the Nazi Holocaust and as a reference to the British Home Office's depersonalizing terminology of "removals." The policy of declaring all immigrants "illegal" is shown as only a few steps away from existing immigration laws, which already criminalize them. As the film suggests, using the label "illegal" for huge parts of the population has a dehumanizing effect. Armed with helmets and shields, the police act as agents of the state's repressive apparatus, their faceless exterior representing its ruthlessly efficient anonymous bureaucracy. The scene's overwhelming impression is of brutality and force, reinforced by the imagery of garbage removal as a bulldozer clears and crushes belongings, classifying the immigrants and their livelihoods, by implication, as human waste.

Bare life in the camp: an unplace for unpeople

Far from presenting immigration as a symptom of social disorder, as is common in popular media, *Children of Men* offers a *critical* discourse, enabling us to decipher the imagery used to justify repressive measures exerted against immigrants and terrorist suspects. This discourse portrays the dehumanizing *result* of policies that reduce human beings to the status of unpeople and bare life – "life that does not deserve to be lived" to translate the German term *lebensunwerten Leben* (Agamben, 1995, p. 137). As Jasper comments, "After escaping the worst atrocities and finally making it to England, our government hunts them [the refugees] down like cockroaches." The film has its denouement in Bexhill refugee camp, into which – with the connivance of a security guard – Theo, Kee, and Miriam enter in order to access the Human Project, whose boat is due to meet them on the south coast. Here, *Children of Men* revives the dark associations of the concentration camp, evoking the Nazis' "Final Solution" and the Soviet gulag, as well as detention facilities around the world. Inviting comparisons with the detention center/penal colony of Stonehaven (a fictionalized Margate) in *The Last Resort* (Pawlikowski, 2000), Bexhill is both a "non-place" (Augé, 1995) since identity is constantly under check and at risk of being stripped away, and what Foucault calls a "heterotopia," a place where otherness is policed and enforced but which at the same time holds alternative possibilities (Bexhill is a platform of escape for the main characters, and is also transformed by the refugees who live there). At the entrance, the sign "Homeland Security. Bexhill Refugee Camp. Restricted Access" arches overhead on a metal support, with the brown building on the left recalling famous photographs of Auschwitz. The use of US nomenclature ("Homeland Security") emphasizes the tendency of the British to adopt the measures and terminology of security from across the Atlantic. Located on the south-east coast of England, known for its detention centers for asylum claimants, Bexhill exemplifies the camp "not as a historical fact and an anomaly belonging to the past ... but in some way as the hidden matrix and *nomos* of the political space in which we are still living" (Agamben, 1995, p. 166). The camp is a place where the state of exception is materialized as the norm. Simultaneously a penal colony and detention center for refugees and terrorist suspects, it enfolds into itself multiple spaces – Nazi death camps and ghettoes, War on Terror prisons, and recent war zones – showing how a set of practices form a continuum and are not confined to one space.[5] These are practices that have their historical roots in the colonies and continue today on a global scale.

The restricted access to the camp and the multiple checkpoints en route underline its status as a place where individuals cede their identity and are deprived of their subjecthood. Busloads of immigrants arrive there, the maximum-security detainees held within cells. As a dumping ground for refugees from all over the world, Bexhill reveals the camp as a biopolitical space for human "garbage." Enclosed and hidden from the wider world, it is a "non-place" in which individuals are turned into "unpeople," prisoners into "detainees," who remain utterly at their guards' disposal. As the bus drives into the camp, numerous images of atrocity are visible through its barred windows. Prisoners are rounded up, perhaps to be summarily executed, some of them semi-naked. Lines of men kneel in abject positions on the floor, with their backs to the camera, evoking photographs of Guantánamo Bay detainees. Filming from the moving bus, the camera pans past prisoners in cage cells, tied to the bars in stress positions (curiously not with handcuffs, but with bands of bright orange reminiscent of Guantánamo Bay prisoner jumpsuits)[6] and arranged in compositions that obliquely allude to the choreography of the Abu Ghraib prison photographs, which featured naked human pyramids. One caged prisoner is a hooded and cloaked figure standing on a box, shaking as if he is being electrocuted – a composite image that merges one of the most notorious photographs from the Abu Ghraib prison scandal (which showed a hooded prisoner with wires hanging from his hands, having been told that he would be electrocuted if he stepped off the box) with accounts of another prisoner who testified that he was electrocuted. On the soundtrack, a siren blares incessantly, proclaiming security threats and alerts – the camp's permanent state of emergency – and creating a cacophony with the victims' screams and Kee's birth pangs (her labor begins as they enter the refugee camp).

Photographs of the Abu Ghraib prison scandal emerged in the international media in April 2004. Taken by US soldiers in charge of "softening up" prisoners for interrogation, their imagery depicts Iraqis in cruel and humiliating poses, evoking the Ku Klux Klan (the Hooded Man), racist lynching (prisoners handcuffed in stress-positions), and Nazi concentration camps (the use of dogs for intimidation). By laying the blame on

Figure 12.2 An immigration official accosts Theo and Kee on the refugee bus, whilst the Hooded Man – a notorious emblem of the use of torture in the War on Terror – is displayed through the near-left window (Source: still *Children of Men*, 2006)

a few low-ranking officers (labeled "bad apples"), both the public and official response to the photographs diverted attention from torture as a policy adopted by the Bush government in its War on Terror. Hinted at by the leaders of the administration in their public rhetoric, supported by memos by White House lawyers prevaricating on the meaning of torture, and aided by expanded presidential powers, this policy was methodically carried out using standard techniques in detention facilities around the world since 9/11. Not just the pranks of a few "bad apples" upon whom blame was pinned, events at Abu Ghraib were the culmination of a systematic program of dehumanization.

The photographs reveal torture as an exercise of power that uses the Other for self-affirmation. Techniques included those calculated to appeal to fear of humiliation in the "Arab mindset" through the use of women, nudity, and homosexuality within the torture scenarios (see Danner, 2004, pp. 19–20). Not only do the photographs, and the techniques they employ, replay Oriental fantasies of the Arab as weak and effeminate, they also dehumanize their victims through the use of hoods, making them anonymous and faceless. Commentators have rightly spoken of the "recreational racism" of the torture and its "profound violation of ontological dignity" (Grossinger, 2004, p. 127; Cavarero, 2009, p. 114). In seeing themselves as bringers of liberation to Iraq, the coalition forces subscribed to the civilizational discourses of empire that characterize subjugated people as primitive, animalistic, degenerate, sexually deviant or lascivious; in an ironic twist, the amateurish staging of the photographs portrays the barbarism within their own endeavor, which the occupiers attempted to project onto their subjects, as well as a culture of imperialist and racist violence and cruelty that goes back in history.

The film's images of atrocity engage in a dialogue with the photographs, laying bare the brutality of the practices without reproducing their Orientalist or voyeuristic sensationalism. The windows of the bus act as frames within the frame, alluding to the still frames of the photographs but putting them in motion by means of the camera's journey past a series of *tableaux vivants* of torture. Although held at a distance, in the background or at the edges of the frame, they do not lack emotional affect. In other words, this is not a typical Brechtian distanciation, for it is in this sequence that foreground and background merge most powerfully. When the bus comes to a standstill, guards with dogs come on board to shift the passengers, including Miriam. Observing the liquid pool beneath Kee's seat as her waters have just broken, an immigration guard, characteristically associating refugees with the abject, shouts "You fucking people disgust me." Meanwhile, the Hooded Man is displayed through the near-left window, inviting spectators to make connections between the racist logic of immigration controls and torture policies.[7] As Miriam is taken outside, the lights on the bus are switched off, silhouetting the main characters and the other passengers on board. This rather theatrical staging makes the narrative drama in the foreground recede momentarily so that figures and events in the background can be witnessed more prominently. The camera pans across the windows, aligning itself with Kee's distraught gaze as she watches Miriam being forcibly hooded in the background. The blaring of the siren yields to a non-diegetic choral track, which lends a melancholy tone, amplifying the affective charge of this sequence which ends by revealing the grim aftermath of the torture procedures in the form of bodies laid out on the ground. Rather than a narrative strategy that centers on the safety and resolution of the white hero overcoming adversity, the merging of foreground and background emphasizes a shared vulnerability to the production of "bare life" under states of exception, and indicts the solipsistic attitudes and policies that would trade the rights of "Others" for the benefits of "our" security.

Imagining resistance

Children of Men identifies key sites of oppression, but it also imagines ways beyond them, tracing sites of resistance and possibilities for a future other than the oppressive realities of the past and present. This it does mainly, as already mentioned, through narrative strategies that promote ethical attitudes that counteract imperialistic ways of thinking and acting. In the form of the Fishes, the grassroots resistance movement that demands immigrants' rights, the film interiorizes its own ethical demands upon its audience, although the Fishes are eventually undermined by their own power play: first, through the leadership struggle that results in Julian's death and, second, by their attempt to co-opt Kee's baby for their own political ends. However, also vital in this respect are the images of the "Stop the Iraq War" campaign glimpsed in the *mise-en-scène* of Jasper's flat where we see images and texts referring to the "mass action and mass protest" of public demonstrations against the invasion of Iraq, which Said referred to as "formidable tools of human resistance" (Said, 2004, pp. 253–4). Displaying the solidarity of huge numbers of people across the globe, they brought together very different voices and subject positions in the struggle against imperialism. The camera pans across newspaper clippings from the past amongst photographs and other family memorabilia, including a photo of Theo and Julian (who met on an anti-war march) together with their son Dylan, who later died in an influenza epidemic. The sequence reveals several of the characters' political pasts: Jasper's award as political cartoonist of the year; his wife Janice's activism as a photojournalist which led to her torture by MI5; and Theo's own former radicalism. That these oppositional voices are now silenced – literally in the case of the mute and paralyzed Janice – does not detract from the impressive reserve of resistance to which the film uses them to allude.

Moreover, far from representing immigrants as a criminal threat, the film gives them a positive valence. This is exemplified by the role of the Roma refugee, Marichka, and the Georgian family who help Kee and Theo and, most of all, by the appropriately named Kee herself as the key to the future. For Barbara Korte, the film's utopian perspective resides in Kee as a black mother figure: "In very explicit terms, the film makes the point that a black woman, and a refugee woman, for that matter, might guarantee a future for Britain and the whole world" (Korte, 2008, p. 322). In the face of calls for more restrictions, the film favors immigration as a solution to such trends as an ageing population, which the science-fiction infertility scenario represents in an exaggerated fashion.

Children of Men ends with two rival utopian moments: on the one hand, there is Theo's sacrifice. He dies from a bullet he received earlier, in order to "save" Kee and accompany her to the Tomorrow ship; on the other hand, there is the revolution taking place in the refugee camp where, amongst the film's most abysmal and dystopic scenes, the Muslims begin an uprising in a sequence which evokes both the Palestinian *intifada* and the insurgency in Iraq. Theo, Kee, and Marichka encounter a stream of marchers shouting "*Allahu Akbar*" ("God is great"). The camera follows the characters as they thread through the crowd, the handheld style facilitating a sense of immediacy. The sense of threat is not presented as emanating from the marchers, who are shown as a popular resistance movement, demonstrating the resolve of people to govern themselves against an occupation that seeks to impose its own law. Rather, the violent presence in the scene is that of the British military, who brutally respond to the uprising with tanks and bomber aircraft, and later, that of the Fishes, who enter the fray partly to retrieve Kee and partly to aid the uprising. In its reportage style, the camera runs ahead of the characters or follows them, dodging bullets, employing long takes and whip pans. In one *tour de force* sequence, a seven-minute long take, blood spatters on the camera lens; at another point, the camera briefly pauses from its chase and pans left to focus on a wailing woman holding her son, an image recalling a photograph from the Bosnian War, underlining the film's assumed role as guide into the history of our present.

Conclusion

This essay has argued for postcolonial theory's powerful bearing on the politics of the present, in which states placing themselves above international law manifest a contemporary form of imperialism. It has shown how a postcolonial reading of *Children of Men*'s rich matrix of imagery helps to decipher the hidden and changing forms of neo-imperial sovereignty, including the War on Terror global prison network and detention centers for refugees as the biopolitical spaces in which the West's others are dehumanized and reduced to the condition of bare life. Through its science fiction premise, the film dwells upon the legacy of the past in its own present, asserting continuities that are compatible with a postcolonial perspective. Making connections between foreign invasion and occupation and measures that justify the denigration of minorities and destruction of civil liberties at home, it invites its audience to recognize the consequences of the incitement of fears of terrorists and asylum seekers. The neo-imperial politics of the present raise urgent questions to which *Children of Men* responds by highlighting the links between discourses about "our" security and the creation of unpeople everywhere.

Notes

1 As Agamben writes, the analysis of biopolitics is exemplified in Michel Foucault's work, which explores "the concrete ways in which power penetrates subjects' very bodies and forms of life" (Agamben, 1995, p. 5).
2 For an insightful discussion of the ways in which asylum seekers are stripped of recognition and rights, see Tyler (2006, p. 189).
3 See Desser (1999) for a taxonomy of binaries in science-fiction films.
4 The 7/7 bombings refer to the attacks carried out by four suicide bombers during the morning rush hour on the London public transport network on 7 July 2005; their bombs exploded on three underground trains and one bus, killing 52 people and injuring hundreds.

5 In P.D. James's novel, upon which the film is based, the counterpart of Bexhill is a penal colony located in the Isle of Man.
6 Anne McClintock provides an illuminating gloss on the orange color of Guantánamo Bay jumpsuits, connoting "danger and security threats to Western viewers," whilst also reminding Muslim prisoners of the orange robes traditionally worn for execution. See McClintock (2009, p. 67).
7 As Tyler notes, the rhetoric of popular UK media makes frequent associations between asylum-seekers and abject qualities that evoke feelings of disgust, fear and anger. See Tyler (2006, pp. 191–2).

Bibliography

Agamben, G., 1995. *Homo Sacer: Sovereign Power and Bare Life*. Translated from Italian by D. Heller-Roazen. Stanford, CA: Stanford University Press.

Agamben, G., 2005. *State of Exception*. Translated from Italian by K. Attell. Chicago, IL: University of Chicago Press.

Augé, M., 1995. *Non-places: Towards an Anthropology of Supermodernity*. London: Verso.

Blair, T., 2003. *Newsnight*. Interviewed by J. Paxman [television] BBC2, 7 February 2003, 10:30 pm.

Butler, J., 2004. *Precarious Life: The Powers of Mourning and Violence*. London: Verso.

Cavarero, A., 2009. *Horrorism: Naming Contemporary Violence*. Translated from Italian by W. McCuaig. New York: Columbia University Press.

Chaudhary, Z., 2009. Humanity Adrift: Race, Materiality, and Allegory in Alfonso Cuarón's *Children of Men*. *Camera Obscura*, 24(3 27), pp. 73–109.

Curtis, M., 2004. *Unpeople: Britain's Secret Human Rights Abuses*. London: Vintage.

Danner, M., 2004. *Torture and Truth: America, Abu Ghraib, and the War on Terror*. London: Granta.

Desser, D., 1999. Race, Space and Class: The Politics of Cityscapes in Science-Fiction Films. In: A. Kuhn, ed., 1999. *Alien Zone II: The Spaces of Science- Fiction Culture*, London: Verso, pp. 80–96.

Goldberg, E.S., 2007. *Beyond Terror: Gender, Narrative, Human Rights*. New Brunswick, NJ: Rutgers University Press.

Grossinger, R., 2004. Abu Ghraib: A Howl. In: M. Benvenisti, M. Danner, B. Ehrenreich, J. Gray, R. Grossinger, D. Maitlin, C. Stein, D. Levi-Strauss and B. Warner, eds., 2004. *Abu Ghraib: The Politics of Torture*. Berkeley, CA: North Atlantic Books, pp. 123–33.

Gregory, D., 2010. Vanishing Points: Law, Violence, and Exception in the Global War Prison. In: E. Boehmer and S. Morton, eds., 2010. *Terror and the Postcolonial*. Malden, MA: Wiley-Blackwell, pp. 55–98.

James, P.D., 2006. *The Children of Men*, London: Faber.

Jenkins, S., 2008. Britain is Slithering Down the Road Towards a Police State. *The Guardian*, 6 February, p. 29.

Korte, B., 2008. Envisioning a Black Tomorrow? Black Mother Figures and the Issue of Representation in *28 Days Later* (2003) and *Children of Men* (2006). In: L. Eckstein, B. Korte, E.U. Pirker and C. Reinfandt, eds., 2008. *Multicultural Britain 2000+: New Perspectives in Literature, Film and the Arts*. Amsterdam: Rodopi, pp. 315–28.

McClintock, A., 2009. Paranoid Empire: Specters from Guantánamo and Abu Ghraib. *Small Axe*, 13(1), pp. 50–74.

Said, E., 1991. *Orientalism: Western Conceptions of the Orient*. Harmondsworth: Penguin.

Said, E., 2004. *From Oslo to Iraq and the Roadmap*. New York: Pantheon Books.

Tyler, I., 2006. Welcome to Britain: The Cultural Politics of Asylum. *European Journal of Cultural Studies*, 9(2), pp. 185–202.

Ware, V., 2010. The White Fear Factor. In: E. Boehmer and S. Morton, eds. 2010. *Terror and the Postcolonial*. Malden, MA: Wiley-Blackwell, pp. 99–112.

Žižek, S., 1995. *Looking Awry: An Introduction to Lacan through Popular Culture*. Cambridge, MA: MIT Press.

Žižek, S., 2007. Commentary. *Children of Men* [DVD], 2 Disc Special Edition, Los Angeles, CA: Universal Studios.

Filmography

Children of Men, 2006. [film] Directed by A. Cuarón. USA: Universal Pictures.

Night and Fog, 1955. [film] Directed by A. Resnais. France: Argos Films.

The Last Resort, 2000. [film] Directed by P. Pawlikowski. United Kingdom: BBC.

Chapter 13

Mira Nair's *Monsoon Wedding* and the transcoded audiologic of postcolonial convergence

Kanika Batra and Rich Rice

Working to interpret overlapping layers of media and culture in Mira Nair's film *Monsoon Wedding* (2001), this paper focuses on what new media theorists call "transcoding" – a convergence of layers of media, technology, and culture that generates new layers of meaning. In *The Language of New Media* (2002), Lev Manovich describes transcoding as one of the most substantial outcomes of the computerization of media. For Manovich, the "ontology, epistemology, and pragmatics" of technology influence the "organization," "emerging genres," and "contents" of the cultural layer (2002, p. 63). *Monsoon* is an example of postcolonial convergences that include culture and technology, and in this essay we explore transcoding in Bollywood and Hollywood film genres. We argue that Nair refashions elements of previous films, a process in new media theory known as "remediation," borrowing from and transforming existing media (Bolter and Grusin, 2000, p. 49). These two principles of new media – transcoding and remediation – that relate to cinematic intertextuality are important in understanding the entry of Indian cinema into a globalized cultural economy.[1]

Homegrown, digital, and new media technology are shaping the cultural framework of a new generation in India, which now looks at and speaks to countries in North America, the Middle East, and Australia as equal partners in economic and cultural exchanges. As Nair's remediation of existing film and digital genres in *Monsoon* reveals, the privatization of the Indian economy and young upwardly mobile Indians' acquisition of education and "globalized" lifestyles increasingly free of parental restraints, have transformed and diversified media discourses in postcolonial India. The trope of marriage introduces the issue of sexuality into this discussion, since the matrimonial relationship is a necessary and approved means of legalizing sexuality among middle-class Indian families like the one depicted in the film. The transformation of such culturally-approved modes of alliance, as opposed to "Westernized" lifestyles involving extra-marital and promiscuous sexuality propagated through the media, is introduced early on in the film.

In fact, just seven minutes into the film the viewer is pulled into a fiery debate taking place on- and off-stage in the context of a television program called *Delhi.com*. As some participants vociferously defend media censorship by pointing to a decline in Indian cultural values, one of the more cosmopolitan debaters states, "Let's take the example of America, the First Amendment . . ." only to be cut short by a *khadi* (handloom) clad man who categorically declares, "This is not America." The Americanized debater retorts, seamlessly mixing English and Hindi, "*Aap kya samjhte hain* [Do you think that], just because you wear handloom and speak Hindi you represent the common man. You don't."[2] The argument that the common man desires to see sex on screen, like some Westernized young men and women in India, is clinched when the Hindiwallas call on a scared-looking middle-class woman who dubs sex scenes for films apparently not made with a Hindi-speaking audience in mind. This is just one instance of Nair's acknowledgment of the exposure of Indian audiences to Hollywood. With the introduction of multiplexes in India in the 1990s came the release of Hollywood films, though often snipped of their sex scenes by the Censor Board of India. The freedom to watch sex on screen, though, is claimed by the Americanized debater as a natural right in a globalized India.

Nair uses this debate about the screening of sexuality to introduce the bride-to-be, Aditi, whose wedding preparations provide the title of the film. Aditi subverts the cinematic stereotype of the virginal bride by choosing to enter an arranged marriage as a way out of her affair with her married boss, who is the *Delhi.com* moderator and guiding spirit of the show. As Jenny Sharpe has pointed out, Nair brings together the "sexual frankness of Hollywood with the visual and affective extravagance of Bollywood in order to establish her heroine as a desiring subject" (2005, p. 71). In this way, Nair both remediates the genre of 1990s Bollywood wedding films, such as Yash Chopra's *Hum Aapke Hain Kaun/Who Am I To You?* and Yash and Aditya Chopra's *Dilwale Dulhania Le Jayenge/The Bravehearted Will Take The Bride*, and acknowledges her debt to televisual culture and technology.

Local, reflexive remediations

The wedding video is a particular, localized genre, characteristic of the contemporary, global India that Nair's film remediates. In middle- and upper-class Indian families, a videographer is often hired to cover the ceremonies before and on the wedding day. In the 1980s the videographer supplemented (but did not replace) the wedding photographer as recorder of wedding events. Given the confusion and noise surrounding the wedding, the audio later inserted in most wedding videos was a mélange of popular wedding songs from Bollywood films. At one level, *Monsoon* can be seen as an homage to this era when photographers and videographers had the final say on the visual and audio representation of marriage celebrations. By the 1990s, with ready access to video and digital equipment, this authority was wrested from the professional videographers and photographers. Increasingly members of the family were assigned to record ceremonies, which gave a more personal perspective to the official record.

"Hypermediation," another new media concept, refers to the use of the properties of specific media to make cultural points. For instance, in *Monsoon*, the "same" family is portrayed differently by the traditional, professionally-produced family photograph and the behind-the-scenes hand-held video. Differences between what is captured in one medium and what in another are telling. While the prospective in-laws are being served drinks at Aditi's engagement ceremony, Lalit Verma (played by a veteran actor

Figure 13.1 The Verma family photograph just before Aditi's wedding ceremony. Ria is asked by the photographer to sit at the "Gentleman's" (Tej's) feet; insert of Ria's face one video frame after the picture is taken demonstrating video and views over time can capture in some cases what context-less photography does not (Source: stills *Monsoon Wedding*, 2001)

Naseeruddin Shah, who has acted both in mainstream Bollywood and independent cinema in India), Aditi's father and the organizer of her wedding, summons his nephew Rahul to capture the event on camera, urging him to focus on the ring: "Come on, camera on kar na [turn on the camera] on the ring, on the ring." This reflexive moment early in the film prefigures a memorable scene that takes place just before the wedding ceremony itself when the extended family gathers together for a group portrait. The photographer advises Aditi's cousin, Ria, to sit at the feet of her uncle Tej (see Figure 13.1). There is a bitter irony in Tej's being honored as the head of the family by being seated next to the bride, which is brought out cinematically by a close-up of Ria's attempt to smile and hold back tears. She is remembering Tej molesting her as a child. While the wedding *photograph* shows Ria looking at the camera and almost smiling, the next frame of the *film* captures her lowering her tear-filled eyes. The professional picture captures a specific version of reality that is limited by the medium of still photography. The video, allowing perception over time, creates meaning differently and creates a different meaning.

Major events that lead up to the wedding are all shot in Super-16, the format used to make the film. These events include the hustle and bustle involved in constructing the venue, supervised by the "event manager," Dubey, the engagement ceremony, the *mehendi* or henna ceremony for the bride preceding the wedding, the cocktail-dinner on the day of the *mehendi*, and finally the wedding itself, amid sudden monsoon rains. Several times during the confusion surrounding the occasion, Nair signals the camera's presence as a mediating recorder of events. A romance between Dubey and a servant girl named Alice, for instance, is framed not only by Bollywood film songs but also by Dubey's own blocking, scripting, and setting the scene for his love story. Seated atop the scaffolding of the wedding tent, dreamily eating marigolds as he supervises the arrangements for the Verma family, Dubey closes his eyes to envision an ideal relationship with a "simple, decent" girl, forming a rectangle with his hands to frame his wedding as a film director frames a shot.

Nair explains in the Director's Notes on the DVD that this important scene was shot with an 8mm. lens to create a "distorting" effect. The camera captures the color and vibrancy of the wedding celebrations as a mix of fantasy and reality. The blocking of the actors playing the assistants allowed the focus to remain on Dubey as he envisaged his marriage to Alice as framed by his raised hands. These scenes, like the one with the family photographer, foreground the camera as a mediator of events, even as they show its inability to capture the reality of the lives of the people on screen. Additionally, these scenes provide a gloss on class and caste inequality, the basis of the middle-class weddings, like that between Lalit Verma's daughter, Aditi, and her fiancé Hemant, the Non-Resident Indian son of the Rai family. The source of this gloss is Dubey, whose own dreams of a wedding with the Christian maid, Alice, defy and challenge caste and religious taboos.

In a subsequent scene that develops these class and caste differences, Dubey and his assistants look at Alice through a glass window while she is looking at herself in a mirror. Alice has been trying on the jewelry of her employer, the bride's mother, imagining herself as a bride, while Dubey looks in without her being aware of his gaze. As Alice returns the wedding ornaments to the box where they are kept, Dubey's assistants join him in looking at her. But because they transcode the situation photographically, as opposed to Dubey's more contextualized videographic view of the scene, they believe Alice intends to steal the jewels. It could be said that Alice is refashioning her identity, remediating herself by placing cultural artifacts in new contexts. Media savvy Alice – familiar with the Bollywood idiom of the shy bride whom she imitates – here tries on the bride's ornaments. Later she adopts the modern means of communication, email. The viewer of *Monsoon* sees a dimensionality in Alice's actions, as does Dubey, whereas what the assistants see is limited. Where the viewers and Dubey see Alice remediating her position and growing as a person through making connections between transcoded layerings of culture and media, the assistants see her illegitimately trying to occupy the position of her employer/exploiter.

A similar instance of clashing mediations occurs when Ria foils the attempt of Tej to take a young female member of the family, Aliya, out for a drive. Ria looks at Tej through the car window, pulls Aliya out of the car, and publicly accuses Tej of having sexually abused her when she was a girl. The look of incredulity on Lalit Verma's face following Ria's disclosure matches Dubey's incredulous expression when his minions accuse Alice of stealing. Eventually both clashes are privately and publicly resolved. Dubey's assistants collectively apologize to Alice, and Lalit Verma seeks Ria's forgiveness for failing to protect her from the family patriarch. As he opens the glass doors to the room where Ria lies sobbing, he enters a space in which his surrogate daughter's rights weigh as heavily as the honor of the family. His later public apology is made in proximity to the framed photograph of Ria's father, Lalit's elder brother, to

Figure 13.2 Lalit Verma opens the glass doors to Ria's room in order to see her situation more clearly (Source: still *Monsoon Wedding*, 2001)

whom the family pays its respects immediately after posing for the group portrait. Both Lalit Verma and Dubey frame their own transcoded remediations through which new situations are composed.

Two paintings refract Ria's predicament as a victim of sexual abuse. The first is of a woman, half her face in darkness, and half in color, visible on the wall during Tej's declaration to Lalit that that he will sponsor Ria's education in America. The patriarchs of the family converse while the painting in the background asserts an angry, silent, yet accusing presence. When the camera moves over the room to the faces of the relatives gathered there, it rests on Ria's face behind which we see another painting. It depicts a baby Krishna before an overturned butter churn, allegorizing Ria's loss of innocence at Tej's hands. As the film also does with new and old music technologies, here the layers of new and old visual technologies are used to explore layers of culture – how respect for elders is complicated by the "disturbing topic of sexual molestation – a subject that would be too controversial for popular Indian cinema" (Sharpe, 2005, p. 61).

At another crucial moment, an abstract representation of a woman clad, almost bundled, in a white sari forms the background to the scene in which the family pays its respects to the photograph of Ria's father just before the wedding ceremony. Aditi enters the house to bow her head to the framed picture of her father's elder brother. The painting of the woman in white seems to be watching her, reflecting Ria's grief as the family pays homage to her father. The media of painting, photography, and cinematography are transcoded as grief is expressed simultaneously in the painting and in close-ups of Ria's expressive face. Like other postcolonial filmmakers, Nair de-hierarchizes background-foreground relationships, exploiting them instead for purposes of contextualized transcoding (see Chaudhuri, Doran, and Waller in this volume).

Photographic and videographic remediations are allegorized in the mirrors and glass frames through which the characters see themselves and others. In these versions of what Anne Friedberg has called "frame-within-a-frame compositions," the "interior screen materializes under special variables – windshields of automobiles, a torn curtain, different demarcations of the view" (2009, pp. 200–1). For Friedberg these interior screens serve as metacinematic techniques thematizing the history of the moving image in single frames. One could extend this formulation to say that Nair's film remediates media forms themselves. Mirrors, glass doors, windows, framed photographs, and paintings emerge as interior screens that not only reflect and refract; they create palimpsests of the representational logics of different subplots in the narrative.

This remediation enables what David Harvey calls an "immediate" communication of text, audio, and video information that foreshortens distance, hierarchy, and cultural difference. Through the remediation and ubiquity of technology, socio-economic and cultural boundaries are erased, collapsing dis-junctions of time and space in radically new ways in order to create what Henry Jenkins refers to as a "convergence culture" (2006, p. 37).

Nair characteristically directs the audience's gaze to local settings that allow a reflected/refracted look at life in a culturally convergent India. The city of Delhi, for example, impinges on the viewer's consciousness through both low-key, soft-focus shots of the city at night and sharply-focused shots of both day and night. The sharply-focused shots depict "India shining" for the upper middle-classes like the Vermas, while the low key night shots focus on those for whom postcolonial India is not such a shining place after all.[3] In the tradition of socially conscious documentary filmmaking and independent cinema, Nair provides viewers with both panoramic scenes of the city and close-ups of the lives of a particular selection of people across classes, religions, and geographies. By collapsing these disparities into a kaleidoscope of mutually transcoded patterns, though, her critique approximates a postcolonial analysis that inter-weaves (see Doran in this volume) these social realities in the tradition of postcolonial thinkers from Frantz Fanon onward.

Globalized audiologic

Nair's technique of remediation extends brilliantly to the audio track of the film, serving to highlight the status of the film as digital artifact. What we might call "globalized audiologic" can be defined as an interaction of cultural and computer layers that plays out in multiple dimensions of the film's production and reception (Manovich, 2002, pp. 63–4). This audiologic is also the site of postcolonial ambivalence. *Monsoon* confidently borrows from various Indian musical traditions such as folk music and Bollywood film song, but under the direction of a Canadian music director, a point to which we will return shortly.

Literary critic Paul Jay has suggested that, "the development of electronic media forms . . . has changed entirely the nature of social, cultural, economic, and political relations" (2010, p. 33). The cultural impact of digitized sound technologies through cell phones, pagers, and sounds of televised programs constantly reminds the audience of a listening India, as tuned in to MTV as it is to Bollywood (Sharpe, 2005, p. 59). This audiologic incorporates two forms of globalization that Stuart Hall has identified: first, an older, corporate, and enclosed form in which a national cultural identity is asserted in a highly defensive way; second, a form of the "global post-modern," which is trying to live with, as well as incorporate, difference (1997, p. 33). Within the logic of convergence, new media sound technologies (such as cell phone conversations, dubbing – usually of Hollywood films into Hindi – and remixing), and the complex layering of carefully selected music over certain scenes make up what Nair has called the "aural design" of the film (2001).

The now ubiquitous cell phone, for instance, is popular among all classes in India, particularly since there is a model to suit every pocket. Not bound by one or two-year contracts through telephone companies, middle- and upper-class professionals quite commonly own more than one mobile communication device – usually two phones from two different companies –paying monthly use-based charges. In *Monsoon*, Dubey, while planning the wedding, climbs up the scaffolding of the wedding tent in order to ensure a clearer signal on his phone (although ironically the signal turns out to be much clearer when his feet are on firm ground). At another moment, when he's having a conversation with Lalit Verma about the flower arrangements, we hear the beeping of his mobile phone. Not one to stand on politeness, he barks his reply in a typical mixture of Hindi and English words "Arre pager pe call kaliye [Call me on the pager]." The use of more than one communication device is, of course, a professional necessity for Dubey, particularly during the busy wedding season. Layering communication devices and being receptive to multiple viewpoints is crucial to cultural understanding. What is curious is that Dubey confuses the functionalities of the two modes when he asks a client to "call" him on his pager, forgetting in his stressful situation that the cell phone in his hand has remediated the pager, a cheaper device prefiguring but preceding the telecommunication boom in India. Dubey's confusion is perhaps symptomatic of the class distinctions that the ubiquity of cell phone usage in India has not leveled.

A visual referent for the audiologic of the mobile phone occurs during Aditi's last rendevouz with Vikram, the sleazy talk show host of *Delhi.com*, the night before her wedding. The encounter with Vikram turns into a smutty version of reality TV when two Delhi cops with distinctively rural Haryanvi accents accost them on noticing Vikram's car parked in an isolated spot in the middle of the night. As the officers shine their flashlights on the kissing couple, drag Vikram out of the car, and sexually harass Aditi, Vikram's cell phone rings. A call from his wife is enough to make Vikram abandon Aditi to the interrogation of the cops. In fact, Vikram explains Aditi's screams for help as part of the noise of a "show" he's recording. In this scene, then, there is a reversal of sorts since the cell phone becomes the means through which Vikram remediates the incident as one taking place on screen and not in real life, thereby absolving himself of any culpability.

Audiologic also works to layer the talk show mentioned at the beginning of this chapter. Hosted by Vikram, the program begins with a serious and heated debate about censorship in India, only to become a way of entertaining the audience at the expense of the frightened woman who dubs sex scenes. The audience's laughter at the incongruity of

Figure 13.3 Aditi and Hemant sit down for tea at a campus café. Posters from both Hollywood and Bollywood films layer the wall behind Hemant, signifying cultural convergence (Source: still *Monsoon Wedding*, 2001)

the woman's titillating dubbing with her homely appearance first introduces the ubiquity of representations of sexuality in new millennium India, where films like *Biwi No. I,* top revenue grosser in 2000 – directed by David Dhawan, one of the acknowledged masters of sleaze and comedy in Bollywood – and Hollywood movies, with their combination of action and sex, share the same screen space in multiplexes all over the country. This superimposition is also captured by the posters in the roadside *dhaba* (street café) where Aditi's fiancé, Hemant, takes her for a cup of tea (see Figure 13.3).

As they enter the *dhaba* and as they leave after Aditi confesses her affair with Vikram, the camera partially focuses on a faded poster of Nicolas Cage's 2000 film *Gone in 60 Seconds.* At the bottom left of the same wall there is an advertisement for the latest Abhishek Bachchan film *Tera Jadoo Chal Gaya*/You Worked Your Magic, released in the same year. It is as if the magical romance Hemant had envisioned with Aditi is gone in sixty seconds with Aditi's confession. At the same time, Nair also presents the convergence of media in India in the year 2000. The ramshackle café becomes a space that brings together Hollywood and Bollywood in the minds of the people. Likewise on Dubey's walk home through the streets of old Delhi, the filmmaker focuses on a cinema in Darya Ganj, one of the oldest neighborhoods in Delhi, which is advertising the Bollywood release, *Dhai Akshar Prem Ke*/*Two and a Half Words of Love*, starring Abhishek Bachchan and Aishwarya Rai, the leading couple in Bollywood at the time Much as the posters in the café comment on Aditi and Hemant's relationship, this one gestures to the complications in Dubey's budding romance with Alice. He would like to utter the two and a half words "I love you" to Alice, but he cannot bring himself to do so while she is angry with him.

Bollywood is thus a constant point of reference and influence in a cultural milieu in which, although classes are not abolished, people of all classes are transcoding media, especially popular songs, which are invoked at critical moments in the film. The songs from Hindi films that Nair includes are the filmmaker's personal favorites. The most catchy is "Chunari Chunari," a club favorite in Delhi at the time of the film's shooting, and the song to which the bride's cousin, Ayesha, and her brother, Varun, are planning to dance at the cocktail party the night before the wedding. Originally from *Biwi No.1*, the song as it is used diegetically within *Monsoon* thus serves as an example of characters performing remediated transcoding. Such is the reach of music, though, that Nair's own transcoding of the song is scarcely remembered. It is assumed to have been originally composed for *Monsoon*. In this case, then, transcoding becomes a postcolonial cultural translation of a Bollywood song to a non-Bollywood, diasporic film.

Much has been written about the generic and musical conventions used by Nair in *Monsoon*. Critics have either focused on the film's relationship with the aesthetic of the Bollywood wedding film genre, popularized in the 1990s (Sharpe, 2005, p. 61), or placed it in the "bourgeoning nuptial film genre" of Hollywood in the same decade (Capp, 2001). But the film is better illuminated when it is set within the postcolonial context suggested by Vijay Mishra, who assigns the wedding song a crucial place in his analysis of Bombay cinema and diasporic desire. In Mishra's opinion, the wedding song "forthrightly confirms through the space of the elaborate Hindu wedding the ultimate longing (as Bombay Cinema sees it) of the diaspora" (2002, p. 262). This reading is applicable not only to the songs but to the film itself, which "directs the diasporic gaze to the 'ideal arranged love marriage' unlikely to be unrealized in the diaspora" (Mishra, 2002, p. 266). The hummable songs from old Hindi films sung by the elders at the family gatherings emphasize romance on the personal and the national level by reconnecting the Indian diaspora to its roots. Thus, while first generation diasporics are steeped in the mellifluous melodies of *ghazals* and *thumris*, the younger generation learns to be Indian by dancing to "Chunari Chunari" As Gopal and Moorti have asserted, "through its mobility, Bollywood music as trope is not only deterritorialized but also reterritorialized with significant effects" (Gopal and Moorti, 2008, p. 38). The *filmigit* or film song functions across the diaspora as "a placeholder for memory and ethnic identity" (2008, p. 43). Incorporating several recognizable songs, both new and old, Nair locates her film in a space that is not quite Bollywood, but partakes of the transnational reach of Bollywood's cinematic idiom. Songs, according to Nair, are used to "weave in the fabric of everyday life in Delhi," and the film itself is "a love song to the city" where the filmmaker spent a part of her life (Nair, 2001). Continuing this trajectory of transcoding and remediation, there is news of a Broadway musical based on the film due to appear in 2011.

The audiologic of the film, however, is also a site of postcolonial ambivalence, involving the perhaps inadvertent sidelining of local talent. The theme song of *Monsoon*, "Aaj Mera Jee Karda," [Today My Heart Desires], sung by the acclaimed Punjabi folk and Bollywood singer Sukhwinder, is an inspired creation drawing on the earthy tunes of his native traditions as well as the Bhangra beats popular among the younger generation both in India and abroad. While the music of the film did extremely well, fame did not accrue as much to the singer as to the music director of *Monsoon*, the Canadian Mychael Danna. Sukhwinder's ill luck with recognition continues in the controversy over the

superhit number "Jai Ho" that he sang for Danny Boyle's *Slumdog Millionaire*. Both the lyricist Gulzar and the singer of "Jai Ho," Sukhwinder, were sidelined by the Academy Awards committee in its invitation to A.R. Rahman to perform in 2008. Almost all the credit for the song and the music went to Rahman, the music director of *Slumdog*, who has carved a name for himself in and outside India through collaborations with Indian directors based in the West such as Shekhar Kapur and Deepa Mehta. In a country where songs can make or break a film, it was a canny move on Nair's part to tap into local talent for vocalists while reserving the music director's role for Mychael Danna, who has an international reputation as well as experience in working with Indian artists and directors. Does Indian talent thus serve as the raw material to be shaped and given a form by a foreign music director? If so, how do we assess *Monsoon* as a postcolonial cultural artifact participating in the channels of global distribution and recognition? The marginalization and sidelining of Indian musical talent, in effect, serves to overshadow and undermine the brilliant cinematic reflexivity of the film, and emerges as a postcolonial concern.

Foreplays, backdrops, and digital cinema

As the family is presented as a supportive but flawed entity, reflexive cinematic techniques are used in ways that call attention to the film as, itself, a flawed artifact. In the almost but not quite perfect mix of documentary filmmaking, and independent, low budget cinema traditions that Nair invokes in *Monsoon*, there are at least two flaws that highlight the presence of the computer layers transcoding the cultural and generic layers. The two "flaws" occur within a few minutes of each other: the first is the repetition of shots of Ayesha putting a chunni (scarf) around Rohit, as he walks in on Varun's and her dance rehearsal. As she asks him, "Come on Sydney boy, can you move to this?" the shot is repeated three times in a loop, in a special instance of cinema montage that points to the digitization of filmmaking (Manovich, 1995, p. 191).

The second "flaw" occurs later in the film as Dubey abandons his helpers' clumsy attempts to put up a colorful tent with the excuse that he's not feeling well. As he rises and walks forward, the camera moves in to make it seem as if he has crossed the bamboo scaffold which intersects the previous frame. But the scaffold appears again in the next shot as Dubey bends down to get under it and emerge on the other side. While this reemergence could be the result of faulty continuity, either in the shooting or the editing, it could also be a deliberate gesture on the part of the filmmaker, as a sort of hypermediated perspective on editing technique, implicitly critiquing the strictures of "continuity."

On a cultural level, the transcoded remediations of local and global technologies – cell phones, still cameras, analog and digital film cameras, and the internet – contribute to a proliferation of explicit representations of sexuality in postcolonial India. Media layering converges with cultural transformation. But how to read such transformations is far from obvious. One of *Delhi.com's* panelists asks, "Just because India has gone global, should we embrace everything? What about our ancient culture, our traditions, our values? The film does not allow these questions to remain in such binary oppositional terms. Amid the babble of voices debating whether such proliferation can be allowed or whether it needs to be censored, what gets lost sight of are the thousands of routine, banal, and sometimes exploitative forms of sexual expression in India.[4] Gayatri Gopinath, for example, astutely points to the suppression of the queer forms of expression in *Monsoon* in order for a "modern, heterosexual, liberal, feminist subject to emerge" (2005, p. 162). It is, in fact, Ria, avid reader of Tagore and Naipaul, aspiring creative writer, and firm believer in marrying for love, who provides the film's denouement. Having survived Tej's sexual abuse and saved little Aliya from its repetition, she emerges as a feminist subject whose position has far-reaching implications for the sexuality of the Indian middle classes. Daughters must be married at the right age; sons must be taught to become "professional" men and not chefs or dancers at weddings. Traditional middle-class families like the Vermas rely on preventing (if not absolutely suppressing) any sexuality, whether incestuous or queer, outside the heteronormative framework.

Conclusion

The spaces of traditional and contemporary cultures accessed in the film through layering digitized and personal recordings of experience make this film as much a digital as a cultural artifact. In addition, the borrowing, mixing, splicing, and layering of sound – ringtones, pager beeps, MTV hits, Hindi film songs, director's commentary – contribute to a global audiologic that is itself a result of several transcoded remediations. No longer is it possible to prioritize the national over the global when invoking the postcolonial because borders do not limit the reach of cultures and technologies. The spectacle of the film is as much for "Indian" as for "foreign" audiences, a distinction the film itself does not maintain. (Is "Sydney boy" Australian or Indian or a little bit of both?) Much of the film is devoted to the celebratory, potentially nostalgic occasion of a wedding between an "Indian" woman and a "diasporic" man, yet the subplot of sexual abuse reveals the spectacle as comparable to a static photographic rather than a seamless videographic representation. While the film's closing shots of the three unmarried cousins – Ria, Aliya, and Ayesha – dancing in the rain may indicate a celebration of uninhibited sexuality and a respite from patriarchal oppression (as the Indian monsoon tempers the oppressive heat), these shots are preceded by the wedding of Dubey and Alice, and the credits are intercut with shots of of Aditi and Hemant's wedding. Above all *Monsoon Wedding* constructs a postcolonial space inundated with, and to some extent constituted by, technology, where the sights seen and the sounds heard of a recently discovered sexual freedom are not binarily opposed to the notions of "chastity," "honor," "respectability," and "family values" that enable the "arranged love" marriage of Aditi and Hemant.

Notes

1 One of the early readers of this essay took this to mean that "technology is Western and hence external to Indian cinema." That is certainly not our implication when we say that Indian cinema has entered the globalized cultural economy. In terms of numbers of movies

produced each year and their reach in various countries around the world, the Indian film industry surpasses Hollywood. However, the low budget of most of Indian movies makes them technologically inferior to Hollywood films. In a scenario where multiplexes in India simultaneously screen Hollywood and Bollywood films, Bollywood productions are far more popular despite the marketing and technological superiority of Hollywood productions.

2   Cloth woven by hand known as handloom was popularized by Mahatma Gandhi as a mark of resistance against British rule in India. In postcolonial India it no longer signifies resistance against Westernization as much as a chic indigenous identity.

3   The slogan "India Shining" was used by the right-wing Bharatiya Janta Party (BJP) to brag about its military and economic achievements during its electoral term from 1999 to 2004. The term was coined around 2003 as the BJP was gearing up to contest another round of elections and hoping for a clear majority in the parliament. We use the phrase somewhat anachronistically to refer to Nair's clever play with light as well as to indicate the postcolonial hierarchies between the have and the have-nots in Delhi.

4   In 2004 the nation was alerted to the misuse of cellular phone and camera technology by the MMS scandal at Delhi Public School, R.K. Puram when a 17-year old boy filmed sexual acts with his girlfriend and circulated the video through his cellphone. Multimedia Messaging Service (MMS) remediates SMS much as Dubey's cellphone remediates pager technology. Two recent Bollywood films, *DevD* (2009) and *Love, Sex aur Dhoka* (2010) refer to this incident.

Bibliography

Appadurai, A., 1996. *Modernity at Large: Cultural Dimensions of Globalization*. Minneapolis: University of Minnesota Press.

Bolter, J.D. and Grusin, R., 2000. *Remediation: Understanding New Media*. Cambridge, MA: MIT Press.

Burke, K., 1969. *A Rhetoric of Motives*. Berkeley: University of California Press.

Capp, R., 2001. Delhi Deluge of Colour and Movement in Mira Nair's *Monsoon Wedding. Senses of Cinema*, [online] December 2001, Available at: http://archive.sensesofcinema.com/contents/01/18/monsoon_wedding.html [accessed 8 February 2011].

Friedberg, A., 2009. *The Virtual Window: From Alberti to Microsoft*. Cambridge, MA: MIT Press.

Gopal, S. and Moorti, S., 2008. Introduction: Travels of Hindi Song and Dance. In: S. Gopal and S. Moorti, eds., 2008. *Global Bollywood: Travels of Hindi Song and Dance*. Minneapolis: University of Minnesota Press, pp. 1–60.

Gopinath, G., 2005. Bollywood Spectacles: Queer Diasporic Critique in the Aftermath of 9/11, *Social Text*, 23(3-4), pp. 157–69.

Hall, S., 1997. The Local and the Global: Globalization and Ethnicity. In: A. King, ed., 1997. *Culture, Globalization, and The World System: Contemporary Conditions for the Representation of Identity*. Minneapolis: University of Minnesota Press, pp. 19–40.

Harvey, D., 1990. *The Condition of Postmodernity: An Enquiry Into the Origins of Cultural Change*. Malden, MA: Blackwell.

Jay, P., 2010. *Global Matters: The Transnational Turn in Literary Studies*. Ithaca, NY: Cornell University Press.

Jenkins, H., 2006. *Convergence Culture: Where Old and New Media Collide*. New York: New York University Press.

Manovich, L., 1995. What is Digital Cinema? In: P. Lunenfeld, ed., 1995. *The Digital Dialectic: New Essays on New Media*, Cambridge, MA: MIT Press, pp. 172–92.

Manovich, L., 2002. *The Language of New Media*. Cambridge, MA: MIT Press.

Mishra, V., 2002. *Bollywood Cinema: Temples of Desire*. New York: Routledge.

Nair, M., 2001. Feature Commentary with the Director. *Monsoon Wedding* [DVD]. USA: Universal.

Sharpe, J., 2005. Gender, Nation, and Globalization in *Monsoon Wedding* and *Dilwale Dulhania le Jayenge*, *Meridians: Feminism, Race, Transnationalism*, 6(1), pp. 58–81.

Filmography

Biwi No. I, 1999. [film] Directed by D. Dhawan. India.

DevD, 2009. [film] Directed by A. Kashyap. India: Anurag Kashyap Films.

Dilwale Dulhania Le Jayenge, 1995. [film] Directed by Y. Chopra and A. Chopra. India: Yash Raj Films.

Dhai Akshar Prem Ke, 2000. [film] Directed by R. Kanwar. India: Inderjit Films Combine.

Gone in 60 Seconds, 2000. [film] Directed by D. Sena. USA: Buona Vista.

Hum Aapke Hain Kaun, 1994. [film] Directed by R. Barjatya. India: Rajshri Productions.

Love, Sex aur Dhoka, 2010. [film] Directed by D. Banerjee. India: Balaji Telefilms.

Monsoon Wedding, 2001. [film] Directed by M. Nair. USA/India: Mirabai films.

Slumdog Millionaire, 2001. [film] Directed by D. Boyle. UK: Celador Films.

Tera Jadoo Chal Gaya, 2000. [film] Directed by A. Muthu. India: Tips Music Films.

Chapter 14

Nollywood in transit

The globalization of Nigerian video culture

Claudia Hoffmann

Introduction

In recent decades, Nigerian video films have experienced astounding popularity and are consumed in homes, street corners, and video parlors in Nigeria, other parts of the continent, and the African diaspora. Nigerian filmmakers produce anywhere between 1,000 (Haynes, 2006) and 1,500 (Barrot, 2008) films per year, shot with handheld video or digital cameras, edited on personal computers, and featuring actors who might not have enjoyed extensive training, but whose names attract audiences in their native Nigeria and its diaspora and whose stardom can make it difficult for them to navigate the streets of Lagos, the epicenter of English Nollywood films.[1] Upon arrival for a research trip to Nigeria during the summer of 2008, I was only vaguely familiar with the staggering popularity of these straight-to-video productions that were handed to me through the car window for purchase during every traffic stop in Lagos. Ultimately it was my Nigerian host family who introduced me to a form of film consumption that is entirely in tune with Nigerian realities and takes place in the familiarity of the home, the video parlor, at the hair dresser, or the market stall. Films are shown on television almost around the clock, and the neighborhood rental stalls are always up to date with the latest release.

But for all the intimacy these settings seem to suggest, the films elicit a greater degree of audience interaction than I had ever witnessed. Whether at home, at the market stall, or at the university staff club, people animatedly discussed characters, plot lines, and issues, offered scathing criticism and exuberant praise, and went back and forth between discussing the action on the screen and its relationship with personal and national realities. In short, I witnessed a form of interaction between the films and their audience I had never encountered before, which stands in stark contrast to the historical tendency of African cinema not to reach general populations. In order to bring a national cinema to the people, something unprecedented in the history of African cinema, Nigerian filmmakers cater to the needs and desires of their audience and circumvent the problems of a national reality in which resources are scarce and filmmaking training practically non-existent.[2] Nollywood's unabashed and self-sustained commercialism and concern with entertainment pits it against African cinema conventions that more overtly take stock of postcolonial and contemporary conditions, but rely heavily on

Western funding and exposure at international film festivals. Moreover, Nollywood as a commercial enterprise has transcended Nigerian borders, and has established itself as one of the most popular forms of cinema on the continent and within diasporic African communities around the world. Films are easily available in African food stores in much of Europe and North America, as well as for purchase on the internet.

Inspired by the success of Nollywood abroad, Nigerian expatriate filmmakers in Europe and North America have turned to producing and directing their own films in which immigrant characters and migration stories provide high degrees of immediacy for African diasporic communities. In his pioneering essay about the Nollywood diaspora, Jonathan Haynes (forthcoming) observes that a great majority of films made in the Nigerian diaspora feature storylines about migration and life in exile. They not only reflect the filmmakers' diasporic identities, but, on a larger scale, constitute a cinema that complicates our discussions of African cinema and its traditional critical affiliation with the politicized engagement of Third Cinema.[3] The dismissal of Nollywood as a purely profit-oriented entertainment industry, which lacks the serious cinematic activism of, for example, Francophone African films, neglects the profound success of Nigerian filmmakers in creating and distributing films without the need for outside funding or support. The creation of these self-sustained production and distribution channels make Nollywood the first entirely self-supporting African cinema. Moreover, the mobility of Nollywood across Africa and the diaspora through the commercialization of popular Nigerian culture defies the historical and contemporary control of the global North over Africans and African culture, including visual representation, and constitutes one of Nollywood's most empowering features. Babson Ajibade (2009, p. 418) goes so far as to describe the Nollywood phenomenon as a "coup against the colonial domination of film, enacted outside the state's control, and in such a way as to undermine the authority of filmmakers and critics whose tastes reflected colonial and/or Western castes of mind." Ramón Lobato (2010, p. 350) makes the important point that Nollywood should be taken seriously in its success in finding "a third way" of distribution, which leads to its current status as "a viable, popular and accessible film culture." In this essay I wish to situate the Nigerian video film industry more firmly within the critical discourse on African cinema and complicate the way in which we assess and define "political" cinema. Drawing on Lobato, I argue that Nollywood's "third way" of production and distribution and its popularity among African audiences around the world makes it an unprecedented phenomenon of African expression and cultural, as well as political, engagement.

Recent scholarship has begun to acknowledge that the "emergence of Nollywood is emblematic of serious structural transformations in Nigeria, and indicates new standards both within the form of cinema and in the social structure" (Adesokan, 2009, p. 2). Through his analysis of what he terms "democracy films," Adesokan affirms that the disjuncture between Francophone African cinema and Nollywood should not lead us to dismiss any sort of political engagement on the part of the latter. Similarly, Haynes (2006, p. 530) points to the political dimension in a number of Nollywood films across a variety of genres and concludes that "the Nigerian video industry has taken up political issues with a wide, varied, and ever-increasing range of generic strategies." I would like to add to these authors' assessment of an "alternative political" by tracing the themes and concerns of selected Nigerian video films made in Nigeria and the diaspora. By doing so, I attempt to show how Nollywood's break with the conventions and dependencies of postcolonial African filmmaking has profoundly revolutionized African popular culture. More specifically, I argue that Nollywood's most political feature is its defiance against forces, colonial, postcolonial, and neo-colonial, that have traditionally controlled and continue to control not only the cinematic representations of Africans, but also their circulation.

Nigerian video films might not fit into our discussion of the ideology-driven postcolonial cinema created by filmmakers such as Ousmane Sembène, Djibril Diop Mambéty, Med Hondo, and Souleymane Cissé, among many others. The works of these filmmakers overwhelmingly take stock of difficult postcolonial and neocolonial conditions. As Jude Akudinobi points out in Chapter 4 of this volume, "cinema was construed by the African filmmakers as a novel platform for the national project of rebirth and reconstruction" (p. 78). The emergence of African cinematic production out of the nation-building endeavor of the 1960s has created this form of politically engaged cinema which served many purposes: to correct self-serving portrayals of "primitive" African natives on the part of Westerners, to creatively engage with a newly-independent political landscape, and to function as "platforms for radical social change and inspirational principles" (Akudinobi, p. 78). While critical discourse has rightly situated African cinema within the political context of its creation and development, it has until very recently overwhelmingly favored the Francophone productions of West Africa which were "known as *the* African cinema before the emergence of Nollywood" (Okome, 2007, p. 1). The problem with this critical focus lies in its conflation of African cinema and Francophone African cinema, which erroneously suggests that African cinema as a whole embodies a political engagement born out of a Francophone African reality.

Postcolonial Anglophone African cinema and the emergence of Nollywood

The beginnings of African film production vary significantly across the continent as each colonial government implemented its own rules in accordance with ideology, colonial practices, and administrative needs.[4] Film production in Anglophone Africa formally began with the Bantu Educational Cinema Experience in 1935, which was established for the purpose of introducing Africans to, and educating them about, living under colonial rule. In 1939, the Colonial Film Unit was set up, and although it made an effort to educate Africans in filmmaking, it retained full control over film production in the colonies and perpetuated a continuing dependence in the former colony after independence (Diawara, 1992). Following independence, the British administrators left filming equipment behind, and Nigerian filmmakers emerged, among them Segun Olusola, Ola Balogun, and Francis Oladele. Their films, however, had to compete with the influx of Western films, which were screened all over Anglophone West Africa, partially by means of mobile cinemas that brought the viewing experience into remote rural areas (Diawara, 1992).

Many critics credit the popular Yoruba traveling theatre with being a predecessor of today's video phenomenon. Performers traveled in the Nigerian Southwest and parts of Benin to stage plays in front of audiences from the Yoruba ethnic group. Eventually the ensembles started recording their performances on video. Despite its focus on Yoruba value systems and traditions, the traveling theatre also appealed to a non-Yoruba Nigerian audience, thus transcending divisions along ethnic lines in the country (and beyond). Before its economic decline, Nigeria did experience a brief phase of cinema culture and featured over 100 theatre houses, but their prosperity was short-lived. Nigerian cinema culture experienced a downturn due to increased criminal activity in city streets and significant economic woes. Nigerian cities became increasingly unsafe as crime rates skyrocketed; when the Nigerian film audiences deemed it too dangerous to leave the house during the evening hours, the number of cinema houses declined sharply. However, with easier access to VHS video cameras and tapes and a good intuition for what the Nigerian audience wanted to watch, a new breed of filmmakers catered to the immediate need of Nigeria's film consumers. By turning to the production and sale of VHS films, and later VCDs, which most Nigerians can watch in the safety of their home, young filmmakers were able to make popular films on small budgets.[5] Generally, Nollywood themes range from elaborate love stories, often frayed by betrayal, witchcraft, and the occult (although less so in recent years, partly due to government efforts) to corruption, polygamy, gender conflicts, and much more. Most films follow a main plotline with varying numbers of subplots that break off, sometimes into the distance never to be seen again, other times in preparation for one of often many sequels. Nollywood themes encompass all conceivable social issues that make up the fabric of daily realities in Nigeria and are often related to gender, family, and business relations. For the purpose of this discussion, it is highly significant that Nollywood is a form of cinema that thrived because the national film industry modeled after colonial film culture failed.

John McCall argues that "[what] positions Nollywood as a catalyst for pan-African discourse is precisely that it has no view, no agenda, no ideology. It is a sprawling marketplace of representations" (2007, p. 96). However, McCall also agrees with Haynes that "the political" has traditionally been a Western intellectual concept and urges caution when trying to apply it to the Nollywood storylines. The film credited most often as the catalyst for Nollywood's success is Kenneth Nnebue's *Living in Bondage* (1992), which sold 200,000 copies. *Living in Bondage* tells the story of Andy whose unsuccessful attempts at economic success lead him to sacrifice his wife in a cult ritual in exchange for riches. After drinking her blood and indeed becoming a rich man, he finds himself haunted by her ghost and, after a series of events, seeks redemption through religion. The film's commentary on the immoral accumulation of wealth in a country plagued with corruption is hard to miss: "the film also suggests that the new wealth in Nigeria is the result of demonic practices – and the source of inequality in the country and the suffering of too many people" (Krahe, 2010). *Living in Bondage*, like many Nollywood films, foregrounds a personal political realm that takes place in the interpersonal relations of character and that does not perpetually foreground a colonial legacy and therefore the West. In other words, Nollywood has successfully removed itself from the confines of critical expectations that demand an African cinematic narrative, which evokes liberation struggles that are not immediately relevant for many Africans.

Haynes (2006, p. 514) acknowledges the alternative expression of political engagement in many Nollywood films: "the concept of the political should encompass the level of the banal, everyday reproduction of authority ... – all the myriad social tensions and controversies to which the videos have responded with literally thousands of stories ..." Haynes argues furthermore that the Nigerian social reality is infused with anxieties caused by political conditions, which the videos reflect through their concern with localized issues. The main difference between Nollywood's political engagement and that of Francophone cinema lies in the question of what issues are relevant and, perhaps more importantly, immediate for their respective audiences. Furthermore, the films often provide much-needed outlets for frustrations within lower-class populations coming to terms with a reality that stands in stark contrast to the riches of officials and other selected few: "Nollywood films provide us with the images and language to represent this new imagined community with the same frustrations and aspiration" (Diawara, 2010, p. 177). Despite their entertainment value, Nollywood films successfully capture and distribute the complications within a society that is coming to terms with a postcolonial past and a neocolonial presence. But more importantly, they do so in a way that a non-intellectual audience can relate to.

This immediacy has made Nollywood popular throughout Africa. The tradition of appropriating existing resources to fit the needs of local audiences continues outside the Nigerian borders where Nollywood has become a cinematic staple. Films are shown in little parlors with translators at hand who put on their very own show to make the Nollywood films appealing to non-Nigerian audiences. One example is given in Matthias Krings' (2009) fascinating study of Tanzanian interpreters who provide simultaneous translations of the English dialogues of Nigerian and foreign films in a video parlor in Dar es Saalam. Krings (2009, p. 18) describes these parlors as being equipped with "hard wooden benches, small TV-screen, bad video copies, and bad sound" and notes that the interpreters add information and commentary where they see fit to "localize" the film. In the narration for a Nigerian video film about the religious battle between good and evil, the interpreter, for example, explicitly tells the audience that he likes Nigerian films because "[these] are the evil things that take place around us every day. That's why I like Nigerian films, because they talk about every-day life" (cited in Krings, 2009, p. 18). Krings further (2009, p. 19) points out that the added comments on the part of the interpreter grant the film authenticity for the local context even though it was not made in Tanzania or even Eastern Africa: "Such commentary in fact serves to authorize Nigerian films as depicting *authentic* images of the battle between good and evil, despite their being foreign and fictitious. Their moral lessons may therefore be adapted to local every-day realities."

Ajibade (2009, p. 417) observes similar appropriations in Cameroon: "youth in Cameroon ... are keeping current about the goings-on in the popular video industry because Nigerian videos move through cities like Douala, Bamenda, Yaoundé, and villages in-between in increasing volume." During his fieldwork in a Cameroonian village, Ajibade, like Krings, observed that the popularity of Nollywood films remains unbroken by linguistic barriers. In this case, Cameroonian youths watch English films and discuss them in French, thus collectively trying to make sense of what happens on the screen. Ajibade (2009, p. 423) concludes that "it is the powerful lure of images about contemporary African life-worlds that has made Nigerian video films a significant presence in spaces across the Cameroonian nation." Moreover, through appropriating Nollywood conventions and modes of filmmaking within Africa, Nigerian filmmakers have, for the first time, created a truly pan-African creative phenomenon, which has now led to Nollywood-style filmmaking across the continent.

Nollywood and the allure of the global north

Issues of migration and the desire to leave Nigeria for seemingly greener pastures were part of Nollywood films before diasporic filmmaking even began. Kenneth Egbuna's *American Visa 1* (2004) depicts the futile efforts of a Nigerian citizen to obtain a visa for a visit to the United States, thus addressing questions of global mobility and the particular challenges faced by nationals of third world countries.[6] Adim Williams' *Mr. Ibu in London* (2004) takes on the collective imagination of the West and transcultural pitfalls. Ibu, a security employee, decides to travel to London to get international experience after unsuccessfully wooing a woman with an American boyfriend. London, however, turns out to be a taxing place for Ibu, and in the end he returns to Nigeria with empty hands. The trope of the unsuccessful returnee has been common in both film and literature, often in the context of unreasonable expectations and the migrant's inability to return.

While the previous two films present the West as a desirable space, Kingsley Ogoro's extremely successful comedies *Osuofia in London 1 and 2* (2003 and 2004, respectively) cleverly subvert notions of the desirable West. Village-dweller and hunter Osuofia travels to London to collect his inheritance after learning of his brother's death. In London he meets Samantha, his brother's fiancée, who unsuccessfully tries to scam him out of his money. In the end she resorts to following Osuofia to Nigeria as his second wife in the hope of being able to claim the money there. *Osuofia in London 2* sets out where the first part ends and shows a series of intercultural clashes during which Samantha's dishonest intentions are revealed by Osuofia's first wife. The story concludes with reconciliation between Samantha and Osuofia and her return to London. Despite their apparent entertainment value, the *Osuofia in London* films provide a distinctly subversive take on African-Western encounters. Osuofia is consistently scandalized by the conditions in London and seeks to improve them. He covers the legs of a young woman to preserve her decency, lectures a fast food employee on the establishment's unacceptable food offerings, and is entirely flabbergasted when the same employee does not accept his Nigerian naira in lieu of British pounds. Osuofia's indignation and utter surprise constitutes a clever take on the Western desire to improve African conditions. In fact, at the end of part 2, Samantha admits that life in the village has made her realize that stereotypes about "primitive" Africa do not hold true, which suggests the village as the place of enlightenment rather than the progressive and "civilized" Western space.[7]

But Nollywood films have also gained profound significance in Nigerian expatriate communities: "Around 600,000 VCDs are pressed daily in Lagos, and crates of these films leave on planes every day, making Nigeria one of the leading digital media content producers, and Nollywood one of Nigeria's most important exports after oil" (Saro Wiwa, cited in Highet, 2010, p. 18). Nigeria's oil industry, unlike the video film industry, has never been an economic force for the general population in Nigeria, the majority of which lives on less than $1 per day. Oil revenues rarely trickle down to benefit the general population, while profits from the export of video films are much more likely to return to the informal economy that produced them. Nollywood has also achieved an independence from cinema imports, while even the oil industry remains dependent on fuel imports. According to the BBC (2010), poor maintenance and subsequent poor conditions limit the capacity of Nigerian oil refineries to an estimated 40 percent. While even Nigeria's oil industry, despite its abundant supply of crude oil, cannot sustain itself on international markets, Nollywood, which is also the second-largest employer in Nigeria, has successfully circumvented any form of dependence on a global economy that is almost exclusively controlled by Western corporations and distribution channels, which is yet another tribute to the industry's fierce independence.

Nollywood USA and diasporic anxieties

Expatriate Nigerian filmmakers recognized the appeal of Nollywood films for diasporic African audiences and the potential of their films to cater even more directly to Africans abroad. Just as Nigerian video films address the anxieties of living in contemporary Africa in general and Nigeria in particular, many diasporic Nollywood films concern themselves with issues of contemporary migration out of Nigeria as a direct result of neocolonial economic pressures and resulting anxieties about living abroad. These attempts at coming to terms with migrant life also serve to bridge the gap between Nigeria and North America and result in films that embody both human migration and the circulation of visuals influencing migration. Diasporic video films are located at the intersection of global technologies, transnational actors, and creative practices and embody visual representations that humanize the often opaque concept of "African immigrant." Furthermore, by bringing the home nation Nigeria (or the home continent Africa) into the migrant space, Nollywood films bridge the distance between the homeland and the diaspora: "the films answer a longing for home and serve as a vehicle for showing children and non-Nigerian friends what Nigerian culture is like" (Haynes, forthcoming).

But Nollywood films also politicize the immigrant experience and take this political concern into a globalized arena in which people, ideas, images, and the films themselves circulate. The relationship between on-screen spaces and the filmmaker's relationship with these spaces are often obvious and relevant. US-based Nigerian filmmakers like Oliver Mbamara, Bethels Agomuoh, Pascal Atuma, Sola Osofisan, Eve Ikuenobe-Otaigbe, and Femi Agbayewa have created a brand of Nollywood that is entertaining, educating, political, and self-consciously concerned with the allure that moving images can create.[8] Each of these filmmakers has made films that focus on the experience of Nigerian expatriates who navigate an unexpectedly difficult life in the United States. The protagonist of Bethels Agomuoh's *This America* (2005) Ozobio, assumes that New York City offers new opportunity after he loses his banking position in Lagos, but he soon finds out that without a green card he will not be employed in accordance with his education. Ozobio ends up entering a green card marriage. In Sola Osofisan's *Missing in America* (2004), protagonist Agatha travels from Nigeria to New Jersey in search of her missing husband, only to find that he has married an American woman for a green card. Eve Ikuenobe-Otaigbe's newly-arrived immigrant character Biu considers a green card marriage in *The God Daughter* (2006), but gets tangled in a web of fraud and deception which eventually leads to her arrest. Besides the need for legal papers, these filmmakers address immigrant-specific topics such as cross-cultural encounters in which the protagonist feels misunderstood and alienated. In an interview with Nigeria International, Agbayewa (2008) addresses the appeal of Nollywood movies to Nigerian expatriates: "When you come over to America, you want a piece of home ... It has a lot to do with nostalgia because you want to be part of where you are from." Agbayewa (cited in Goffe, 2010, p. 21) furthermore says about his attempt at creating a "Nollywood USA" that "[there] had never really been any films in America that in a popular, everyday Nollywood style, talked about the African experience." He continues: "I wanted to bring the Nigerian and the American experience together. I wanted to bring the hamburger together with fu fu."

In *This America*, screenwriter and director Bethels Agomuoh recreates the important link between circulating media images and immigration. The film begins with a street scene in a New York City neighborhood in which immigrants sell and buy DVDs and possibly VCDs (Figure 14.1). A police car arrives, and the sellers take to running, indicating the illegality of the sales. This opening scene reflects on the cycle of media images that inspire immigrants who might very well end up having to engage in the illegal selling of these media images, including this film itself. The drive to "move upward" geographically and economically necessitates imagining the target country as a place where economic survival is possible. People then shape their movement according to their perception of the world and how they want to situate themselves in its diasporic spheres, which are themselves constantly on the move. Out of this interplay, new images are created that start the cycle all over again. Or to say it in terms of cinema, the circulation of, and easy access to, films, especially in the digital age, create imaginaries, and the migrants who have developed those imaginaries realize them through movement and might make films that again circulate these imaginaries.

Diasporic Nollywood films consistently evoke the homeland Nigeria, often in the context of nostalgia, but also in terms of alienation and resentment. Instead of vilifying the host nation as a place that won't give immigrants a chance, these diasporic filmmakers also take the opportunity to problematize Nigeria. The cinematic Nigerian home country is often chaotic, dangerous, corrupt, or lacking opportunity. Although Nigeria remains a beloved home country in most films mentioned here, some film-makers make it a point to explain why their protagonists attempt to leave. Agbayewa's *God's Own Country* (2007) offers an interesting take on the space of Nigeria, which is commonly associated

Figure 14.1 Illegal DVD sale in *This America* (Source: still *This America*, 2005)

with crime, fraud, and corruption. Nigerian protagonist Ike arrives in New York City to take up residence with his uncle. Upon learning that his uncle is not the successful businessman he had made himself out to be, Ike is under pressure to find employment. Unable to find employment as an attorney, his trained profession, Ike begins to work in the same hotel kitchen as his uncle, along with several other immigrants. Upon learning that his sick sister in Nigeria is in need of money, Ike, unable to retrieve the money through legal means, participates in 419 credit card fraud.[9] Although he eventually manages to raise the money, the experience leaves him disillusioned. For Ike, America is the place that introduces him to criminal activity, while Nigeria is a place that promises peace and a reconnection with home. Agbayewa's film is the only one in which Nigeria is re-branded into a desirable space to which the protagonist would return if it offered more opportunity. At the same time, Ike never gains access to the established immigrant community.[10]

Agbayewa's (2008) reason for making *God's Own Country* clearly carries a political and revisionist message for inclusion of an African perspective into mainstream media outlets:

> It represents the taking back of the black image. Right now the media landscape has us dancing like fools, shooting and disrespecting each other for a dollar. Black people are only thought of in certain terms, what's even crazier is that we are trying to live up to those stereotypes. That's why the making of *God's Own Country* is important because it's a self-financed project whose sole purpose is to introduce culture into the image equation.

Agbayewa's explanation evokes colonial filmmaking in which Africans were the subjects of white films and as such were represented in ways that served the colonial masters. His emphasis on self-financing is therefore important not only for contemporary diasporic filmmaking, but for African cinema as a whole. To dismiss the self-reliance and control that Nollywood filmmakers have over their films based on a supposedly shoddy end product is to ignore the implications of dependence all throughout African history. Therefore, the fact that the Nollywood end products are made with an audience in mind and reach this audience at home and abroad is a remarkable feat in itself, both in Nigeria and the diaspora. *God's Own Country* reflects this reach and the negotiation of modern technology in that it was, and still is, available for download on the internet. This channel of distribution not only eases access for diasporic audiences, but achieves what has as of yet been a struggle for diasporic filmmakers, namely the distribution of their films in Nigeria itself. *God's Own Country* localizes form and content for its diasporic audience. Although Agbayewa immigrated to the United States at the age of four and therefore has not himself experienced the problems of newly arrived immigrants, his film focuses on the trials and tribulations of those who arrive with high hopes soon to face a sobering reality. Haynes (forthcoming) points to the "enduring basis for films about Nigerians abroad: the existence of many communities of expatriate Nigerians in Europe, America, and elsewhere, which provide both practical succor and imaginative inspiration to their compatriots stuck in the seemingly permanent morass of the Nigerian economy."

Writer, producer, director, and actor Pascal Atuma addresses similar migrant anxieties in his films, but through comedic interpretations. His films *Only in America* (2005), *My American Nurse 1* and *2* (2006 and 2010, respectively), and *Hurricane in the Rose Garden* (2009) are all concerned with culture clashes either between the seasoned immigrant and the newcomer or between generations within immigrant communities. Atuma's career path also reflects on the way in which Nollywood as a film industry empowers individuals through providing a market for films that do not require sophisticated equipment and large budgets. After he graduated from acting college in Dallas, Texas, Atuma moved to Hollywood and auditioned for film roles. During the process, he was repeatedly told that his Nigerian English accent would be a hindrance to his chances of being cast, an experience which inspired him to become a filmmaker himself to give a new generation of African expatriate actors an opportunity to work (Atuma, personal conversation). As I have maintained elsewhere (Hoffmann, forthcoming a), all the above-mentioned films employ a consistently didactic interaction between the seasoned and settled Nigerian immigrant and the naïve newcomer. Moreover, the filmmakers recreate what Arjun Appadurai refers to as the ethnoscape (1996): we watch Nigerian customs in settings like New York City, Atlanta, and Los Angeles, characters eat Nigerian food (or at least talk about wanting it), and even Nigerian scammers find their way into this cinematic diaspora. Nigeria itself is evoked through dress, food, speech, and mannerisms. It is identified both as a place of longing and a place characters are longing to leave.

Figure 14.2 Hurricane in the Rose Garden (Source: still *Hurricane in the Rose Garden*, 2009)

Conclusion

Oliver Mbamara is calling for efforts to uphold the strength of Nigeria video filmmaking, namely its openness and ability to embrace whatever circumstance arises:

> Those in Diaspora are as relevant to those in the local African countries just as the local countries are to those in Diaspora. The market is now global and would take all the output. There is no need for infighting or division born out of the fear that one group would stifle the other. The two need to work together and grow or face the danger of dwindling fortune or the consequence of isolated irrelevancy.
>
> (Mbamara, 2009)

Clearly Nollywood has proven itself capable of embracing diversity. As long as Western portrayals of Africa and Africans dominate global imaginations, African cinema takes on a special role in telling its own stories. To say it with Femi Agbayewa, "not everything about Africans has to be *Hotel Rwanda* or *Blood Diamond* or even *God's Own Country*. There are a billion stories that Nollywood USA can tell" (cited in Goffe, 2010, p. 21).

I have tried to make a case for Nollywood as a form of cinema that derives a political contribution from its independence from colonial, postcolonial, and neo-colonial power structures in terms of production and distribution. Nollywood filmmakers never put themselves in the position of having to contend with agencies and organizations in the formerly colonizing nations, corrupt and ineffective political leaders, and neo-colonial market forces controlled by the first world. Nollywood's contribution, as Lobato so eloquently points out, stems not from an appropriation of Third Cinema politicized aesthetics, but from literally a "third way," namely a creative force coming out of an African general population rather than an intellectual elite. Furthermore, Nollywood has broken out of the confines of celluloid film production which has previously kept the Western stronghold on African cinema by creating a dependence that could not be eliminated from within the African creative context. With no need for expensive 35mm cameras, extensive training, and Western-style global marketing strategies, Nollywood has been able to "effectively leverage their cultural assets and integrate them into global economic networks, thus providing new sources of revenue, employment and growth" (Lobato, 2010, pp. 338). Hopefully the critical acknowledgment of Nollywood's contribution to African cinema cultures, but also to global media flows, will continue and situate Nollywood in its rightful place as a dynamic, influential, and highly mobile form of African creative expression.

Acknowledgment

I would like to thank the editors Marguerite Waller and Sandra Ponzanesi for their invaluable feedback and constructive criticism throughout this process. Furthermore, I am indebted to the Andrew W. Mellon Foundation, the UCLA Mellon Postdoctoral Program in the Humanities, and Françoise Lionnet and Shu-mei Shih for awarding me the fellowship that provided the time and resources for this creative process.

Notes

1 Another thriving center for film production is Kano, a major city in Northern Nigeria. The Kano-based film industry is sometimes referred to as "Kannywood" and produces videos aimed at a Hausa audience, reflecting the predominantly Islamic orientation of the region and the profound influence of Bollywood films which are extremely popular here. For a comprehensive account of the Hausa film industry, see Brian Larkin's groundbreaking book *Signal and Noise: Media, Infrastructure, and Urban Culture in Nigeria* (2008), as well as the chapter "Itineraries of Indian cinema: African videos, Bollywood, and global media," by the same author (2003).

2 In fact, many of the most celebrated African filmmakers received filmmaking training outside Africa. Ousmane Sembène, Souleymane Cissé, and Abderrahmane Sissako, for example, attended different film schools in Moscow, Idrissa Ouedraogo and Jean-Marie Téno were trained in Paris, and Haile Gerima graduated from the University of California in Los Angeles with a degree in filmmaking.

3 For an excellent and insightful discussion of Third Cinema, see Teshome Gabriel's *Third Cinema in the Third World. The Aesthetics of Liberation* (1982).

4 For an overview of colonial and postcolonial filmmaking in Anglophone, Francophone, and Lusophone Africa well as of the history of FESPACO, see Manthia Diawara's *African Cinema – Politics and Culture* (1992) and Frank Ukadike's *Black African Cinema* (1994).

5 As of 2003, the Gallup-Nigeria Institute estimates that roughly 67 percent of Nigerians own VCD players (Barrot 2008).

6 During my stay in Nigeria, many people expressed that they would be happy to have a Western passport because it ensures a much higher level of mobility than a Nigerian passport. My ability to freely travel between many Western countries and comparably easy

access to most visas seemed much more desirable to many people than supposed Western riches.

7   The depiction of the "primitive" village is also clearly satirical and exaggerated.

8   My focus is on diasporic Nollywood films in the United States, but these films are also made in European countries. In her work on Nollywood filmmakers in the Netherlands, Belgium, and Germany, Sophie Samyn describes her subjects as "Nigerian expatriates who left Nigeria between 1990 and 2000 and have experienced the difficulties of arriving in a European country as an African immigrant" (Samyn, 2010, p. 3). The five filmmakers interviewed by Samyn express very similar motivations behind their creative expressions as their United States-based counterparts. Samyn also mentions the Nollywood industry in the United Kingdom, which she describes as "more intensely intertwined with the Nigerian-based film industry" (p. 6).

9   The number "419" references section 419 of the Nigerian Criminal Code, which prohibits the fee advancement schemes and letter impersonations that have come out of Nigeria in massive numbers within the past decade. At this point, "419" is used to refer to many different types of e-mail and letter scams and perpetrators are frequently called "419ers." Although fee advancement scams originate not only in Nigeria, they are still commonly associated with Nigerian scammers, probably due to Nigeria's reputation as a haven for corruption. The Nigerian government has launched a wide-spread campaign against 419 scams.

10 For a more in-depth analysis of the interaction between newly-arrived and established immigrants in diasporic Nollywood films, see Hoffmann (forthcoming b).

Bibliography

Adesokan, A., 2009. Practising "Democracy" in Nigerian Films. *African Affairs*, 108(433), pp. 599–619.

Agbayewa, F., 2008. *Director Femi Agbayewa interview*. [video online] Available at: http://www. youtube.com/watch?v=taCAi6vAZAQ [Accessed 15 July 2009].

Ajibade, B., 2009. Speaking French, Seeing English: Cameroon's Youth Audience for Nigerian Videos. *The Review of Education, Pedagogy, and Cultural Studies*, 31, pp. 409–25.

Appadurai, A., 1996. *Modernity at Large. Cultural Dimensions of Globalization*. Minneapolis: University of Minnesota Press.

Atuma, P., 2011. Conversation About Nollywood. Personal Conversation. USA. 18 February 2011.

Barrot, P. ed., 2008. *Nollywood: The Video Phenomenon in Nigeria*. Bloomington, IN: Indiana University Press.

BBC, 2010. China to Build $8bn Oil Refinery in Nigeria. *BBC*, [online] 6 July. Available at: http://www.bbc.co.uk/news/10527308 [Accessed 2 March 2011].

Diawara, M., 1992. *African Cinema: Politics and Culture*. Bloomington, IN: Indiana University Press.

Diawara, M., 2010. *African Film: New Forms of Aesthetics and Politics*. Berlin: Prestel Verlag.

Gabriel, T.H., 1982. *Third Cinema in the Third World. The Aesthetics of Liberation*. Ann Arbor, MI: UMI Research Press.

Goffe, L., 2010. Nollywood Goes to America. *New African*, April, pp. 20–1.

Haynes, J., 2006. Political Critique in Nigerian video films. *African Affairs*, 105(421), pp. 511–33.

Haynes, J., Forthcoming. The Nollywood Diaspora: a Nigerian Video Genre. In: M. Krings, O. Okome, eds., *Nollywood and Beyond: Transnational Dimensions of an African Video Film Industry*.

Highet, J., 2010. Inside Nollywood. *New African*, 18, pp. 18–9.

Hoffmann, C., Forthcoming a. Localizing the Transnational: The Negotiation of Immigrant Spaces in "Accented" Nollywood films. In: M. Krings, O. Okome, eds., *Nollywood and Beyond: Transnational Dimensions of an African Video Film Industry*

Hoffmann, C., Forthcoming b. Negotiating the Transnational Discourse: Undocumented Immigrants and Identity Formation in Nigerian Cinema. In: Akintunde Akinyemi ed. *African Creative Expressions: Mother Tongue and Other Tongues*.

Krahe, D., 2010. Nollywood's Film Industry Second Only to Bollywood in Scale. *Spiegel Online International,* [online] Available at: http://www.spiegel.de/international/world/ 0,1518,690344-3,00.html [Accessed 22 January 2011].

Krings, M., 2009. Turning Rice into *Pilau*. The Art of Video Narration in Tanzania. In: V. Bouchard, U. Fendler, G. Lacasse, eds. 2009. *Intermédialités*, 4, [online] Available at: http:// cri.histart.umontreal.ca/cri/fr/INTERMEDIALITES/interface/numeros.html [Accessed 15 January 2011].

Larkin, B., 2008. *Signal and Noise: Media, Infrastructure, and Urban Culture in Nigeria*. Durham, NC: Duke University Press

Larkin, B., 2003. Itineraries of Indian Cinema: African Videos, Bollywood, and Global Media. In: E. Shohat and R. Stam, eds., 2003. *Multiculturalism, Postcoloniality, and Transnational Media*. New Brunswick, NJ: Rutgers University Press, pp. 170–92.

Lobato, R., 2010. Creative Industries and Informal Economies. Lessons from Nollywood. *International Journal of Cultural Studies*, 13(4), pp. 337–54.

Mbamara, O., 2009. Nollywood in Danger: The Need For a Fresh Direction. *Nollywood Films, Movies and Events*, [online] August. Available at: http://www.nollywoodmovies.com /Esy-om-NollywoodInDanger.html [Accessed 18 December 2010].

McCall, J., 2007. The Pan-Africanism We Have: Nollywood's Invention of Africa. In O. Okome, ed. *Film International* 4, pp. 92–7.

Okome, O., 2007. Nollywood: Spectatorship, Audience and the Sites of Consumption. *Postcolonial Text*, 3(2), pp. 1–21.

Samyn, S., 2010. Nollywood in the Diaspora: An Exploratory Study on Transnational Aesthetics. Master's Thesis University of Gent.

Ukadike, F., 1994. *Black African Cinema*. Berkeley: University of California Press.

Filmography

American Visa 1, 2004. [video] Directed by K. Egbuna. Nigeria: Elonel International Ltd.

Blood Diamond, 2006. [film] Directed by E. Zwick. USA: Warner Bros. Pictures.

God's Own Country, 2007. [short film] Directed by F. Agbayewa. USA: Real Living Films.

Hotel Rwanda, 2004. [film] Directed by T. George. USA: United Artists.

Hurricane in the Rose Garden, 2009. [video] Directed by I. Etuk. USA: Pascal Atuma Productions.

Living in Bondage, 1992. [video] Directed by C. Obi Rapu. Nigeria: NEK Video Links.

Missing in America, 2004. [film] Directed by S. Osofisan. USA: Creative Chronicles and Concepts/ Buky's Place Enterprises Inc.

Mr. Ibu in London, 2004. [film] Directed by A. Williams. Nigeria: Kas-Vid International.

My American Nurse 1, 2006. [film] Directed by P. Atuma. USA: Pascal Atuma Productions.

My American Nurse 2, 2010. [film] Directed by P. Atuma. USA: Pascal Atuma Productions.

Only in America, 2005. [film] Directed by D. Decrane. USA: 360 World Pictures.

Osuofia in London, 2003. [video] Directed by K. Ogoro. Nigeria: Kingsley Ogoro Production.

Osuofia in London 2, 2004. [video] Directed by K. Ogoro. Nigeria: Kingsley Ogoro Production.

This America, 2005. [film] Directed by B. Agomuoh. USA: African Film Company/United African Artists.

The God Daughter, 2006. [film] Directed by E. Ikuenobe-Otaigbe. USA: Afrimedia Entertainment International.

Chapter 15

Postface

An interview with Priya Jaikumar

On February 18, 2011, editor Marguerite Waller met with noted colonial and postcolonial cinema studies scholar Priya Jaikumar of the School of Cinematic Arts at the University of Southern California to discuss Professor Jaikumar's thoughts about bringing postcolonialism and cinema together in the classroom. What emerges in the pages that follow is a profound appreciation of the pressures that postcolonial thought puts on pedagogy. Professor Jaikumar also demonstrates the fruitfulness of the complex interdisciplinarity that postcolonial cinema studies calls for. We offer this interview, then, not as an ending, but as a "postface" that looks outward toward the teachers and students who will carry on this rewarding project.

On teaching postcolonialism and cinema: an interview with Priya Jaikumar

P.J. Colonialism creates a combative terrain, but as Edward Said says, it also produces a shared space. I take it as axiomatic that colonization was the political, social, economic, affective process that made the world truly global for the first time. How can we think of colonialism as the context that brought into being heterogeneous cultures while splintering the experience of modernity? This poses conceptual and methodological problems that I dealt with in my first book (2006). It has also fed into subsequent thinking about courses on postcolonialism and cinema.

In my training, I encountered divides between film studies, empire studies, and subaltern studies. Non-Hollywood films were framed by national cinema discourses. Subaltern studies, very influential on me, went against nationalist historiography. It presented the subaltern as an alternative sphere of self-definition, with a certain autonomy. Here were subjects not entirely grasped by the terms of colonial-national states, because these state-formations and paradigms came into existence through the subject's exclusion. Subaltern subjects are those who exist both within and outside such circuits and institutions. This raised important questions for me about how to theorize any subject or discourse not immediately visible or readable within political frameworks such as the colonial, the national, maybe even the global. How do you get at the incompletely realized subject of discourse, or the non-hegemonic discourses? How can they be historiographically articulated?

At the same time, thinking about film stretched my readings in subaltern studies. While subaltern scholars were writing from the impossible place of subjects removed from all lines of social mobility – that's Spivak's phrase – popular media were all about creating the fantasy of social mobility. In media studies we were having conversations about taste, pleasure, markets, affective technologies, and the expansion of the idea of social mobility. About the discursive regimes of media.

Historiographies and knowledges

There has been a lively debate about whether postcolonial theory is still effective in what it claims to do. Because they primarily frame postcolonial studies as studies of hybridity, Michael Hardt and Antonio Negri (2000) argue that postcolonial theory is ineffective in studying new patterns or arrangements of power. They argue that hybridity is precisely what is assimilated by corporate cultures, so postcolonialism, along with the other "posts" such as postmodernism and poststructuralism, embraces an outdated ideal, fighting an old binary paradigm of power that is no longer operative. This is a limited understanding of postcolonialism. I do, however, take seriously the criticisms of political allies like Antonio Negri, Ella Shohat, and Stuart Hall (1996), among others.

Shohat (1992) argues that postcolonialism doesn't address its own politics of location. It emerged temporally when Third World nationalism stopped being an effective axis around which to organize. Around the 1980s and 1990s – with the intensification of market economics and neoliberal policies globally, the fall of the Wall, the disappearance of a world divided between two power blocs – there was a loss or rearticulation of the Third World politics/Third Cinema paradigm. So, she asks, have we given up too easily on a more radical politics?

These criticisms do not lead to an impasse if we ask certain questions: "What is the history of postcolonial studies as a critical tool? What is its function as a political optic?" This is what I want my students to understand. What are its failings? What debates is it a part of? How has it extended other fields? These questions, I feel, are useful in my classes, as students get a sense of the historical movement of postcolonial studies essential to comprehending its relevance today. As Dipesh Chakrabarty (2000, 1992) points out, subaltern and postcolonial studies depart from the English Marxist tradition of "history from below" by thinking the "political" in new ways. The political is not defined purely in relation to the state. It is a history of power separate from, if in negotiation with, universalist histories of capital. It takes seriously the persistence of spaces – the feudal, the tribal, the supernatural – incongruous with the vocabulary of capitalism and modernity, without thinking of them as anachronisms. So a constant question for postcolonialism is, what epistemologies underwrite our historiography of the world and our understanding of its present?

Spivak's (1988b) criticism of the subalternists is relevant here. She notes that the apparent investment of subaltern studies in recovering an effaced subject consciousness distracted attention from its interest in the construction of knowledge as discourse. One of the most important contributions of postcolonial studies is that modernity/ modernism, postmodernity/postmodernism, and their universalization of a particular industrial experience of the west are transformed when you put the colonial in the mix. The take-away question for me is, how do we organize history and therefore understand the present – of power, of culture, of people – without relying on singular transition narratives. R. Radhakrishnan (2000) says it well. He says postcolonialism wants to describe radically different knowledges with a politics of mutual recognition. It is, for me, a form of writing and thinking that seeks an alternative to stagist histories, by considering articulations of power in different but materially linked parts of the world and producing a politics of engagement across them.

Methodology

M.W. Is postcolonial thinking too complicated for any one discipline or any one theoretical position? It is so full of singularities, and the work lies in making the connections rather than in mastering one position or another.

P.J. It's a necessary complexity, which always existed but was not sufficiently articulated by available modes of knowledge. We don't have to be apologetic about the difficulty of our task, if we can show students what is gained by broader conversations across theory and disciplines. As an instance, as part of his work on the ambivalent place of numbers in liberal social theory, Arjun Appadurai (2006) talks of enumerative minorities – people who are a small percentage of national demographics – who attract disproportionately large anxieties from majorities threatened by the forces of globalization. You can't attack globalization, but you can attack minorities. This disaggregation of enumerative minorities from their metaphysical function is a wonderful move, and Appadurai walks us through the ways in which individuals have been counted in relation to populations in the deep history of liberal democracy. He worked this out first in thinking about imperial liberalism, finding these patterns recursive in the global era of neoliberal democracies. Social theory has had a lot to teach and a lot to learn from postcolonial studies.

In staging multiple conversations, the disciplinary fear is that we are promoting dilettantism and a loss of methodological rigor. This is why we have to be good historians as we attempt to be cultural theorists, always understanding that historical consciousness comes from particular theoretical positions. This is also why I cannot name particular cinemas as postcolonial. Doing so would reify postcolonial cinema as a commodity. But I can say that cinema was invented and circulated in the context of colonial domination. Colonialism disturbed the sense of territorial unity and temporal and spatial continuity for colonizer and colonized. Photography and cinema also radically manipulated time and place with their ability to capture, transport, and replicate images. These were forces fracturing and reassembling the world according to a series of new logics that must be considered together, because they worked together to shape our world. So it isn't just about how we study or teach a class on postcolonial cinema, but how we view cinema and how we teach survey courses on international cinema, which easily defaults into the national canons paradigm. It's easier to think within the paradigm of nations, but if you start accounting for the circuitous mappings, the conjoined histories, the nation as an influential but contingent political formation, that's when it becomes more complex. It puts greater demands on scholarship. You have to learn different languages. You have to understand different aesthetic forms and talk about how they influence each other, which compounds your work.

M.W. Or requires people to work collaboratively.

P.J. Yes. It's humbling as well. The goal in qualifying our universalist ideas is not to fall into apathetic relativism, but to move to mutual recognition and engagement. To create narratives of this sort, by thinking about the recursiveness of the colonial and the way it haunts our world, is to think about the fragility of any of our current states. It is not to be stuck in the past or to lapse into a rhetoric of blame, as Said (1994) warns us. It is to think of new power alignments in relation to longer histories, in order to build coalitions in the present with a sense of hope.

New media

Once we begin to think of postcolonial studies as an optic or thematic, it can be a tool to study many forms of visual or aural expression. To say "postcolonial cinema" is to start a broader conversation that is not just about cinema. It doesn't have to be cinema *qua* cinema. Let's include radio, television, and social media. With what has been happening in the Egyptian Uprising recently, we have to consider social media within this framework. How does it allow people to oppose secular dictatorships set up by colonial powers? How does it articulate spaces between secularism and Islamicist movements, in coalitions that defy western liberal imaginations or vocabularies?

M.W. Everything becomes interwoven. You have people making movies with cell phones and putting them on YouTube. The technologies contaminate or collaborate with one another.

P.J. Exactly. People who say cinema is dead, who think of new media as a completely distinct, discrete object, might be missing part of the story. New forms and technologies do render older forms obsolete, do create new possibilities. But there are also ways in which one medium keeps another alive, with everyone working as a citizen journalist or filmmaker, uploading their film or digital video. The social issues remain relevant, and if anything the historical optic of postcolonial studies is more important now because the excitement over newness makes us all very forgetful.

Access and distribution

M.W. Is there anything to be done about getting these films distributed more widely, so that students in California, for example, or the Netherlands, can see them? It can be very hard to get these films.

P.J. I think universities are a good place, though funding may be embattled. Digitization is another possibility, though there is the question of who is digitizing this work, who is giving money for it. Some film archives in India resist digitization because it involves a loss of control over the material. They ask, if the BFI (British Film Institute) or any of the American universities invests in their digitization, will this relationship erode the authority of the people administering the film archive. I do see the problems, but I also see the possibility of a network of interested people like filmmakers, scholars, and librarians bringing these films to people's attention. The audience is likely to be small, but books, films, and digital spaces can collaborate with each other. Books and on-line discussion groups might increase the awareness of certain visual materials. I don't want to pose them as antithetical. There can be good overlap.

Postcolonial theory and cinema: the course

I do not give the students a definition for postcolonial cinema. I introduce them to classics in colonial and postcolonial theory and have them think about what this opens up in their consideration of cinema. The main goal is to encourage them to see the world in a different way, to allow them to shift perspectives.

I make it clear at the start of my seminar, and in my syllabus, that we will read postcolonial theories that don't always apply to cinema. Making connections between theory, concept, and image or narrative is our task. I try to keep it open-ended. The midterm prompt is: "What is postcolonial theory? What do you think of its relevance to the analysis of culture in general and film in particular?" I don't seek a definitive answer, but I provide them with guidelines driven by questions like, what is the "post" in postcolonialism? What are its investments and motivations, its historical trajectory and significance? Readings and screenings are clustered around thematics in postcolonial studies, and each session is preceded by the circulation of student notes on readings and film screenings. For example, we consider binary, Manichean formulations of the colonizer and colonized against ideas about the hauntings of colonialism and mutually constitutive histories or subjectivities; questions of nationhood and colonial modernity; identity and hybridity; postcolonial poetics; postmodernism, and globalization. Using these thematic lenses, each student may choose to analyze a screened film in a particular way.

For one of the "Postcolonialism in the era of globalization" weeks, for example, students saw *Kandahar* (Makhmalbaf, 2001). The film is the story of an Afghan-born Canadian woman who returns home to save her sister from suicide and the Taliban regime. It came out the year of the US war in Afghanistan. Students had read sections of Hardt and Negri's (2000) *Empire*, essays from Afzal-Khan and Seshadri-Crook's (2000) *The Preoccupation of Postcolonial Studies*, Masao Miyoshi's (1996) essay on a borderless world, among other texts. One student discussed the film in terms of the "rescue narrative" genre. The film's narrative is complicated by images of amputees from the war chasing artificial limbs thrown from the sky by the Red Cross. So students asked, what is the difference between the sister's desire to save, and the story of the amputees? What does the film say about First World aid, charity, responsibility, and guilt? In previous sessions, they had read critiques of the "comprador intellectual," the postcolonial scholar who has institutional comforts, access, and mobility denied to those they write about. Students used this to think about the Canadian sister's position. We also attempted to move beyond narratives and images to thinking of the film's circulation in festivals. Students do well if you set those frames for the films, and then allow them to draw their own observations and conclusions.

M.W. Is there a film that has had a particular impact on the way you think about postcolonialism?

P.J. I think for me it's more a question of what I put together in terms of films and readings. It is not about a particularly startling film so much as the creation of a context and of dialogue between different visions. For instance, for our first class, I have screened *The "Teddy" Bears* (Porter, 1907), *Black Girl* (Sembene, 1966), and excerpts from Euzhan Palcy's documentary *Aimé Césaire: A Voice for History* (1994). For that week, students read excerpts from Aimé Césaire's (1994) *Discourse on Colonialism*, Lenin on imperialism (1939; 1993), Hannah Arendt (1951) on totalitarianism, Abdul JanMohammad's (1988) *The Manichean Aesthetic*, and Kristen Whissel's (1999) article on the Porter film. I wanted them to think about the history of capitalism differently. All the readings stage the gaze turned back on European history, recasting the European bourgeoisie in a colonial-global context. Hannah Arendt writes about colonialism as the political emancipation of the bourgeoisie. Lenin writes about the bourgeoisie as a kind of parasitic class, resonating with Césaire's language, which is very powerful, almost surreal. Europe is indefensible, Césaire says, and what horrified the world about Fascism was that it brought to Europe practices long directed at non-Europeans. How does this vision of the essential savagery of the bourgeoisie find its way into film and art, alter our thinking about images and about history? It's good to show Buñuel or Godard in this context as well.

Black Girl has elements of realism but ends with a boy wearing a mask, following a French man after the suicide in France of the man's young Senegalese maid, who was the little boy's sister. The mask is an object that has changed hands several times, becoming different things. A kind of surreal vision of Europe emerges when you follow the visual and hermeneutic trajectory of certain objects traversing these films, haunting the present with their forms and meanings. Whissel's article allows students to include the Spanish American war and colonialisms within the U.S. in our discussion. So we end up considering films from 1907, 1966, and 1994, from the U.S., Senegal, and the Caribbean, placed in their specific contexts but also raising larger questions about how we can speak of the history of colonialism and its aftereffects, how this speaking constitutes a certain vision, and how the normative vision of history can be displaced by this more surreal vision where temporality works differently, where the past is also always present.

M.W. Showing recursiveness is one of the things that cinema is so good at. Showing the patterns.

P.J. Exactly. And speaking of repetition, *The "Teddy" Bears* is a retelling of the Goldilocks story. The little blond white girl finds one of Teddy Roosevelt's "Rough Riders" who kills all the bears except the baby, who becomes her captive. It offers a vision of the racialization of the U.S. imaginary and its society of the spectacle. In these discussions, the surreal allows a refracted aesthetic. It makes a darker commentary on what appears to be normal. Isn't that partly what we are doing? We read below the surface of what is presented as normal, to understand its historical, statist, epistemic conditions of possibility. There are, of course, many differences between these films. And they are not all dark in terms of themes or styles. But when combined with the readings, the emotional gamut you cover make for very intense classes.

Despite that intensity, one thing really pleasurable about the process has been guiding students through a vocabulary with which they can talk about global power dynamics that they have already felt or encountered. I have also been fortunate that students from different disciplines have enrolled in my seminar. The last time I taught it, I had students from history, art history, cinema, and literature. Each one pushed the others in a different way. The student from history was trained in the material history of class conflict, and the cinema students would challenge him to think about film as a medium not transparently readable through social history. He would push them, in turn, to account for the social context of images. They were also from different countries. I had a student from Burkina Faso, a couple of students from India, a Mexican-American – it made for a great class.

I think a failing on my part was that in my syllabus, I defined empire mainly through European and Anglo-American political regimes. This is still vast, but I was teaching from what I knew. It has the problem of replicating a certain Eurocentricity in its frame. We did talk about Hong Kong, but I didn't address the imperialisms of Japan, of China. I think what I offered needs to be more decentralizing. I am learning from my students some of whom have recently received Ph.D.s and are now teaching and publishing. One, for example, is working on early Korean cinema and its audiences during the Japanese occupation.

M.W. I think it is easy to confuse what is on a syllabus with what the optic is. Is it necessarily Eurocentric to teach from where you are coming from, as long as you don't confine your students to that position, which you obviously don't?

P.J. There is some valid criticism that South Asia, and a particularly influential generation of South Asian scholars, dominated early writings in postcolonial studies and so shaped the field. If one of our constitutive claims is that no one experience can stand in for the universal, then a syllabus constructed around the postcolonial has to be very conscious that the particular instances are not building to a comprehensive conclusion, or becoming the theoretical template. We have to make clear that it is not about a collection of all experiences of colonization and decolonization. Derrida's dismantling of the mission of totalization in knowledge is a useful guide. Each context is a supplement to our knowledge about the postcolonial, not a normative example. If we don't think of knowledge in territorial ways, but as igniting other thoughts, then our different knowledges become more useful. A productive area of exchange has been between subaltern studies and Latin American studies, for instance.

"Pessimism of the intellect; optimism of the will"

M.W. Are there generational mutations or evolutions taking place in the field of postcolonial (and/or cinema) studies? And what about the splintered perspectives within postcolonial studies? I am reading Zygmunt Baumann and Édouard Glissant. One seems completely depressed about the same circumstances that the other finds exhilarating. Is this just because they are coming from such different histories and locations, or are they enacting other kinds of division as well?

P.J. Variances in history and location matter, so context is very important. But the pessimism/optimism distinction may also have to do with Gramsci's formulation: "pessimism of the intellect, optimism of the will." Think of Spivak's "Can the Subaltern Speak?" (1988a). Her definitive answer seems to be that they cannot speak, but then how or why is she writing the article? A certain place is being made for a subject whose very position is effaced by what she is writing about. There is a dynamism in that. A lot of the material we look at or read is pretty dark, but when we talk about it, we are creating a community engaged by these issues, a community making these questions important. Film gives us powerful affective connections to motivate thought about our postcolonial world.

Bibliography

Afzal-Khan, F. and Seshadri-Crooks, K., eds., 2000. *The Preoccupation of Postcolonial Studies*. London: Routledge.

Appadurai, A., 2006. *Fear of Small Numbers: An Essay on the Geography of Anger*. Durham, NC: Duke University Press.

Arendt, H., 1951. *The Origins of Totalitarianism*. New York: Schocken.

Césaire, A., 1994. *Discourse on Colonialism*, translated from French by R. D. G. Kelly. New York: Monthly Review Press.

Chakrabarty. D. 1992. Postcoloniality and the Artifice of History: Who Speaks for "Indian" Pasts? *Representations*, Special Issue: Imperial Fantasies and Postcolonial Histories. 37, pp. 1–26.

Chakrabarty. D., 2000. Subaltern Studies and Postcolonial Historiography. *Nepantala: Views from the South,* 1(1), pp. 9–32.

Hall, S., 1996., When was the "Postcolonial"? Thinking at the Limit. In: I. Chambers and L. Curti, eds., 1996. *The Postcolonial Question: Common Skies, Divided Horizons*. London: Routledge, pp. 242–60.

Hardt, M. and Negri, A., 2000. *Empire*. Cambridge, MA: Harvard University Press.

Jaikumar, P., 2006. *Cinema at the End of Empire: A Politics of Transition in Britain and India*. Durham, NC: Duke University Press.

JanMohamed, A. R., 1988. *Manichean Aesthetics: The Politics of Literature in Colonial Africa*. Amherst: University of Massachusetts Press.

Lenin, V. I., 1993. *Imperialism, the Highest Stage of Capitalism* (reprint edition 1939). London: International Publishers.

Miyoshi, M., 1996. A Borderless World? From Colonialism to Transnationalism and the Decline of the Nation-State. In: R. Wilson and W. Dissanayake, eds., 1996. *Global/Local: Cultural Production and the Transnational Imaginary*. Durham, NC: Duke University Press, pp. 76–106.

Radhakrishnan, R., 2000. Postmodernism and the Rest of the World. In: F. Afzal-Khan and K. Seshadri-Crooks, eds., 2000. *The Pre-Occupation of Postcolonial Studies*. Durham, NC: Duke University Press, pp. 37–70.

Said, E., 1994. *Culture and Imperialism*. New York: Vintage Books.

Shohat, E., 1992. Notes on the Postcolonial. *Social Text*, 31/32, pp. 99–113.

Spivak, G. C., 1988a. Can the Subaltern Speak? In: C. Nelson and L. Grossberg, eds., 1988. *Marxism and the Interpretation of Culture*. Urbana and Chicago: University of Illinois Press.

Spivak, G. C., 1988b. Subaltern Studies: Deconstruction Historiography. In: R. Guhat and G. C. Spivak, eds., 1988. *Selected Subaltern Studies*, pp. 3–33.

Whissel, K., 1999. Uncle Tom, Goldilocks, and the Rough Riders: Early Cinema's Encounter with Empire. *Screen*, 40(4), pp. 384–404.

Filmography

Aimé Césaire: A Voice for History, 1994. [documentary film] Directed by E. Palcy. USA: Saligne and So On.

Black Girl, 1966. [film] Directed by O. Sembene. Senegal: Filmi Domirev.

Kandahar, 2001. [film] Directed by M. Makhmalbaf. Iran: Makhmalbaf Productions.

The "Teddy" Bears, 1907. [short film] Directed by E. S. Porter. USA: Edison Manufacturing Company.

Index

In this index film titles are alphabetised under the first noun or adjective, e.g. *A costa dos murmúrios* is listed under 'C'.